Language Complexity as an Evolving Variable

STUDIES IN THE EVOLUTION OF LANGUAGE

General Editors
Kathleen R. Gibson, *University of Texas at Houston,*
and James R. Hurford, *University of Edinburgh*

PUBLISHED

[For a list of books in preparation for the series, see p 310]

Language Complexity
as an Evolving Variable

Edited by
GEOFFREY SAMPSON, DAVID GIL,
AND PETER TRUDGILL

OXFORD
UNIVERSITY PRESS

OXFORD
UNIVERSITY PRESS

Great Clarendon Street, Oxford OX2 6DP

Oxford University Press is a department of the University of Oxford.
It furthers the University's objective of excellence in research, scholarship,
and education by publishing worldwide in

Oxford New York

Auckland Cape Town Dar es Salaam Hong Kong Karachi
Kuala Lumpur Madrid Melbourne Mexico City Nairobi
New Delhi Shanghai Taipei Toronto

With offices in

Argentina Austria Brazil Chile Czech Republic France Greece
Guatemala Hungary Italy Japan Poland Portugal Singapore
South Korea Switzerland Thailand Turkey Ukraine Vietnam

Oxford is a registered trade mark of Oxford University Press
in the UK and in certain other countries

Published in the United States
by Oxford University Press Inc., New York

British Library Cataloguing in Publication Data
Data available

Library of Congress Cataloging in Publication Data
Data available

Typeset by SPI Publisher Services, Pondicherry, India
Printed in Great Britain
on acid-free paper by
CPI Antony Rowe, Chippenham, Wiltshire

ISBN 978–0–19–954521–6 (Hbk.)
        978–0–19–954522–3 (Pbk.)

1 3 5 7 9 10 8 6 4 2

Contents

Preface

This book is the outcome of a workshop held at the Max Planck Institute for Evolutionary Anthropology, Leipzig, in April 2007. The workshop was convened in response to the fairly sudden emergence, in many diverse quarters internationally, of scepticism about a longstanding linguistic axiom – that all languages and language varieties are similar in complexity, and have been so at all times in the past.

The organizers set out to assemble in one place as many as possible of those who have been questioning this axiom, so that they could thrash out how far they were genuinely discussing the same issue, what they agreed on, and where they diverged. Almost everyone invited was able to come – and the three who could not make it to Leipzig in person, Ngoni Chipere (who as a Zimbabwean encountered visa problems), Guy Deutscher, and Johanna Nichols, have nevertheless contributed in writing.

The Leipzig workshop was by common consent exceptionally successful as a meeting of minds, with an intellectual fizz that will not be quickly forgotten by those who were there. Contributors represented institutions in twelve countries and a broad spectrum of discipline backgrounds, ranging for instance from Southeast Asian field anthropology (David Gil) through generative linguistic theory (Ljiljana Progovac) to ancient Near Eastern philology (Guy Deutscher). Yet despite this diversity, both in the formal sessions and in the breaks, everyone was talking to each other rather than past each other.

After the workshop, the editors invited a selection of the speakers to write up their material in the light of the discussions at Leipzig. (A minority of the presentations which were less closely related to the central topic are not included here.) Contributors were encouraged to pay special attention to what had emerged in the course of proceedings as common themes – these were codified by Jack Hawkins in a helpful written aide-memoire.

The first of the chapters that follow was written as an attempt to survey the overall issue in its various aspects. The sequence of later chapters was chosen so as to bring together contributions which address similar topics or which can be read as responding to one another. However, there are so many overlapping relationships between the various contributions that any ordering principle is inevitably fairly arbitrary.

We should like to express our warmest thanks to the Max Planck Institute for Evolutionary Anthropology, and to Bernard Comrie, Director of its

Linguistics Department, for making this workshop financially possible, and to support staff at the Institute for their help in making this such a welcoming and smoothly running occasion. We hope that the following pages will enable the reader to share not only the ideas but some of the intellectual effervescence that was in the air at Leipzig.

G.R.S.

D.G.

P.T.

Interlinear glosses

Interlinear glosses for language examples in this book conform to the Leipzig Glossing Rules (for which, see www.eva.mpg.de/lingua/resources/glossing-rules.php). Where possible, codes for grammatical morphemes are drawn from the standard list of abbreviations shown below. Person–number combinations are represented as 3S (third person singular), 1P (first person plural), etc.; and the categories "present participle", "past participle" are shown as PRP, PAP respectively. Other abbreviations are defined at the place where they are used.

Standard abbreviations

1	first person
2	second person
3	third person
A	agent-like argument of canonical transitive verb
ABL	ablative
ABS	absolutive
ACC	accusative
ADJ	adjective
ADV	adverb(ial)
AGR	agreement
ALL	allative
ANTIP	antipassive
APPL	applicative
ART	article
AUX	auxiliary
BEN	benefactive
CAUS	causative
CLF	classifier
COM	comitative
COMP	complementizer

COMPL	completive
COND	conditional
COP	copula
CVB	converb
DAT	dative
DECL	declarative
DEF	definite
DEM	demonstrative
DET	determiner
DIS	distal
DISTR	distributive
DU	dual
DUR	durative
ERG	ergative
EXCL	exclusive
F	feminine
FOC	focus
FUT	future
GEN	genitive
IMP	imperative
INCL	inclusive
IND	indicative
INDF	indefinite
INF	infinitive
INS	instrumental
INTR	intransitive
IPFV	imperfective
IRR	irrealis
LOC	locative
M	masculine
N	neuter
N-	non- (e.g. NSG nonsingular, NPST nonpast)
NEG	negation, negative
NMLZ	nominalizer/nominalization

NOM	nominative
OBJ	object
OBL	oblique
P	patient-like argument of canonical transitive verb
PASS	passive
PFV	perfective
PL	plural
POSS	possessive
PRED	predicative
PRF	perfect
PROG	progressive
PROH	prohibitive
PROX	proximal/proximate
PRF	present
PST	past
PTCP	participle
PURP	purposive
Q	question particle/marker
QUOT	quotative
RECP	reciprocal
REFL	reflexive
REL	relative
RES	resultative
S	single argument of canonical intransitive verb
SBJ	subject
SBJV	subjunctive
SG	singular
TOP	topic
TR	transitive
VOC	vocative

Notes on the contributors

WALTER BISANG is Professor of General and Comparative Linguistics at the Johannes Gutenberg-Universität, Mainz. He is editor in chief of the *Zeitschrift für Sprachwissenschaft*.

NGONI CHIPERE is a lecturer in Language Arts in the School of Education, University of the West Indies at Cave Hill, Barbados. He is author of *Understanding complex sentences* (Palgrave Macmillan, 2003).

ÖSTEN DAHL is Professor of General Linguistics at Stockholm University. His books include *The growth and maintenance of linguistic complexity* (John Benjamins, 2004).

GUY DEUTSCHER is an Assyriologist in the Department of Languages and Cultures of Mesopotamia and Anatolia, Leiden University. He is author of *Syntactic change in Akkadian* (Oxford University Press, 2000) and *The unfolding of language* (Heinemann, 2005).

After years as a missionary in Brazil, **DANIEL EVERETT** now chairs the Department of Languages, Literatures, and Cultures at the Illinois State University. His book *'Don't sleep, there are snakes': life and language in the Amazon jungle* will appear from publishers in several countries in 2008.

DAVID GIL is a researcher in the Department of Linguistics, Max Planck Institute for Evolutionary Anthropology, Leipzig. Much of his life is spent on fieldwork in remote areas of Indonesia.

JOHN HAWKINS is Professor of English and Applied Linguistics at Cambridge University. His books include *Efficiency and complexity in grammars* (Oxford University Press, 2004).

FRED KARLSSON is Professor of General Linguistics at the University of Helsinki. His books in English include *Finnish: an essential grammar* (2nd edn, Routledge, 2008).

BERND KORTMANN is a Chair Professor in the Faculty of Philology at the Albert-Ludwigs-Universität, Freiburg im Breisgau. He co-edited *A handbook of varieties of English* (Mouton de Gruyter, 2004).

UTZ MAAS is Professor of Education and Germanic Linguistics at Osnabrück University. His books include *Sprachpolitik und politische Sprachwissenschaft* (Suhrkamp, 1989).

JOHN MCWHORTER is a Senior Fellow at the Manhattan Institute. Apart from books on linguistics, including *Defining creole* (Oxford University Press, 2005), he has written extensively on American racial and cultural issues.

MATTI MIESTAMO is a Research Fellow at the Helsinki Collegium for Advanced Studies, and teaches linguistics at the University of Helsinki. He was the lead editor of *Language complexity* (John Benjamins, 2008).

JOHANNA NICHOLS is a Professor in the Department of Slavic Languages and Literatures at the University of California, Berkeley. Her books include *Linguistic diversity in space and time* (University of Chicago Press, 1992).

LJILJANA PROGOVAC is a Professor in the College of Liberal Arts and Sciences, Wayne State University, Detroit. She is author of *A syntax of Serbian* (Slavica, 2005) and co-editor of *The syntax of nonsententials* (John Benjamins, 2006).

GEOFFREY SAMPSON is Professor of Natural Language Computing at Sussex University. His books include *English for the computer* (Clarendon, 1995) and *The 'language instinct' debate* (2nd edn, Continuum, 2005).

KAIUS SINNEMÄKI is a Ph.D. student in the Finnish Graduate School in Language Studies and is based in Helsinki. With Miestamo and Karlsson he co-edited *Language complexity* (John Benjamins, 2008).

EUGÉNIE STAPERT is a researcher in the Department of Linguistics, Max Planck Institute for Evolutionary Anthropology, Leipzig, and is working on a Manchester University doctoral thesis on the Pirahã language.

BENEDIKT SZMRECSANYI is a member of the Freiburg Institute for Advanced Studies, Albert-Ludwigs-Universität, Freiburg im Breisgau. He is author of *Morphosyntactic persistence in spoken English* (Mouton de Gruyter, 2006).

PETER TRUDGILL is Professor Emeritus of English Linguistics, Université de Fribourg. His books include *The dialects of England* (Blackwell, 1990) and *New-dialect formation* (Edinburgh University Press, 2006).

Frank Cotham cartoon from New Yorker, 28 May 2007, ID 123995

"We'll start out by speaking in simple declarative sentences."

1

A linguistic axiom challenged

GEOFFREY SAMPSON

1 Background

This book responds to the fact that an idea which ranked for many decades as an unquestioned truism of linguistics is now coming under attack from many different directions. This introductory chapter sketches the history of the axiom, and goes on to draw together some of the diverse ways in which it is now under challenge.

For much of the twentieth century, linguistics was strongly attached to a principle of *invariance of language complexity* as one of its bedrock assumptions – and not just the kind of assumption that lurks tacitly in the background, so that researchers are barely conscious of it, but one that linguists were very given to insisting on explicitly. Yet it never seemed to be an assumption that linguists offered much justification for – they appeared to believe it because they wanted to believe it, much more than because they had reasons for believing it. Then, quite suddenly at the beginning of the new century, a range of researchers began challenging the assumption, though these challenges were so diverse that people who became aware of one of them would not necessarily link it in their minds with the others, and might not even be aware of the other challenges.

Linguists and non-linguists alike agree in seeing human language as the clearest mirror we have of the activities of the human mind, and as a specially important component of human culture, because it underpins most of the other components. Thus, if there is serious disagreement about whether language complexity is a universal constant or an evolving variable, that is surely a question which merits careful scrutiny. There cannot be many current topics of academic debate which have greater general human importance than this one.

2 Complexity invariance in early twentieth-century linguistics

When I first studied linguistics, in the early 1960s, Noam Chomsky's name was mentioned, but the mainstream subject as my fellow students and

I encountered it was the "descriptivist" tradition that had been inaugurated early in the twentieth century by Franz Boas and Leonard Bloomfield; it was exemplified by the papers collected in Martin Joos's anthology *Readings in linguistics*, which contained Joos's famous summary of that tradition as holding "that languages can differ from each other without limit and in unpredictable ways" (Joos 1957: 96).

Most fundamental assumptions about language changed completely as between the descriptive linguistics of the first two-thirds of the twentieth century and the generative linguistics which became influential from the mid-1960s onwards. For the descriptivists, languages were part of human cultures; for the generativists, language is part of human biology – as Chomsky (1980: 134) put it, "we do not really learn language; rather, grammar grows in the mind". The descriptivists thought that languages could differ from one another in any and every way, as Martin Joos said; the generativists see human beings as all speaking in essence the same language, though with minor local dialect differences (N. Chomsky 1991: 26). But the invariance of language complexity is an exception: this assumption is common to both descriptivists and generativists.

The clearest statement that I have found occurred in Charles Hockett's influential 1958 textbook *A course in modern linguistics*:

… impressionistically it would seem that the total grammatical complexity of any language, counting both morphology and syntax, is about the same as that of any other. This is not surprising, since all languages have about equally complex jobs to do, and what is not done morphologically has to be done syntactically. Fox, with a more complex morphology than English, thus ought to have a somewhat simpler syntax; and this is the case. (Hockett 1958: 180–81)

Although Hockett used the word "impressionistically" to avoid seeming to claim that he could pin precise figures on the language features he was quantifying, notice how strong his claim is. Like Joos, Hockett believed that languages could differ extensively with respect to particular subsystems: e.g. Fox has complex morphology, English has simple morphology. But when one adds together the complexity derived from the separate subsystems, and if one can find some way to replace "impressions" with concrete numbers, Hockett's claim is that the overall total will always come out about the same.

Hockett justifies his claim by saying that "languages have about equally complex jobs to do", but it seems to me very difficult to define the job which grammar does in a way that is specific enough to imply any particular prediction about grammatical complexity. If it really were so that languages varied greatly in the complexity of subsystem *X*, varied greatly in the complexity of subsystem *Y*, and so on, yet for all language the totals from the separate subsystems added together could be shown to come out the same, then I would not agree with Hockett in finding this unsurprising. To me it would feel almost like magic.

3 Apparent counterexamples

And at an intuitive level it is hard to accept that the totals do always come out roughly the same. Consider for instance Archi, spoken by a thousand people in one village 2,300 metres above sea level in the Caucasus. According to Aleksandr Kibrik (1998), an Archi verb can inflect into any of about 1.5 million contrasting forms. English is said to be simple morphologically but more complex syntactically than some languages; but how much syntactic complexity would it take to balance the morphology of Archi? – and does English truly have that complex a syntax? Relative to some languages I know, English syntax as well as English morphology seems to be on the simple side.

Or consider the Latin of classical poetry, which is presumably a variety of language as valid for linguists' consideration as any other. Not only did classical Latin in general have a far richer morphology than any modern Western European language, but, in poetry, one had the extraordinary situation whereby the words of a sentence could be permuted almost randomly out of their logical hierarchy, so that Horace could write a verse such as (*Odes* Book I, XXII):

> *namque me silva lupus in Sabina,*
> *dum meam canto Lalagen et ultra*
> *terminum curis vagor expeditis,*
> *fugit inermem*

which means something like:

for a wolf flees from me while, unarmed, I sing about my Lalage and wander, cares banished, in the Sabine woods beyond my boundary

but expresses it in the sequence:

for me woods a wolf in the Sabine, while my I sing about Lalage and beyond my boundary cares wander banished, flees from unarmed

We know, of course, that languages with extensive case marking, such as Latin, tend to be free word order languages. But it seems to me that what linguists normally mean by "free word order" is really free constituent order – the constituents of a logical unit at any level can appear in any order, when case endings show their respective roles within the higher-level unit, but the

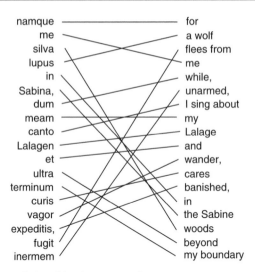

FIG. 1.1. Text-sense relationships in a verse of Horace

expectation is that (with limited exceptions) the logical units will be kept together as physical units. In Latin poetry that expectation is comprehensively flouted, creating highly complex relationships (Fig. 1.1) between the physical text and the sense structure it encodes.[1]

4 Ideological motives

For the descriptivist school, I believe the assumption of invariance of total language complexity as between different languages was motivated largely by ideological considerations. The reason why linguistics was worth studying, for many descriptivists, was that it helped to demonstrate that "all men are brothers" – Mankind is not divided into a group of civilized nations or races who think and speak in subtle and complex ways, and another group of primitive societies with crudely simple languages. They assumed that more complex languages would be more admirable languages, and they wanted to urge that the unwritten languages of the third world were fully as complex as the well-known European languages, indeed the third world languages often contained subtleties of expression having no parallel in European languages.

---

[1] In the example, the logical constituency of the Latin original can be inferred straightforwardly from that of my English translation, except that *inermem*, "unarmed", belongs in the original to the main rather than the subordinate clause – a more literal translation would run "... flees from unarmed me...".

One point worth making about this is that it is not obvious that "more complex" should be equated with "more admirable". We all know the acronym KISS, "Keep it simple, stupid", implying that the best systems are often the simplest rather than the most complex ones. Whoever invented that acronym probably was not thinking about language structure, but arguably the principle should apply as much to our domain as to any other. We English-speakers do not seem to spend much time yearning to use languages more like Archi or poetic Latin.

Still, it is certainly true that the layman's idea of language diversity was that primitive Third World tribes had crude, simple languages, whereas the languages of Europe were precision instruments. The descriptivists were anxious to urge that this equation just does not hold – unwritten third world grammars often contain highly sophisticated structural features; and they were surely correct in making that point.

It is worth adding that the founders of the descriptivist school seem often to have been subtler about this than those who came after them, such as Hockett. Edward Sapir, for instance, did not say that all languages were equally complex – he did not believe they were, but he believed that there was no correlation between language complexity and level of civilization:

Both simple and complex types of language ... may be found spoken at any desired level of cultural advance. When it comes to linguistic form, Plato walks with the Macedonian swineherd, Confucius with the head-hunting savages of Assam. (Sapir [1921] 1963: 219)

Franz Boas was more knowledgeable about detailed interrelationships between language, race, and culture than later descriptivist linguists, who tended to focus on language alone in a more specialized way; and Boas was responsible for the classic discussion of how Third World languages sometimes enforced precision about intellectual categories that European languages leave vague:

In Kwakiutl this sentence [*the man is sick*] would have to be rendered by an expression which would mean, in the vaguest possible form that could be given to it, *definite man near him invisible sick near him invisible.* ... in case the speaker had not seen the sick person himself, he would have to express whether he knows it by hearsay or by evidence that the person is sick, or whether he has dreamed it. (Boas [1911] 1966: 39)

But Boas did not claim, as later linguists often have done, that there was no overall difference in the intellectual nature of the ideas expressed in the languages of culturally primitive and culturally advanced societies. Boas believed that there *were* important differences, notably that the languages of primitive cultures tended to lack expressions for abstract ideas and to focus almost exclusively on concrete things, but he wanted to say that this was because life in a primitive society gave people little practical need to think about abstractions, and whenever the need did arise, languages would quickly be adapted accordingly:

Primitive man ... is not in the habit of discussing abstract ideas. His interests center around the occupations of his daily life ... (p. 60)

... the language alone would not prevent a people from advancing to more generalized forms of thinking if the general state of their culture should require expression of such thought; ... the language would be moulded rather by the cultural state. (p. 63)

5 Complexity invariance and generative linguistics

If we come forward to the generative linguistics of the last forty-odd years, we find that linguists are no longer interested in discussing whether language structure reflects a society's cultural level, because generative linguists do not see language structure as an aspect of human culture. Except for minor details, they believe it is determined by human biology, and in consequence there is no question of some languages being structurally more complex than other languages – in essence they are all structurally identical to one another. Of course there are some parameters which are set differently in different languages: adjectives precede nouns in English but follow nouns in French. But choice of parameter settings is a matter of detail that specifies how an individual language expresses a universal range of logical distinctions – it does not allow for languages to differ from one another with respect to the overall complexity of the set of distinctions expressed, and it does not admit any historical evolution with respect to that complexity. According to Ray Jackendoff (1993: 32), "the earliest written documents already display the full expressive variety and grammatical complexity of modern languages".

I have good reason to know that the generativists are attached to that assumption, after experiencing the reception that was given to my 1997 book *Educating Eve*, written as an answer to Steven Pinker's *The language instinct*. Pinker deployed many different arguments to persuade his readers of the reality of a biologically inbuilt "language instinct", and my book set out to refute each argument separately. I thought my book might be somewhat controversial – I intended it to be controversial; but I had not foreseen the extent to which the controversy would focus on one particular point, which was not specially central either in my book or in Pinker's. I argued against Ray Jackendoff's claim just quoted by referring to Walter Ong's (1982) discussion of the way that Biblical Hebrew made strikingly little use of subordinate clauses, and also to Eduard Hermann's belief (Hermann 1895) that Proto-Indo-European probably contained no clause subordination at all.

On the electronic Linguist List, this led to a furore. From the tone of some of what was written, it was clear that some present-day linguists did not just factually disagree with Ong and Hermann, but passionately rejected any possibility that their ideas might be worth considering.

This did not seem to be explainable in terms of politically correct ideology: people who use words like "imperialism" or "racism" to condemn any suggestion that some present-day human societies may be less sophisticated than others are hardly likely to feel a need to defend the Jews of almost 3,000 years ago, and still less the mysterious Indo-Europeans even further back in the past: those peoples cannot now be touched by twenty-first-century neo-imperialism. So it seemed that the generative doctrine of innate knowledge of language creates an intellectual outlook within which it becomes just un-thinkable that overall complexity could vary significantly between language and language, or from period to period of the historical record. The innate cognitive machinery which is central to the generative concept of language competence is taken to be too comprehensive to leave room for significant differences with respect to complexity.

6 "Some issues on which linguists can agree"

Summing up, the idea that languages are similar in degree of complexity has been common ground between linguists of very different theoretical persua-sions. In 1981 Richard Hudson made a well-known attempt to identify things that linguists all agreed about, and his list turned out to be sufficiently uncontentious that the updated version of it is nowadays promulgated as "Some issues on which linguists can agree" on the website of the UK Higher Education Academy. Item 2.2d on the list runs:

There is no evidence that normal human languages differ greatly in the complexity of their rules, or that there are any languages that are "primitive" in the size of their vocabulary (or any other part of their language [*sic*]), however "primitive" their speakers may be from a cultural point of view. (The term "normal human language" is meant to exclude on the one hand artificial languages such as Esperanto or computer languages, and on the other hand languages which are not used as the primary means of commu-nication within any community, notably pidgin languages. Such languages may be simpler than normal human languages, though this is not necessarily so.)

Echoing Hockett's comparison of English with Fox, Hudson's item 3.4b states: "Although English has little inflectional morphology, it has a complex syntax..."

This axiom became so well established within linguistics that writers on other subjects have treated it as a reliable premiss. For instance, Matt Ridley's popular book about recent genetic discoveries, *Genome*, illustrates the concept of instinct with a chapter uncritically retailing the gospel according to Noam Chomsky and Steven Pinker about language, and stating as an uncontentious fact that "All human people speak languages of comparable grammatical complexity, even those isolated in the highlands of New Guinea since the Stone Age" (Ridley 1999: 94). At a more academic level, the philosopher Stephen Laurence, in a discussion of the relationship between language and thought, writes:

there seems to be good evidence that language *isn't* just [*sic*] a cultural artefact or human "invention". For example, there is no known correlation between the existence or complexity of language with cultural development, though we would expect there would be if language were a cultural artefact (Laurence 1998: 211)

Laurence cites Pinker as his authority.[2]

7 Complexity invariance over individuals' lifespans

So far I have discussed the existence or nonexistence of complexity differences between different languages: linguists either believe that no sizeable differences exist, or that what differences do exist do not correlate with other cultural features of the respective societies. That is not the only sense in which linguists have believed in complexity invariance, though. One can also hold that an individual's language remains constant in complexity during his or her lifetime.

If the period considered were to include early childhood, that would be an absurd position: everyone knows that small children have to move through stages of single-word utterances and then brief phrases before they begin to use their mother tongue in the complex ways characteristic of adults. But the generative school believe that the language acquisition period of an individual's life is sharply separate from the period when the individual has become a mature speaker, and that in that mature period the speaker remains in a linguistic "steady state". According to Chomsky:

---

[2] The word "just" in the first line of the Laurence quotation seems to imply that products of cultural evolution will be simpler than biological structures. This may well be a tacit assumption among proponents of the "language instinct" concept more generally, but if so it is a baseless one. The English legal system, for instance, with its common-law foundation overlaid by massive corpora of statute and case law, its hierarchy of courts, its rules of evidence, arrangements for legal education, dress codes, and so forth is certainly a product of cultural rather than biological evolution, but no-one would describe it as simple.

children proceed through a series of cognitive states...[terminating in] a "steady state" attained fairly early in life and not changing in significant respects from that point on.... Attainment of a steady state at some not-too-delayed stage of intellectual development is presumably characteristic of "learning" within the range of cognitive capacity. (N. Chomsky 1976: 119)

Chomsky's word "presumably" seems to imply that he was adopting the steady-state hypothesis because he saw it as self-evidently plausible. Yet surely, in the sphere of day-to-day commonsense social discussion, we are all familiar with the opposite point of view: people say "You never stop learning, do you?" as a truism.

And this is a case where the generative position on complexity invariance goes well beyond what was believed by their descriptivist predecessors. Leonard Bloomfield, for instance, held a view which matched the commonsense idea rather than Chomsky's steady-state idea:

there is no hour or day when we can say that a person has finished learning to speak, but, rather, to the end of his life, the speaker keeps on doing the very things which make up infantile language-learning. (Bloomfield 1933: 46)

8 Complexity invariance between individuals

There is a third sense in which language complexity might or might not be invariant. Just as one can compare complexity between the languages of separate societies, and between the languages of different stages of an individual's life, one can also compare complexity as between the idiolects spoken by different members of a single speech community. I am not sure that the descriptivists discussed this issue much, but the generativists have sometimes explicitly treated complexity invariance as axiomatic at this level also:

[Grammar acquisition] is essentially independent of intelligence.... We know that the grammars that are in fact constructed vary only slightly among speakers of the same language, despite wide variations not only in intelligence but also in the conditions under which language is acquired. (N. Chomsky 1968: 68–9)

Chomsky goes on to say that speakers may differ in "ability to use language", that is, their "performance" levels may differ, but he holds that their underlying "competence" is essentially uniform. Later, he wrote:

[Unlike school subjects such as physics] Grammar and common sense are acquired by virtually everyone, effortlessly, rapidly, in a uniform manner.... To a very good first approximation, individuals are indistinguishable (apart from gross deficits and abnormalities) in their ability to acquire grammar... individuals of a given community each acquire a cognitive structure that is... essentially the same as the systems acquired by others. Knowledge of physics, on the other hand, is acquired selectively.... It is not quickly and uniformly attained as a steady state ... (N. Chomsky 1976: 144)

In most areas of human culture, we take for granted that some individual members of society will acquire deeper and richer patterns of ability than others, whether because of differences in native capacity, different learning opportunities, different tastes and interests, or all of these. Language, though, is taken to be different: unless we suffer from some gross disability such as profound deafness, then (according to Chomsky and other generativists) irrespective of degrees of native wit and particular tastes and formative backgrounds we grow up essentially indistinguishable with respect to linguistic competence.

Admittedly, on at least one occasion Chomsky retreated fairly dramatically from this assumption of uniformity between individuals. Pressed on the point by Seymour Papert at a 1975 conference, Chomsky made remarks which seemed flatly to contradict the quotation given above (Piattelli-Palmarini 1980: 175–6). But the consensus among generative linguists has been for linguistic uniformity between individuals, and few generativists have noticed or given any weight to what Chomsky said to Papert on a single occasion in 1975. When Ngoni Chipere decided to work on native-speaker variations in syntactic competence for his MA thesis, he tells us that his supervisor warned him that it was a bad career move if he hoped to get published, and he found that "a strong mixture of ideology and theoretical objections has created a powerful taboo on the subject of individual differences", so that "experimental evidence of such differences has been effectively ignored for the last forty years" (Chipere 2003: xv, 5).

9 Diverse challenges to the axiom

Now let us consider some of the ways in which the consensus has recently been challenged. I cannot pretend to survey developments comprehensively, and many of the challengers will be speaking for themselves in later chapters. But it is worth listing some of the publications which first showed that the constant-complexity axiom was no longer axiomatic, in order to demonstrate that it is not just one facet of this consensus that is now being questioned or contradicted: every facet is being challenged simultaneously. (For further references that I have no room to discuss here, see Karlsson et al. 2008.)

10 Complexity growth in language history

For me, as it happened, the first item that showed me that my private doubts about complexity invariance were not just an eccentric personal heresy but a topic open to serious, painstaking scholarly research was Guy Deutscher's year-2000 book *Syntactic change in Akkadian*. Akkadian is one of the earliest languages to have been reduced to writing, and Deutscher claims that if one looks at the earliest recorded stages of Akkadian one finds a complete absence of finite complement clauses. What's more, this is not just a matter of the surviving records happening not to include examples of recursive structures that did exist in speech; Deutscher shows that if we inspect the 2,000-year history of Akkadian, we see complement clauses gradually developing out of simpler, non-recursive structures which did exist in the early records. And Deutscher argues that this development was visibly a response to new communicative needs arising in Babylonian society.

That is as direct a refutation as there could be of Ray Jackendoff's statement that "the earliest written documents already display the full expressive variety and grammatical complexity of modern languages". I do not know what evidence Jackendoff thought he had for his claim; he quoted none. It seemed to me that we had an aprioristic ideological position from Jackendoff being contradicted by a position based on hard, detailed evidence from Deutscher.

This was particularly striking to me because of the Linguist List controversy I had found myself embroiled with. I had quoted other writers on Biblical Hebrew and Proto-Indo-European, and I was not qualified to pursue the controversy from my own knowledge, because I have not got the necessary expertise in those languages. One man who knew Biblical Hebrew well told me that Walter Ong, and therefore I also, had exaggerated the extent to which that language lacked clause subordination. But I have not encountered anyone querying the solidity of Deutscher's analysis of Akkadian.

If the complexity invariance axiom is understood as absolutely as Stephen Laurence expressed it in the passage I quoted in section 6 above, it was never tenable in the first place. For instance, even the mainstream generative linguists Brent Berlin and Paul Kay, in their well-known cross-linguistic study of colour vocabularies, recognized that "languages add basic color terms as the peoples who speak them become technologically and culturally more complex" (Berlin and Kay 1969: 150), in other words there is a correlation between this aspect of language complexity and cultural development. But vocabulary size was not seen by linguists as an ideologically charged aspect of language complexity. Grammatical structure was, so Deutscher was contradicting a significant article of faith.

The way that linguists were muddling evidence with ideology was underlined by a book that appeared in English just before the turn of the century: Louis-Jean Calvet's *Language wars and linguistic politics* (a 1998 translation of a French original published in 1987). You could not find a doughtier enemy of "linguistic imperialism" than Calvet; but, coming from a separate national background, his conception of what anti-imperialism requires us to believe about language structure turned out to differ from the consensus among English-speaking linguists. One passage (chapter 9) in his book, based on a 1983 doctoral dissertation by Elisabeth Michenot, discusses the South American language Quechua, and how it is being deformed through the influence of Spanish. According to Calvet, the Quechua of rural areas, free from Spanish contamination, has very little clause subordination; the "official" Quechua of the towns has adopted a richly recursive system of clause subordination similar to Spanish or English.

Many American or British linguists might take Calvet's statement about rural Quechua as a shocking suggestion that this peasant society uses a crudely simple language; they would want to insist that rural Quechua speakers have recursive structures at their disposal even if they rarely use them. For Calvet, the scenario was a case of domineering European culture deforming the structural properties which can still be observed in Quechua where it is free from imperialist contamination. I do not doubt the sincerity of any of these linguists' ideological commitments; but surely it is clear that we need to establish the *facts* about variation in structural complexity, before it is reasonable to move on to debating their ideological implications?

11 Differences among individuals' levels of linguistic competence

I have already mentioned Ngoni Chipere's 2003 book *Understanding complex sentences.* Chipere sets out from a finding by the scholar who was his MA supervisor, Ewa Dąbrowska (1997), that adult members of a speech community differ in their ability to deal with syntactic complexity. Chipere quotes the English example:

The doctor knows that the fact that taking care of himself is necessary surprises Tom.

The grammatical structure here is moderately complicated, but any generative grammarian would unquestionably agree that it is a well-formed example of English. Indeed, the grammar is less tangled than plenty of prose which is in everyday use in written English. But Dąbrowska found that native speakers' ability to understand examples like this varied fairly dramatically.

When she asked participants in her experiment to answer simple comprehension questions... she found that university lecturers performed better than undergraduates, who, in turn, performed better than cleaners and porters, most of whom completely failed to answer the questions correctly. (Chipere 2003: 2)

What is more, when Chipere carried out similar experiments, he

found, unexpectedly, that post-graduate students who were *not* native speakers of English performed better than native English cleaners and porters and, in some respects, even performed better than native English post-graduates. Presumably this was because non-native speakers actually learn the grammatical rules of English, whereas explicit grammatical instruction has not been considered necessary for native speakers ... (Chipere 2003: 3)

If our mother tongue is simply part of our culture, which we learn using the same general ability to learn complicated things that we use to learn to play chess or keep accounts or program computers, then it is entirely unsurprising that brighter individuals learn their mother tongue rather better than individuals who are less intelligent, and even that people who go through explicit language training may learn a language better than individuals who are born into the relevant speech community and just pick their mother tongue up as they go along.

The linguistic consensus has been that mother tongue acquisition is a separate issue. According to the generativists, "we do not really learn language", using general learning abilities; "rather, grammar grows in the mind." Descriptivist linguists did not believe that, but they did see native speaker mastery as the definitive measure of language ability. For many twentieth-century linguists, descriptivist or generativist, I believe it would simply not have made sense to suggest that a non-native speaker might be better at a language than a native speaker. Native speaker ability was the standard; to say that someone knew a language better than its native speakers would be like saying that one had a ruler which was more precisely one metre long than the standard metre, in the days when that was an actual metal bar.

However, in connection with syntactic complexity there are quite natural ways to quantify language ability independently of the particular level of ability possessed by particular native speakers, and in those terms it is evidently not axiomatic that mother tongue speakers are better at their own languages than everyone else.

12 Complexity growth during individuals' lifetimes

The minor contribution I made myself to this process of challenging the linguistic consensus related to the idea of complexity invariance over individuals' lifetimes. It concerned what some are calling *structural complexity* as opposed to *system complexity*: complexity not in the sense of richness of the set of rules defining a speaker's language, but in the sense of how many cycles of recursion speakers produce when the rules they use are recursive.

The British National Corpus contains transcriptions of spontaneous speech by a cross-section of the British population. I took a subset and looked at how the average complexity of utterances, in terms of the incidence of clause subordination, related to the kinds of people the speakers were (Sampson 2001). It is well known that Basil Bernstein (1971) claimed to find a correlation between structural complexity and social class, though by present-day stand-ards his evidence seems quite weak.

I did not find a correlation of that sort (the BNC data on social class are in any case not very reliable); but what I did find, to my considerable surprise, was a correlation with age.

We would expect that small children use simpler grammar than adults, and in the BNC data they did. But I had not expected to find that structural complexity goes on growing, long after the generativists' putative steady state has set in. Forty-year-olds use, on average, more complex structures than thirty-year-olds. People over sixty use more complex structures than people in their forties and fifties. Before I looked at the data, I would confidently have predicted that we would not find anything like that.

13 New versus old and big versus small languages

Meanwhile, John McWhorter moved the issue about some languages being simpler than others in an interesting new direction, by arguing not only that new languages are simpler than old ones, but that big languages tend to be simpler than small ones.

Everybody agrees that pidgins are simpler than established, mother tongue languages; but the consensus has been that once a pidgin acquires native speakers it turns into something different in kind, a creole, and creoles are said to be similar to any other languages in their inherent properties. Only their past history is "special". McWhorter (2001a) proposed a metric for measuring language complexity, and he claimed that, in terms of his metric, creoles are commonly simpler than "old" languages. He came in for a lot of flak (e.g. DeGraff 2001) from people who objected to the suggestion that politically powerless groups might speak languages which in some sense lack the full sophistication of European languages.

But, perhaps even more interestingly, McWhorter has also argued (e.g. 2001b) that English, and other languages of large and successful civilizations, tend to be simpler than languages used by small communities and rarely learned by outsiders. Indeed, similar ideas were already being expressed by Peter Trudgill well before the turn of the century (e.g. Trudgill 1989). It possibly requires the insularity of a remote, impoverished village community to evolve and maintain the more baroque language structures that linguists have encountered. Perhaps Archi not only is a language of the high Caucasus but could only be a language of a place like that.

14 An unusually simple present-day language

Possibly the most transgressive work of all has been Dan Everett's description of the Pirahã language of the southern Amazon basin (Everett 2005). Early Akkadian, according to Guy Deutscher, lacked complement clauses, but it did have some clause subordination. Pirahã in our own time, as Everett describes it, has no clause subordination at all, indeed it has no grammatical embedding of any kind, and in other ways too it sounds astonishingly crude as an intellectual medium. For instance, Pirahã has no quantifier words, comparable to *all, some,* or *most* in English; and it has no number words at all – even "one, two, many" is a stage of mathematical sophistication outside the ken of the Pirahã.

If the generativists were right to claim that human biology guarantees that all natural languages must be cut to a common pattern, then Pirahã as Dan Everett describes it surely could not be a natural human language. (It is reasonable to include the proviso about correctness – faced with such remarkable material, we must bear in mind that we are dealing with one fallible scholar's interpretations.) Despite the oddity of their language, though, the Pirahã are certainly members of our species. The difference between Pirahã and better-known languages is a cultural difference, not a biological difference, and in the cultural sphere we expect some systems to be simpler than others. Nobody is surprised if symphonic music has richer structure than early mediaeval music, or if the present-day law of England requires many more books to define it than the Anglo-Saxon common law out of which it evolved. Cultural institutions standardly evolve in complexity over time, often becoming more complex, sometimes being simplified. But we have not been accustomed to thinking that way about language.

15 Language "universals" as products of cultural influence

Finally, David Gil documents a point about isomorphism between exotic and European languages. Where non-Indo-European languages of distant cultures in our own time do seem to be structurally more or less isomorphic with European languages, this is not necessarily evidence for biological mechanisms which cause all human languages to conform to a common pattern. It may instead merely show that the "official" versions of languages in all parts of the world have nowadays been heavily remodelled under European influence.

Gil has published a series of comparisons (e.g. Gil 2005b) between the indigenous Indonesian dialect of the island of Riau and the formal Indonesian language used for written communication, which outsiders who study Indonesian are encouraged to see as the standard language of that country. Formal Indonesian does share many features of European languages which generative theory sees as necessary properties of any natural language. But colloquial Riau Indonesian does not: it fails to conform to various characteristics that generativists describe as universal requirements. And Gil argues (if I interpret him correctly) that part of the explanation is that official, formal Indonesian is to some extent an artificial construct, created in order to mirror the logical properties of European languages.

Because the formal language has prestige, when a foreigner asks a Riau speaker how he expresses something, the answer is likely to be an example of formal Indonesian. But when the same speaker talks spontaneously, he will use the very different structural patterns of Riau Indonesian.

In modern political circumstances Gil's argument is very plausible. Consider the opening sentence of the United Nations Charter, which in English contains 177 words, consisting of one main clause with three clauses at one degree of subordination, eight clauses at two degrees of subordination, four clauses at three degrees of subordination, and one clause at four degrees of subordination (square brackets delimit finite and angle brackets delimit non-finite clauses):

[We the peoples of the United Nations <determined <to save succeeding generations from the scourge of war, [which twice in our lifetime has brought untold sorrow to mankind]>, and <to reaffirm faith in fundamental human rights, in the dignity and worth of the human person, in the equal rights of men and women and of nations large and small>, and <to establish conditions [under which justice and respect for the obligations <arising from treaties and other sources of international law> can be maintained]>, and <to promote social progress and better standards of life in larger freedom>, and for these ends <to practise tolerance and live together in peace with one another as good neighbours>, and <to unite our strength <to maintain international peace and security>>, and <to ensure, by the acceptance of principles and the institution of methods, [that armed force shall not be used, save in the common interest]>, and <to employ international machinery for the promotion of the economic and social advancement of all peoples>>, have resolved <to combine our efforts><to accomplish these aims>].

Although the sentence was composed by speakers of modern European or European-derived languages (specifically, Afrikaans and English), it would translate readily enough into the Latin of 2,000-odd years ago – which is no surprise, since formal usage in modern European languages has historically been heavily influenced by Latin models.

On the other hand, the early non-European language I know best is Old Chinese; so far as I can see, it would be quite impossible to come close to an equivalent of this sentence in that language (cf. Sampson 2006). Old Chinese did have some clause subordination mechanisms, but they were extremely restricted by comparison with English (Pulleyblank 1995: e.g. 37, 148ff.) However, if the community of Old Chinese speakers were living in the twenty-first century, their leaders would find that it would not do to say, "You can say that in your language, but you can't say it in our language." In order to survive as a society in the modern world they would have to change Old Chinese into a very different kind of language, in which translations were available for the UN Charter and for a great deal of other Western officialese.

And then, once this new language had been invented, generative linguists would come along and point to it as yet further corroboration of the idea that human beings share innate cognitive machinery which imposes a common structure on all natural languages. A large cultural shift, carried out in order to maintain a society's position vis-à-vis more powerful Western societies, would be cited as proof that a central aspect of the society's culture never was more than trivially different from Western models, and that it is biologically impossible for any human society to be more than trivially different with respect to cognitive structure. Obviously this scenario is purely hypothetical in the case of Old Chinese of 3,000 years ago. But I believe essentially that process has been happening a lot with Third World languages in modern times.

That turns the generative belief that all languages are similar in structural complexity into something like a self-fulfilling prophecy. What European or North American linguists count as the "real language" of a distant part of the world will be the version of its language which has been remodelled in order to be similar to European languages. Because of the immense dominance nowadays of European-derived cultures, most or all countries will have that kind of version of their language available; and for a Western linguist who arrives at the airport and has to spend considerable time dealing with officialdom, that will be the version most accessible to study. It takes a lot of extra effort to penetrate to places like Riau, where language varieties are spoken that test the axiom of constant language complexity more robustly.

If we are concerned about the moral duty to respect alien cultures, what implies real lack of respect is this insistence on interpreting exotic cognitive systems as minor variations on a European theme (Sampson 2007) – not the recognition that languages can differ in many ways, including their degree of complexity.

16 A melting iceberg

The traditional consensus on linguistic complexity was accepted as wholly authoritative for much of the past century. Developments of the last few years, such as those surveyed above, suggest that it finds itself now in the situation of an iceberg that has floated into warm waters.

2

How much grammar does it take to sail a boat?

DAVID GIL

1 Complexity of language, complexity of civilization

Human languages are of much greater complexity than the communicative systems of great apes, dolphins, bees, and other animals.[1] Similarly, human culture, technology, and civilization are also immensely more complicated than anything observed in other species, such as the ways in which chimpanzees fashion tools to crack nuts or fish for termites. Clearly, these two facts are related: comparing humans to other species leads inexorably to the conclusion that linguistic complexity is *correlated* with complexity in other, non-linguistic domains. But what exactly is the nature of this correlation?

A widespread assumption is that linguistic complexity is necessary in order to support complexity in other domains. This accords with a functional approach towards the evolution of language, whereby greater linguistic complexity enables humans to accomplish more tasks, and in doing so confers an evolutionary advantage. It also forms the basis for archaeological investigations into the evolution of language, in which the existence of material artifacts from a certain era is interpreted as evidence that humans at that time were also endowed with the cognitive and linguistic abilities necessary for the production of such artifacts (Lee and DeVore 1968; G. Clark 1977; Roebrooks 2001; de la Torre 2004; and many others). Similarly, the discovery of the remains of an apparently new species of hominin on the Indonesian

[1] Most of the naturalistic data discussed in this paper were collected by the staff at the Max Planck Institute Jakarta Field Station and its Padang and Manokwari branches. For their administrative and professional assistance I am indebted to Uri Tadmor and Betty Litamahuputty (Jakarta), Yusrita Yanti (Padang), and Yusuf Sawaki (Manokwari); and for collecting and transcribing the data I am grateful to Sarah Chakrawati, Erni Farida Sri Ulina Ginting, Ferdinand Okki Kurniawan, Dalan Mehuli Peranginangin, and Tessa Yuditha (Jakarta), Santi Kurniati, Silvie Antisari Anhar, and Yessy Prima Putri (Padang), and Fitri Djamaludin, Yehuda Ibi, Nando Saragih, and Olivia Waren (Manokwari). For the *pantun* I am thankful to Kudin (Sungai Pakning).

island of Flores raises the possibility that such hominins were capable of constructing and sailing boats, which in turn may suggest that *Homo floresiensis* was endowed with whatever linguistic abilities are necessary for the collective planning and execution of such a complex set of activities (see Morwood and Cogill-Koez 2007 for recent critical discussion).

But what, exactly, are the necessary linguistic abilities: how much grammar does it really take to build a boat and sail it to a distant island? Or more generally: how much grammar does it take to do all of the things that, amongst all living species, only humans are capable of doing, such as, for example, worshipping God, waging war, and working in offices; inventing, manufacturing, and using sophisticated hi-tech tools; and engaging in multifarious commercial, scientific, and artistic activities?

This chapter argues that the amount of grammar that is needed in order to support the vast majority of daily human activities is substantially less than is often supposed, in fact less than that exhibited by any contemporary human language, and far less than that exhibited by most such languages. In other words, much of the observable complexity of contemporary human grammar has no obvious function pertaining to the development and maintenance of modern human civilization. More specifically, it is argued that the level of grammatical complexity necessary for contemporary culture, technology, and civilization is no greater than that of *Isolating-Monocategorial-Associational* (or *IMA*) *Language*.

2 Isolating-Monocategorial-Associational Language

Isolating-Monocategorial-Associational Language, introduced in Gil (2005a), is an idealized language prototype with the following three properties:

(1)　(a)　*morphologically isolating*: no word-internal morphological structure;
　　　(b)　*syntactically monocategorial*: no distinct syntactic categories;
　　　(c)　*semantically associational*: no distinct construction-specific rules of semantic interpretation (instead, compositional semantics relies exclusively on the Association Operator, defined in (2) below).

As argued in Gil (2005a, 2006), IMA Language characterizes an early stage in the phylogenetic evolution of human language, and also an early stage in the ontogenetic development of contemporary child language. In addition it can be observed in artificial languages such as that of pictograms. However, no known contemporary human language instantiates IMA Language; all such languages are endowed with additional kinds of structure beyond those sanctioned by the definition in (1) above.

The defining properties of IMA Language represent the limiting points of maximal simplicity within each of three distinct domains: morphology, syntax, and semantics. Hence, for each domain, one may imagine languages approaching these endpoints along a scale of decreasing complexity. Accordingly, a language is increasingly isolating as it has less and less morphological structure, increasingly monocategorial as its syntactic categories decrease in number and importance, and increasingly associational as its construction-specific rules of semantic interpretation become fewer and less distinct. Alongside *Pure IMA Language,* as in (1) above, one may thus entertain the possibility of a range of *Relative IMA Languages,* approaching Pure IMA Language to various degrees within each of the above three domains.

The first defining property, *morphologically isolating,* is the one that is most familiar, since it forms the basis for a typology that has been the focus of considerable attention in the linguistic literature. As is well known, isolating languages such as Vietnamese have considerably less word-internal morphological structure than synthetic languages such as Russian, which in turn have considerably less morphology than polysynthetic languages such as Mohawk. However, no natural language is purely isolating; all known isolating languages still have *some* morphology – affixation, compounding, or other kinds of process such as reduplication, stem alternation, and so forth.

The second defining property, *syntactically monocategorial,* pertains to a domain within which the presence of cross-linguistic variation has only recently, and still only partially, been recognized. In the past, syntactic categories have generally been presumed to be universal; however, in recent years an increasing body of literature has begun to examine the ways in which the inventories of syntactic categories may vary across languages. One major area of focus has been the case of languages purportedly lacking in various part-of-speech distinctions, such as languages with no adjectives, or languages in which nouns and verbs cannot be distinguished. However, to the best of my knowledge, no language has ever actually been proposed to be purely monocategorial. In particular, most or all descriptions of languages still involve, at the very least, a distinction between one or more open syntactic categories containing "content words" and one or more closed syntactic categories containing various "grammatical" or "functional" items; see, for example, Gil (2000).

The third defining property, *semantically associational,* relates to the domain of compositional semantics, the way in which the meanings of complex expressions are derived from the meanings of their constituent parts. This property makes reference to the *Association Operator,* defined as follows:

(2) The Association Operator A

Given a set of n meanings $M_1 \ldots M_n$, the Association Operator A derives a meaning $A(M_1 \ldots M_n)$ read as "entity associated with M_1 and ... and M_n".

Setting n equal to 1 results in the *Monadic Association Operator*, manifest, for example, in constructions containing a genitive, possessive, or associative marker. Allowing n to equal 2 or more results in the *Polyadic Association Operator*, in accordance with which, whenever two or more expressions group together to form a larger expression, the meaning of the combined expression is associated with, or has to do with, the meanings of each of the individual expressions. The Polyadic Association Operator is responsible for the fact that in a two-word expression in which, say, one of the words contains a stem meaning "chicken" while the other contains a stem meaning "eat", the meaning of the expression as a whole must be related to "chicken" and "eat", for example "The chicken is eating", "The chickens that were eaten", "The reason chickens eat"; it can never mean "Beavers build dams". The Polyadic Association Operator is thus a universal default mechanism for semantic interpretation, albeit one that is in most cases overridden and narrowed down substantially by the application of additional construction-specific rules. A purely associational language would be one in which there were no such further construction-specific rules of semantic interpretation, and in which, therefore, the compositional semantics were effected exclusively by the Polyadic Association Operator. It is almost certainly the case that no natural language is purely associational; however, as argued in Gil (2007; 2008), some languages make relatively less use of such additional semantic rules, and may thus be characterized as more highly associational.

3 Riau Indonesian as a Relative IMA Language

No naturally occurring contemporary human language completely satisfies the definition of IMA Language. However, whereas many languages, such as English, Hebrew, Dani (Rosch Heider and Olivier 1972), and Pirahã (Chapters 15 and 16 below), go way beyond the confines of IMA Language, exhibiting much greater levels of complexity with respect to morphological structure, syntactic category inventories, and compositional semantics, others approach the IMA prototype to various degrees, thereby warranting characterization as Relative IMA Languages. One example of a Relative IMA Language is Riau Indonesian, as described in Gil (e.g. 1994, 2000, 2001, 2002a, b, 2004a, b, 2005a, b).

In Riau Indonesian, basic sentence structure is in fact purely IMA. Consider the following simple sentence:

(3) *Ayam   makan*
     chicken   eat
     A(CHICKEN, EAT)

The above sentence consists entirely of two "content words", and is devoid of any additional grammatical markers. The *isolating* character of the language is instantiated by the fact that each of the two words is monomorphemic. The *monocategorial* nature of the language is reflected by the fact that the two words, although referring to a thing and an activity respectively, exhibit identical grammatical behaviour: rather than belonging to distinct parts of speech, such as noun and verb, they are thus members of the same syntactic category, which, on the basis of its distributional properties, is most appropriately identified as the category "sentence" (see Gil 2000). Accordingly, sentence (3) as a whole is a simple juxtaposition, or coordination, of two sentences. The *associational* character of the language can be seen in the wide range of available interpretations: the first word, *ayam*, is underspecified for number and definiteness; the second word, *makan*, is indeterminate with respect to tense and aspect; and the sentence as a whole is underspecified with regard to thematic roles, with *ayam* being able to bear agent, patient, or any other role in relation to *makan*, and in addition also indeterminate with respect to ontological categories, with possible interpretations belonging to categories such as activity, thing, reason, place, time, and others. However, although the sentence can be understood in very many different ways, such as "The chicken is eating", "The chickens that were eaten", "The reason chickens eat", and so forth, it is not multiply ambiguous; rather, it is extremely vague, with a single very general interpretation which may be represented, as in (3) above, with the Polyadic Association Operator, A(CHICKEN, EAT), to be read as "entity associated with chicken and eating", or, more idiomatically, "something to do with chicken and eating". Sentence (3) above is a typical sentence in Riau Indonesian; it is not "telegraphic" or otherwise stylistically marked in any way. Longer and more complex sentences can be constructed which, like (3), instantiate pure IMA structure.

Nevertheless, Riau Indonesian contains a number of features which take it beyond the bounds of a pure IMA Language. That Riau Indonesian is not purely isolating is evidenced by the presence of a handful of bona fide affixes, plus various other morphological processes, such as compounding, reduplication, and truncation. None of these processes, however, are inflectional, and none of them are obligatory in any particular grammatical environment. That

Riau Indonesian is not purely monocategorial is due to the fact that in addition to the single open syntactic category sentence, it also contains a single closed syntactic category containing a few dozen semantically hetero-geneous words whose grammatical behaviour sets them apart from words belonging to the category of sentence. However, although most members of this second, closed syntactic category are what are generally considered to be grammatical function words, none of these items are obligatory in any specific grammatical construction. Finally, that Riau Indonesian is not purely associ-ational is clear from the presence of additional rules of compositional seman-tics that make reference to specific lexical items or to particular syntactic configurations, for example, word order. Still, the effect of such rules is much more restricted than is the case in many other languages. Thus, Riau Indo-nesian is most appropriately characterized as a Relative IMA Language.

The present analysis of Riau Indonesian runs counter to arguments put forward by Walter Bisang (Chapter 3 below) that in the isolating languages of Southeast Asia "less is more", overt grammatical simplicity being compen-sated for by "hidden complexity" in the semantics or pragmatics, as well as (in passing) by John Hawkins (Chapter 18 below), who makes a similar claim for "simple SVO structures with complex theta-role assignments" in English. Elsewhere, however, I have argued that in Riau Indonesian there is no evidence for such a trade-off producing "hidden complexity"; rather, simple forms map onto simple meanings with no reason to believe that the prag-matics then automatically steps in to fill in any number of additional more complex details (Gil 2008: 124–9).

4 IMA Language is all that's needed to sail a boat

Riau Indonesian is a colloquial language variety used in informal situations as a vehicle of interethnic and increasingly also intraethnic communication by a population of about five million in the province of Riau in east-central Sumatra. Riau Indonesian is but one of a wide range of colloquial varieties of Malay/Indonesian, spoken throughout Indonesia and neighbouring Ma-laysia, Brunei, and Singapore by a total population of over 200 million people. Although differing from each other to the point of mutual unintelligibility, a majority of these colloquial varieties resemble Riau Indonesian in their basic grammatical structures, and accordingly share the characterization as Relative IMA Languages. However, in addition to these basilectal language varieties, there are also versions of Standard Indonesian and Malay, typically acquired in mid-childhood or later as a second or subsequent language variety for use in formal situations; as might be expected, these more acrolectal varieties of Malay/Indonesian are less IMA than their colloquial counterparts.

As Relative IMA Languages, Riau Indonesian and other colloquial varieties of Malay/Indonesian make it possible to address the question: how much grammar does it take to sail a boat? By peeling off the extra layers of non-IMA complexity and homing in on the IMA core, one may examine the expressive power of pure IMA Language, and see exactly what levels of culture, technology, and civilization it can support. In order to do this, we shall take a look at some fragments of pure IMA Language culled from naturalistic corpora in a few varieties of colloquial Malay/Indonesian. In such corpora, most utterances contain at least some additional structure beyond what is purely IMA: an affix, a word belonging to the closed class of grammatical function words, or a construction-specific rule of semantic interpretation. Nevertheless, it is also possible to find stretches of text in which, by probabilistically governed accident, no such additional structure is present, and in which, therefore, exhibit pure IMA structure. Following are some such examples of pure IMA text:

(4) *"Ck,　emang　lu　libur　besok?"　tadi　　kan　Erto.*
　　tsk　really　2　holiday　tomorrow　PST.PROX　Q　Erto
　　"Then Erto asked, right, 'Tsk, do you really have a day off tomorrow?'"

(5) *Tadi　　ogut　pas　telefon,　Eto　lagi　mandi.*
　　PST.PROX　1S　precise　telephone　Eto　more　wash
　　"Right when I phoned, Eto was taking a shower."

(6) *Kenapa　kamu　ngga　pengen　ikut?*
　　why　2　NEG　want　follow
　　"Why don't you want to come along?"

(7) *Semester　tujuh　sampe　skarang　semester　delapan　ni.*
　　semester　seven　arrive　now　　semester　eight　DEM.PROX

　　Semester　delapan　tinggal　sampe　kemarin　baru　bayar　SPP.
　　semester　eight　　remain　arrive　yesterday　new　pay　tuition_fee

　　Baru　bayar　SPP　　selesai　tra　tau　tong　masuk
　　new　pay　tuition_fee　finish　NEG　know　1P　enter

　　kulia　　kapan　ni.
　　university_class　when　DEM.PROX

　　"From the seventh semester until now, the eighth semester. Through the eighth semester until yesterday, we only just paid the tuition fee. But even though we just paid the tuition fee, we don't know when we're going to start classes again."

(8) *Baru de dapa sepak langsung kaki pata.*
　　 new 3S get kick direct leg break

　　 Jadi   semester enam tu   de cuti.
　　 become semester six DEM.DIST 3S holiday

　　 "Then he was kicked and broke his foot. So he was out for semester six."

(9) *Pas   SMA   tu   sa bilang "mama kam beli*
　　 precise senior_high_school DEM.DIST 1S say   mother 2P   buy

　　 sa gitar baru dulu". Dong beli sa gitar   baru suda mo.
　　 1S guitar new before 3P   buy 1S guitar new IMPF want

　　 "When I went into senior high school I said 'Mum, you should buy me a new guitar'. So they bought me a new guitar."

(10) *Kan dia pengen orang   luar nikah samo   dio, samantaro.*
　　 Q   3   want   person out   marry together 3   temporary

　　 Orang   tuo   nyo kan ndak buliah,
　　 person old   3   Q   NEG   can

　　 dio pingin anak   nyo nikah samo   anak   Datung.
　　 3   want   child 3   marry together child Datung

　　 "She wanted an outside person to marry her, temporarily, right. But her parents wouldn't allow it, right, they wanted their child to marry the son of Datung."

(11) *Karam   tu.   Ntah   ndak tau   wak ntah*
　　 collapse DEM.DIST NEG.know NEG   know 1   NEG.know

　　 a   karam   rumah tu   pas   urang duduak ateh rumah.
　　 what collapse house DEM.DIST precise person sit   up   house

　　 "It collapsed. I don't know how the house could collapse while people were sitting in it."

(12) *Udah tu,   hari ujan. Hari ujan masuak lah,*
　　 IMPF DEM.DIST day rain day rain enter   FOC

　　 ado gua dakek kampuang tu,   masuak lah gua tu   nyo.
　　 exist cave near   village   DEM.DIST enter   FOC cave DEM.DIST 3

　　 Masuak dalam gua tu   kan, paruik   lah   lapa   ko.
　　 enter   inside cave DEM.DIST Q   abdomen IPFV hungry DEM.PROX

　　 "After that, it rained. As it was raining, he went in, there was a cave near the village, and he went into the cave. Having gone into the cave, he was hungry."

(13) *Korsi   kami   korsi   kayu,*
      chair   1   chair   wood

      Korsi   miko   korsi   buloh;
      chair   2P   chair   bamboo

      Orang   kami   orang   Dayak,
      person   1   person   Dayak

      Orang   miko   orang   Batak.
      person   2P   person   Batak

      "Our chairs are wooden chairs / Your chairs are bamboo chairs / Us people
      are Dayak people / You people are Batak people."

Examples (4–6) above are from Jakarta Indonesian, the colloquial variety of Indonesian spoken as the primary everyday language by over 20 million residents of the capital city of Indonesia and its surrounding metropolitan area, and increasingly adopted as a stylistically trendy register by middle- and upper-class inhabitants in the provinces. Examples (7–9) are from Papuan Malay, used by possibly 2 million people as the lingua franca in the western half of the island of New Guinea under Indonesian control. Examples (10–12) are from Minangkabau, spoken by an estimated 6–7 million members of the eponymous ethnicity in the province of West Sumatra as well as in migrant communities elsewhere. (Minangkabau is usually considered to be a "different language"; however, it is very closely related to Malay/Indonesian, and not much more different from many varieties of Malay/Indonesian than such varieties are from each other. For ease of exposition, we shall thus subsume it under the heading of colloquial Malay/Indonesian.) And example (13) is from Siak Malay, a rural dialect spoken by a few hundred thousand people in the Siak river basin in Riau province in east-central Sumatra.[2]

The dialects represented in the above examples span a variety of sociolinguistic types. Whereas Jakarta Indonesian and Papuan Malay are the possible products of radical restructuring such as that characteristic of creole languages, and are now spoken by ethnically mixed populations, Minangkabau and Siak Malay are more appropriately viewed as direct descendants of proto-Malayic, and now constitute emblematic vehicles of the respective ethnic

---

[2] Jakarta Indonesian has been the subject of a number of recent investigations, including Wouk (1989, 1999), Cole, Hermon, and Tjung (2006), and Sneddon (2006). Papuan Malay has featured less prominently in the literature, one recent study being that of Donohue and Sawaki (2007); it is also discussed briefly in Gil (2002b), where it is referred to as Irian Indonesian. Minangkabau is described in a reference grammar by Moussay (1981). And Siak Malay has been discussed in the context of its contact relationship with Riau Indonesian in Gil (2001, 2002a, 2004a). The other authors mentioned above do not necessarily subscribe to the present characterization of these language varieties as Relative IMA Languages.

identities. Speakers of these different varieties range from westernized and upwardly mobile office workers in high-rise buildings in Jakarta, through shopkeepers and rice-farmers across the archipelago, all the way to New Guinea highlanders in penis gourds and grass skirts. Together, these four varieties of colloquial Malay/Indonesian provide a representative sample of the unity in diversity inherent in what is by all accounts a major world language.

The above examples provide an indication of the expressive power of pure IMA Language, showing how it matches up to other, non-IMA Languages, by capturing notions that in other languages make recourse to specialized grammatical constructions. Demonstratives occur in examples (7), (8), (9), (11), and (12); numerals in (7); and negatives in (6), (7), (10), and (11) – all completely within the confines of IMA Language, without any of the structurally specialized constructions used to express the corresponding notions in many other languages. Tense and aspect are expressed in pure IMA structure in several of the above examples – proximate past *tadi* in (4) and (5), progressive *lagi* in (5), sequential *baru* in (7) and (8), and perfectives *suda* in (9) and *udah* and *lah* in (12). And words with first, second, or third person reference but not belonging to a grammatically dedicated category of pronoun can be found in each and every one of the above examples; this is because the words in question belong to an open class of items containing names, titles, kinship terms, and other similar expressions.

Other, more relational notions are also expressed within the confines of pure IMA Language. Various semantic types of attribution are all expressed by simple juxtaposition of head and modifier: *gitar baru* "new guitar" in (9), *anak nyo* "their child" and *anak Datung* "Datung's child" in (10), and eight other instances in (13). The formation of a content question is exemplified in (6); the shift in perspective characteristic of a passive construction is illustrated in (8); while some of the ways in which co-reference can be maintained are shown in (9), (10), and (12) – all remaining within the limits of pure IMA Language.

Complex meanings which in other languages call for various kinds of embedded clauses may also be expressed within pure IMA Language. Among these are temporal clauses in (5), (9), and (11); complements of mental acts in (10); embedded polar questions in (4); embedded content questions in (7) and (11); reported speech in (4) and (9); and tail–head linkage, in which the final sequence of an utterance is repeated, in backgrounded form, at the beginning of the next utterance, in (7) and (12). In fact, example (11), with its temporal clause occurring within the embedded question, shows how such meanings can be nested, thereby underscoring the recursive potential of pure IMA Language.

Thus, as suggested by the above examples, pure IMA Language is endowed with substantial expressive power. In fact, comparing the above pure IMA fragments to the totality of the Relative IMA Language varieties from which they are taken suggests that getting rid of the non-IMA accoutrements – as per the above exercise – has no systematic effect on expressive power in any semantic domain. The affixes and grammatical markers that take these language varieties beyond the bounds of pure IMA Language form a semantically heterogeneous set, a functional hodge-podge sprinkled like confetti over their fundamentally IMA architecture. A few examples should make this point clear. First, consider the well-known voice markers *di-* and *N-*, which, as prefixes or proclitics (depending on the dialect and on the phonological properties of the host word), go beyond pure isolating and monocategorial structure. However, unlike prototypical passive and active voice markers, *di-* and *N-* have no effect on the grammatical structure of the clause; they are thus optional semantic embellishments (Gil 2002b). Next, consider the marker *yang*, often described as a relative-clause marker. Although colloquial varieties of Indonesian do not have bona fide relative clauses, the grammatical behaviour of *yang* – it can only occur in front of another expression which functions as its host – places it outside the single open syntactic category and therefore beyond the limits of monocategoriality. However, its use is always optional; for example, "the chickens that were eaten" can be rendered as either *ayam yang makan* or, simply, as in (3) above, *ayam makan*. Finally, consider forms with meanings corresponding to English prepositions, such as *dengan* "with". Like *yang*, it can only occur in front of a host expression and is therefore not a member of the single open syntactic category of sentence. However, any expression containing *dengan* can be paraphrased with an alternative expression not containing *dengan* and falling within the scope of pure IMA Language. Often, such paraphrases will contain the word *sama* "with", "together", "same", whose range of meanings wholly contains that of *dengan*, but which differs from *dengan* in being a member of the single open syntactic category of sentence (Gil 2004b). Examples such as these demonstrate that the various non-IMA grammatical markers do not make much of a difference when it comes to assessing the overall expressive power of colloquial Malay/Indonesian varieties. In principle, anything that can be said in such languages can be paraphrased within the confines of pure IMA Language.

This being the case, pure IMA fragments such as those in (4–13) paint a reasonably accurate picture of the functionality of IMA Language, and the amount of culture, technology, and civilization that IMA Language can support. In a nutshell: IMA Language is enough to run a country of some two hundred million people and, by extension, most contemporary human activity throughout the world. Most of the examples in (4–13) are conversational, but this merely reflects the fact that conversation is the most common human linguistic activity, and the one that our corpora accordingly focus upon. Still, as suggested by these examples, the restriction to IMA Language does not impose any constraints on the range of things that can be talked about, or on what can actually be said about those things. As the above examples show, IMA Language is enough to talk about school, sports, love, and life. And it is sufficient to support most daily activities throughout one of the world's largest countries, from the giant metropolis that is Jakarta to the most far-flung of island provinces. Moreover, lest this come across as too utilitarian a view of language, example (13) – a *pantun*, the most widespread genre of oral poetry in Malay/Indonesian – demonstrates that IMA Language can also provide the raw material for verbal art.

Admittedly, there are contexts, mostly of a more formal and official nature, where the colloquial language is inappropriate, and instead the somewhat more complex standard language is used. This raises the possibility that there may exist some domains for which the Relative IMA character of colloquial Malay/Indonesian is functionally inadequate. However, in many cases at least, the use of the standard language is motivated not by any functional gain in expressive power but by social conventions. For example, the president addressing the nation on television could easily get his message across in colloquial Jakarta Indonesian, but to do so would result in loss of face, thereby endangering his elevated standing. One important domain in which the standard language is typically preferred over colloquial varieties is that of writing. However, it is striking that although most Indonesians nowadays can read and write, Indonesia remains a functionally illiterate society: people prefer to communicate orally rather than in writing. A ubiquitous example is provided by public transportation, where almost every vehicle – bus, minibus, boat, or whatever – has somebody hanging onto the outside and calling out the destination to prospective passengers; even if there is also a written sign conveying the same information, people still listen rather than look. Moreover, this holds true not only in the "street", but in all walks of life, even academia. For example, conference organizers may nowadays distribute brochures, send out e-mail announcements, and even, in exceptional cases, create a website, but prospective participants still expect to be invited orally, by word of mouth. Thus, even if there do exist some contexts where the greater grammatical complexity of the standard language really plays a necessary communicative role (something that is not at all obvious), such contexts are marginal and few in number, paling into insignificance alongside the much greater number of domains for which IMA Language proves sufficient to do the job.

What colloquial Malay/Indonesian shows us, then, is that IMA Language is all that it takes to sail a boat. This means that, if indeed *Homo floresiensis* sailed across a major body of water to reach the island of Flores, the most that we can infer from this with regard to his linguistic abilities is that he had IMA Language. More generally, what this suggests is that no amount of non-linguistic archeological evidence will ever be able to prove the presence, at some earlier stage of human evolution, of grammatical entities of greater-than-IMA complexity: prefixes and suffixes, nouns and verbs, not to mention complementizers, relative clauses, government, movement, functional categories, antecedents binding empty positions, and all the other things that so delight the souls of linguists.

5 Why is grammar so complex?

If indeed IMA Language is all it takes to sail a boat and to run a large country, why is it that no languages are pure IMA Languages, and most languages are not even Relative IMA Languages, instead exhibiting substantially greater amounts of grammatical complexity? One cannot but wonder what all this complexity is for. This paper has only been able to provide a negative answer, by identifying one albeit enormous thing that this complexity is not for, namely, the maintenance of contemporary human civilization: IMA Language is enough for all that.

As noted at the outset, comparing humans to other species suggests that grammatical complexity is in fact positively correlated with complexity in other non-linguistic domains. However, more fine-grained observations within the human species reveal a more ambivalent picture. Admittedly, within certain specific contexts, it is possible to identify what appear to be significant correlations between grammatical complexity and complexity in other domains, for example in colloquial Malay/Indonesian, where the development of a non-IMA and hence more complex coordinator may be shown to be related to the introduction of mobile telephony and text messaging (Gil 2004b). However, in other contexts, the correlation seems to go in the opposite direction, as in the well-known case of language simplification being associated with the greater sociopolitical complexity of contact situations (e.g. McWhorter 2005 and Trudgill in Chapter 7 below). Thus, across the diversity of contemporary human languages and cultures, grammatical complexity just does not seem to correlate systematically with complexity in other, non-linguistic domains. (Compare the comment by Sapir quoted by Geoffrey Sampson on p. 5 above.)

These facts cast doubt on a central tenet of most functionalist approaches to language, in accordance with which grammatical complexity is there to enable us to communicate the messages we need to get across. In spite of overwhelming evidence showing that diachronic change can be functionally motivated, the fact remains that language is hugely dysfunctional. Just think of all the things that it would be wonderful to be able to say but for which no language comes remotely near to providing the necessary expressive tools. For example, it would be very useful to be able to describe the face of a strange person in such a way that the hearer would be able to pick out that person in a crowd or a police line-up. But language is completely helpless for this task, as evidenced by the various stratagems police have developed, involving skilled artists or, more recently, graphic computer programs, to elicit identifying facial information from witnesses – in this case a picture actually being worth much more than the proverbial thousand words. Yet paradoxically, alongside all the things we'd like to say but can't, language also continually forces us to say things that we don't want to say; this happens whenever an obligatorily marked grammatical category leads us to specify something we would rather leave unspecified. English, famously, forces third person singular human pronouns to be either masculine or feminine; but in many contexts we either don't know the person's gender or actually wish to leave it unspecified, and we are thus faced with the irritating choice between a stylistically awkward circumlocution such as *they*, *he or she*, or (in writing) *s/he*, or, alternatively, the non-politically correct generic *he* or its overly politically correct counter-part *she*. Examples such as this can be multiplied at will. What these facts suggest, then, is that grammatical structure with its concomitant complexity is not a straightforward tool for the communication of pre-existing messages; rather, to a large degree, our grammars actually define the messages that we end up communicating to one another.

Instead of wondering what grammatical complexity is for, one should ask how and why grammars have evolved to their current levels of complexity. Clearly, many factors are involved, some common to all languages, underlying the development of grammatical complexity in general, others specific to individual languages, resulting in the observed cross-linguistic variation with respect to grammatical complexity. Among the many different factors involved, a particularly important role is played by diachrony. Contemporary grammatical complexity is the result of thousands of years of historical change, with its familiar processes of grammaticalization, lexicalization, and the like. Rather than having evolved in order to enable us to survive, sail boats, and do all the other things that modern humans do, most contemporary grammatical complexity is more appropriately viewed as the outcome of natural processes of self-organization whose motivation is largely or entirely system-internal. In this respect, grammatical complexity may be no different from complexity in other domains, such as anthropology, economics, biology, chemistry, and cosmology, which have been suggested to be governed by general laws of nature pertaining to the evolution of complex systems.

3

On the evolution of complexity: sometimes less is more in East and mainland Southeast Asia

WALTER BISANG

1 Setting the stage

Recent functional typological approaches to complexity (McWhorter 2001a, 2005; Dahl 2004) define their field of research in terms of grammatical categories and rules as they are manifested in overt morphological and syntactic structures. As will be argued in this chapter, complexity has two sides – one side is accessible through overt morphosyntactic patterns, while the other side is hidden and must be inferred from context. The former side is extensively discussed in the above functional typological approaches and will be referred to as "overt complexity". The latter side has been neglected in the literature. It will be called "hidden complexity" and will be the main topic of this paper.

The two sides of complexity are deeply rooted in the observation that morphosyntactic structures and their properties can never fully express the meaning they have in a concrete speech situation. The reason for this is related to what Levinson (2000: 6, 27–30) calls the "articulatory bottleneck". Human speech encoding is by far the slowest part of speech production and comprehension – processes like pre-articulation, parsing, and comprehension run at a much higher speed. This bottleneck situation leads to an asymmetry between inference and articulation, which accounts for why linguistic structures and their properties are subject to context-induced enrichment:

[I]nference is cheap, articulation expensive, and thus the design requirements are for a system that maximizes inference. (Levinson 2000: 29)

Given this situation, linguistic structures somehow need to keep the balance between expensive articulation or explicitness and cheap inference or economy.

This scenario of competing motivations has been known since von der Gabe-lentz (1891: 251) and has become part of more recent approaches as divergent as Haiman's (1983) iconic v. economic motivations and faithfulness v. markedness constraints in Optimality Theory.

Overt complexity reflects explicitness: the structure of the language simply forces the speaker to explicitly encode certain grammatical categories even if they could easily be inferred from context. Hidden complexity reflects econ-omy: the structure of the language does not force the speaker to use a certain grammatical category if it can be inferred from context. Linguists dealing with overt complexity see it as the result of a historical development in terms of grammaticalization processes. In McWhorter's view, creole grammars are characterized by a comparatively low degree of complexity because these languages did not have the time that is needed to produce more elaborate grammatical systems. Dahl understands complexity as a process of matur-ation through history. Both approaches are ultimately based on a notion of grammaticalization that takes the coevolution of form and meaning for granted, i.e. high degrees of grammaticalization are typically associated with inflection and obligatory expression.

As will be shown in section 2, this assumption is problematic (Bisang 2004; Schiering 2006). East and mainland Southeast Asian languages[1] are character-ized by a rather limited degree of coevolution of form and meaning and by almost no obligatory marking of grammatical categories. As a consequence, they are more open to economy and attribute a greater importance to inference. The absence of the overt marking of a grammatical category or of a construction-indicating marker does not imply that the speaker may not want to express it – he may simply have omitted it due to its retrievability from context. If one takes the coevolution of form and meaning as universal, the perspective of hidden complexity as the result of a long-term development is unthinkable. In spite of this, the languages of East and mainland Southeast Asia provide considerable evidence that this is in fact possible. Languages with a long history can be characterized by seemingly simple surface structures – structures which allow a number of different inferences and thus stand for hidden complexity. What David Gil (Chapter 2 above) calls "IMA Languages" are not necessarily as simple as Gil believes; their overt structural simplicity may mask hidden complexity.

If one understands grammatical structures as at least partially motivated by the competing forces of economy and explicitness, overt complexity and hidden complexity are both to be expected. There are phenomena in individ-ual languages that tend more to explicitness and others that give preference to

---

[1] For a precise definition of this linguistic area see Bisang (2006).

economy; but for a language to be influenced by only one of the two principles would be extremely unlikely, if not impossible. For that reason, the present paper does not claim that overt complexity and hidden complexity are mutually exclusive. Hidden complexity is more prominent in a number of grammatical domains in East and mainland Southeast Asian languages than in languages like English, but there are instances in which complexity is overt (cf. end of section 2). Similarly, hidden complexity also operates in languages which score higher for overt complexity (cf. beginning of section 4).

The points made in this introduction will be developed more deeply in the remainder of this chapter. For that purpose, it will be organized as follows: section 2 will discuss hidden complexity and its relation to instances of grammaticalization with no coevolution of form and meaning. As will be shown, there are two different types of hidden complexity. The first type, illustrated in section 3, is defined by individual markers that carry a wide range of functions. The second type, introduced in section 4, is characterized by seemingly simple surface structures which can represent more than one construction. Finally, a short summary in section 5 will address some of the problems created by the tension between overt complexity (explicitness) and hidden complexity (economy) for typological approaches to complexity.

2 Grammaticalization and hidden complexity

In structure-based approaches like those of McWhorter and Dahl, high complexity is typically associated with processes of grammaticalization and higher positions in grammaticalization clines such as the following:

(1) Grammatical patterns and the stages of their development (Dahl 2004: 106):
      free > periphrastic > affixal > fusional

In addition to McWhorter, Dahl also sees a correlation between obligatoriness and the maturation of complexity:

[I]f we find an obligatory grammatical marker in a language, there must have been a stage of that language where the same marker was used in the construction(s) in question, although in a less systematic fashion. In other words, a certain degree of maturity could be claimed for any obligatory marker. (Dahl 2004: 106)

Approaches of this type certainly apply to a large number of languages, but they only work under the assumption that there is coevolution of form and meaning. The more abstract and grammatical a linguistic sign becomes, the more it will lose its autonomy (cf. C. Lehmann 1982; Bybee et al. 1994). As a consequence, it will tend to become obligatory and to be expressed inflectionally.

As I tried to show in Bisang (2004, 2008), there is no or only limited coevolution of form and meaning, and almost no obligatory marking of grammatical categories, in East and mainland Southeast Asian languages. This situation is due at least to the following three factors that mutually support each other:

- phonological properties of the languages involved;
- morphological paradigms cannot emerge because grammatical markers are not obligatory and have a broad functional range;
- effects of language contact.

In the languages of East and mainland Southeast Asia, grammaticalization is expressed by phonetic erosion in terms of duration and vowel quality rather than by morphological reduction (Mandarin Chinese has markers -*le* and -*zhe* which are exceptions to that generalization, but such exceptions are rather rare in this area). As was pointed out by Ansaldo and Lim (2004), this is due to two very strong factors: the discreteness of syllable boundaries, and phonotactic constraints. Phonetic erosion is often limited to the reduction of tonality. McWhorter (2005: 12) describes tonality as "the result of a long-term change", i.e. as a clear indicator of maturity. Many examples from East and mainland Southeast Asia show that grammaticalization processes can also take the opposite direction from tonality to the loss of it. Thus, McWhorter's (2005) generalization is incorrect, the lack of tonality in grammatical markers can also be an indicator of maturity.

The absence of the coevolution of form and meaning as a universal property of grammaticalization fits into a more general picture presented by Schiering (2006), who has shown in his rhythm-based typology that the loss of phonological substance (erosion) is not a defining property of grammaticalization.

The lack of obligatoriness and the wide functional range of individual markers leads to a system in which even highly grammaticalized markers that are integrated into rigid word order patterns (syntagmatic variability in terms of C. Lehmann (1982) is often the only clear indicator of grammaticalization) depend heavily on pragmatic inference. From a surface perspective, such a system seems to entail low complexity associated with a comparatively small number of markers. But this is not the whole story. Surface simplicity is counterbalanced by two types of hidden complexity:

(i) There is a relatively small number of non-obligatory grammatical markers

   but

   these markers have a wide range of meaning that must be inferred from context.

(ii) Utterances often look simple at their surface

but

they may represent a number of different constructions.

In both cases, *less is more.* In the case of (i), a small number of markers can be used for the expression of a rather broad range of grammatical functions. In the case of (ii), a simple-looking structure is compatible with more than one construction and thus open to more than one interpretation. As a consequence, what looks simple at the surface is based on a complex background of potential inferences which adds hidden complexity to seemingly simple structures. Both types will be illustrated by examples from East and mainland Southeast Asian languages. Hidden complexity of type (i) will be the topic of section 3; hidden complexity of type (ii) will be discussed in section 4.

To conclude this section, I would like to point out that there are also many instances of overt structural complexity in East and mainland Southeast Asia. Thus, the alleged correlation between typologically isolating languages and structural simplicity is undermined by a number of constructions, most of them situated at the intersection between the lexicon and productive syntax. This fact has been pointed out recently by Riddle (2008), who presents evidence from grammatical phenomena like classifiers (also cf. Bisang 1999), reduplication, compounding, stylized four-part expressions, and verb serialization (also cf. Bisang 1992). These are very important facts that need to be considered in studies comparing complexity across languages – and at least the last two of them are rarely integrated into studies dealing with structural complexity (cf. also section 5).

3 Individual markers that carry a wide range of functions

Hidden complexity due to polyfunctionality can occur in two different ways. An example in which polyfunctionality exclusively depends on context will be shown in subsection 3.1. An instance of construction-based hidden complexity in which a given marker is subject to different interpretations in different constructions will be presented in subsection 3.2. Both subsections report on phenomena I have described more extensively elsewhere (Bisang 2004, 2008). I briefly take them up here to illustrate what is meant by hidden complexity.

3.1 *Context-dependent polyfunctionality: the case of "come to have" in Khmer*

The grammaticalization of verbs with the meaning of "come to have" into a wide range of different functions is an areal characteristic of East and mainland

Southeast Asian languages. Enfield (2003) wrote an excellent monograph on this source concept of grammaticalization, which has otherwise been widely ignored in the literature. The verbs involved are *dé* in Chinese, *dây* in Thai, *tau* in Hmong, and *ba:n* in Khmer, to mention just a few. In most languages, grammaticalized instances of these verbs can occur in the preverbal as well as in the postverbal position. In the present section, I only discuss the verb *ba:n* in Khmer with its preverbal functions. As is typical of grammaticalization, one and the same lexeme can occur in its source function as well as in its grammatical function. The following example shows *ba:n* in its function as a full verb:

(2) *Chnam   nìh   yɤ̀:ŋ   ba:n*   *sro:v   craən   nas*
     year   this   we   come_to_have   rice   a_lot   very
     "This year, we came to have a lot of rice."

In its preverbal position, the same lexeme marks Tense-Aspect-Modality (TAM). The rather broad functional description of "come to have" verbs in terms of TAM is particularly well suited to this marker because, depending on context, the following functions can be inferred (cf. Enfield 2003; Bisang forthcoming):

(3) Possible inferences of "come to have" in East and mainland Southeast
     Asian languages (the symbol +> stands for "conversational implicature",
     as in Levinson 2000: 16):

     a. The event E is [+ desired]:
        +> modal interpretation: "can" (potential meaning either in terms
        of ability or permission)
     b. The event E is [− desired]:
        +> modal interpretation: "must, to have to" (obligation)
     c. In order for X to come to have E, E must have taken place:
        +> Past (E) (particularly if E is negated)
     d. In order for X to come to have E, E must be true:
        +> truth, factuality

In Khmer, *ba:n* can have the meaning of (3a), (3c), and (3d) – inference of obligation (3b) is rare. This is first illustrated by a constructed example in (4):

(4) *ba:n* in preverbal position: ability/permission, past, truth:
     khɲom   *ba:n*   *tɤ̀u*   *phsa:(r)*
     I   come_to_have   go   market
     According to (3a):   "I was able to go to the market." / "I was allowed
                           to go to the market."

> According to (3c):   "I went to the market."
> According to (3d):   "I do go/I really go to the market."

The different interpretations given in (3) can even be combined to a certain extent. Thus, (4) can also be translated as "He did go to the market" (interpretations 3c and 3d). The inferences listed in (3) do not work equally well in the languages where "come to have" verbs are grammaticalized. There are always some types of inference that are frequent (cf. 3a, 3c, and 3d in Khmer), while others are not (cf. Khmer 3b). Although I have no explanation for this at the moment, what I can say is that it adds further complexity to the overall system of inference.

The next example is a real one from a novel. It consists of two instances of *ba:n*. In its first occurrence (*ba:n₁*), past tense interpretation is excluded because *ba:n₁* is immediately preceded by the future marker *nùɳ*. Since it is known from the context that the event marked by *ba:n₁* is desired, an interpretation in terms of ability is the most likely interpretation. This also applies to the second occurrence of the "come to have" verb (*ba:n₂*), although a past interpretation or a factual interpretation cannot be excluded (cf. Bisang 2004: 120):

(5)   Khmer *ba:n* in preverbal position (Bisang 1992: 414):

cù:ən-ka:l   nì:əy   kɔ: nùk-sɔɳkhùm   tha: <u>ba:n₁</u>   cù:əp
sometimes   she   then   think-hope   QUOT   come_to_have   meet

borɔs   nùh   tìət,   tae-kɔ: pùm   <u>ba:n₂</u>   cù:əp
man   that   again   but   NEG   come_to_have   meet

dò:c   bɔmnɔ:ɳ
as   wish

"Sometimes she hoped to be able to meet that man again, but she wasn't able to/*didn't* meet [him] as she wished."

As was shown in the above description, one and the same marker covers semantic domains as different as modality, tense, and factuality/truth. The adequate interpretation is highly context-dependent, i.e. it is based on processes of inference whose complexity is hard to measure.

3.2 The construction-based polyfunctionality of classifiers in Thai

East and mainland Southeast Asian languages are well known for their systems of numeral classifiers (Aikhenvald 2000; Bisang 1999). This is due to the lack of obligatory number marking in these languages (transnumerality) – an implicational typological correlation discovered by Greenberg (1974).

In Thai, the language to be studied in this subsection, the classifier is obligatory with numerals. The sequence [numeral–classifier] always follows the noun:

(6) a. *còtmǎaj*   *sǎam*   <u>*chabàb*</u>
        letter   three   CLF
        "three letters"

     b. **còtmǎaj*   *sǎam*
        letter   three

The minimal function of numeral classifiers in the world's languages are those of classification and individuation. Since transnumeral nouns only refer to a given concept, that concept needs to be individuated before it can be used with numerals and other markers of quantification. The function of classification is related to individuation because individuation is associated with certain properties of the noun involved (e.g. dimension, rigidity, animacy). By individuating a concept, a classifier thus automatically assigns it to a certain class or set of objects that is defined by one of these properties. In addition to classification and individuation, classifiers can also express other functions. In Thai, these functions are singulative, definiteness, and contrast. In contrast to the different functions of "come to have" verbs, these functions cannot be freely inferred from context – they depend on the construction in which the classifier occurs. The following list presents all the functions of the Thai classifier except classification itself, because this is the function from which all the other functions can be derived:

(7) Functions of Thai classifiers beyond classification:
     Individuation: numeral construction (example 6 above)
     Singulative: demonstrative construction (example 8)
     Definiteness: adjective construction (example 9)
     Contrast: demonstrative and adjective construction (example 10
                     on the adjective construction)

To illustrate the plurifunctionality of the Thai classifier, its functions of singulative, definiteness, and contrast will be briefly discussed in the remainder of this subsection. The case of individuation has been described above.

If there is no classifier in the demonstrative construction, i.e. if we have the structure [NOUN DEM], the noun can be singular or plural, i.e. it remains transnumeral (8a). If the classifier is present, the construction has the structure of [NOUN CLF DEM] and a singular interpretation can be inferred (8b):

(8) Demonstrative construction [NOUN (CLF) DEM]:

  a. *rót   níi*
     car   this
     "this car"/"these cars"

  b. *rót   khan   níi*
     car   CLF   this
     "this car"

In combination with stative verbs, which will be called adjectives (ADJ) here, the presence of the classifier triggers referential interpretation in terms of definiteness or specificity. In the adjective construction with no classifier [NOUN ADJ], the noun is referentially neutral, i.e. it can be definite, specific, indefinite, etc. depending on the context (9a). If the classifier is present the construction has the structure of [NOUN CLF ADJ] and the noun is interpreted as definite or specific (9b).

(9) Adjective construction [NOUN (CLF) ADJ]:

  a. *rót   sǐi dɛɛŋ*
     car   red
     "a red car/the red car; the red cars/red cars"

  b. *rót   khan   sǐi dɛɛŋ*
     car   CLF   red
     "the red car/the red cars"

Thai classifiers can express contrast if the items to be discussed are presupposed, i.e. if they have already been introduced and if the classifier has already been used. The general rule in Thai is that once a noun has been marked as definite or specific, it will remain unmarked as long as it is used in the same discourse paragraph. If this rule is broken, i.e. if a noun that has already been introduced as definite or specific is marked by the classifier again, the hearer can infer that the adjective (10) or the demonstrative must be understood contrastively (for a consistent account of the use of classifiers in ongoing text, see N. Becker 2005). Thus, the following example can be used in a context in which a small car and a big car are presupposed. Speaker A says that B likes the big car. B can now correct this wrong presupposition by uttering (10a) or (10b):

(10) a. *Mâj   châj,   chɔ̂ɔp   rót   khan   lék   mâak kwàa*
        NEG   true   like   car   CLF   small   more
        "This is not true, I prefer the *small* car."

     b. *chɔ̂ɔp   rót   khan   lék,   mâj   chɔ̂ɔp   rót   khan   jàj*
        like   car   CLF   small   NEG   like   car   CLF   big
        "I like the *small* car, I don't like the *big* car."

The same can be shown for demonstratives. If there are two cars, of which one is closer to the speech act participants than the other, a speaker can use the classifier to mark a contrast in spatial deixis.

4 Simple surface, inference of various grammatical structures: the case of Late Archaic Chinese

The fact that one and the same surface structure can be subject to different analyses is well known. In example (11) below, the prepositional phrase *in the park* can modify the noun *man* or the clause *I saw the man*. Similarly, the PP *with the telescope* either modifies the noun *park* or the clause *I saw the man in the park*:

(11)   I saw the man in the park with the telescope.

Thus, (11) can be analysed in the following three ways:

(12)   a. I [$_{VP}$ saw [$_{NP}$ the man] [$_{PP}$ in the park] [$_{PP}$ with the telescope]].

  b. I [$_{VP}$ saw [$_{NP}$ the [$_{N}$ man [$_{PP}$ in the park]]] [$_{PP}$ with the telescope]].

  c. I [$_{VP}$ saw [$_{NP_1}$ the [$_{N}$ man [$_{PP}$ in [$_{NP_2}$ the [$_{N}$ park [$_{PP}$ with the telescope]]]]]]].

In the case of machine translation, multiple syntactic analyses and the problem of selecting the one that is appropriate in a given text is still a challenge. As is claimed by Lytinen (1987: 305), the following example stands for no less than 156 possible syntactic analyses:

(13)   The stock cars raced by the spectators crowded into the stands at over 200 mph on the track at Indy.

One of the problems is the analysis of *raced* and *crowded*, which may be interpreted as finite verbs in the past or as past participles. Another problem is that constituents like *at over 200 mph* may modify any of the preceding nouns, if meaning is disregarded. Similarly, *at Indy* may be an independent PP or it may modify *track*, and so on.

The above examples clearly illustrate that complexity is not just a matter of looking at surface phenomena like word order rules or the presence of obligatory and overt grammatical markers. The existence of different analyses of one and the same surface structure adds a considerable degree of hidden complexity to a language. In the case of East and mainland Southeast Asian languages, this type of structural complexity is considerably higher than in a language like English because many markers that are associated with a given construction are not obligatory. Thus, the absence of a marker does not exclude the presence of the construction it is related to. To start with a simple example, the Thai sequence *rót lék* [car small] can either be analysed as (a) "the small car" or (b) "the car is small". By adding the classifier *khan* as in *rót khan lék*, interpretation (b) is excluded, the only possible interpretation is that of a noun phrase. If the tense-aspect marker *lɛ́ɛw* is added as in *rót lék lɛ́ɛw* only the clausal analysis in terms of (b) is possible: "The car has become small". Of course, adding a marker also adds meaning. In the case of the classifier, the noun phrase must now be interpreted as definite, while using *lɛ́ɛw* yields an interpretation that needs a rather peculiar context (maybe an inflatable toy car that is losing air).

The lack of construction-indicating obligatory markers creates a situation in which very simple surface structures can be analysed in a number of ways. I will first illustrate this with a constructed example from Late Archaic Chinese, the language that was used by famous philosophers such as Confucius, Mencius, Laozi, and Zhuangzi in the fifth to third centuries BC. An example like (14) can be analysed in at least four ways:

(14)   病不幸

　　　　bìng　*bú*　*xìng*
　　　　ill　　NEG　be_fortunate
　　　　(a)　　Simple sentence: "Illness is unfortunate."
　　　　(b)　　Headless relative clause: "The one who is ill is unfortunate."
　　　　(c)　　Subject clause: "That he is ill is unfortunate."
　　　　(d)　　Conditional clause: "If s/he is ill this is unfortunate."

Interpretation (14a) is straightforward – no additional marking is possible, the word *bìng* is interpreted as a noun. For the other three interpretations, specification by additional marking is possible in each case.

To understand how the interpretation of headless relative clauses works, it is necessary to look at relative-clause formation more generally. Relative clauses precede their head noun and may be marked by the attributive marker (ATTR) *zhī*:

(15)　Relative clause marked by the attributive marker (Mencius 7B.11):

　　　　好名之人

　　　　[*hào*　*míng*　*zhī*]　*rén*
　　　　love　　fame　　ATTR　　man
　　　　"a man who loves fame"

In a headless relative clause, the position of the head noun may be taken by the nominalizer *zhě* as in (16). If there is an overt subject in a headless relative clause it may be set off from the rest of the relative clause by the attributive marker *zhī*, as in (17):

(16)   Headless relative clause (Mencius 4B.28):

愛人者人恆愛之

[*ài*   *rén*   *zhě*]   *rén*   *héng*   *ài*   *zhī*
love   people   NMLZ   people   always   love   OBJ.3
"He who loves others, people will always love him."

(17)   Headless relative clause with subject marked by *zhī* (Mencius 4B.19):

人之所以異於禽獸者幾希

[*rén*   *zhī*   *suǒ yǐ*   *yì*   *yú*   *qín shòu*   *zhě*]   *jǐ*   *xī*
man   ATTR   whereby   differ   from   animal   NMLZ   very   small
"That whereby man differs from animals is very small."

Example (14) in its interpretation as a headless relative clause may thus be specified as follows:

(14)   b′. 病者不幸

bìng   *zhě*   *bú*   *xìng*
ill   NMLZ   NEG   be_fortunate
"The one who is ill is unfortunate."

The nominalizer *zhě* is not only used to mark headless relative clauses, it also nominalizes whole clauses as in (18):

(18)   Nominalized clause in the subject position (Mencius 3B.9):

子弒其父者有之

[*zǐ*   *shì*   *qí*   *fù*   *zhě*]   *yǒu*   *zhī*
son   kill   POSS.3   father   NMLZ   exist   OBJ.3
"That a son kills his father does occur."

Since *zhě* is a nominalizer, the above specification in (14b′) may also be interpreted in terms of a subject clause. If the subject is additionally marked by the possessive form of the third person *qí*, which marks the subject in embedded clauses, only the interpretation in terms of the subject clause remains:

(14)   c′. 其病者不幸

qí   *bìng*   *zhě*   *bú*   *xìng*
POSS.3   ill   NMLZ   NEG   be_fortunate
"That he is ill is unfortunate."

Conditionals are often expressed by the unmarked juxtaposition of two clauses:

(19) Xun Zi 17.7:

星墜木鳴國人皆恐

xīng	*zhuì,*	*mù*	*míng,*	*guó*	*rén*	*jiē*	*kǒng*...
star	fall	tree	groan	state	people	all	be_frightened

"If the stars fall and the trees groan everybody in the state is frightened..."

If necessary, there are markers like *rú* "if" or *ruò* "if" in the protasis (20) and *zé* "then" in the apodosis (21):

(20) Conditional construction with marked protasis (*Shiji* 65.6):

若君不修德，舟中之人殺之

<u>*ruò*</u>	*jūn*	*bù*	*xiū*	*dé,*	*zhōu zhōng zhī*	*rén*	*shā zhī*
if	prince	NEG	cultivate	virtue boat in	ATTR	people	kill OBJ.3

"If the prince does not cultivate virtue, the people in the boat kill him."

(21) Conditional construction with *zé* in the apodosis (*Lunyu* 13.3):

名不正則言不順

míng	*bú*	*zhèng,*	<u>*zé*</u>	*yán*	*bú*	*shùn*
name	NEG	correct	then	speaking	NEG	be_in_accordance

"If the names are not correct, speaking is not in accordance [with the truth]."

Thus, example (14d) can be disambiguated as follows:

(14) d'. 若病則不幸

<u>*ruò*</u>	*bìng,*	<u>*zé*</u>	*bú*	*xìng*
If	ill	then	NEG	be_fortunate

"If s/he is ill this is unfortunate."

Having illustrated hidden complexity in Late Archaic Chinese by a constructed example, it is now time to present real examples. For that purpose, I will select two examples in which the same content is expressed by two different overt expression formats in the same passage.

The first example starts out from example (19), which is repeated in the first line of (22):[2]

(22) Xun Zi 17.7:

星墜木鳴國人皆恐曰是何也

[*xīng*	*zhuì*],	[*mù*	*míng*],	*guó*	*rén*	*jiē*	*kǒng,*	*yuē*
star	fall	tree	groan	state	people	all	be_frightened	say

shì	*hé*	*yě*
this	what	EQ

---

[2] The code EQ represents the equative particle *yě*: *A B yě* translates "A is B".

"If the stars fall and the trees groan everybody in the state is frightened, saying 'What is this?'"

夫星之墜木之鳴，是 ⋯ 物之罕至者也

fú	[*xīng*	*zhī*	*zhuì*],	[*mù*	*zhī*	*míng*],	*shì...*	*wù*	*zhī*
now	star	ATTR	fall	tree	ATTR	groan	this	things	ATTR

hǎn	*zhì*	*zhě*	*yě.*
rarely	arrive	NMLZ	EQ

"Now, the falling of stars and the groaning of trees are things that happen rarely."

In the first line, *xīng zhuì* [star fall] and *mù míng* [tree groan] are two clauses in the protasis position of a conditional construction. In the second line, the same lexemes occur in a possessive construction formed by the attributive marker: *xīng zhī zhuì* "the falling of the stars" and *mù zhī míng* "the groaning of the trees".

In the second example, the lexemes *jiàn* "remonstrate" and *yán* "say, speak" occur twice. In the first instance (23), one may analyse the two lexemes in the underlined text as nouns:

(23)   Two lexemes in nominal interpretation (Mencius 4B.3):

諫行言聽，膏澤下於民，有故而去，則君使人導之出疆

[*jiàn*	*xíng*	*yán*	*tīng*],	*gāo*	*zé*	*xià*
remonstrate	be_realized/enacted	say	hear	fat	moist	descend

yú	*mín,*	*yǒu gù*	*ér*	*qù,*	*zé*	*jūn*	*shǐ*	*rén*
on	people	for_some_reason	and	leave	then	ruler	send	man

dǎo	*zhī*	*chū*	*jiāng*
conduct	OBJ.3	go_out	boundary

"If the remonstrations [of a minister] are enacted and [his] words are heard [by the ruler] and thus the blessings [lit.: fat and moist] have descended on the people, if then for some reason [such a minister] leaves [his country], the ruler [will] send people to conduct him beyond the boundaries."

Even though it may look "more natural" from the perspective of an English translator to interpret *jiàn* "remonstrate" and *yán* "say" nominally in (23), a conditional analysis as in "A minister, if he remonstrates and it will be enacted, if he speaks and it will be heard by his ruler – and as a consequence blessings descend on the people, if such a minister..." is equally possible, and may even be more adequate if it comes to the overall information structure of (23). And in fact, a few lines below, the same lexical items are embedded in the protasis of a conditional construction overtly marked by *zé* "then":

(24) The same two lexemes in a verbal position (Mencius 4B.3):

今也為臣，諫則不行，言則不聽，膏澤不下於民，有故而去，
則君搏執之

| *jīn* | *yě* | *wéi* | *chén,* | [*jiàn* | *zé* | *bù* | *xíng*], | [*yán* |
| today | TOP | be | minister | remonstrate | then | NEG | enact | speak |

| *zé* | *bù* | *tīng*], | *gāo* | *zé* | *bú* | *xià* | *yú* | *mín,* |
| then | NEG | hear | fat | moist | NEG | descend | on | people |

| *yǒu gù* | | *ér* | *qù,* | *zé* | *jūn* | *bó* | *zhí* | *zhī* |
| for_some_reason | and | leave | then | ruler | seize | capture | OBJ.3 |

"Today, the ministers, if they <u>remonstrate</u>, it will not be enacted, if they <u>speak</u>, it will not be heard and blessings do not descend to the people – if [such ministers want to] leave for some reason, the ruler seizes them and holds them prisoners."

5 Summary

The present chapter has discussed hidden complexity as a second aspect of complexity. It has tried to show that hidden complexity and overt complexity are related to each other by the two competing motivations of economy and explicitness. Since there are different options between the poles of economy and explicitness, languages differ with regard to the extent to which overt complexity and hidden complexity are developed. In spite of this difference, both types of complexity are the result of a historical development that leads to maturation.

From what has been said so far, it may be concluded that measuring the complexity of an individual language should take account of hidden complexity as well as overt complexity. Since the articulatory bottleneck (Levinson 2000) will always leave some areas that are open to pragmatic inference, there will be in each language an area that is difficult to measure. As a consequence, attempts at measuring complexity and at comparing it cross-linguistically will have to cope with the problem that there are structures whose complexity is hard to quantify. A common way out seems to be to look only at overt complexity. This method is selected more or less implicitly by McWhorter (2001a, 2005) as well as by Dahl (2004).

Quantitative comparative studies that are based exclusively on overt complexity face a number of problems. Since they only look at one type of complexity, they obviously do not quantify complexity as a whole. What they can provide is evidence about processes of grammaticalization and their geographic distribution – but only as far as these processes more or less follow the coevolution of form and meaning; potential regularities that deviate from coevolution remain largely invisible to this type of study. Another problem concerns the range of language features surveyed. For the sake of strict comparability, it may seem necessary to survey the same fixed range of features for all the languages of a sample. However, any such fixed list may overlook specific domains of structural complexity that are significant for particular languages. At the end of section 2, it was pointed out that phenomena like four-part expressions and verb serialization (cf. Riddle 2008) significantly contribute to overt complexity in East and mainland Southeast Asian languages. None of these phenomena are considered in current studies of overt complexity (McWhorter 2005: 108–11 only looks at different degrees of complexity within verb serialization in creole languages compared to other languages). If they were part of a typological questionnaire on complexity, East and Southeast Asian languages would score comparatively higher degrees of complexity, while other languages would score comparatively lower degrees.

To conclude this summary, let us go back again to the articulatory bottle-neck, and the fact that languages make different trade-offs between overt complexity/explicitness and hidden complexity/economy. The fact that hidden complexity always involves pragmatic considerations does not merely make quantification of complexity difficult; it may even make it systematically impossible. This is particularly true in the case of particularized conversational implicatures that are characterized by "specific contextual assumptions that would not invariably or even normally obtain" (Levinson 2000: 16). Thus, it seems to be ultimately impossible to disentangle questions of linguistic complexity from questions of everyday complexity as humans perceive it in their environment (speech situation) and in their cultural background. It remains to be seen to what extent typological studies of a well-defined area of complexity may provide insights into structural properties that covary with complexity, and to what extent research on complexity contributes to our knowledge of the general nature of human language.

4

Testing the assumption of complexity invariance: the case of Elfdalian and Swedish

ÖSTEN DAHL

1 Introduction

In Chapter 1, Geoffrey Sampson discusses what he calls "the assumption of (total) invariance of grammatical complexity", and quotes the claim by Hockett (1958): "the total grammatical complexity of any language, counting both morphology and syntax, is about the same as that of any other."

This chapter is an attempt to test the complexity invariance assumption on two closely related North Germanic languages, Swedish and Elfdalian (*älvdalska*, Älvdalen Dalecarlian). The idea is that by comparing such a pair of languages, it will be possible to identify the points at which the languages differ in complexity and see whether these differences are compensated for elsewhere in the grammar. Before doing so, however, I have to briefly discuss the notion of grammatical complexity (fuller discussions are found in Dahl 2004 and forthcoming).

To begin with, we have to make a distinction between two major ways of understanding complexity, which I shall call "absolute" and "agent-related" complexity, respectively.

The first notion (for which I have sometimes used the term "objective complexity") is the one that is employed in information theory and the theory of complex systems, and involves the idea that complexity is an objective property of an object or a system. It is notoriously difficult to give a rigid definition of complexity in this sense. The general idea is that the complexity of an object is related to the amount of information needed to re-create or specify it (or alternatively, the length of the shortest possible complete description of it). I shall give a simple example to show how this idea could be applied in practice. Suppose we have three strings of characters, *hahaha, byebye,* and *pardon.* Although these all consist of six characters, they differ in that the two first strings can in fact be represented in a more compact way, e.g. as $3 \times ha$ and $2 \times bye$, whereas there is no way of compressing the string *pardon* in a similar way. We might therefore say that *hahaha* is the least complex string, since it can be reduced to four characters, while *byebye* takes minimally five and *pardon* six characters. As applied to strings, this notion of complexity, which is sometimes called "Kolmogorov complexity" or "algorithmic information content", comes out as an inverse of compressibility: the most complex string is one which cannot be compressed at all. However, this would mean that maximal complexity would be represented by a random combination of characters, since such a combination cannot be compressed in any way. An alternative would be what Gell-Mann (1994) calls "effective complexity", which differs from Kolmogorov complexity in that it does not measure the length of the description of an object as a whole, but rather the length of the description of the "set of regularities" or structured patterns that it contains. A random string of characters, such as "w509mfowr6435217r00l71734", will have maximal Kolmogorov complexity (the string is its own shortest description), but no effective complexity since it contains no structured patterns. This corresponds better to an intuitive understanding of the notion of complexity. We also come close to a notion which may feel more familiar to linguists: the set of patterns that an object contains can be said to equal its structure, so the complexity of an object is really a measure of the complexity of its structure.

In linguistics, such an absolute complexity measure could apply to different things. Most importantly, it could apply on the one hand to a language seen as a system – what I call system complexity – and on the other to the structure of utterances and expressions – what I call structural complexity. In this chapter, I shall try to adhere as consistently as possible to the notion of system complexity. Simply put, this means that the "grammatical complexity" of a language equals the complexity of the grammar of that language, not the complexity of expressions in the language.

System complexity could be seen as a measure of the content that language learners have to master in order to be proficient in a language, in other words, the content of their competence. It does not as such tell us anything about the difficulty they have in learning, producing, and understanding the language – that would take us to the other notion of complexity, viz. agent-related complexity. Although agent-related complexity is perhaps the most popular way of understanding complexity in linguistics, I would in fact prefer to reserve the term "complexity" for absolute complexity and use other terms such as "cost", "difficulty", and "demandingness" to denote different aspects of "complexity for a user".

In Dahl (2004), I focused on the complexity of rules that relate meaning to form – that is, the question was: given a certain content, how complex are the rules that allow you to express that content in a language? This question makes more sense for grammar proper than for components of the language such as phonology and lexicon. One often-heard reason for scepticism about using complexity measures that build on length of descriptions is that they seemingly make a language with a large vocabulary more complex than one with a small vocabulary. A similar objection is that the complexity of a language would be dependent on the average length of words. It seems to me that these objections can be met by going up one level: we are not so much concerned with the actual length of the lexicon as with the specification of the form of a lexical item. That is, what we ask is how complex is the format of a lexical item – this could be termed "lexical metacomplexity". This means among other things that the length of lexical items would not be essential, since adding another phoneme to a word just gives you "more of the same" – the format of the lexical item is not affected. If, on the other hand, one adds information of a different kind – such as lexical tones – that complicates the format and adds to the lexical metacomplexity of the language.

Cross-component comparison of language complexity is a notoriously difficult issue. In principle, it should be possible to apply the criterion of description length, but in actual practice it is not at all clear how to do so, for example, how much syntactical complexity is needed to compensate for a difference in morphological complexity. The argument here has to be that if the invariance assumption is true, it would lead us to expect that a significant difference in complexity in one component ought to be matched by a similar difference (although going in the opposite direction) in another component – we may not be able to state exactly how great the compensating difference should be, however.

Turning now to the objects of comparison, both Elfdalian and Swedish belong to the North Germanic languages. Elfdalian is an endangered vernacular spoken by about 3,000 persons in Älvdalen in the Swedish province of Dalarna. It is sufficiently far from Swedish not to be mutually comprehensible with it. Elfdalian and Swedish differ in many respects more than Swedish differs from standard Danish and standard Norwegian, but Elfdalian and Swedish are still of course quite closely related. On the whole, Elfdalian is conservative in the sense that many features of Old Nordic that have disappeared from Swedish (as well as from Danish and Norwegian) are preserved in it. Being under high pressure from Swedish, Elfdalian has undergone significant changes during the twentieth century and is now in a rather unstable state; what I am describing here is basically what the language was like around 1900 (sometimes called "Classical Elfdalian", as described in Levander (1909), an excellent grammar with good coverage also of syntax, which was not very common at the time). The orthography used here, however, is compatible with the recently proposed standard way of writing Elfdalian, although I have kept some traits specific to the village of Åsen, whose dialect Levander based himself on.

2 Phonology

The complexity invariance assumption has usually been taken to apply to grammar proper, that is to morphology and syntax. In spite of this, I shall also briefly compare the phonological systems of Elfdalian and Swedish with respect to their complexity.

Starting with segmental phonology, both Elfdalian and Swedish have fairly large vowel systems, and both languages have nine basic oral vowel phonemes (written *a e i o u y å ä ö*), and in addition share a long/short distinction. In Standard Central Swedish, the two phonemes written *e* and *ä* differ only when they are pronounced long, which makes the Elfdalian oral vowel inventory just slightly larger. In Elfdalian, however, there is also a full set of nasal vowels. Thus, with regard to the vowel system, Elfdalian must be said to be more complex.

The consonant systems are also quite similar – there are two main differences. The Swedish fricatives /ʃ/ and /ç/ correspond to affricates in Elfdalian (with varying pronunciation and spelled <tj> and <dj> in the new spelling proposal), and Elfdalian lacks /h/ – this would make the Swedish consonant system a little more complex than the Elfdalian one.

As for suprasegmental phonology, Swedish and Elfdalian are alike in many respects. I have already mentioned the distinction between long and short vowels. Elfdalian also shares with Swedish and Norwegian the distinction between two word pitch accents – referred to as "acute" and "grave" or "Accent 1" and "Accent 2"; and in both languages the placement of word stress is lexically determined. However, in Swedish, there is a coupling between vowel length and consonant length in such a way that stressed syllables are always long: they contain either a long vowel or a long consonant (or a consonant cluster). This restriction does not hold generally in Elfdalian. To start with, the principle that a stressed syllable must be long applies only to monosyllabic words: in a bisyllabic word, the stressed syllable can consist of two short segments. In addition, stressed syllables can also be "over-long", as in *si'tt* "seen".

The existence of short stressed syllables also has repercussions for the word accents. Traditionally, words containing such syllables are said to have "balanced accent" (*jämviktsaccent*); it is perhaps more adequate to say that the word accent distinction is neutralized for those cases.

With regard to complexity, then, Elfdalian must be said to have a slightly higher degree of phonological metacomplexity, in that more information is needed to specify the phonological form of a lexical item – in Swedish, if we know if a stressed vowel is long or short, we also know the length of the following consonant; in Elfdalian, we have to specify these separately, at least for words with more than one syllable.

3 Morphology

3.1 *Nouns*

In the area of nominal morphology, Swedish and Elfdalian share the categories of number (singular and plural) and definiteness (indefinite and definite). The clearest difference concerns the category of morphological case. With some exaggeration, it can be said that Swedish has got rid of the Germanic four-case system while Elfdalian preserves it. The exaggeration concerns the status of the genitive: arguably, there is a genitive in both languages but it has a somewhat marginal status. The other three noun cases are very much alive in Classical Elfdalian, however, although neutralizations are frequent. In the following sentence the three nouns are unambiguously nominative, dative, and accusative, respectively:

(1) *Kulļa*   *djäv*   *kallem*   *spåðån*
     girl.DEF.NOM.SG   give.PRS.SG   man.DEF.DAT.SG   spade.DEF.ACC.SG
     "The girl gives the man the spade."

(cf. *Kalln djäv kullun spåðån* "The man gives the girl the spade").

Thus, Elfdalian nouns have a more complex morphology than Swedish ones in that they distinguish more inflectional forms. The realization of these forms is also at least prima facie more complex in Elfdalian. Levander (1909) lists twenty-one "declensions"; in addition, some words are indeclinable. Many of his "declensions" have variants that he refers to as "paradigms" – the total number of these is thirty-two. For Swedish, the Swedish Academy Grammar (Teleman et al. 1999) lists seven "declensions", but also notes that there are many smaller groups of nouns that are not subsumable under these.

It is therefore difficult to judge differences in complexity here. On the other hand, the existence of an additional morphological category, that of case, makes it natural for there to be more variation in Elfdalian.

In addition to the inflectional categories, we find that nouns in both Elfdalian and Swedish must be specified with respect to their gender, in ways that are partly unpredictable. However, Elfdalian has preserved the old three-gender system with masculine, feminine, and neuter, whereas Swedish has a reduced system with two genders usually referred to as "uter" and "neuter" (historically, "uter" arose through a merger of masculine and feminine).

Summing up the comparison of noun morphology, Elfdalian comes out as significantly more complex in this area.

3.2 *Adjectives*

What can be said about the morphology of adjectives is mainly in accordance with what has already been noted about nouns. In both Swedish and Elfdalian, adjectives have comparative and superlative forms. Elfdalian adjectives have additional forms due to case and gender distinctions that are not present in Swedish. The distinction between strong and weak endings presents some problems. With some marginal exceptions, Elfdalian adjectives lack overt counterparts to the weak endings -*e* and -*a* of Swedish. The adjectives that would receive those endings are either incorporated (as in *gam-kalln* "the old man") or endingless (e.g. after demonstratives: *eð-dar stùr auseð* "that old house"), but in the latter case the original weak ending is still to be seen in the grave accent of the adjective.

3.3 *Pronouns*

In pronouns, Swedish has a nominative/oblique case distinction, so the difference between the two languages is smaller than for nouns; but Elfdalian pronominal case is still more complex, since it distinguishes also dative forms of pronouns. On the other hand, Swedish actually distinguishes more genders in pronouns than Elfdalian since there is a four-gender system here: *han* (male), *hon* (female), *den* (inanimate uter), *det* (neuter), whereas Elfdalian has the same three-gender system as for nouns. Counting forms of personal pronouns, it turns out that Elfdalian has the same number of distinct forms as standard written Swedish, although spoken Central Swedish has one or two less. (This disregards differences between stressed and unstressed forms.)

We thus find that Elfdalian morphology is more complex with regard to adjectives, but that there is no clear difference in complexity in any direction in the pronoun system between Elfdalian and Swedish.

3.4 Verbs

In verb morphology, Elfdalian and Swedish are alike in distinguishing two tenses, present and past, and two fully productive moods, indicative and imperative. The subjunctive is rather marginal in both languages: in Elfdalian, there are only two subjunctive forms, *edde* from *åvå* "have" and *wäre* from *wårå* "be"; in Swedish, only *vore* from *vara* "be" is reasonably frequent, although subjunctive forms are possible for many strong verbs at least in theory. In addition, both languages have a morphological passive formed with the suffix -*s*. So far, there are thus no significant differences between the two languages. However, Elfdalian verb paradigms are considerably larger than Swedish ones due to the categories of person and number. In the present of all verbs and in the past of strong verbs, Elfdalian distinguishes four forms, one for the singular, and one for each of the persons in the plural. Cf. the present tense of the verb "paint":

singular	*mǫler*
1 plural	*mǫlum*
2 plural	*mǫlið*
3 plural	*mǫla*

In the past of weak verbs, the third person plural is identical to the singular form, but there are still separate forms for the first and second person plural:

sing. and 3 pl.	*mǫleð*
1 plural	*mǫleðum*
2 plural	*mǫleðið*

Thus, similarly to what we found for noun morphology, the system of verb forms in Elfdalian is more complex than that of Swedish in that there are extra categories in Elfdalian that are not found in Swedish. If we look at the ways in which the forms are manifested, it is again more difficult to make any judgements – it does seem that weak verbs in Elfdalian are slightly more varied than in Swedish.

Summing up morphology then, Elfdalian comes out as considerably more complex than Swedish, in that the categories of noun case and person and number in verbs, which are absent or almost absent in Swedish, are well developed in Elfdalian. It may be noted here that the greater morphological complexity of Elfdalian can be related to its more peripheral geographical position, which prevented Elfdalian from undergoing the largely simplifying changes undergone by the standard continental North Germanic languages and more centrally positioned dialects, together with most other Germanic languages around the North Sea and the Baltic (and which presumably have something to do with the more intensive contacts these varieties have had with each other and other languages). Furthermore, recent influence from Swedish has led to changes in Elfdalian, such as the erosion of the case system, which has in fact made it less different from Swedish with regard to morphological complexity. This, however, is incidental to the issues discussed here.

If the complexity invariance assumption is correct, we would expect Swedish to compensate for the lack of complexity in morphology by a corresponding surplus of complexity in syntax. So the question is now what we find in syntax.

4 Syntax

To start with, we can see that there are some areas where the complexities we saw in Elfdalian morphology are by necessity accompanied by a corresponding complexity in syntax, since the phenomena in question have both a syntactic and a semantic side. Thus, there could hardly be a distinction between nominative, dative, and accusative case without there being syntactic rules that determine their distribution, and the person and number distinctions in verbs entail rules that regulate the agreement between subjects and verbs. Strangely enough, this positive correlation between certain types of morphological and syntactic complexity, which must be more or less universally valid, is rarely noted in discussions of the complexity invariance assumption. It follows that if there is a mechanism that compensates for lacking complexity in one area by increased complexity in another, it must operate between different kinds of syntactic complexity rather than between syntactic complexity on the one hand and morphological complexity on the other. I shall return to the areas where we could possibly find such a compensatory mechanism; but to start with I shall look a bit more closely at case marking on nouns and noun phrases and subject marking on verbs.

Case marking, as I said, involves complexity both in morphology and in syntax; in addition, it can also be said to involve lexical complexity insofar as verbs have idiosyncratic case assignment features. In Elfdalian, a large number of verbs and adjectives govern the dative case; Levander (1909) lists around a hundred verbs and fifteen adjectives. Even if these partly fall into semantically definable groups, this undoubtedly adds to the general complexity of the language. In addition, Elfdalian prepositions can govern either dative or accusative case. As in many other conservative Indo-European languages, some prepositions can govern more than one case, sometimes with subtle meaning distinctions (cf. Åkerberg 2004):

(2) *Dier   åk   min   wåsainum   este.*
     they.NOM.PL go.PRS.3P with one_each.DAT.SG.M horse.DAT.SG
     "They are going each with one horse."

(3) *Ig al   aut min rakkan.*
     I   shall.PRS.SG out with dog.ACC.SG
     "I'm going out with the dog."

– where the preposition *min* "with" governs the dative in the first case and the accusative in the second. When the morphological case system breaks down, this kind of complexity also disappears.

Turning now to subject marking on verbs, it is usually assumed that overt morphological marking of subjects on verbs goes with the phenomenon known as "pro-drop", i.e. non-obligatoriness of subject pronouns. The cross-linguistic correlation here is weaker than is often assumed, but in Elfdalian we do find a version of pro-drop that indeed seems to be motivated at least partly by the presence of overt person-number endings on verbs. Thus, subject pronouns tend to be left out in the first and second person plural, i.e. precisely when there is an overt subject marker on the verb:

(4) *ulum   jätå   nu*
     shall.PRS.1P eat.INF now
     "We'll eat now."

The correlation is not perfect, however, since word order also plays a role. According to Levander (1909), first and second person subject pronouns are usually not omitted when they follow the verb in declarative sentences, as in:

(5) *nu   kåitum   wir*
     now run.PRS.1P we.NOM
     "Now we run."

In questions, on the other hand, these pronouns are normally left out except when the question is introduced by *wiso* "why" and the subject is first person:

(6) *wiso ulum   wir djärå   eð?*
     why   shall.PRS.1P we   do.INF it
     "Why shall we do it?"

It is not quite clear if Levander's account is wholly correct here (Gunnar Nyström, pers. comm.), but I have included it here to show that there are syntactic principles of considerable complexity linked up with subject marking on verbs in Elfdalian.

Where could one expect to find compensatory complexity? At least two possibilities come to mind. One is that morphological marking may be replaced by periphrastic constructions, the other is that word order obtains a more prominent role.

As for periphrastic constructions, it is often said that loss of case marking is compensated by the increased use of adpositional constructions. For instance, in languages such as English and Swedish which lack a dative case, the recipient can instead be indicated by a preposition such as English *to* or Swedish *åt*. The problem here, though, is that such constructions exist also in Elfdalian (as also for instance in German, despite the continued existence of the dative case). Thus, the preposition *að*, corresponding etymologically to Swedish *åt*, is used to mark the recipient in the following sentence from Levander (1909):

(7) *dier*   *åvå*   *selt*   *gardn*
    they.NOM have.PRS.3P sell.PAP.N farm.DEF.ACC.SG

    að buälaę
    to company.DEF.DAT.SG

    "They have sold the farm to the company."

There may of course be a difference in frequency between the use of this construction in Swedish and in Elfdalian, but this would not influence the complexity of the grammar. Notice also that in Elfdalian, the periphrastic construction also involves case marking. Most importantly, however, there are many instances where the disappearance of a bound (morphological) marking is not matched by any form of free grammatical marking. For instance, the distinction between nominative and accusative is not compensated in this way. Here, on the other hand, it is natural to assume that word order has a role to play. There is an old and widespread idea that there is an inverse correlation between fixed word order and morphological marking of syntactic structure, and we would accordingly expect Elfdalian to have a looser word order than Swedish.

The general word order principles are fairly similar in Swedish and Elfdalian. Both languages are verb-second languages, adpositions precede noun phrases, demonstratives and adjectives precede nouns, etc. There are a number of differences. For instance, possessive pronouns usually come after the noun in Elfdalian but before it in Swedish.

One of the most important differences in this context is found in the application of the verb-second principle: in Swedish, it does not operate in subordinate clauses, which results in differences in placement of some adverbial elements and in particular of negation, which is placed after the verb in main clauses but before it in subordinate clauses, e.g.:

(8) *han kommer   inte*
     he   come.PRS   not
     "He is not coming."

(9) *jag är   rädd   att   han   inte   kommer*
     1S   am   afraid that he   not   come.PRS
     "I am afraid that he is not coming."

In Elfdalian, on the other hand, negation words follow the verb also in subordinate clauses:

(10) *an kumb   int*
      he come.PRS not
      "He is not coming."

(11) *ig ir   redd   an   kumb   int*
      1S be.PRS.SG   afraid he.NOM   come.PRS.SG   not
      "I am afraid that he is not coming."

The verb-second principle would thus seem to be more complex in Swedish than in Elfdalian, since it applies in a more restricted way. On the other hand, word order in Elfdalian subordinate clauses also has its complexities, making it difficult to compare the systems. Thus, Levander notes that in short relative clauses, verb-final order is possible:

(12) *dier so   gamblest   iro*
      they REL   old.SUPERLATIVE   be.PRS.3P
      "those who are oldest"

Let us now turn to an issue that is more directly pertinent to the question of balancing complexity: the ordering of the major arguments of the verb. Levander (1909: 122) says (my translation):

The circumstance that most nouns in the Åsen dialect [the dialect of the village that was Levander's primary object of study] distinguish nominative and accusative inflections often has as an effect that a word order that is unclear in the standard language can be used advantageously in the Åsen dialect.

He gives a couple of examples:

(13) *kullu   tuäg   gamkalln   min   sig*
      girl.DEF.ACC.SG   take.PST.SG   old_man.DEF.NOM.SG   with   REFL.3
      "The old man took the girl with himself."

(14) *påitjin*   *daingd*   *skaulmiestern* [*so'n wart boð guäl i blår*]
     boy.DEF.ACC.SG   beat.PST.SG   school-master.DEF.NOM.SG
     "The schoolmaster beat the boy [so he became both yellow and blue]."

It is not clear how wide the application of Levander's statement is. In the copy of Levander's grammar in Stockholm University Library, an earlier reader changed "most nouns" to "many nouns", which probably comes closer to the truth – the nominative/accusative distinction is neutralized in many declension types, notably in all masculine proper names. It should also be noted that potential subject–object ambiguities are fairly rare in spoken discourse: in general, they only show up when both the subject and the object are animate. In a Swedish spoken corpus that I investigated, the proportion of such clauses was about 10 per cent of all transitive clauses and about 3 per cent of all finite clauses. On the other hand, OVS word order is also fairly common in Swedish (21 per cent in my material), in particular when the object contains a demonstrative pronoun with an antecedent in the immediately preceding context – it may be noted that examples of this type are disambiguated by their meaning alone if the subject is a lexical NP:

(15) *det*   *trodde*   *Pelle* *inte*
      that   believe.PST   Pelle   not
      "Pelle did not believe that."

In other words, the actual increase of freedom in word order when going from Swedish to Elfdalian is probably rather limited. It may well be that Levander was guided more by his expectations than by empirical data about the languages under comparison.

The basis for the hypothesis about the relationship between word order and morphological marking of arguments is the possibility of reordering constituents without any increase in ambiguity as long as the syntactic function of the constituents is unequivocally shown by their morphological marking. This is then related to the issue of syntactic v. morphological complexity. However, it is not clear that syntactic complexity in any coherent sense is involved here. At least among European languages, even those which are said to have free word order do have preferred or default orderings of major constituents, and an obligatory word order rule is not necessarily more complex than an optional one. The differences between languages with greater and lesser freedom in constituent ordering are predicted from the incidence of unambiguously marked noun phrases and a general principle "Do not scramble if it leads to ambiguity".

There seems to be confusion here between complexity and division of labour. In a language without case marking, word order is likely to have a more prominent role or to do more work in the parsing and disambiguation of syntactic structure; but it does not mean that the word order component in the grammar is necessarily more complex in a caseless language.

One objection that I have encountered when presenting the comparison of Elfdalian and Swedish syntax is that if Swedish has a less complex morphology, this could be compensated by a more complex pragmatics. Basically, it seems that this is an example of the same kind of confusion: what is meant is not so much that the pragmatics is more complex but rather that the pragmatics has to do more work, in the sense that there will be more parsing and/or disambiguation to take care of by pragmatic inference when the grammatical information has been exhausted. On the whole, it is to be expected that the pragmatic principles at work are similar cross-linguistically; at least, this ought to be the case in languages which are culturally as close as Elfdalian and Swedish.

5 Concluding discussion

What conclusions can be drawn from the above? What we saw was that it can hardly be questioned that Elfdalian has a more complex morphology than Swedish. The issue was then really whether this difference is compensated by a corresponding difference in the other direction with regard to syntactic complexity.

At the very least, I think it can be said that such a difference is not readily demonstrable. Indeed, the most important conclusion that can be drawn from the discussion in my opinion is that the overall complexity of the syntactic component of a language is not easily measured – in fact, it seems that we have no very clear criteria for judging which language has the more complex syntax. This is reflected in the rather contradictory judgements that are found in the literature (including electronic publications) on concrete instances. For instance, the authors of the *sci.lang* discussion group FAQ (Covington and Rosenfelder 2002), after having formulated the complexity invariance assumption, say: "Latin, for instance, has a much richer system of inflections than English, but a less complicated syntax." The statement is seen to be too obviously true to need to be argued further – it is apparently easy to verify that Latin is indeed less complex than English with respect to syntax. We may assume, however, that what is behind the statement is the view that assigning a heavier functional load to word order in a language is tantamount to complicating its syntax. Sampson (p. 3 above), on the other hand, quotes

Latin as an equally obvious counterexample to the complexity invariance assumption, basing himself mainly on the "the extraordinary situation whereby the words of a sentence could be permuted almost randomly out of their logical hierarchy" in Latin poetry and the assumption that non-contiguous semantic constituents are harder to process. In both views, syntactic complexity is something different from the complexity of the syntactic component of the grammar. It is obvious that as long as we do not have a common understanding of what syntactic complexity is, we will not reach an agreement on the complexity invariance assumption.

There are, though, some further significant points to make. What we saw was that in a number of cases, complexities in morphology are accompanied by complexities in syntax. This makes it impossible for there to be a simple trading relationship between morphological and syntactic complexity. Furthermore, we saw that assumptions about such trading relationships are often founded on confusion between complexity and functional load, that is, it is assumed that if word order plays an important role in the processing of sentences, it also has to be complex.

I said above that a difference in syntactic complexity between Elfdalian and Swedish is not easily demonstrable. In view of the points just made, however, I would argue that the claim that the lesser morphological complexity of Swedish is compensated by a greater syntactic complexity is not only hard to demonstrate but is also quite likely a false one. Formulating this in positive terms, I would claim that it is in fact reasonable to assume that Elfdalian has a more complex grammar than Swedish.

Someone might object to this claim by saying that it is not possible to assess the global grammatical complexity of a language, and consequently that one cannot compare the grammars of two languages with respect to global complexity. It is important to see that this is not the same thing as the complexity invariance assumption, which does in fact presuppose that such comparisons are possible. Moreover, it involves a rather strong claim about the relationship between the complexity of different components of a grammar, while the null hypothesis must be that there is no such relationship, that is, that the complexity of one component does not carry any information about the complexity of another.

Thus, now that we have seen that there is a significant difference in morphological complexity between Elfdalian and Swedish, the burden of proof must be on the person who wants to argue that this complexity will necessarily be compensated in the syntactic component.

5

Between simplification and complexification: non-standard varieties of English around the world

BENEDIKT SZMRECSANYI AND BERND KORTMANN

1 Introduction

This contribution is an empirical study of morphosyntactic complexity variance in more than four dozen varieties of English, based on four different complexity notions and combining two different data sources.[1] Our point of departure is previous research (e.g. Szmrecsanyi and Kortmann forthcoming) according to which varieties of English – be they native L1 vernaculars, non-native L2 varieties, or English-based pidgins and creoles (P/Cs) – can be thought of as varying along two underlying dimensions of morphosyntactic variance. Crucially, Szmrecsanyi and Kortmann (forthcoming) demonstrate that variety type (L1, L2, or P/C) and not, for example, geographical distance or proximity, is the best predictor of a given variety's location relative to these two dimensions.

The work reported here seeks to complement this line of research in three ways. First, we endeavour to analyse and interpret language-internal variation in English in terms of varying complexity and simplicity levels. More specifically, we will be concerned with measuring local morphological and syntactic complexities. The following notions of linguistic complexity will be subject to numerical quantification in the present study:

ornamental rule/feature complexity – the number of "ornamentally complex" features (cf. McWhorter 2001a) attested in a given variety's morphosyntactic inventory;

[1] We wish to thank Christian Mair (Freiburg) for giving us access to the Jamaican component of the International Corpus of English (ICE) (being compiled at Freiburg University) even though the component is not officially released yet, and Johanna Gerwin, our research assistant, who manually coded a large portion of our corpus database with utmost precision.

L2 acquisition difficulty, also known as "outsider complexity" (cf. Kusters 2003;
Trudgill 2001) or "relative complexity" (cf. Miestamo 2008);

grammaticity and redundancy – the token frequency of grammatical markers,
synthetic or analytic, in naturalistic discourse (cf. Greenberg 1960);

complexity deriving from *irregularities* – more specifically, the text frequency
of irregular, lexically conditioned grammatical allomorphs in naturalistic
discourse (cf. McWhorter 2001a; Trudgill 2004a).

Second, in addition to survey data (the classic data type in typological–
dialectological research), we shall also tap naturalistic corpus data, a procedure
which will yield a range of frequency-based complexity measures. And third,
building on sociolinguistic work suggesting that there is a typological continuum of L1 varieties (cf. Trudgill forthcoming a), we expand our earlier
threefold typological classification to a fourfold split: high-contact L1 vernaculars (e.g. Australian E),[2] v. low-contact L1 vernaculars (e.g. East Anglia E),
v. English-based P/Cs (e.g. Tok Pisin), v. L2 varieties (e.g. Hong Kong E).
In this connection we would like to note that L2 varieties are rather under-
researched, especially from a dialectological/typological point of view, which is a
gap in the literature that the present study will seek to remedy. Our overall
research interest in this chapter will lie in the degree to which variety type
correlates with complexity variance.

2 Data sources

2.1 *The World Atlas of Morphosyntactic Variation in English*

The *World Atlas* accompanies the *Handbook of Varieties of English* (Kortmann
et al. 2004). It is available – along with a phonological survey (which will not
be subject to analysis in this chapter) – on CD-ROM and online (<http://
www.mouton-online.com>). A catalogue of seventy-six features – essentially,
the usual suspects in previous dialectological, variationist, and creolist research – was compiled and sent out to the authors of the chapters in the
morphosyntax volume of the *Handbook*. For each of the seventy-six features,
the contributors were asked to specify whether the feature in question is
attested in the variety at hand. Kortmann and Szmrecsanyi (2004: 1142–5)
discuss the survey procedure in considerable detail. Suffice it to say here that
forty *Handbook* authors provided us with data on forty-six non-standard
varieties of English. All seven Anglophone world regions (British Isles, America,
Caribbean, Australia, Pacific, Asia, Africa), as well as a fair mix of traditional

---

[2] Since the many language-varieties discussed in this chapter are all varieties of or derived from
English, the name "English" is abbreviated as "E" in order to enable readers to focus on the distinctive
parts of the variety names.

(low-contact) L1 vernaculars ($N = 8$), high-contact L1 varieties ($N = 12$), L2 varieties ($N = 11$), and English-based P/Cs ($N = 15$), are represented in the survey.[3] Table 5.1 gives the breakdown by variety type.

The features in the survey are numbered from 1 to 76 (see the Appendix for the entire feature catalogue) and include all major phenomena discussed in previous survey articles on grammatical properties of (individual groups of) non-standard varieties of English. They cover eleven broad areas of morpho-syntax: pronouns, the noun phrase, tense and aspect, modal verbs, verb morphology, adverbs, negation, agreement, relativization, complementation, and discourse organization and word order.

2.2 *Corpus data*

To supplement the survey data described above – which provide a clear "attested"/"not attested" signal, albeit at the price of being essentially dichot-omous (and thus simplistic) in nature – we also sought to investigate natur-alistic corpus data, a data type which can yield gradient frequency information. We accessed four major digitized speech corpora sampling

Table 5.1. Varieties sampled in the *World Atlas*

Varieties	Variety type
Orkney and Shetland, North, Southwest and Southeast of England, East Anglia, Isolated Southeast US E, Newfoundland E, Appalachian E	Traditional L1
Scottish E, Irish E, Welsh E, Colloquial American E, Ozarks E, Urban African-American Vernacular E, Earlier African-American Vernacular E, Colloquial Australian E, Australian Vernacular E, Norfolk, regional New Zealand E, White South African E	High-contact L1
Chicano E, Fiji E, Standard Ghanaian E, Cameroon E, East African E, Indian South African E, Black South African E, Butler E, Pakistan E, Singapore E, Malaysian E	L2
Gullah, Suriname Creoles, Belizean Creole, Tobagonian/Trinidadian Creole, Bahamian E, Jamaican Creole, Bislama, Solomon Islands Pidgin, Tok Pisin, Hawaiian Creole, Aboriginal E, Australian Creoles, Ghanaian Pidgin E, Nigerian Pidgin E, Cameroon Pidgin E	P/C

[3] In this study, categorization of individual L1 varieties into the categories at hand (traditional L1 v. high-contact L1) was carried out somewhat impressionistically, taking into account factors such as the size of speech community, a prolonged history of adult L2 acquisition (as in the case of, e.g., Welsh E), and so on. Observe that our categorization also glosses over the notion of "shift varieties" (cf. Mesthrie 2004: 806).

Table 5.2. Speech corpora and varieties of English investigated

Corpus	Subcorpus	Variety/varieties	Variety type
Freiburg Corpus of English Dialects (FRED) (cf. Hernández 2006)	FRED-SE	English Southeast + East Anglia (SE + EA)	Traditional L1
	FRED-SW	English Southwest (SW)	Traditional L1
	FRED-MID	English Midlands (Mid)	Traditional L1
	FRED-N	English North (N)	Traditional L1
	FRED-SCH	Scottish Highlands (ScH)	Traditional L1
	FRED-WAL	Welsh English (WelE)	High-contact L1
International Corpus of English (ICE) (cf. Greenbaum 1996)	ICE-NZ-S1A	New Zealand E (NZE)	High-contact L1
	ICE-HK-S1A	Hong Kong E (HKE)	L2
	ICE-JA-S1A	Jamaican E (JamE)	L2
	ICE-PHI-S1A	Philippines E (PhilE)	L2
	ICE-SIN-S1A	Singapore E (SgE)	L2
	ICE-IND-S1A	Indian E (IndE)	L2
	ICE-GB-S1A	colloquial British E (collBrE)	High-contact L1
Northern Ireland Transcribed Corpus of Speech (NITCS) (cf. Kirk 1992)		Northern Irish E (NIrE)	High-contact L1
Corpus of Spoken American English (CSAE) (Du Bois et al. 2000)		colloquial American E (collAmE)	High-contact L1

fifteen spoken varieties of English, including traditional (low-contact) vernaculars ($N = 5$), high-contact L1 varieties ($N = 5$), and L2 varieties of English ($N = 5$) (see Table 5.2 for an overview).[4]

All of the corpus material subject to analysis in the present study is spoken-conversational (ICE, CSAE) or drawn from rather informal interview situations (FRED, NITCS). Technically, we utilized an automated algorithm to extract 1,000 random, decontextualized tokens (i.e. orthographically transcribed

---

[4] Note though that we did not include corpus data on English-based pidgins and creoles here, the reason being that this step would have necessitated devising a set of tailor-made coding schemes, which would have gone beyond the scope of the present study.

words) per variety and (sub)corpus, yielding in all a dataset of 15,000 tokens (15 varieties × 1,000 tokens). This dataset was then subjected to morphological/grammatical analysis, on the basis of which we eventually computed a set of Greenberg-inspired indices (cf. Greenberg 1960). Sections 5 and 6 will provide more detail on the procedure.

3 Ornamental rule/feature complexity

We define *ornamental rule/feature complexity* as complexity deriving from the presence, in a given variety's morphosyntactic inventory, of features or rules that add contrasts, distinctions, or asymmetries (compared to a system that does not attest such features/rules) without providing a clearly identifiable communicative or functional bonus. In a nutshell, we mean to capture here "ornamental accretions" (McWhorter 2001c: 390) similar to human hair, which serves no real functional purpose and is thus "a matter of habit, doing no harm and thus carried along" (p. 389). A popular example for such complexity is grammatical gender (Trudgill 1999: 148).

Let us illustrate on the basis of our feature catalogue. Among the seventy-six features covered there are, indeed, many features that add contrasts, distinctions, or asymmetries – for instance, feature [26], *be* as perfect auxiliary (yielding additional selection criteria concerning verb type), and feature [3], special forms or phrases for the second person plural pronoun (adding an additional singular/plural contrast). Notice though that in our definition, only the former (*be* as perfect auxiliary) would qualify as complexifying. This is because special forms or phrases for the second person plural clearly add complexity, but they also yield a clearly identifiable functional/communicative advantage – the ability, that is, to distinguish one from two or more addressees. In the spirit of considerations like these, we classified the following items in our survey as "ornamentally complex":

[7]   *she/her* used for inanimate referents (e.g. *She was burning good* [said of a house])

[12] non-coordinated subject pronoun forms in object function (e.g. *You did get he out of bed in the middle of the night*)

[13] non-coordinated object pronoun forms in subject function (e.g. *Us say 'er's dry*)

[26] *be* as perfect auxiliary (e.g. *They're not left school yet*)

[32] *was sat/stood* with progressive meaning (e.g. *when you're stood* [are standing] *there you can see the flames* – a construction with highly specific verb selection criteria, coexisting with the -*ing* progressive though not replacing it)

Table 5.3. Mean ornamental rule/feature complexity (number of ornamentally complex items) by variety type

Variety type	Mean no. of ornamentally complex features/rules attested[a]
Traditional L1	2·40
High-contact L1	1·17
L2	1·00
P/C	1·14

[a] marginally significant at $p = ·06$ (ANOVA: $F = 2·97$).

[41] *a*-prefixing on *ing*-forms (e.g. *They wasn't a-doin' nothin' wrong*)
[60] Northern Subject Rule (e.g. *I sing* [v. **I sings*], *Birds sings, I sing and dances*)

So, which of the forty-six varieties in our survey attest most of these features? Table 5.3 cross-tabulates ornamental rule/feature complexity with variety type. The overall thrust of the effect is clear: the typical traditional L1 vernacular attests between two and three ornamentally complex features/rules, while high-contact L1 varieties, L2 varieties, and English-based P/Cs typically attest only about one ornamentally complex feature.[5] Thus, ornamental complexity is clearly a function of the degree of contact (and, possibly, of a history of L2 acquisition among adults), which is a result that ties in well with the literature (Trudgill 2001, 2004a, forthcoming).

4 L2 acquisition difficulty

We will now consider a measure of *outsider complexity* (cf. Kusters 2003; Trudgill 2001) or *relative complexity*. Following the terminology in Miestamo (2008), we shall refer to this type of complexity as *difficulty* (and, correspondingly, to "relative" simplicity as *ease*). The particular reference point that we will use is an adult L2 learner as an outsider whose difficulty or ease of acquiring a language or language variety is theoretically highly relevant, especially in a sociolinguistic perspective. Against this backdrop, we operationalize *L2 acquisition difficulty* as the degree to which a given variety does *not* attest phenomena that L2 acquisition research has shown to recur in interlanguage varieties. The following interlanguage universals (or near-universals), then, may be extrapolated from the literature:

---

[5] The difference between high-contact L1 vernaculars, L2 varieties, and English-based pidgins and creoles is not statistically significant (ANOVA: $F = ·19$, $p = ·83$).

- avoidance of inflectional marking (− INFLECTION), preference for analyticity (+ ANALYTICITY) (Klein and Perdue 1997: 311; Seuren and Wekker 1986; Wekker 1996)
- pronoun systems are minimal (− PRONOUN) (Klein and Perdue 1997: 312)
- preference for semantic transparency (+ TRANSPARENCY) (Seuren and Wekker 1986)
- tendency to overgeneralize, as in *he goed* (+ GENERALIZATION) (Towell and Hawkins 1994: 227)
- typically, one particle for negation (Klein and Perdue 1997: 312) which is preverbal, especially in early stages of L2 acquisition (Hawkins 2001: 84; Littlewood 2006: 510) (+ PREVERBAL NEG)
- avoidance of agreement by morphological means, for instance, third person singular -*s* (− AGREEMENT) (Dulay and Burt 1973, 1974; Klein and Perdue 1997: 311)
- widespread copula absence (− COPULA) (Klein and Perdue 1997: 320)
- resumptive pronouns are frequent (+ RESUMPTIVE) (Hyltenstam 1984)
- overt syntactic subordination is dispreferred (− SUBORDINATION) (Klein and Perdue 1997: 332)
- inversion as a relatively late development (− INVERSION) (Littlewood 2006: 510)

Given this body of research, we classified the following twenty-four items in our seventy-six-feature catalogue as diagnostics for ease of L2 acquisition:

[6]	lack of number distinction in reflexives (− INFLECTION)
[8]	generic *he/his* for all genders (− PRONOUN)
[14]	absence of plural marking after measure nouns (− INFLECTION)
[27]	*do* as a tense and aspect marker (+ ANALYTICITY)
[28]	completive/perfect *done* (+ ANALYTICITY)
[29]	past tense/anterior marker *been* (+ ANALYTICITY)
[31]	*would* in *if*-clauses (+ TRANSPARENCY)
[36]	regularization of irregular verb paradigms (+ GENERALIZATION)
[37]	unmarked verb forms (− INFLECTION)
[40]	zero past tense forms of regular verbs (− INFLECTION)
[45–47]	*ain't* (− INFLECTION)
[48]	invariant *don't* in the present tense (− INFLECTION)
[50]	*no* as preverbal negator (+ PREVERBAL NEG)
[52]	invariant non-concord tags (− INFLECTION)
[53]	invariant present tense forms: no marking for third person singular (− AGREEMENT)
[55]	existential/presentational *there's* etc. with plural subjects (− AGREEMENT)

Table 5.4. Mean L2-ease (number of L2-easy items) by variety type

Variety type	Mean no. of L2-easy features[a]
Traditional L1	6·14
High-contact L1	6·23
L2	6·00
P/C	12·73

[a] highly significant at $p < ·01$ (ANOVA: $F = 16·63$).

[57] deletion of *be* (− COPULA)
[65] use of analytic *that his* etc. instead of *whose* (+ TRANSPARENCY)
[67] resumptive/shadow pronouns (+ RESUMPTIVE)
[72] serial verbs (− SUBORDINATION)
[73] lack of inversion/auxiliaries in *wh*-questions (− INVERSION/− COPULA)
[74] lack of inversion in main clause *yes/no* questions (− INVERSION)

Table 5.4 illuminates how the number of L2-easy features in a variety's inventory tallies with variety type. English-based P/Cs clearly stand out in that they attest, typically, between twelve and thirteen L2-easy features, while other varieties of English only attest about six L2-easy features on average.[6] This is another way of saying that English-based P/Cs are substantially more L2-easy than any other variety type in our survey. In itself, it is not actually surprising that P/Cs are particularly L2-easy, given the nature of creole genesis and the great deal of adult L2 acquisition that accompanies it (cf. Seuren and Wekker 1986). Yet it is noteworthy that L2 varieties of English do not attest significantly more L2-easy features than L1 varieties of English, as one might have expected. This is a puzzle that the subsequent sections will attempt to shed light on.

5 Grammaticity and redundancy

Let us go on to a discussion of some frequency-based, corpus-derived complexity metrics, all of which are "absolute" (cf. Miestamo 2008) because they do not draw on an extragrammatical reference point. We operationally define a given variety's morphosyntactic *grammaticity* as the text frequency with which that variety attests grammatical markers in naturalistic, spontaneous spoken discourse. We take more grammaticity to be indicative of higher complexity, and draw a further distinction between (i) *overall grammaticity*, (ii) *synthetic*

---

[6] The difference between low-contact L1 vernaculars, high-contact L1 varieties, and L2 varieties is not statistically significant (ANOVA: $F = ·02$, $p = ·98$).

Table 5.5. Grammaticity indices by variety type

Variety type	Mean syntheticity index[a]	Mean analyticity index[b]	Mean overall grammaticity index[c]
Traditional L1	·13	·48	·61
High-contact L1	·11	·46	·57
L2	·09	·45	·54

[a] significant at $p = ·02$ (ANOVA: $F = 5·80$).
[b] marginally significant at $p = ·07$ (ANOVA: $F = 3·35$).
[c] significant at $p = ·02$ (ANOVA: $F = 6·04$).

grammaticity (i.e. the incidence of bound grammatical morphemes), and (iii) *analytic grammaticity* (i.e. the incidence of free grammatical morphemes). We suggest that *grammaticity*, thus defined, can be roughly equated with (grammatical) *redundancy*, in the sense of *repetition of information* (cf. e.g. Trudgill forthcoming a).

Our particular method here is broadly modelled on Joseph Greenberg's (1960) paper, "A quantitative approach to the morphological typology of language". This means that we conducted a morphological/grammatical–functional analysis of our corpus database spanning 15,000 tokens (recall here from section 2 that we compiled fifteen sets – one for each variety of English investigated – of 1,000 orthographically transcribed, randomly selected words). For each token in the database, we established:

- whether the token contains a bound grammatical morpheme (fusional or suffixing), as in *sing-s* or *sang*;
- and/or whether the token is a free grammatical morpheme, or a so-called function word, belonging to a closed grammatical class (essentially, determiners, pronouns, *wh*-words, conjunctions, auxiliaries, prepositions, negators).[7]

On the basis of this analysis, we established three indices: a *syntheticity index* (the percentage of bound grammatical morphemes per 1,000 tokens), an *analyticity index* (the percentage of free grammatical morphemes per 1,000 tokens), and an *overall grammaticity index* (the sum of the former two indices). Table 5.5 cross-tabulates these indices with variety type.

The figures in Table 5.5 may be interpreted as follows: in traditional L1 vernaculars, 13 per cent of all orthographically transcribed words (tokens) carry a bound grammatical morpheme, 48 per cent of all tokens are function words,

---

[7] In the case of inflected auxiliaries (e.g., *he is singing*), the token was counted as being both inflected and belonging to a closed class.

and approximately 61 per cent of all tokens bear grammatical information. There is a strikingly consistent hierarchy that governs grammaticity levels: traditional L1 vernaculars > high-contact L1 vernaculars > L2 varieties. Hence, traditional L1 varieties exhibit most grammaticity, L2 varieties exhibit least grammaticity, and high-contact L1 varieties occupy the middle ground. Assuming, as we do, that grammaticity is just another name for redundancy, this hierarchy dovetails nicely with claims in the literature that a history of contact and adult language learning can eliminate certain types of redundancy (cf. Trudgill 1999, 2001, and esp. forthcoming a). We also note along these lines that the fact that L2 varieties generally exhibit the smallest amount of grammatical marking resolves our earlier puzzle (cf. section 4) as to why L2 varieties do not exhibit particularly many L2-easy features. It just seems as though L2 speakers do not generally opt for "simple" features in preference to "complex" features. As a matter of fact, L2 speakers appear to prefer zero marking – and thus, possibly, hidden pragmatic complexity (cf. Walter Bisang's Chapter 3 above) – over explicit marking, be it L2-easy or complex.

The interplay between the different types of grammaticity is visualized as a scatterplot in Fig. 5.1. The Southeast/East Anglia and Hong Kong E are the extreme cases in our dataset. The former are highly analytic *and* synthetic

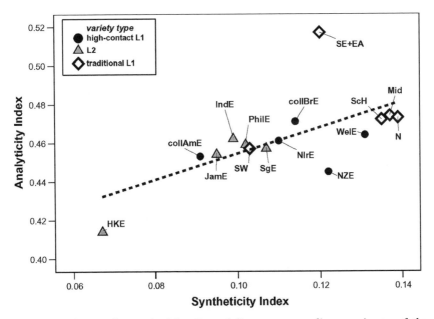

FIG. 5.1. Analyticity by syntheticity. Dotted line represents linear estimate of the relationship (R^2 = 0·40).

varieties, while HKE is neither of these things. In sum, the traditional L1 vernaculars are to be found in the upper right half of the figure (exhibiting above-average grammaticity), whereas L2 varieties are located in the lower left half, being neither particularly analytic nor synthetic. High-contact L1 varieties occupy the middle ground, along with the two standard varieties (collAmE and collBrE) and the Southwest of England. What merits particular attention in Fig. 5.1, we believe, is the slope of the dotted trend line: as a rather robust ($R^2 = 0.40$) statistical generalization, this line indicates that on the inter-variety level, there is *no* trade-off between analyticity and syntheticity. Needless to say, such a trade-off is often claimed to be one that has governed the history of English. In reality, according to Fig. 5.1, analyticity and syntheticity correlate positively, so that a variety that is comparatively analytic will also be comparatively synthetic, and vice versa. Once again, in terms of L2 varieties this is another way of saying that these tend to opt for less overt marking, rather than trading off synthetic marking for analytic marking, which is purportedly L2-easy (cf. e.g. Seuren and Wekker 1986).

6 Irregularity and transparency

This section will look more closely at the text frequency of bound grammatical morphemes, adding a twist to our findings on syntheticity in the previous section by distinguishing, additionally, between regular and irregular grammatical allomorphs. We propose that a given variety A is more complex than another variety B if, in naturalistic spoken discourse, variety A exhibits a greater percentage of bound grammatical allomorphs which are irregular and lexically conditioned (in turn, variety A would be *less complex* and *more transparent* if it exhibited a higher share of regular-suffixing allomorphs). The rationale is a theme in the complexity literature (e.g. McWhorter 2001a: 138) that while inflectional marking and syntheticity is not *per se* complex, it typically adds to linguistic complexity thanks to collateral "nuisance factors" such as allomorphy and morphophonemic processes (cf. Braunmüller 1990: 627).

    We investigated all bound grammatical morphemes in our 15 × 1,000 token corpus database, classifying them into either (i) regular-suffixing, phonologically conditioned allomorphs (e.g. *he walk-ed*) or (ii) irregular, lexically conditioned allomorphs (e.g. *he sang*), and establishing corresponding *transparency indices*, which yield the share of regular allomorphs as a percentage of all bound grammatical morphemes (cf. Table 5.6). As can be seen, in typical L2 discourse, 82 per cent of all bound grammatical allomorphs are regular; the figure decreases to 71 per cent in the case of high-contact L1 varieties and to 65

Table 5.6. Mean transparency indices (percentage of regular-suffixing bound grammatical morphemes) by variety type

Variety type	Mean transparency index[a]
Traditional L1	·65
High-contact L1	·71
L2	·82

[a] highly significant at $p < ·01$ (ANOVA: $F = 11·31$).

per cent in traditional L1 vernaculars. The upshot, then, is that in terms of irregularity L2 varieties are least complex and most transparent while traditional, low-contact L1 vernaculars are most complex and least transparent (high-contact L1 varieties, once again, occupy the middle ground). These results can be taken to suggest that higher degrees of contact and – in particular – adult language acquisition both appear to level irregularities. The likely reason is that "[i]mperfect learning...leads to the removal of irregular and non-transparent forms which naturally cause problems of memory load for adult learners, and to loss of redundant features" (Trudgill 2004a: 307).

To visualize the variance at hand here, the scatterplot in Fig. 5.2 plots transparency indices against grammaticity indices, i.e. the total text frequency of grammatical markers (see the preceding section for the technicalities). Traditional L1 vernaculars, displaying much grammatical marking but not being transparent, cluster in the lower right half of the diagram, whilst L2 varieties are to be found in the upper left half of the diagram, where one finds varieties characterized by low grammaticity but high transparency. As for the extreme cases, the Southeast and East Anglia are the single most verbose (in the sense of high grammaticity) and least transparent varieties in our sample; conversely, Hong Kong E exhibits, as we have seen already, the lowest levels of grammaticity overall, and Indian E turns out to be the most transparent, least irregular variety considered in our study. The Southwest of England, once again, rather patterns with the high-contact L1 varieties, and the two standard vernaculars (Standard American and British E) maintain a low profile – one that is akin to high-contact non-standard L1s – in every respect, a finding which is fully consonant with claims (cf. Trudgill forthcoming a) that these standard dialects constitute just another type of high-contact variety. The overall generalization emerging from Fig. 5.2, as suggested by the dotted trend line, is that transparency trades off against grammaticity – thus, morphosyntactic grammaticity implies irregularity, and vice versa.

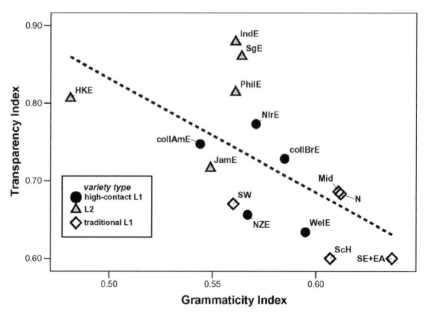

FIG. 5.2. Transparency by grammaticity. Dotted line represents linear estimate of the relationship (R^2 = 0.38).

7 Summary and conclusion

We have sought to present quantitative evidence in this study that variety type is a powerful predictor of complexity variance in varieties of English around the world.

In particular, we detailed how low-contact, traditional L1 vernaculars are on almost every count (ornamental complexity, grammaticity, irregularity) more complex than high-contact L1 varieties of English. Therefore, contact clearly is a crucial factor (cf. Trudgill 1999, forthcoming a). At the same time, "young", native varieties of English (i.e., English-based pidgins and creoles) turned out not to be any less ornamental than high-contact L1 varieties of English (partially contradicting e.g. McWhorter 2001a), although English-based pidgins and creoles are, according to our metric, more benign in terms of L2 acquisition difficulty than any other variety type in our sample.

This takes us to L2 varieties of English. Our implicit working hypothesis was that these should be objectively "simpler" than native varieties of English in terms of almost any measure. This hypothesis does not mesh with the facts, though. L2 varieties are not any less ornamental than, say, high-contact L1 varieties, and intriguingly, they also do not appear to be any L2-easier than

L1 varieties. Instead, our corpus-based analysis of text frequencies of grammatical markers showed that while traditional L1 vernaculars are most redundant, in the sense that they attest high text frequencies of grammatical markers (be they analytic or synthetic), L2 varieties tend towards the lower, non-redundant end of the grammaticity spectrum. Specifically, L2 varieties do *not* trade off purportedly L2-difficult inflectional marking (cf. e.g. Klein and Perdue 1997; Seuren and Wekker 1986) for analytical marking. Rather, in spontaneous discourse L2 speakers appear to avoid grammatical marking of any kind, rather than opting for analytic marking or overtly L2-easy marking. Be that as it may, our analysis did indicate that L2 varieties are significantly more transparent than L1 varieties in that they exhibit the highest share of regular bound grammatical allomorphs. Hence, L2 varieties trade off grammaticity against transparency.

In terms of methodology, we should like to argue that language-internal variation is an ideal research site for developing, testing, and calibrating different complexity metrics. Varieties of English, in particular, constitute for a host of reasons (rich variation in sociohistorical settings, broad availability of data, and so on) an ideal opportunity to understand the comparatively simple (i.e. language-internal complexity variance) before probing the comparatively complicated (i.e. cross-linguistic complexity variance).

Appendix: the feature catalogue

For a version of the feature catalogue illustrated with linguistic examples, see Kortmann and Szmrecsanyi (2004: 1146–8).

Pronouns, pronoun exchange, and pronominal gender

  1 *them* instead of demonstrative *those*
  2 *me* instead of possessive *my*
  3 special forms or phrases for the second person plural pronoun
  4 regularized reflexives paradigm
  5 object pronoun forms serving as base for reflexives
  6 lack of number distinction in reflexives
  7 *she/her* used for inanimate referents
  8 generic *he/his* for all genders
  9 *myself/meself* in a non-reflexive function
  10 *me* instead of *I* in co-ordinate subjects
  11 non-standard use of *us*
  12 non-coordinated subject pronoun forms in object function
  13 non-coordinated object pronoun forms in subject function

Noun phrase

  14 absence of plural marking after measure nouns
  15 group plurals

16 group genitives
17 irregular use of articles
18 postnominal *for*-phrases to express possession
19 double comparatives and superlatives
20 regularized comparison strategies

Verb phrase: tense and aspect

21 wider range of uses of the Progressive
22 habitual *be*
23 habitual *do*
24 non-standard habitual markers other than *do*
25 levelling of difference between Present Perfect and Simple Past
26 *be* as perfect auxiliary
27 *do* as a tense and aspect marker
28 completive/perfect *done*
29 past tense/anterior marker *been*
30 loosening of sequence-of-tense rule
31 *would* in *if*-clauses
32 *was sat/stood* with progressive meaning
33 *after*-Perfect

Verb phrase: modal verbs

34 double modals
35 epistemic *mustn't*

Verb phrase: verb morphology

36 levelling of preterite and past participle verb forms: regularization of irregular verb paradigms
37 levelling of preterite and past participle verb forms: unmarked forms
38 levelling of preterite and past participle verb forms: past form replacing the participle
39 levelling of preterite and past participle verb forms: participle replacing the past form
40 zero past tense forms of regular verbs
41 *a*-prefixing on *ing*-forms

Adverbs

42 adverbs (other than degree modifiers) have same form as adjectives
43 degree modifier adverbs lack *-ly*

Negation

44 multiple negation/negative concord
45 *ain't* as the negated form of *be*

46 *ain't* as the negated form of *have*
47 *ain't* as generic negator before a main verb
48 invariant *don't* for all persons in the present tense
49 *never* as preverbal past tense negator
50 *no* as preverbal negator
51 *was/weren't* split
52 invariant non-concord tags

Agreement

53 invariant present tense forms due to zero marking for the third person singular
54 invariant present tense forms due to generalization of third person *-s* to all persons
55 existential/presentational *there's, there is, there was* with plural subjects
56 variant forms of dummy subjects in existential clauses
57 deletion of *be*
58 deletion of auxiliary *have*
59 *was/were* generalization
60 Northern Subject Rule

Relativization

61 relative particle *what*
62 relative particle *that* or *what* in non-restrictive contexts
63 relative particle *as*
64 relative particle *at*
65 use of analytic *that his/that's, what his/what's, at's, as'* instead of *whose*
66 gapping or zero-relativization in subject position
67 resumptive/shadow pronouns

Complementation

68 *say*-based complementizers
69 inverted word order in indirect questions
70 unsplit *for to* in infinitival purpose clauses
71 *as what/than what* in comparative clauses
72 serial verbs

Discourse organization and word order

73 lack of inversion/lack of auxiliaries in *wh*-questions
74 lack of inversion in main clause *yes/no* questions
75 *like* as a focusing device
76 *like* as a quotative particle

6

Implicational hierarchies and grammatical complexity

MATTI MIESTAMO

1 Introduction

This chapter examines the usability of Greenbergian implicational hierarchies (Greenberg 1966) in cross-linguistic research on language complexity.

Recently an increasing number of linguists have started to question the conventional wisdom according to which all languages are equally complex. McWhorter (2001a) proposes a metric for measuring the overall complexity of grammars of languages. One of the criteria employed in the metric pays attention to the number of grammatically expressed semantic or pragmatic distinctions: for example, a language that has a singular, a plural, and a dual is more complex in this respect than a language where only two number categories, singular and plural, are found. McWhorter further argues (p. 160) that such complexity differences can be translated into implicational hierarchies. Thus, the existence of number categories is regulated by the implicational hierarchy in (1) (adapted from Greenberg 1963; Greenberg formulated his Universal 34 as follows: "No language has a trial number unless it has a dual. No language has a dual unless it has a plural.").

(1) The number hierarchy
     (SINGULAR) < PLURAL < DUAL < TRIAL

The hierarchy is interpreted as follows: if a language exhibits a given category on the hierarchy, it will also exhibit all the categories to the left of this category (i.e. in the direction of the arrowheads). Thus, if we know that a language has a dual, then we can expect it to have a plural (and a singular) as well, but we cannot infer anything about the existence of a trial in that language. McWhorter's criterion can then be recast as: the higher a language climbs on a given hierarchy, the more complex its grammar is in that respect.

In this chapter, I shall develop and critically examine this idea, and relate the concept of implicational hierarchy to the ongoing discussion on language complexity.

In section 2, I will discuss and define the notion of complexity adopted here. Section 3 presents the sample used in the study, and section 4 discusses in detail the implicational hierarchies investigated. The cross-linguistic results are given in section 5. Finally, section 6 discusses the relationship between implicational hierarchies and complexity in more depth and presents the main conclusions of the chapter.

2 Some background on the notion of complexity

As discussed in Miestamo (2006, 2008) and by Östen Dahl on pp. 50–2 above, complexity can be and has been approached in two different ways in linguistics: in *absolute* and in *relative* terms.

The absolute approach defines complexity in objective terms as the number of parts in a system, of connections between different parts, etc. Absolute complexity can be cast in information-theoretic terms, defining a phenomenon as the more complex, the longer its shortest possible description is (see also Dahl 2004 for more discussion). This is the basic idea behind the notion of Kolmogorov complexity (Li and Vitányi 1997). However, defining complexity as straightforward length of description would take total chaos as maximally complex: that is not the concept of complexity which interests us. Gell-Mann's (1994) notion of effective complexity pays attention only to the regularities within a system. The length of the description of the regularities in a system provides a usable definition of grammatical complexity. Examples of the absolute approach to complexity in recent typologically oriented discussion include McWhorter (2001a) and Dahl (2004).

The relative approach to complexity defines complexity in relation to language users: what is costly or difficult to language users (speakers, hearers, language learners) is seen as complex. Complexity is thus identified with cost and difficulty of processing and learning. However, the notion of relative complexity is problematic in typological research.

First, language use involves very different situations and roles, and what is costly or difficult for one class of language users (e.g. speakers) may ease the task of another user type (e.g. hearers). As noted by Kusters (2003), adopting a relative definition of complexity requires one to answer the question "Complex to whom?" For example, fission (many forms corresponding to one meaning syntagmatically), for example, discontinuous negation as in French *Je ne chante pas*, will be an extra burden for the speaker, but eases the hearer's task of comprehension. Complexity would thus mean different things depending on whether we adopt the speaker's or the hearer's perspective (or that of the L1 or L2 learner).

How should we then decide which type of language use is primary and criterial for our definition? And do we want to make such a decision in the first place? In Kusters' (2003) study, the sociolinguistic orientation justifies the choice of L2 learners as criterial, but if we are aiming at a general definition of language complexity, the relative approach has no solution to this problem.

Secondly, our understanding of what is costly or difficult and what is easy for language users is far from being complete. For some phenomena we might have a fairly good understanding of cost and difficulty, but when looking at different domains of grammar, especially when doing this with an extensive sample of languages, we are likely to encounter many phenomena for which we cannot decide unequivocally what is easy and what is difficult in them for different classes of language user. There is simply not enough psycholinguistic research on all the relevant aspects of all the relevant phenomena. Kusters (2008) also acknowledges this problem.

Given these problems with the relative definition of complexity (see Miestamo 2006, 2008 for more detailed discussion), cross-linguistic studies of grammatical complexity should adopt an absolute definition of complexity. Accordingly, I follow Dahl (2004) in restricting the term "complexity" to absolute complexity, and using the terms cost and difficulty when cost and difficulty are intended. Whether complexity defined in absolute terms correlates with cost and difficulty is a highly important follow-up question – indeed one of the main factors that make the study of language complexity theoretically interesting.

Another important distinction is to be made between *global* and *local* complexity, the former term referring to the global or overall complexity of (the grammar of) a language, and the latter to a particular domain of grammar such as (to take two random examples) verbal morphology, or the system of spatial deixis.

The received view of global complexity is that all languages are equally complex, and that complexity in one area is compensated by simplicity in another – this is the equi-complexity hypothesis. There is, however, little empirical work to support this thesis. The most explicit attempt to measure the global complexity of grammars is the metric proposed by McWhorter (2001a, 2007). The 2007 version of the metric contains three criteria of complexity: *overspecification* (the extent to which a grammar makes semantic and pragmatic distinctions beyond communicative necessity), *structural elaboration* (number of rules mediating underlying forms and surface forms), and *irregularity*.

Miestamo (2006, 2008) identifies two general problems that any such metric of global complexity must deal with. The *Problem of Representativity* means that it is very difficult to account for all aspects of grammar in such detail that one could have a truly representative measure of global complexity. It may, however, be possible to achieve a sufficient level of representativity to show global complexity differences when these are very clear. The *Problem of Comparability* refers to the fact that the different criteria used to measure the complexity of a grammar are incommensurable. It is not possible to quantify the complexity of, for example, syntax and morphology so that the numbers would be comparable in any useful sense. This incommensurability obtains between the domains and subdomains of grammar in general. Therefore, only in cases where one language is more complex than another on (almost) all criteria can we identify differences in global complexity. Given these problems, one should focus in large-scale typological studies on the complexity of specific areas of grammar.

As argued in Miestamo (2006, 2008), functional domains provide a useful *tertium comparationis* for approaching the complexity of specific areas of grammar. Thus, we may study and compare the complexity of e.g. tense systems across languages, and say that according to the *Principle of Fewer Distinctions*, a language with two grammatical tense distinctions is less complex than one with five. Similarly, we may look at the way these tense distinctions are formally encoded and say that the more the formal coding of tense deviates from the *Principle of One Meaning–One Form*, the more complexity it involves. When we have gathered data from many different domains, we may see whether the complexities of different domains (e.g. tense, aspect, mood, deixis) show correlations, and this will then provide partial answers to the big question behind the equi-complexity hypothesis, namely whether the complexity of one domain is compensated by simplicity in another.

Implicational hierarchies provide one means of examining the complexity of functional domains. Many of them are straightforward complexity measures in terms of the Principle of Fewer Distinctions. This is the case with for example the number hierarchy in (1) above: a language that climbs higher on the number hierarchy makes more distinctions in the domain of number.

However, the connection between complexity and the hierarchies is not so straightforward in all cases, for example in the case of the accessibility hierarchy proposed by Keenan and Comrie (1977):

(2)   The accessibility hierarchy
      SBJ < DIRECT OBJ < INDIRECT OBJ < OBL < GEN

The syntactic structures used with subject relativization are usually the simplest, and complexity tends to increase when we climb up the hierarchy.

In this case, we are naturally dealing with language-specific structures, the complexity of which we have to describe separately in each language. (See J. A. Hawkins 2004 for a way to analyse the complexity of these structures, and cf. also Kirby 1997.) In what follows, I will explicate the connection between complexity and the hierarchies I discuss. In addition to the fact that many hierarchies are complexity measures as such, a further interest can be seen in that related hierarchies may be expected to show (inverse) correlations, and thus also allow us to test the equi-complexity hypothesis.

3 Sampling

The study is based on a sample of fifty languages. The sampling method follows the principles introduced in Miestamo (2005). It has two main goals: the sample should be as representative of the world's linguistic diversity as possible, and the languages should be areally and genealogically as independent of each other as possible. The latter goal is especially important in view of the statistical aims of the study. The sampling frame is therefore stratified both genealogically and areally.

The stratification is based on the notions of *genus* and *macroarea*, as understood by Dryer (1989, 2005). Instead of taking an equal number of languages from each macroarea, the method pays attention to the genealogical diversity of each area. The number of languages selected from each macroarea is determined by the proportion that the number of genera in that macroarea represents of the total number of genera in the world. Genealogically more diverse areas are thus represented by a higher number of languages in the sample than areas that show less diversity. In Dryer's (2005) classification, the world's languages are divided into 458 genera. Table 6.1 shows the distribution of the genera in the six macroareas.

Table 6.1. Genera and sample languages by macroarea

	Genera	%	Sample
Africa	64	14·0	7
Eurasia	38	8·3	4
Southeast Asia and Oceania	46	10·0	5
Australia and New Guinea	125	27·3	14
North America	91	19·9	10
South America	94	20·5	10
Total	458	100·0	50

The middle column shows the percentage that the number of genera in each macroarea represents of the total number of genera in the world. For example, Africa has sixty-four genera in Dryer's classification, which equals 14 per cent of the world's total of 458 genera. According to the sampling method adopted here, 14 per cent of the sample languages should come from Africa. With a sample size of fifty languages, this means seven African languages. The number of languages included in the fifty-language sample is shown in the rightmost column of Table 6.1. Every language in the sample must come from a different genus (and so far as possible, also from different families). The languages sampled from each macroarea are listed in Table 6.2; Fig. 6.1 shows the geographical distribution of the sample languages.[1]

Table 6.2. Sample languages by macroarea (primary sources consulted in brackets)

AFRICA (7 languages)
Khoekhoe (Hagman 1977), Hdi (Frajzyngier 2002), Koyra Chiini (Heath 1999), Krongo (Reh 1985), Ma'di (Blackings and Fabb 2003), Somali (Saeed 1999), Supyire (Carlson 1994)

EURASIA (4 languages)
Basque (Hualde and Ortiz de Urbina 2003), Lezgian (Haspelmath 1993), Lithuanian (Ambrazas 1997), Yukaghir (Kolyma) (Maslova 1999)

SOUTHEAST ASIA AND OCEANIA (5 languages)
Hmong Njua (Harriehausen 1988), Kambera (Klamer 1998), Meithei (Chelliah 1997), Semelai (Kruspe 2004), Thai (Iwasaki and Ingkaphirom 2005)

AUSTRALIA AND NEW GUINEA (14 languages)
Alamblak (Bruce 1984), Arapesh (Conrad and Wogiga 1991), Daga (Murane 1974), Gaagudju (Harvey 2002), Imonda (Seiler 1985), Inanwatan (de Vries 2004), Kayardild (Evans 1995), Lavukaleve (Terrill 2003), Maybrat (Dol 1999), Nabak (Fabian et al. 1998), Sentani (Cowan 1965), Tauya (MacDonald 1990), Yelî Dnye (Henderson 1995), Yimas (Foley 1991)

NORTH AMERICA (10 languages)
Greenlandic (West) (Fortescue 1984), Halkomelem (Galloway 1993), Koasati (Kimball 1991), Mixtec (Chalcatongo) (Macaulay 1996), Osage (Quintero 2004), Pipil (Campbell 1985), Purépecha (Chamoreau 2000), Slave (Rice 1989), Tiipay (Jamul) (A. Miller 2001), Wintu (Pitkin 1984)

SOUTH AMERICA (10 languages)
Awa Pit (Curnow 1997), Hixkaryana (Derbyshire 1979), Jarawara (Dixon 2004), Kwazá (van der Voort 2004), Mapudungun (Smeets 1989; Zúñiga 2000), Mosetén (Sakel 2004), Rama (Grinevald-Craig 1988), Sanuma (Borgman 1990), Trumai (Guirardello 1999), Yagua (Payne and Payne 1990)

---

[1] The names of the languages appear in the form they are listed in *The World Atlas of Language Structures* (WALS, Haspelmath et al. 2005). The map was generated using the WALS Interactive Reference Tool developed by Hans-Jörg Bibiko.

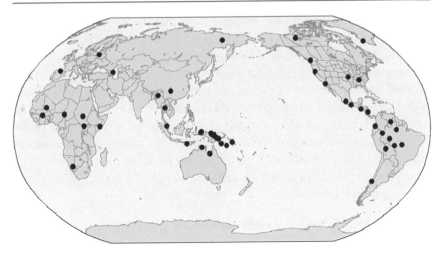

FIG. 6.1. Sample languages

4 The implicational hierarchies

To find suitable hierarchies for the study, I consulted the Universals Archive (UA),[2] which covers a large number of universals proposed in linguistic literature.

One methodological possibility would be to examine the cross-linguistic variation on all or most of the hierarchies found in such a database. This path was not followed, because with most of the hierarchies no connections to – and thus correlations with – other hierarchies would be expected (some unexpected correlations could of course turn up).

The research strategy adopted in this chapter concentrates on hierarchies that might be expected to show correlations. Two pairs of hierarchies found in the UA, surmised to be connected in the relevant sense, were chosen for case studies in this chapter: the agreement and case hierarchies on the one hand and the verbalization and copula hierarchies on the other.

4.1 *The agreement and case hierarchies*

The agreement and case hierarchies operate in the domain of the marking of clausal participants.[3] It should be noted that in this context case and agreement

---

[2] <http://typo.uni-konstanz.de/archive/intro/index.php>
[3] Note that the agreement hierarchy examined here is different from what Corbett (1979) refers to by that term.

are not understood as referring to bound morphology only, but "case" will also include dependent marking of grammatical relations with adpositions and "agreement" will also include head marking of grammatical relations with adverbal clitics or particles. The following representation (3) of the hierarchies is adapted from C. Lehmann (1988):

(3)   Agreement and case hierarchies

	1		2		3		4
Agreement:	ABS	<	OBJ	<	INDIRECT OBJ	<	DIRECT ADJUNCT
	SBJ	<	ERG	<	LOC ADJUNCT	<	ABL ADJUNCT
					INS ADJUNCT	<	COM ADJUNCT
	4		3		2		1
Case:	ABS	>	OBJ	>	INDIRECT OBJ	>	DIRECT ADJUNCT
	SBJ	>	ERG	>	LOC ADJUNCT	>	ABL ADJUNCT
					INS ADJUNCT	>	COM ADJUNCT

The hierarchies in (3) read as follows. If a language codes a participant in a given column with agreement, it will code (at least some) participants in the columns to the left of this column with agreement. If a language codes a participant in a given column with case, it will code (at least some) participants in the columns to the right of this column with case. We may give the following interpretation to the hierarchies in terms of complexity: a language is the more complex the higher it climbs on either hierarchy, since agreement and case marking are means of coding relations overtly – overt marking is more complex than no marking because, other things being equal, it requires a longer description than no marking.

In this chapter I have restricted my investigation of agreement and case to verbal main clauses; furthermore, I have counted case only on full NPs, not on pronouns. As can be seen in (4a, b) (data from Hualde and Ortiz de Urbina 2003: 209, 411, 413), Basque has verbal agreement for absolutives, ergatives, and indirect objects (datives), but no agreement for the directional (allative) relation in (4c); overt case marking occurs on ergatives, indirect objects, and directional participants, but not on absolutives. For reasons of space, it is not possible to exemplify all the relations in the rightmost and next-to-rightmost columns of (3), but, apart from indirect objects, it is true in general in Basque that those relations show case marking but no agreement.

(4)   a. *dakar-ki-zu-t*
             bring.3.ABS-PRS-2S.DAT-1S.ERG
             "I bring it to you."

b. *jon-ek   miren-i   ardoa   ekarri dio*
   Jon-ERG Miren-DAT wine[ABS] bring   AUX.3.ABS.3.ERG.3.DAT
   "Jon brought wine for Miren."

c. *autobus-era bultzatu gaituzte*
   bus-ALL   push   AUX.1P.ABS.3P.ERG
   "They pushed us into the bus."

Basque is thus assigned three points on the agreement hierarchy and three points on the case hierarchy.

All languages in the sample have case marking for at least one item in each of the rightmost and next-to-rightmost columns. Furthermore, in the fifty languages examined, there is only one instance of agreement with any of the adjunct relations, namely in Imonda, where comitatives have number agreement; this is the only instance of agreement extending to the rightmost column.[4] There is therefore little reason in the present study to distinguish between the rightmost and next-to-rightmost columns. Instead I have adopted simplified versions of the two hierarchies, as shown in (5):

(5) Agreement and case hierarchies, simplified

	1		2		3
Agreement:	SBJ/ABS	<	OBJ/ERG	<	OBL
	3		2		1
Case:	SBJ/ABS	>	OBJ/ERG	>	OBL

In (5) the two rightmost columns of (3) have been merged under the label "oblique". It is still the case that all languages score at least one point on the case hierarchy, i.e. in all languages we find dependent marking for at least some of the oblique relations,[5] but in order to preserve the symmetry between the two hierarchies, the oblique column was retained in the case hierarchy. Using the simplified hierarchies, Basque (4) is assigned three complexity points for agreement and two for case.

Restrictions on space preclude detailed discussion of the limits of what counts as case and what counts as agreement. Nevertheless, a few issues need to be mentioned here.

---

[4] There are naturally cases of head marking of different oblique relations, e.g. directional and instrumental affixes, but as they do not index the participant in question, these are not agreement or cross-reference.

[5] In the sample, Arapesh, where the use of prepositions is rather marginal, comes the closest to having no dependent marking for the oblique relations.

First, the agreement and case hierarchies are about grammatical relations, not directly about the expression of semantic roles. Thus, for example, direct objects may code various semantic roles in languages, but in the present context we pay attention to their status as grammatical relations, not to the semantic roles they may express. More concretely, when a language expresses recipients as direct objects, these are not counted as indirect objects in the hierarchy. Thus a language with a secondary object system, for example Mosetén, where subjects and objects are cross-referenced on the verb and where ditransitives mark the recipient rather than the theme as direct object, is assigned two points on the agreement hierarchy.

Secondly, the marking of participants with serial verb constructions (as in Maybrat) or with adpositional verbs (as in Halkomelem) is dependent marking and counted as case in the present context; note that it is common for such serial verbs to grammaticalize as adpositions – a development that is currently under way in Maybrat.

Finally, it should be noted that a few counterexamples to the hierarchies can be found in the fifty-language sample. There is one counterexample to the agreement hierarchy, namely Khoekhoe, where direct and indirect objects may be cross-referenced on the verb if there is no overt object or indirect object NP in the clause, but subjects are not cross-referenced. As to the case hierarchy, there are three languages where subjects show overt case marking but objects do not: Osage, Somali, and Jamul Tiipay. In these cases the complexity points are assigned according to the highest point the language reaches on the hierarchy regardless of the gap observed lower on the hierarchy: Khoekhoe scores three points on the agreement hierarchy, and Osage, Somali, and Jamul Tiipay score three points on the case hierarchy.

4.2 *The verbalization and copula hierarchies*

The verbalization and copula hierarchies concern the linguistic encoding of location, object, property, and action predicates.

Coding with a copula is here understood as referring to coding with any support item, be it a true copula or a locational support verb. Verbalization means, to put it simply, that the predicates show morphosyntactic properties of verbs in the language in question. The representation of the verbalization and copula hierarchies in (6) is adapted from Stassen (1992) and Croft (1991), respectively. Croft's copula hierarchy does not include locative predicates, but they have been included here to make the hierarchies symmetrical; extended this way (and defined as covering coding with any support item), the copula hierarchy is a valid cross-linguistic generalization in my sample.

(6)   Verbalization and copula hierarchies

	4		3		2		1
Verbalization:	LOCATION	>	OBJECT	>	PROPERTY	>	ACTION
	1		2		3		4
Copula:	LOCATION	<	OBJECT	<	PROPERTY	<	ACTION

The hierarchies can be read as follows. If a given type of predicate is coded by using a copula (a support item), then the predicate types to its left will also be. Similarly, if a given type of predicate is coded by verbalization, then the predicate types to its right will also be. In my fifty-language sample, there are no clear counterexamples to either hierarchy. Requiring a longer description (other things being equal), overt coding with a copula or by verbalization is more complex than its absence, and a language is thus the more complex the higher it climbs on either hierarchy.

As Stassen (1992: 193) notes, action predicates are verbalized by default and do not belong to the hierarchy in the same sense as the three others; in Stassen's (1997: 124) data, non-verbal coding of action predicates is very rare and never the sole option in languages. Cross-linguistic variation relevant in the present context can only be found in the coding of location, object, and property predicates. In this study, I have therefore disregarded action predicates, and focused on the three remaining predicate types. Furthermore, I have only taken into account stative predications, and left inchoative predications outside the study. The simplified form of the hierarchies adopted in this study is given in (7):

(7)   Verbalization and copula hierarchies, simplified

	3		2		1
Verbalization:	LOCATION	>	OBJECT	>	PROPERTY
	1		2		3
Copula:	LOCATION	<	OBJECT	<	PROPERTY

In this chapter I have restricted my investigation of verbalization and copular coding to main clauses. The assignment of complexity points on the hierarchies is illustrated in (8) with examples from Kambera (Klamer 1998: 49, 107, 123, 166):

(8)   a. *mbeni-ya-ka*   *nú*
          be_angry-3S.ACC-PFV   DEICTIC
          "People are angry."

       b. *tau*   *mayila-mbu-kai*   *nyimi*   *ná*
          person   poor-also-2P.ACC   you   DEICTIC
          "Moreover, you are also poor people."

c. *la*   *'uma-ya*
   LOC   house-3s.ACC
   "(S)he is at home."

d. *ni-nya*   *la*   *uma*
   be-3s.DAT   LOC   home
   "(S)he is at home."

The language does not have a separate class of adjectives, property words being intransitive verbs (8a). Object and location predicates are also coded verbally, as the accusative verbal enclitic cross-references the subject (8b, c). Example (8a) shows that this is indeed a verbal enclitic (marking an impersonal subject in this example). Location predications can alternatively be construed with a support verb, as in (8d). Therefore Kambera is assigned three points on the verbalization hierarchy and one point on the copula hierarchy.

Again, lack of space prevents more detailed discussion and exemplification of the limits of what counts as copula coding and verbalization; but a couple of issues must be addressed. First, the support items that the copula hierarchy covers may be maximally abstract copular verbs or more concrete locational verbs, for example, posture verbs such as "stand", "sit", or "lie", but they may also be non-verbal copulas as in Ma'di, where the element ʔɨ that is originally a focalizer acts as a non-verbal copula with object predicates.

Secondly, verbalization may mean fully verbal coding, as is the case in the cross-linguistically common pattern where property concepts are (stative) verbs and the language has no separate (open) class of adjectives, e.g. in Kambera (8a). In some cases, as in Kambera object and location predications (8b, c), the stative predicates do not show the full morphosyntactic characteristics of verbs in the language, but their coding is clearly verbal as verbal cross-reference markers (or other verbal marking) is used whenever these predicates occur.

There are two less clear cases of verbalization in the data. In Tauya, object words in predicate position show the same declarative mood marker as verbs, but unlike verbs, they lack cross-reference markers; however, since the mood marker is verbal, the language shows (at least some) verbal marking for object predicates, and therefore receives two complexity points on the verbalization hierarchy. In Semelai, location and object words are usually zero-coded as predicates, but they may carry the imminent aspect proclitic, which is a verbal marker, and again we must conclude that verbalization of location and object predicates occurs in the language.[6]

---

[6] It should be noted that Stassen's (1997) criteria of verbalization are somewhat more conservative than the ones used here.

5 Results

Tables 6.3 and 6.4 show the scores for each of the fifty sample languages on the hierarchies examined. (Language names are represented by their first three letters.) Figs 6.2 and 6.3 further visualize the cross-linguistic complexity variation along the hierarchies: Figs 6.2a, b and 6.3a, b show the individual scales, whereas Figs 6.2c and 6.3c combine the related hierarchies, and thus show the overall complexity of each domain in terms of these hierarchies. The cross-linguistic means and medians are given in Table 6.5.

In Tables 6.3 and 6.4, complexity increases as we go higher on the x and y axes. If the hierarchies balanced each other out perfectly, only the shaded cells would be populated; in these cells the overall complexity of the domain is 3. The cells below and to the left of the shaded cline contain less complex cases (overall complexity 0–2), where one or more of the functions are not overtly marked with the marking devices observed in the hierarchies. The cells above

Table 6.3. Agreement and case data

AGREEMENT		CASE		
		0	1	2	3
3			dag gaa kam yim	bas imo kho pur	koa som
2			ala ara hal hix ina jar lav mad map mos nab pip sen sla	awa gre hdi kwa tau win yel	osa tii
1			kro may mix ram	tru yag yuk	lit sem
0			hmo sup koy tha	lez mei san	kay

Table 6.4. Verbalization and copula data

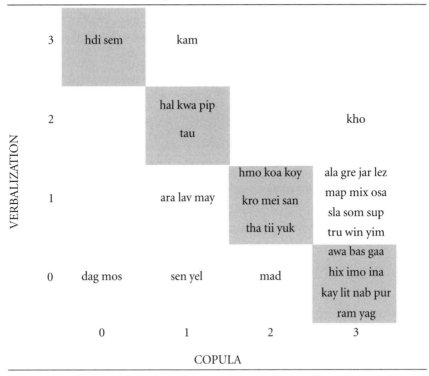

VERBALIZATION	COPULA 0	COPULA 1	COPULA 2	COPULA 3
3	hdi sem	kam		
2		hal kwa pip tau		kho
1		ara lav may	hmo koa koy kro mei san tha tii yuk	ala gre jar lez map mix osa sla som sup tru win yim
0	dag mos	sen yel	mad	awa bas gaa hix imo ina kay lit nab pur ram yag

COPULA

Table 6.5. Means and medians

	Mean	Median
Agreement	1·70	2
Case	1·62	1
Agreement + Case	3·32	3
Verbalization	0·88	1
Copula	2·16	3
Verbalization + Copula	3·04	3

and to the right of the shaded cline contain more complex cases (overall complexity 4–6), where one or more of the functions are marked with more than one device.

The mean overall complexities of both domains are close to 3, but we can see some clear differences between them. The agreement and case hierarchies

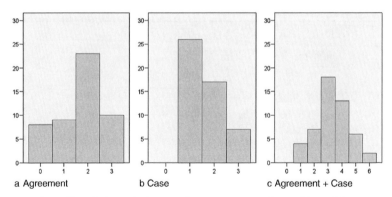

FIG. 6.2. Cross-linguistic variation on the agreement and case hierarchies

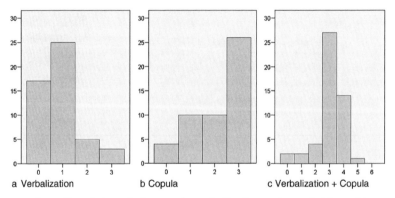

FIG. 6.3. Cross-linguistic variation on the verbalization and copula hierarchies

do not show any clear patterning along the shaded cline and the simplest and the most complex areas of the grid are well populated. (The picture is a bit skewed by the fact that all languages are assigned at least one point on the case hierarchy: cf. section 4.1.) The means and medians are slightly higher for the agreement hierarchy, as is the sum of all complexity points assigned in all sample languages: agreement 85, case 81. The overall complexity of the domain is normally distributed. The verbalization and copula hierarchies show fewer cases where overall complexity is very low or very high. The overall complexity values come close to the shaded descending cline, suggesting an inverse correlation between the hierarchies (we will come back to the correlations below). Overall complexity is not as clearly normally distributed as in the domain of agreement and case. Compared to each other, the verbalization and copula hierarchies are very different, the former showing a skewing at the lower end of the scale and the latter at the higher end, the total points assigned in all languages being 44 for verbalization and 108 for copula.

It may be noted that the amount of redundancy cannot be directly read off the tables. Agreement and case may often occur simultaneously coding a given relation in a clause, but there are some cases in the data where they are in complementary distribution, e.g. Inanwatan and Khoekhoe. The hierarchies as presented here only pay attention to whether the language may have case or agreement coding for the relation in at least some (verbal main) clauses, without paying attention to whether they may occur simultaneously. As to verbalization and copular coding, they are mutually exclusive in a clause, so they can only co-occur in a language on the system level (in different contexts or as free variants). Tables 6.3 and 6.4 and Figs 6.2c and 6.3c therefore show the overall complexity of their respective domains on the level of the system, not on the level of individual constructions.

Correlations are to be expected between the agreement and case hierarchies on the one hand and the verbalization and copula hierarchies on the other. In the data of my fifty-language sample there is no significant correlation, positive or negative, between the agreement and case hierarchies (Kendall's tau-b $= 0 \cdot 012$, $p = \cdot 921$),[7] but there is an inverse correlation between the verbalization and copula hierarchies which turns out to be significant at the $0 \cdot 01$ level (Kendall's tau-b $= -0 \cdot 353$, $p = \cdot 005$).[8] One of the two hierarchy pairs expected to show correlations thus meets this expectation and the other one does not. I also checked if there were any (unexpected) correlations between the unrelated hierarchies (i.e. between copula and case, copula and agreement, verbalization and case, verbalization and agreement) and between the overall complexities of the two domains (i.e. between copula + verbalization and agreement + case): no significant correlations emerged.

Relating these correlations to the discussion of complexity, we can conclude that there is no compensation between the agreement and case hierarchies; but the complexities of copular and verbal marking of stative

---

[7] As a non-parametric test, Kendall's tau correlation test is not subject to the main criticisms in Janssen et al. (2006).

[8] I also selected a 50-language sample from Stassen's (1997) data following the principles of areal and genealogical stratification discussed above. I merged the locational and copula strategies in Stassen's data. As already mentioned, his definition of verbalization is slightly different from the present study. In this dataset, the verbalization and copula hierarchies showed a correlation that was almost significant at the $\cdot 05$ level (Kendall's tau-b $= -0 \cdot 250$, $p = \cdot 052$).

predicates do show a trade-off effect. This points towards the conclusion that while compensations are found in some domains of grammar, they are not an all-encompassing phenomenon; see Sinnemäki (2008) for a similar result. Why there is compensation in one domain but not in another needs to be explained in each case – and this naturally also requires a more detailed investigation of the domains in question; but such explanations will not be attempted in this methodological essay.

6 Discussion and conclusions

So far, we have seen that implicational hierarchies may be used for measuring aspects of the grammatical complexity of the domains in which they operate. Furthermore, we have seen that when we find related hierarchies operating within a given domain, we may look for correlations between them and thereby address the question of the existence of complexity trade-offs. The applicability of this research strategy is, however, to some extent limited by the fact that the implicational hierarchies proposed in the literature so far cover only a limited number of grammatical phenomena, and even fewer are related in such a way that correlations could be expected between them.

Nevertheless, using implicational hierarchies in the study of complexity (regardless of whether they show correlations) has the additional value of deepening our understanding of the relationship between complexity and cost/difficulty. The reasoning goes as follows. First, while cross-linguistic frequencies are not fully determined by ease of processing and learning, these factors play a significant role in what is preferred and what is dispreferred in the world's languages. In other words, the easier a given grammatical category or structure is to process or learn, the more frequently it will appear in discourse in a given language and the more frequently it will be grammaticalized in the world's languages (cf. the Performance–Grammar Correspondence Hypothesis proposed by John Hawkins 2004). Secondly, implicational hierarchies reflect cross-linguistic preferences: on any hierarchy the features at the least marked end are the most frequent ones cross-linguistically, and the marked end contains less frequent features. Drawing these two ideas together, implicational hierarchies can (to some extent at least) be interpreted as measuring cost/difficulty of processing and/or learning from a cross-linguistic point of view.

Moreover, we may assume that linguistic phenomena that are cross-linguistically frequent are relatively easy for all language users (speakers, hearers, learners). As to cross-linguistically less common phenomena, the question is more complicated, since a given category or structure may be rare because it is costly or difficult for a particular class of language users while being easy for other classes. In any case, cross-linguistic preferences can be interpreted as reflecting (to some extent) cost/difficulty shared by all language users. Thus, in implicational hierarchies, the differences between different types of language user have been filtered away to a large extent, and the use of hierarchies as complexity measures allows us (partly) to bypass the question "Difficult to whom?" referred to in connection with the discussion of "relative complexity" above. This makes implicational hierarchies especially attractive in illuminating the link between complexity and cost/difficulty.

As a final note, we have seen that hierarchies may differ as to the location of the cross-linguistically most frequent point that languages reach. The preferred point may be situated anywhere between the simplest and the most complex ends of the scales. As seen above, the most commonly reached point on the verbalization hierarchy is close to the simplest end of the scale, whereas on the copula hierarchy it is at the most complex end. Naturally, the features at the simplest end are always the commonest ones and those at the most complex end the least common ones, i.e. copula coding for locational predications is more frequent than copula coding for property predications, even though property predications are the point that languages most frequently reach on the copula hierarchy.

That the most frequently reached point is not always at the simplest end of the scale shows that some complexity is needed for communication. Both speakers' and hearers' needs are reflected in these preferences.

7

Sociolinguistic typology and complexification

PETER TRUDGILL

1 Background

In previous work in sociolinguistic typology (e.g. Trudgill 1983, 1989, 1992, 1996a, b, 1998, 2002) I have suggested that it might be possible to argue that the distribution of linguistic features over languages may not be just random or areal.[1] Rather, it may be the case that certain types of society, or social structure, tend to produce certain types of language, or linguistic structure. In the context of the present volume, therefore, the suggestion is that certain types of social factor may predispose languages to demonstrate greater or lesser degrees of complexity.

Previous work suggests that amongst the most promising social factors to examine in the typological search for the social correlates of complexification and simplification are the following:

- (i) *degree of contact v. isolation*: the focus of discussion here is on the "critical threshold" (Lenneberg 1967);
- (ii) *denseness v. looseness of social networks*, following especially Milroy and Milroy (1985);
- (iii) *small v. large community size*. Relevant here, amongst others, is the work of André Haudricourt (1961).

2 Contact and the critical threshold

At least one helpful way of looking at the concept of linguistic complexity is to regard it as being synonymous with the difficulty of acquisition of a language,

[1] I am very grateful for help I have received with this paper from Lars Gunnar Andersson, Martin Atkinson, Östen Dahl, Gunther De Vogelaer, Jan Terje Faarlund, Jean Hannah, Martin Haspelmath, Juan Manuel Hernandez Campoy, Andrew Koontz-Garboden, Michael Noonan, Wolfgang Schulze, and Jürg Schwyter. Not all of them necessarily agree with everything or indeed anything that I have written here.

or a subsystem of a language, for adolescent and adult learners. This approach has received support (e.g. Kusters 2003), but it is of course not the only way of looking at complexity, as other chapters in this volume reveal. In particular it has been queried by Dahl (2004: 282), who suggests that "difficult" and "complex" should not be automatically equated: "what an individual finds difficult obviously depends not only on the complexity of the object of learning but also on the individual's previous knowledge." One cannot but agree, but my suggestion is that, *other things being equal,* some systems are more difficult and therefore complex than others. In a paper written in 1979 (Trudgill 1983: 106) I noted:

It is usual for laymen to claim that some languages are easier to learn than others. Linguists have tended to play down this suggestion, and to point out that it depends on what your point of departure is: Spanish is easier for an English speaker to learn than Chinese, but for a speaker of Thai it might be the other way round. However, I think it is legitimate to suggest that some languages actually are easier for adults to learn, in an absolute sense, than others. If one were given a month in which to learn a language of one's choice, I think one would select Norwegian rather than Faroese, Spanish rather than Latin, and Sranan rather than English.

Crucially, the preferred languages for rapid learning are all "languages which have undergone more contact" (see also Trudgill 1989). Not only are some languages more complex than others, but also this very often has something to do with the amount of contact a variety has experienced.

The link between language contact and simplification has often been made in the literature, For example, the link has been demonstrated by Kusters (2003), who examines the history of degrees of complexity and simplicity in verbal inflectional morphology in Quechua, Swahili, Arabic, and the Scandinavian languages. His highly detailed quantitative analyses lead him to conclude that "the level of [linguistic] complexity is related to the type of speech community" (2003: 359), in that language varieties with a history of higher contact also tend to demonstrate higher degrees of simplification.

Language contact has this consequence because of *pidginization.* The most extreme outcome of pidginization is the development of a pidgin language, but this is a very rare occurrence. It is only pidginization at its most extreme, together with a number of other unusual factors, which combine to lead to the development of pidgin and, even more rarely, creole languages. Pidginization can be said to occur whenever adults and post-adolescents learn a new language (Trudgill 1989). This in turn – although other factors such as motivation may be involved – is due to the relative inability of adult humans to learn new languages perfectly. Adult (and adolescent) humans are speakers who have passed the critical threshold for language acquisition (Lenneberg 1967). The critical threshold is the most fundamental instrumental mechanism involved in pidginization, and it has to play an important part in our understanding of language contact phenomena.

Pidginization consists of three related but distinct processes: reduction, admixture, and simplification. Reduction refers to the fact that, in pidginized form, there is simply *less of* a language as compared to the form in which it is spoken by native speakers. Admixture refers to interference or transfer, an obvious feature of adult second-language acquisition.

Simplification, as is well known (see Mühlhäusler 1977, 2001), is a rather complex phenomenon, but it refers crucially to three linked processes (Trudgill 1996a):

  (i) regularization of irregularities;
 (ii) an increase in lexical and morphological transparency;[2]
(iii) loss of redundancy.

All languages contain redundancy, which seems to be necessary for successful communication, especially in less than perfect (i.e. normal) circumstances; but it is probable that some languages have more redundancy than others. Loss of redundancy takes two major forms, corresponding to different forms of redundancy:

  (a) the *loss of morphological categories* (i.e. grammatical categories that are expressed morphologically). Some grammatical categories are more frequent in the world's languages than others. For example, all the languages of the world have the category *person*, but of the other categories some are more and others less common. It appears that these categories may be of different statuses or degrees of importance, and that their functions may be less or more clear. And there are also important differences in how the categories may be expressed, the most important difference for our purposes being between morphological (or synthetic) expression, on the one hand, and lexical and syntactic (or analytic) expression, on the other. Sometimes, but not always, loss of the morphological expression of grammatical categories is compensated for by the use of more analytical structures, such as the usage of adpositions instead of case endings. We can speak of loss of redundancy "with or without repair".
  (b) The second type of redundancy loss occurs in the form of *reduction in repetition of information*. Repetition of information is illustrated for

---

[2] I do not discuss phonology here, but phonological transparency (i.e. low levels of allophony) will also be relevant.

example in grammatical agreement, where there is more than one signal that, say, a noun phrase is feminine; or in obligatory tense marking, such as when all verbs in a past-tense narrative are marked for past tense. Here, reduction in redundancy will take the form of reduction in the number of repetitions, as in the loss of agreement.

Pidginization involves simplification because high irregularity, low transparency, and high levels of redundancy make for difficulties of learning and remembering for adolescent and adult learner-speakers. Simplification is the direct result of the critical threshold. Small children, as is well known, will learn perfectly any language that they have sufficient exposure to. But the less complexity a language has – technically speaking, the less irregularity, opacity, and redundancy – the easier it will be for post-threshold learners to master.

This does not necessarily mean that simplification occurs only in high contact situations – Dahl writes: "it is unlikely that those changes can all depend on language contact" (2004: 283) – rather it is a matter of probabilities. While simplification and complexification may both occur in all languages, it is in the high-contact situations that there is an imbalance between the two, with simplification dominant. This is presumably why Shosted (2006) does not succeed in demonstrating the validity of the "negative correlation hypothesis", which supposes that if one component of language is simplified then another must be elaborated.

It is also very important not to lose sight of the role of the critical threshold, because high-contact situations of certain sorts can also lead to complexification. Nichols writes (1992: 193): "contact among languages fosters complexity, or, put differently, diversity among neighbouring languages fosters complexity in each of the languages." This then is borrowed, *added* complexity. And here of course the contact will have to be of a very particular type, namely stable, long-term, co-territorial, contact situations involving childhood – and therefore *pre-threshold* and proficient – bilingualism (see Trudgill 2008).

3 Community size and social networks

I now suggest that simplification is not an especially challenging phenomenon for students of language change, precisely because it is rather predictable in terms of the less than perfect language acquisition abilities of adolescents and adults. The reverse challenge is much more severe. As Thurston (1994: 603) says, what we need to be able to do is "to explain how complexity arose in languages in the first place". I argue that the more challenging problem is: in which social circumstances do we witness the reverse process, spontaneous (i.e. not additive, long-term contact-induced) complexification? To what extent can we expect to see a greater degree of the spontaneous *development* of irregularity and redundancy in *low*-contact varieties? And to what extent can we expect to see a greater degree of the growth (as opposed to the addition, as a result of borrowing) of morphological categories in such varieties?

The answer would appear to be reasonably clear: are we not forced to assume that it is precisely in (now increasingly rare) low-contact situations that we are most likely to find the development of irregularity, redundancy, and morphological categories, because otherwise none of the world's languages would have them? But why would this be?

This is where the two further sociolinguistic factors cited above, *social network structure* and *community size*, come in. Grace (1990: 126) has written:

A language exists in the people who speak it, but people do not live very long, and the language goes on much longer. This continuity is achieved by the recruitment of new speakers, but it is not a perfect continuity. Children (or adults) learning a language learn it from people who already speak it, but these teachers exercise considerably less than total control over the learning process.

A possibility is that in some communities the "teachers" may have more control over individuals than in others. Insights deriving from the pioneering work of James Milroy and Lesley Milroy (e.g. esp. Milroy and Milroy 1985) clearly indicate that small, tightly-knit communities are more able to encourage the *preservation of* norms, and the continued *adherence to* norms, from one generation to another, however complex they may be. Coupled with the absence of contact and the effects of the critical threshold, it is therefore to be expected that in such communities complexity will be more readily *maintained*.

However, it is also not unreasonable to suppose that small community size and tight social networks will also assist the *production* of complexification. In small isolated communities, change will be slower – witness Icelandic versus Danish – but when it does occur, it is also more likely to be of the complexification type, the other side of the coin of high contact and loose networks leading to rapid change and simplification. I hypothesize that small isolated communities are more able, because of their network structures, to push through, enforce, and sustain linguistic changes which would have a much smaller chance of success in larger, more fluid communities. These would be changes of a relatively complex or unusual type. So not only is there less simplification in low-contact situations, there may also be more complexification.

This suggestion fits in with the observation of Werner (1984: 219) that:

unsere germ. Sprachen zeigen, dass eine kleine, weitgehend isolierte, sozial homogene Sprechergemeinschaft (wie etwa auf Island) am ehesten bereit ist, Akkumulationen an Komprimierung und Komplikation weiterwachsen zu lassen.

And the same kind of idea is also suggested by Braunmüller (1995), who sees morphological opacity as a characteristic of "small languages".

My hypothesis is therefore that it is in small tightly-knit communities that we are most likely to find an increase in irregularity and opacity, and a higher level of redundancy; and that not only are morphological categories most readily lost during (post-threshold) language contact, but also that they are more readily developed in such tightly-knit communities. And there is some suggestion (although the picture is far from clear at the moment: Trudgill forthcoming b) that the major mechanisms involved in the production of these forms of complexity include fast speech processes (Trudgill 2002), grammaticalization (Trudgill 1995), and "exorbitant phonetic developments" (Andersen 1988; Trudgill 1996b).

As far as morphological categories are concerned, creoles provide a wealth of instructive negative evidence for the sorts of morphological-category development we can expect to find in low-contact dense social network languages and dialects. Pre-critical threshold language contact and social upheaval mean that pidgin languages usually lack all morphology: there are no cases, numbers, tenses, aspects, moods, voices, persons, or genders that are morphologically marked. However, the expansion process inherent in creol-ization – the "repair" of the reduction of pidginization – involves the reintro-duction of some of the grammatical categories that have been lost. Creole languages typically have (optional) aspect and tense markers. And they typically have (optional) plural markers. But note that they have no person markers on verbs – they continue the pidgin practice of signalling person by pronouns. There is no morphological case marking – case is marked by word order, even for pronouns. Mood has to be signalled lexically. In particular, creoles also lack features such as switch-reference systems, evidentials, subjunct-ives, noun incorporation, polysynthesis, trial-, quadral-, and quintal-number, pronoun hierarchies, inalienable versus alienable possession markers, and so on. There is no passive voice. And there is still no gender. Creoles lack what Dahl (2004: 2) refers to as "mature linguistic phenomena" of which "we find that the most obvious one is inflectional morphology" (Dahl 2004: 111). It is then no surprise that they lack grammatical gender in particular, since this is a phenom-enon which "crosscuts lexicon, morphology and syntax", and since "gender, inflectional morphology and syntactic agreement make up an interesting cluster of phenomena that all belong to the later stages of maturation processes" (Dahl 2004: 197).

What we are interested in, then, is the type of social situation in which features such as grammatical gender, switch-reference, case marking, noun incorporation, and so on – perhaps changes of the type referred to by Mühlhäusler (2001), following Bailey (1973), as "abnatural" – are engendered. And it will also be relevant to consider when and where repetition of information and irregularity are most likely to develop.

4 Complexification

If it is the case that complexification typically occurs, or occurs more often, in low-contact situations (see Trudgill 2002), then even a high-contact variety like English permits us to explore this type of more opaque linguistic change by doing so comparatively. We can compare the long-established relatively low-contact Traditional Dialects of English with the majority General English varieties, standard and nonstandard. According to Wells (1982), English Traditional Dialects – a term which would appear to be equivalent to labels such as German *Mundarten* and French *patois* – are increasingly hard to find, and occur only in parts of England, especially those further away from London, and in southern and eastern Scotland and parts of Northern Ireland; with the addition of Newfoundland and perhaps parts of the Appalachians. The other varieties of English – General English dialects – are for the most part standardized and/or urban and/or colonial varieties which have a considerable history of dialect and/or language contact, and show very many signs of simplification over the centuries.

The relevance of the Traditional Dialects is that we can check to see if the relatively low-contact linguistic situations in which the Traditional Dialects grew up really have led to the development of features which represent the reverse of simplification: expansion in irregularity, increase in opacity, increase in repetition of information, and the growth of morphological categories. And Traditional Dialects are especially important because it is the sociolinguistic situations in which these varieties developed which most closely resemble the situations in which most language varieties have developed over the past tens of thousands of years of human linguistic history.

Here are just a small but maybe suggestive selection of English Traditional Dialect features, taken from dialects in East Anglia and the English West Country, which do not occur in high-contact Standard English, or high-contact nonstandard mainstream varieties, and which illustrate – although this can only be suggestive – the growth of complexity which, I suggest, may tend to depend for its genesis on low-contact linguistic environments.

4.1 *Irregularization*

Grammatical change may lead to greater irregularity as well as regularity, and it is therefore worth noting that irregularization may be more common in Traditional Dialects than in General varieties. In the Traditional Dialect of the English county of Norfolk, for example, we find a number of irregular preterites which occur in cases where Standard English has regular forms. These include (Forby 1830; Trudgill 2003):

hoe	*hew*
mow	*mew*
owe	*ewe*
row	*rew*
save	*seft*
sew /sou/	*sew* /sʉ:/ (as of stitches)
show	*shew*
snow	*snew*
sow	*sew* /sʉ:/ (as of seed)
thow (thaw)	*thew*
shriek	*shruck*
wave	*weft*
wrap	*wrop*

A few of these verbs had strong or irregular preterites on their first attested appearance in Old English or Middle English. This is true of *mow* and *row*, while *sew* had both strong and weak forms in Old English. In these cases, then, regularization has taken place in Standard English and in the General English nonstandard dialects, while the Traditional Norfolk Dialect has preserved the original irregularity. The other irregular forms, however, are not historical. *Show*, for example, was a weak verb in Old English, with the preterite *sceawed*, as was *thaw*; and the other verbs were also regular from their earliest appearance. The only exception is *owe*, which goes back to Old English *aʒan*, with the early OE preterite *ahte*, which later of course gave rise to *ought*, and was superseded as preterite by regular *awede* > *owed*. So the Norfolk forms *ewe*, *hew*, *sew* (of *sew*), *shew*, *snew*, *thew*, *shruck*, *seft*, *weft*, *wrop* are all innovations which involved irregularization. The changes to *ewe*, *hew*, *sew*, *shew*, *sew*, *thew* are obviously the result of analogy with the *blow* class, but the origins of *shruck*, *seft*, *weft*, and *wrop* are less clear.

It is often said that some forms of American English, including Standard English, have replaced the regular preterite of *dive*, namely *dived*, with an irregular preterite *dove* – clearly by analogy with the class of irregular verbs such as *ride/rode*. However, this is not a case of the development of irregularity in Standard English. According to the OED, *dove* is also a form which occurs in dialectal British English, and, more importantly, the verb was a strong verb in Old English, with the past participle *dofen*.

4.2 *Decrease in morphological transparency*

Growth in allomorphy represents a clear case of loss of morphological transparency, and thus an increase in complexity. Kusters (2003), for example, argues that the loss of allomorphy in Arabic represents an obvious instance of simplification. I give two examples:

(i) One example from an English Traditional Dialect which, crucially, has not been paralleled in any variety of General English concerns the third person singular neuter pronoun. In nearly all English dialects, including Standard English, this is of course *it* as both the subjective and the objective form. In the dialect of Norfolk, however, a complication has developed. In stressed position, the subject form of the neuter singular pronoun is not *it* but *that*. This is particularly clear in the case of the "weather pronoun", where no possibility exists that we are dealing with the homophonous demonstrative:

That's raining.
That's cold in here.

But there is no doubt that it also operates in genuine pronominalization:

He shew me the cat – that was on the wall.

However, in tag questions, the pronoun takes the form *it*, as it does also in the objective case:

That's raining, is it?
That's cold in here, in't it?
The cat? I don't like it.

This allomorphic distinction is not mentioned by the posthumously published Forby (1830), who states that he is describing the Norfolk dialect as it was spoken in the period 1780–1800; and he himself uses stressed *it* in his illustrative examples. And I have found no cases in the fifteenth- and sixteenth-century letters written by the Norfolk Paston family. The distinction may therefore be a relatively recent instance of complexification.

Differences between objective and subjective pronouns are obviously totally unsurprising. The focus here is on the fact that, and on the type of variety where, a differentiation has developed where none existed before.

(ii) In the Traditional Dialect of East Somerset (Ihalainen 1991), a pronominal allomorphy more complex than that found in other dialects has developed, notably in the third person singular masculine. The subject form of the pronoun is the expected *he:*

He's older than what I be

The object form is *'n* /ən ~ n̩/ which generally functions just like *him* in other dialects:

I looked up to un and said "What's say?"

However, there is also an additional form of the subject pronoun which Ihalainen refers to as a question clitic, and which occurs obligatorily in tag questions and other inversions. It is not immediately obvious that this form derives from *he*, *him*, or *'n*. Ihalainen writes it as *her* or *er* and phonologically it is /əɾ ~ ɾ/:

He do live in Latcham, don' er?

This type of pronominal allomorphy is of course not unknown at all in the world's languages. The point is that, where it has developed out of an earlier more simple system in English, it has been in a Traditional Dialect that this has occurred.

4.3 *Increase in redundancy (a): the growth of new morphological categories*

(i) A few Traditional Dialects in a small area of the southwest of England saw the development of a new and fascinating marking of the difference between transitive and intransitive infinitives. Intransitive infinitives (and objectless transitives) in these dialects were marked by the word-final morpheme *-y,* while transitive infinitives were unmarked. So in Dorset we find (Gachelin 1991):

Can you zew up thease zeam? "Can you sew up this seam?"

versus:

There idden many can sheary now "There aren't many who can shear now".

This is unparalleled anywhere else in the English-speaking world, and is quite possibly unparalleled anywhere else at all. My enquiry on the LingTyp list asking for examples of other languages which have morphological marking for intransitive but not transitive infinitives received three answers, none of them producing a precise parallel. The Australian Aboriginal language Warrgamay has two sets of inflections – those that can attach to intransitive verbs and those that cannot attach to intransitive verbs – but this applies to all verb forms and not just infinitives. A similar situation applies in Ulwa, a Misumalpan language of Nicaragua. The closest we can come to it is in the

Anywa language, a Nilo-Saharan language of Ethiopia and Sudan, where special marking does occur on intransitive infinitives, but only on those which are derived from transitives, which are then marked relative to their transitive counterparts: "weave [trans.]" versus "to do weaving" (Reh 1996: 187).

(ii) A number of Traditional Dialects in the southwest of England developed an interesting phenomenon described by Ihalainen (1976) in which there is a category distinction between habitual verb forms such as:

I do go there every day
I did go there every day

versus:

I goes tomorrow
I went last week

This of course is a distinction between two categories which is common enough in languages of the world. In English, however, it represents an innovation, and one which is unknown in any of the General English varieties.

(iii) Also in the English southwest we see the development of the expression of a pronominal category difference between count and mass nouns, such that inanimate count nouns are pronominalized with *he* but mass nouns with it:

Pass the loaf – he's over there

versus:

I likes this bread – it be very tasty

This too is unparalleled elsewhere in the English-speaking world, except in Newfoundland, where it is known to have derived from the English southwest (Paddock 1991) – it is once again unknown in any variety of General English.

4.4 *Increase in redundancy (b): introduction of repetition of information*

(i) One example of introduction of repetition of information can be found in the Traditional Dialect of Norfolk, where double tense marking or "past-tense infinitives" can be found. For example:

Have the fox left?
No that ain't, do Bailey would've let them went.
"No it hasn't, or Bailey would've let them [the hounds] go" (Trudgill 1995)[3]

---

[3] The grammaticalization of *do* as a conjunction is also discussed in Trudgill (1995).

(ii) These same Norfolk dialects also have an overtly expressed second person pronoun in imperatives:

Come you on! "Come on [sing.]"
Come you on together! "Come on [plur.]"
Shut you up!
Be you quiet!

Yet again, this is not unusual, but it is an innovation in English, and one which has not occurred in General English varieties.

5 Conclusion

I have argued that societal type influences language type. I have argued that language contact involving widespread adult language learning leads to an increase in simplification including loss of morphological categories. (Long-term coterritorial child language learning contact, on the other hand, leads to added complexity.) And I have argued, more hypothetically, that small community size and isolation may promote the spontaneous growth of morphological categories; and that they may also promote the growth of irregularity, redundancy, and low transparency. I have cited a small number of examples which might point in that direction, but of course very many more such examples would be needed before we could feel at all confident about the legitimacy of the hypothesis.

If widespread adult-only language contact is a mainly post-neolithic and indeed a mainly modern phenomenon associated with the last 2,000 years, and if the development of large, fluid communities is also a post-neolithic and indeed mainly modern phenomenon, then according to this thesis the dominant standard modern languages in the world today are likely to be seriously atypical of how languages have been for nearly all of human history. We have become so familiar with simplification in linguistic change – in Germanic, Romance, Semitic – that it has been tempting to regard it as normal – as a diachronic universal. Maybe, however, it is complexification that is more normal. Or rather, we should say, *was* more normal; some languages, it seems, are certainly more complex than others, but the current diachronic trend is in the direction of an increasingly higher proportion of languages which are increasingly less complex. A number of the English Traditional Dialect features illustrating complexification listed above have already disappeared, or are in the process of disappearing (e.g. Gachelin 1991).

8

Linguistic complexity: a comprehensive definition and survey

JOHANNA NICHOLS

1 Introduction

The long-received truism that all languages are ultimately about equal in complexity has taken some serious criticism in recent years. McWhorter (2001a) shows that one set of languages (creoles) are systematically less complex than most languages. Gil (1994, 2001; and cf. Chapter 2 above) shows that a non-creole variety of Indonesian is strikingly devoid of most kinds of morphosyntactic specificity and complexity, and Gil (2008) shows that isolating languages vary considerably in aspects of syntactic complexity. Ross (1996, 1997) and Dahl (2004) show that the sociolinguistics of contact and acquisition can greatly affect the complexity and amount of irregularity in a language. Hyslop (1993) shows that complexity in one lexical area (the number of distinctions in spatial demonstrative systems) varies inversely not with some other grammatical or lexical factor but with the size of the speech community; and Kaius Sinnemäki, in Chapter 9, below, demonstrates a subtler relationship between community size and a specific grammatical domain. Shosted (2006) and Sinnemäki (2008) select two components of grammar that might be expected to exhibit inverse levels of complexity if overall grammars were equally complex, and they show that there is little or no evidence of a negative correlation.

What is needed is a cross-linguistic survey of complexity levels in different parts of phonology, grammar, and lexicon. If the sample were large enough and the complexity survey broad and detailed enough, this would tell us whether all languages are in fact equally complex, or at least whether there is some optimal overall level of complexity and/or some upper and lower limit to overall complexity. Measuring the total complexity of a language in cross-linguistically comparable and quantifiable terms would be a massive task and unreasonably costly in time and effort; but a properly comprehensive definition of complexity should make it possible to draw a representative sample of complexity in enough different grammatical domains, relatively easy to survey, to give a reliable indication of whether overall complexity does or does not vary. The present chapter is not that survey, but attempts a first step by giving a comprehensive definition of complexity that should make it possible to draw grammatical samples, and doing a large enough cross-linguistic survey of enough parts of grammar to indicate whether the assumption of equal complexity appears viable.

2 Complexity

What is of interest here is only what I will call *grammatical complexity* – complexity of the strictly linguistic domains of phonology, morphosyntax, lexicon, etc. and their components. I exclude complexity (or difficulty) of processing, mental storage and management, learning, etc.; these are no doubt important symptoms of grammatical complexity, but they are nonetheless different from strict linguistic structure. A definition of grammatical complexity can be based on the usual understanding of a complex system as one consisting of many different elements each with a number of degrees of freedom. In addition, for languages, what is probably relevant is not just the number of elements, etc., but the amount of information needed to describe them, as discussed below. In this approach complexity can be measured as follows.

(a) For each subsystem of the grammar, the number of elements it contains. For instance, the number of consonant phonemes, tones, genders, cases, tenses, alignments, voices, word orders, relativization strategies, derivational means for forming denominal verbs, ways of forming subordinate clauses of time, complementation strategies with verbs of cognition, the number of lexical roots in particular semantic domains such as words for "break" or "know", the number of derivational processes applying in particular semantic domains.

(b) The number of paradigmatic variants, or degrees of freedom, of each such element or set of elements: allophones, allomorphs, declension or conjugation classes.

(c) Syntagmatic phenomena: syntagmatic dependencies among elements such as agreement, non-adjacent allomorph selection, non-adjacent morpheme or category selection, and valence. These things have interesting effects on processing and learnability: they complicate learning but add redundancy, and so facilitate processing by the fluent speaker.

(d) Constraints on elements, alloforms, and syntagmatic dependencies, including constraints on their combination. Examples include co-occurrence constraints on vowels and consonants, on genders and declension classes, and on valence types and conjugation classes. Whether constraints actually increase complexity depends on whether complexity is defined as the number of elements (etc.) or the information required to describe them. As an illustration and thought experiment, consider two languages each with twenty consonant phonemes, five vowel phonemes, and a strict CV syllable canon. The first language allows all possible combinations of consonant and vowel and therefore has 100 possible CV syllables. The second language disallows certain consonant-vowel co-occurrences and has only seventy possible CV syllables. If complexity is the number of elements in the system, the first language is more complex as it has more possible syllables.[1] If information required to describe the system is allowed to figure in the definition of complexity, the second language may be more complex, as describing its possible syllables requires more information than just specifying C + V. I assume that information required for describing the system should enter into the definition of complexity, and therefore constraints should be regarded as increasing complexity; but I do not know how to test this assumption. Constraints reduce the possible combinations of elements, perhaps thereby facilitating learning; and they add redundancy and thereby facilitate processing by fluent speakers (for this point see Trudgill 2004a: 315–16). Therefore the whole question of whether they increase or reduce complexity needs more chewing by more linguists.

The spirit of this approach to complexity has something in common with the approach to morphological typology proposed by Greenberg (1960), who counted not only the number of morphemes in a domain but also the number of allomorphic and derivational paradigmatic alternatives (though his stated goal was to quantify types and not complexity levels).

An accurate measure of complexity would need to somehow count up these four points for all parts of the grammar and lexicon. This would be a huge task, but surveying a range of different parts of the grammar and lexicon – at least the major parts that are routinely covered in grammatical descriptions – should

---

[1] The number of possible syllables is the phonological complexity measure used by Shosted (2006). The amount of cross-linguistic spread he finds is so great that my hypothetical difference of 100 and 70 would hardly count.

capture enough of the overall complexity to let us see whether there is a tendency toward equal complexity.

3 Survey

I chose a number of different grammatical domains for which cross-linguistic information was already available (chiefly in my own files or in Bickel and Nichols 2002ff.) or could be gathered straightforwardly:

Phonology:

- number of contrastive manners of articulation in stops (existing data);
- number of vowel quality distinctions (Maddieson 2005a with additional data gathered);
- tone system (none/simple/complex, following Maddieson 2005c with additional data);
- syllable structure (Maddieson 2005b with additional data).

Synthesis:

- inflectional synthesis of the verb (following Bickel and Nichols 2005): the number of different inflectional categories marked on the maximally inflected verb form;
- polyagreement: two arguments obligatorily marked on the verb;
- noun plural marking;
- noun dual marking.

Classification:

- numeral classifiers;
- overt possessive classes (Nichols and Bickel 2005);
- agreement gender: gender marked by agreement on other words;
- overt inherent gender: gender or gender-like classification marked on the noun itself, as in Bantu languages.[2]

Syntax:

- number of different alignments between noun arguments, pronoun arguments, and verb. Stative-active or split-S alignment was counted as two alignments. Neutral alignment was not counted.

---

[2] Called *head class* by Evans (1997) and *morphological class* by Evans et al. (2002). Since many languages have more than one kind of morphological class of nouns, I use a more precise term. Corbett (1991: 62–3, 117–19) calls it *(alliterative) overt gender*, but Nichols (2008) argues for a term that implies morphological rather than phonological correspondence between gender types, and which does not imply that the overt inherent gender class is the same as the noun's agreement gender.

- number of different basic word orders. A split like that between main and non-main clauses in most Germanic languages counts as two orders.

Lexicon:

- inclusive/exclusive opposition in independent personal pronouns;
- the number of distinct roots, i.e. number of suppletive pairings, in the set of nine pairs of plain and semantically causative verbs (e.g. "fear, be afraid" and "frighten, scare") in Nichols et al. (2004);
- derivations: the number of different overt derivations in the same nine verb pairs.

This survey covers well the number of elements in the phonology and in classification; it covers synthesis fairly well; and it covers syntax and lexicon sketchily. The features surveyed were chosen because they could be surveyed without excessive cost in time (generally because they were already surveyed in part in existing databases). All of them belong to category (a) above, numbers of elements in the system, with the possible exception of agreement gender (agreement is in (c)). Such things as numbers of declension and conjugation classes are almost always covered in grammars but not in any database available to me, so they would require the time-costly procedure of surveying from scratch. Surveying something as simple as what agrees with what can be even more labour-intensive. Restricting the survey to materials already available or surveyable without excessive cost restricts the validity of the findings, but even so the cost in time was exorbitant relative to the usual time outlay for one paper. This survey is therefore a contribution to the line of research begun by Shosted (2006) and Sinnemäki (2008), and extends this kind of work to more grammatical domains and more languages while giving more schematic coverage to the grammatical domains.

4 Findings

In previous work I showed that cross-linguistic frequencies of complexity in various grammatical domains form bell curves (Nichols et al. 2006). The null hypothesis for this study is that languages do tend to be equally complex overall. If there is in fact any such tendency, then in a cross-linguistic survey overall complexity should form a very steep bell curve, steeper than the curves for the individual components. In fact, if all languages really are equally complex, and if the survey is well designed, there should be not even a steep bell curve but just a single complexity level that all languages reach. Furthermore, since equal complexity entails balancing and hence negative correlations between complexity levels in different parts of grammar, some tendency toward negative correlations should be visible between any two grammar components. Not all languages will exhibit a negative correlation for any two components, but some will, and if there is cross-linguistic equal complexity they should be expected to outnumber those that have positive correlations. On the other hand, if there is no cross-linguistic equal complexity, the frequencies of overall complexity levels should form a flatter curve than those for most of the individual components, and negative correlations between pairs of grammar components should not be particularly common.

In the present survey I found that four of the five grammatical domains did in fact form bell curves (Figs 8.1–8.5).[3] The exception is syntax, for which most languages have one basic word order and one basic alignment type; no language can have fewer, and some have more of one or the other or both. Because the simplest type is the logical minimum, it is the most frequent type and the curve is a declining slope. The other four figures are all skewed to the left, indicating that less complex types are favoured. On the other hand, all four extend far to the right, suggesting that there is no upper limit in principle, though of course high extremes are rare. The clearest case is Fig. 8.1, where there is a left-skewed curve with one outlier far to the right: this is the southern African click language !Kung (!Xoõ) with its many manners of consonant articulation; the next highest is another click language, Nama (Khoekhoe).

Figs 8.6 and 8.7 show the total complexity levels, Fig. 8.6 for the sixty-eight languages with all datapoints filled and Fig. 8.7 for the 130 for which all domains but lexical are filled (the first sixty-eight languages are counted here too, without their lexical components). These two curves are not steeper, and in fact are somewhat flatter, than the individual curves, and they have a longer rightward trailing end. This seriously undermines the assumption of equal complexity, though in view of the small sample of sixty-eight languages and the less than comprehensive grammar survey it does not conclusively falsify it.

I tested correlations between the different grammar domains and some of their subcomponents, doing two-way correlations using all possible pairings and recoding all complexity levels as high/medium/low based on the standard deviation. This removes any bias caused by the fact that different features have

---

[3] In all the figures the vertical and horizontal scales are approximately equal, so comparisons purely by eye are meaningful. All horizontal scales begin at the logically possible minimum. Numbers of languages differ because for each domain I considered all the languages that had all datapoints filled for that domain, and this varied from feature to feature depending on what languages had entries in what databases.

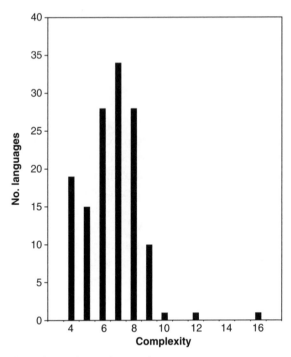

FIG. 8.1. Phonological complexity ($N = 137$)

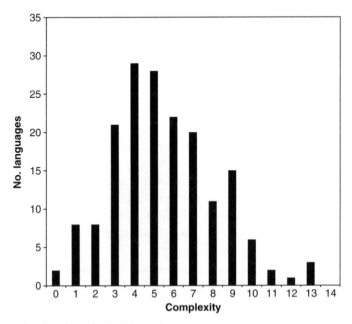

FIG. 8.2. Inflectional synthesis ($N = 176$)

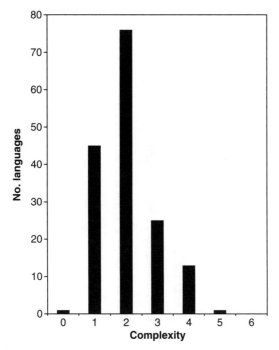

FIG. 8.3. Classification ($N = 161$)

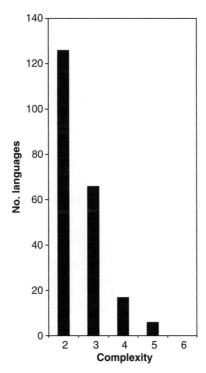

FIG. 8.4. Syntax ($N = 215$)

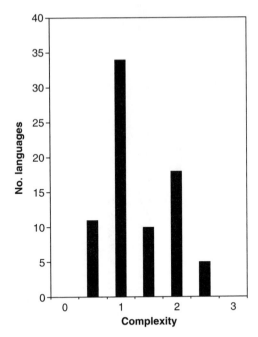

FIG. 8.5. Lexicon (*N* = 78)

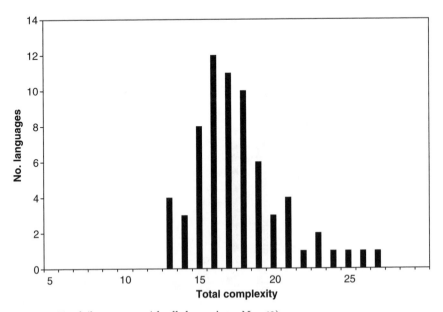

FIG. 8.6. Total (languages with all datapoints, *N* = 68)

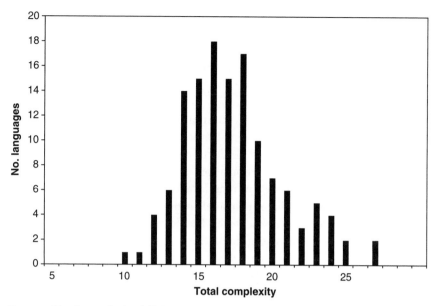

Fɪɢ. 8.7. Total complexity (all datapoints except lexicon; $N = 130$)

different complexity levels, ranging from a maximum of one for yes/no features such as inclusive/exclusive (no $= 0$, yes $= 1$) to scales with no firm upper limit for e.g. consonant manners of articulation (highest value is 10 in my survey) and verb inflectional synthesis (high of 10). There were no significant negative correlations between different components of grammar. There was a significant positive correlation between complexity of syntax and complexity of synthesis ($p = \cdot 0097$, Fisher's Exact Test on high v. nonhigh frequencies). An earlier version (Nichols 2007a, 2007b), using a smaller set of datapoints and a different high/medium/low breakdown, also found a significant positive correlation of phonology (which at that time comprised only consonants and syllable structure) with synthesis, which could not be replicated this time. These differences indicate that results of these comparisons are sensitive to such things as feature breakdowns, which in turn indicates that principled, accurate definitions of complexity levels in different parts of grammar, and proper weightings of different components and subcomponents, are needed before meaningful comparisons can be made (though for a pessimistic view on the possibility of such definitions see Guy Deutscher's Chapter 17 below). In any event, it is more telling that no negative correlations emerged on either set of comparisons, as it is negative correlations that support the hypothesis of equal complexity.

In Nichols (2007a, b) and again here I found a highly significant negative correlation between population size and overall complexity. I determined population sizes from grammars and expert consultations, or failing that from R. Gordon (2005), and where possible I sought not the number of speakers for each language but the size of the ethnic group (assuming that language transmission rates have often dropped recently and ethnic group size is a better measure of speech community size a generation or two ago, when fieldworkers' main consultants learned their languages), coding them simply by order of magnitude of population size (hundreds, thousands, tens of thousands, etc.). A smaller population, then, favours higher complexity, but in fact this could be a purely geographical effect: population sizes are large overall in Africa and Eurasia, much smaller in the Pacific and the Americas, and complexity levels are higher in the Pacific and especially the Americas. *Within* each of these macrocontinents there was no significant correlation between population size and complexity, as there should be if there were a universal tendency; this supports the idea that the correlation is an accident of geography (though the number of languages per continent was not high enough to reach significance easily).

A larger problem is that it is not very clear what a correlation with population size might mean. Population sizes plummeted in the Americas and Australia on European contact and consequent smallpox epidemics; but the comparative method shows that grammars and lexicons similar to today's reconstruct for pre-contact protolanguages; therefore today's levels of complexity do not depend on today's population sizes and have in fact been stable despite drastic population size fluctuations. Additionally, it has never been made clear how much time should be required for grammar to catch up with population size changes (assuming there is a correlation); but if it takes more than a century or two it cannot be expected that there will be clear synchronic correlations between grammar and population size, now or at any other time.

Appendices 1 and 2 list the sixty-eight languages with all datapoints filled, in order of increasing complexity by the two counts (total points and total low/medium/high points).

5 Conclusions

Complexity levels are hard to measure and weight, and the present survey has been too small in both number of languages and number and type of different complexity measures to give a very accurate view of complexity. Still, if there were a preferred complexity level or trade-off between complexity levels of different grammar components, one could expect it to have at least made itself felt in this survey; but it has not done so. That the frequencies of total complexity levels (Figs 8.6 and 8.7) form bell curves at all is probably due not to convergence on a universal or optimal complexity level but to simple probability: for most of the individual components, both high and low extremes of complexity are less common than a medium degree of complexity, and the likelihood that a language would have an uncommon extreme degree of complexity in all individual components (thereby achieving an extreme degree overall) is low.

A language I work closely on, Ingush (Nakh-Daghestanian; Caucasus), has the highest total complexity score in this survey and falls within the second highest rank on the high/medium/low coding. My first reaction was to suspect that my greater knowledge of this language enabled me to find more countable phenomena in it. In fact, though, the showings of the other languages I know well are not out of line; the grammatical features counted here are straightforward and covered well in most grammars; and at most only about two points of verbal synthesis might be artefactual consequences of my knowledge of Ingush.

The showing of Tok Pisin, a creole (English lexicon, Oceanic Austronesian substrate; Papua New Guinea), is interesting. Its overall complexity level is below average, but not at the very low end of the scale and certainly not notably lower than non-creole languages. This is at best only weak support for the claim of McWhorter (2001a) that creole grammars are among the world's simplest.

I tried to anticipate the consequences of including other kinds of complexity in the survey, such as number of noun cases, number of declension classes, number of conjugation classes, and agreement phenomena. Judging from what is found in languages I know, it appears that in a fuller survey the spread between languages and between lowest and highest levels of complexity will increase and will certainly not level out, but the relative positions of languages in the complexity hierarchy will not change greatly.

I conclude that complexity balancing between different components of grammar is not supported cross-linguistically. It still makes the best null hypothesis for surveys, but this does not mean that we should treat it as received wisdom. To judge from the references quoted in my first paragraph, equal complexity is no longer the active received view, and most linguists (and certainly most younger linguists) believe that languages can vary considerably in their overall complexity. It is important to devise better and more comprehensive measures of complexity and track them in larger surveys, but the really interesting questions concern the distribution of complexity: whether and how it correlates with population size and/or sociolinguistic factors, and how much time is required for the grammatical complexity to adjust to the sociolinguistics; whether and how it correlates with pure structural properties of grammar, or with geography; how stable it is in language families; whether sheer complexity (either high or low) can be an areal feature; how contact affects it; whether there is a grammatical (as opposed to psychological, cognitive, neurolinguistic, etc.) upper bound on complexity, and if so what drives it.

Appendix 1

The sixty-eight languages with all datapoints filled, sorted by total complexity. The mean is 18·01, s.d. 3·14.

Basque	13.0	Europe and Near East
Rama	13.0	Central America
Warao	13.3	South America
Ewe	13.6	Africa
Finnish	14.3	North and Central Asia
Mandarin	14.6	South and Southeast Asia
Nenets (Tundra)	14.9	North and Central Asia
Nanai	15.0	North and Central Asia
Araona	15.0	South America
Mongolian (Khalkha)	15.1	North and Central Asia
Spanish	15.3	Europe and Near East
Totonac (Misantla)	15.4	Central America
Lezgi	15.6	Europe and Near East
Tok Pisin	15.8	New Guinea and Oceania
Martuthunira	15.9	Australia
Vietnamese	16.0	South and Southeast Asia
Luganda	16.0	Africa
German	16.0	Europe and Near East
Japanese	16.0	North and Central Asia
Telefol	16.0	New Guinea and Oceania
Nubian (Dongolese)	16.0	Africa
Mixtec (Chalcatongo)	16.0	Central America
Guaraní (Paraguayan)	16.0	South America
Diegueño	16.0	Western North America
Armenian (Eastern)	16.3	Europe and Near East
Thai	16.4	South and Southeast Asia
Tiwi	16.8	Australia
Tarascan	17.0	Central America
Tuva	17.0	North and Central Asia
Kutenai	17.0	Eastern North America
Hindi	17.1	South and Southeast Asia

Tzutujil	17.1	Central America
Russian	17.2	North and Central Asia
Cree (Plains)	17.2	Eastern North America
Hungarian	17.2	Europe and Near East
Somali	17.5	Africa
Ket	17.6	North and Central Asia
Ossetic	17.6	Europe and Near East
Fula	18.0	Africa
Wintu	18.0	Western North America
Kayardild	18.0	Australia
MEAN		
Chukchi	18.1	North and Central Asia
Huallaga Quechua	18.3	South America
Georgian	18.4	Europe and Near East
Tunica	18.7	Eastern North America
Hausa	18.7	Africa
Maung	18.8	Australia
Kiwai	18.8	New Guinea and Oceania
Abkhaz	19.0	Europe and Near East
Tibetan (Standard Spoken)	19.1	South and Southeast Asia
Squamish	19.2	Western North America
Lango	19.5	Africa
Rapanui	19.9	New Guinea and Oceania
Yup'ik (Siberian)	19.9	North and Central Asia
Nunggubuyu	20.0	Australia
Slave	20.6	Eastern North America
Yimas	20.9	New Guinea and Oceania
Tümpisa Shoshone	21.2	Western North America
Hakha Lai	21.4	South and Southeast Asia
Arabic (Egyptian)	21.7	Africa
Maa (Maasai)	21.9	Africa
Motuna	22.0	New Guinea and Oceania
Haida	23.8	Western North America
Oneida	23.9	Eastern North America
Hua	24.1	New Guinea and Oceania
Lakhota	25.6	Eastern North America
Koasati	26.1	Eastern North America
Ingush	27.9	Europe and Near East

Appendix 2

The sixty-eight languages sorted by total low/medium/high complexity levels. The mean is 9·54, s.d. 1·18.

Ewe	7	Africa
Mandarin	7	South and Southeast Asia
Hausa	8	Africa
Nenets (Tundra)	8	North and Central Asia
Thai	8	South and Southeast Asia
Kiwai	8	New Guinea and Oceania
Diegueño	8	Western North America
Rama	8	Central America
Totonac (Misantla)	8	Central America
Warao	8	South America
Araona	8	South America
Luganda	9	Africa
Nubian (Dongolese)	9	Africa
Lango	9	Africa
Basque	9	Europe and Near East
Finnish	9	North and Central Asia
Spanish	9	Europe and Near East
German	9	Europe and Near East
Russian	9	North and Central Asia
Ossetic	9	Europe and Near East
Abkhaz	9	Europe and Near East
Nanai	9	North and Central Asia
Japanese	9	North and Central Asia
Tuva	9	North and Central Asia
Vietnamese	9	South and Southeast Asia
Martuthunira	9	Australia
Tiwi	9	Australia
Tok Pisin	9	New Guinea and Oceania
Telefol	9	New Guinea and Oceania
Rapanui	9	New Guinea and Oceania
Squamish	9	Western North America
Slave	9	Eastern North America
Mixtec (Chalcatongo)	9	Central America
Tarascan	9	Central America
Guaraní (Paraguayan)	9	South America
MEAN		
Somali	10	Africa
Fula	10	Africa
Maa (Maasai)	10	Africa

Lezgi	10	Europe and Near East
Armenian (Eastern)	10	Europe and Near East
Hungarian	10	Europe and Near East
Mongolian (Khalkha)	10	North and Central Asia
Ket	10	North and Central Asia
Yup'ik (Siberian)	10	North and Central Asia
Hindi	10	South and Southeast Asia
Hakha Lai	10	South and Southeast Asia
Kayardild	10	Australia
Maung	10	Australia
Yimas	10	New Guinea and Oceania
Motuna	10	New Guinea and Oceania
Wintu	10	Western North America
Kutenai	10	Eastern North America
Cree (Plains)	10	Eastern North America
Tunica	10	Eastern North America
Tzutujil	10	Central America
Huallaga Quechua	10	South America
Arabic (Egyptian)	11	Africa
Georgian	11	Europe and Near East
Chukchi	11	North and Central Asia
Nunggubuyu	11	Australia
Tümpisa Shoshone	11	Western North America
Haida	11	Western North America
Oneida	11	Eastern North America
Koasati	11	Eastern North America
Ingush	12	Europe and Near East
Tibetan (Standard Spoken)	12	South and Southeast Asia
Hua	12	New Guinea and Oceania
Lakhota	13	Eastern North America

9

Complexity in core argument marking and population size

KAIUS SINNEMÄKI

1 Introduction

A widely accepted presupposition among linguists is that language structure has nothing to do with its geographical or sociocultural setting (e.g. Kaye 1989: 48).[1] However, this claim has not been supported by empirical evidence. On the contrary, there seems to be a growing body of evidence indicating a relationship between, for example, structural complexity of language and its geographical or sociocultural setting. Nichols (1992), for one, has argued that morphological complexity varies geographically. Perkins (1992) has argued that grammatical complexity of deictic categories correlates negatively with cultural complexity. Sociolinguistic aspects of the speech community have also been suggested as causing complexity variation (Nettle 1999; Kusters 2003; Trudgill 1996b, 2004a, b). This chapter develops the ideas of Johanna Nichols (in Chapter 8 above and other recent writing) by studying whether a specific morphosyntactic area, core argument marking, shows complexity varying with speech community size.

I test this relationship statistically with a sample of fifty languages. Complexity is measured as violations of distinctiveness and economy, the two sides of the principle of one-meaning–one-form (discussed in section 2.1). In the following, I formulate the hypothesis (section 2), outline the method (section 3), and present and discuss the results (sections 4 and 5, respectively).

[1] I am grateful to Fred Karlsson, Matti Miestamo, and the editors (especially Geoffrey Sampson) for their many helpful comments on earlier versions of this chapter. I alone am responsible for any remaining errors. Research for this article has been funded by Langnet, the Finnish Graduate School in Language Studies, whose support is gratefully acknowledged.

2 Formulation of the hypothesis

2.1 *Complexity and social typology*

I take as a starting point Trudgill's (2004a) suggestion that the small phoneme inventories of Polynesian languages could be explained by their social characteristics. Although this hypothesis is concerned with phonological complexity, I shall argue that it can be fruitfully applied to other domains as well.

The crux of this hypothesis is that languages spoken by small, isolated/low-contact communities with close-knit social networks will likely have either very small or very large phoneme inventories, whereas languages spoken by large communities with a great deal of adult language learning by outsiders and loose social networks will likely have medium-sized phoneme inventories. The rationale is that the former types of community can afford, and are able, to preserve redundancies, whereas those of the latter type tend towards transparency. The underlying complexity factor here is not necessarily size of phoneme inventory in itself, but rather its effect on distinctiveness of lexical items. Large inventories may increase the distinctiveness of lexical items redundantly, whereas small inventories coincide with either greater word lengths or greater confusability of constituents. These consequences increase memory burden, a factor known to inhibit adult language learning (see Trudgill 2004a: 315–16 and references there).

Since such complexity effects can be connected to the general principles of economy and distinctiveness, the thesis can be fruitfully applied outside phonology as well. Economy and distinctiveness are like the two sides of the same coin: they both relate to the principle of one-meaning–one-form (a.k.a. transparency) but from different perspectives. Adherence to the principle of one-meaning–one-form requires adherence to both economy and distinctiveness. Violations of it involve either excessive encoding of distinctions, which increases distinctiveness at the expense of economy, or insufficient encoding of distinctions (when two intended meanings are encoded by non-unique forms), which increases economy at the expense of distinctiveness. The former causes redundancy, while the latter causes homonymy and ambiguity.

Violations of the one-meaning–one-form principle may increase difficulty of processing as well as structural complexity. In this sense, it matters little whether we measure relative difficulty to a user (Kusters 2003), or structural complexity (e.g. Dahl 2004). However, measuring cost/difficulty would require psycholinguistic tests, which is far beyond the scope of this short chapter. Following Dahl (2004), complexity is here kept distinct from cost/difficulty and is defined as description length of a phenomenon. In terms of description length, adherence to the one-meaning–one-form principle requires shorter description length than violations of it (Miestamo 2008). Economy violations increase description length by adding rules to the description, whereas distinctiveness violations increase description length by requiring greater contextual specification in the rules in order to disambiguate otherwise identical forms. From the user perspective, adherence to the principle means full transparency, which is easy for most types of language users but especially favoured by adult language learners. Most violations of this principle increase memory load, for example redundant agreement or homonymic forms in case marking (Kusters 2003: 52–7). While different types of violation are affordable to different user groups, they are least affordable to adult language learners, who tend to reduce forms and change non-transparent forms to transparent ones (Kusters 2003; Trudgill 2004a: 306–7). All in all, because violations of the principle may increase both complexity and cost/difficulty, measures of the former might well approximate measures of the latter.

Trudgill (2004b: 386; pers. comm.) argues forcefully that the three parameters (size, isolation, network structure) should not be considered independently of one another but rather as jointly effective. Unexpectedly, though, this multifactor scenario seems unnecessary in the light of Hay and Bauer's (2007) cross-linguistic investigation. They tested the relationship between phoneme inventory size and speech community size in 216 languages, and arrived at a statistically very significant positive correlation. This result suggests that it may be fruitful to consider speech community size at least as a tentative parameter of complexity variation: the parameters may be intertwined to such a degree that a univariate approach (which pays attention to a single societal parameter) could already approximate the phenomenon itself.

In addition to Hay and Bauer's (2007) results, there are three other reasons why, in an exploratory typological study, community size may serve as a feasible starting point and a springboard for further research. First, if we assume that the three criteria (size, isolation/amount of contact, network structure) must operate jointly, then the hypothesis will make predictions only about two of eight logically possible classes of language – languages which are small, isolated, and socially close-knit, and languages which are large, non-isolated, and socially loose-knit. (Here I assume for the sake of argument that each criterion is bivalent – in reality the measure of each criterion is more likely a matter of degree: Trudgill 2004b: 384–5.) Strictly speaking, the hypothesis makes no prediction for the six other possible combinations of the criteria; consequently, a sample of fifty languages might contain perhaps no more than a dozen for which the hypothesis can be tested. However, at least some of the criteria seem more or less interconnected. For instance, tight social networks are more characteristic of isolated communities (Milroy and Milroy 1985) and of small communities (Allcott et al. 2007). Large languages, on the other hand, are more likely to attract adult language learning by outsiders for e.g. socioeconomic reasons, but they also generally have loose networks, which potentially bring about rapid change compared to communities with fewer weak ties in the network (Trudgill 2004b: 385; Milroy and Milroy 1985: 375, 380). This actually makes large, non-isolated languages with loose-knit networks prototypical large languages, because the combination of large community size and tight social network is practically impossible.

Secondly, it may be difficult to characterize speech communities with respect to all three criteria. Languages spoken by large communities pose particular problems, since a large community will be composed of smaller communities which may vary greatly in terms of size, isolation, and network structure. Speakers can also belong to many diverse communities simultaneously. Should large communities, therefore, be categorized according to the overall (macro-)level or according to the smaller communities they consist of (micro-level)? For instance in the Russian speech community, many micro-level communities are small, isolated, and relatively tight-knit, whereas the macro-level community is large, has loose networks, and has a good deal of adult language learning by outsiders (Kusters 2003: 44). Small speech communities have their particular classification problems as well. As one reviewer pointed out, culturally specific habits such as exchanging women between otherwise isolated tribes may introduce adult language learning into the speech community and thus simplify the language. Simplification is certainly possible in this situation, but it is not inevitable; the outcome may equally well be that gender-specific registers begin to diverge, or that there is an increase in distinctiveness but no decrease in redundancy (see section 5). These scenarios exemplify the complexity of talking about the issue at large when classifying languages according to the three criteria.

Thirdly, many languages lack reliably documented social histories. This forces one to sample languages for which documented histories are available, which may bring unwanted bias to the sample. Speech community size is much more readily available and does not bias the sample from the outset. I suggest here that in an exploratory typological study it may be worthwhile to focus on speech community size alone. The result will necessarily remain suggestive and require further research, but will do as an initial approximation.

2.2 A hypothesis about core argument marking

In this section I formulate my hypothesis about core argument marking. I focus on the morphosyntactic strategies found in simple main clauses with affirmative polarity and indicative mood (note that this definition covers some pragmatically marked clauses, as in (3)).

In core argument marking, three morphosyntactic strategies – head marking, dependent marking, and word order – interact in distinguishing "who does what to whom". They differentiate the arguments of a prototypical two-place transitive predicate, one more agent-like (A) and the other more patient-like (P) (Comrie 2005: 398). As defined by Nichols (1992), head and dependent marking are morphological strategies that indicate syntactic relations either on the head (as in (1) below) or the dependent of the constituent (as in (2)). (There is some head marking in (2) as well, but this will be discounted in the analysis (see below)). In the clause as a constituent, the predicate is the head and the arguments are its dependents.[2]

(1)   Yimas (Lower Sepik; Foley 1991: 193)

Payum   narmaŋ   na-mpu-tay.
man.PL   woman.SG   3S.P-3P.A-see
"The men saw the woman."

(2)   Kannada (Southern Dravidian; Sridhar 1990: 86)

Cirate   mariy-annu   nekkutti-de.
leopard   cub-ACC   lick.PRS-3S.N
"The leopard is licking the cub."

The role of word order is considered in clauses in which the arguments are part of the clause proper, i.e. where they are not separated from the rest of the clause for example by a pause, or when there is no pronoun in situ replacing a transposed argument. Word order has a role in distinguishing the arguments if the position of the argument relative to the verb and to the other argument expresses its role – in other words, if reversible word order pairs (APV/PAV, AVP/PVA, and VAP/VPA) are disallowed. In the English sentence *John hit Mike, John* can only be interpreted as A and *Mike* as P: the opposite interpretation is disallowed.

Word order may occasionally have a role even when a reversible word order pair is allowed. In these cases, a change in word order is parallelled by a change in the morphological properties of the clause, and (as we analyse the situation) the former would not be allowed without the latter. Slave (Rice 1989) obligatorily marks the head with the co-indexing pronoun *ye-* when the object occurs clause-initially (3):

---

[2] Nonstandard grammatical glossing codes in examples below are: 4: fourth person (in Slave), REAL: realis, TOT: totality of action, VAUG: augmentative vowel.

(3)   Slave (Athapaskan, Rice 1989: 1197)

    a. *lį*   *ˀehkee*   *kayįhshu*
       dog(A)   boy(P)   3.bit
       "The dog bit the boy."

    b. *ˀehkee*   *lį*   *kayeyįhshu*
       boy(P)   dog(A)   3.bit.4
       "The boy, a dog bit him."

It is understood that word order in Slave helps to distinguish the arguments at least in the canonical APV order.

Next we may formulate the hypothesis to be tested. I aim to test whether there is a relationship between complexity in core argument marking of a language and social typology of the community speaking that language. This hypothesis is broken down into a pair of interrelated hypotheses about core argument marking:

    (i) Languages spoken by small speech communities are likely to violate the principle of one-meaning–one-form by either redundant or insufficient morphosyntactic marking of core arguments.
   (ii) Languages spoken by large speech communities are likely to adhere to the principle of one-meaning–one-form.

3 Method

3.1 *Sample*

The two hypotheses were tested against a random sample of fifty languages. I follow Dryer (1992, 2005) in sampling genera rather than languages. A genus is a grouping of languages with a time-depth of *c.* 3,000–4,000 years, corresponding roughly to e.g. the Germanic or the Romance languages (Dryer 1992: 83–5).

The sample is genealogically stratified so that no two languages come from the same genus and no two genera come from the same language family (with minor deviations at the highest strata in Africa and Australia–New Guinea). The sample is areally stratified so that the number of genera chosen in each macro-area is represented in the same proportion to the total number of genera in each macro-area (Miestamo 2005: 31–9). Macro-areas correspond roughly to continent-sized geographical areas: Africa, Eurasia, Southeast Asia–Oceania, Australia–New Guinea, North America, and South America (Dryer 1992). See the Appendix for the classification and sources of the sample languages.

3.2 *Speech community size*

The number of speakers for each language was obtained from grammar descriptions whenever possible. When the grammar description gave no estimate or an unreliable estimate (e.g. including number of speakers of closely related variants not described in the grammar), I took the number of speakers from the Ethnologue (R. Gordon 2005) (more specifically, number of speakers for all countries). Table 9.1 provides the figures for each language.

Basing language-size estimates on the grammar descriptions rather than the Ethnologue has advantages. For one, neither speech community size nor complexity remains constant over time, although the former seems to change more readily than the latter (Hay and Bauer 2007: 398). Consequently, the most recent estimate of community size may differ from the community size during the writing of the grammar description. It is therefore desirable to use the count whose date most closely matches the grammar description.

Community size during the formation time of the grammatical phenomena recorded in the grammar descriptions may also differ from community size when the grammar was written (and may differ even more compared to the most recent estimates). One sign of this discrepancy could be a disproportionately large ethnic population no longer speaking the language. According to the Ethnologue, Lakhota has 6,000 speakers but the ethnic population is 20,000 people. This raises the question how accurately the present-day figure would represent Lakhota as a "small" or a "large" language. It would be tempting to make the leap and include the ethnic group in the speech community size (as Johanna Nichols did for the research reported in the preceding chapter); I chose not to do this, because it would introduce further problems that could not be addressed within the limits of this chapter.

3.3 Complexity metric

Complexity is here measured as adherence to versus deviation from the principle of one-meaning–one-form. Two types of deviation are recognized: violations of economy and violations of distinctiveness. No account is taken of different *degrees* of deviation.

As a starting point, the number of morphosyntactic strategies interacting in core argument marking was counted for each language. Note that, for head marking, only languages which mark both A and P on the verbal head were counted. Head marking of only one of the arguments would require other strategies in order fully to distinguish the arguments from one another – at least when both participants are third person and identical in number and gender. Also, head marking of just A, in particular, is very widespread cross-linguistically, and does not seem to correlate with anything else in languages (Nichols et al. 2006: 97).

Languages were analysed as adhering to the principle of one-meaning–one-form if a single strategy distinguishes the arguments in all or nearly all contexts. As an example, word order in Ngiti (Kutsch Lojenga 1994) distinguishes the arguments from one another in all contexts. Various minor deviations were discounted in categorizing certain languages as adhering to the principle. In Imbabura Quechua (Cole 1985), the arguments are distinguished from one another in all contexts by dependent marking. In addition, head marking of A is obligatory, but that of P occurs optionally and only for the first person singular. This slight redundancy of optionally using both dependent marking and head marking of both A and P when P is first person singular was treated as a negligibly small deviation from the principle. Some languages use more than one morphosyntactic strategy in roughly complementary manner. In Kannada (Sridhar 1990), dependent marking distinguishes the arguments obligatorily when P has a human referent or when it is emphasized, and optionally elsewhere, but word order is used when both arguments are inanimate. This kind of complementary distribution is interpreted as adhering to the principle.

The two types of deviation are treated next. Languages violate economy if they use more than one strategy and not in a complementary manner. Maricopa uses both head and dependent marking in all relevant contexts:

(4)   Maricopa (Yuman; L. Gordon 1986: 74)

Va   vany-a   nyip   '-n'ay-sh   chew-k.
house   DEM-VAUG   me   1-father-SBJ   3>3.make-REAL
"My father built *that house*."

Languages violate distinctiveness if they use only one strategy but in limited contexts, or allow a lot of syncretism in the head or dependent marking paradigms. As an example, Iau (Bateman 1986) uses neither head marking nor word order but uses some type of dependent marking in limited contexts. Noun phrases "which are part of the new information being predicated about the topic" and are preceded by a non-A are marked with a postpositional particle *be* whose tone indicates the role of the NP in question (Janet Bateman, pers. comm.):

(5)   Iau (Lakes Plain; Janet Bateman, pers. comm.)

Da^7 Das$^{7-8}$ be-^{8} di^3
dog   Das   FOC-A   kill.TOT.DUR
"Das killed the dog."

In most contexts, therefore, Iau uses no morphosyntactic strategy for distinguishing the arguments from one another.

One might ask whether languages which violate distinctiveness to a great extent have actually grammaticalized the distinction at all. Although not all sample languages seemed to identify A and P uniquely, at the least they all seemed to distinguish A from non-A, which suffices for the present purposes. Table 9.1 presents the complexity analysis for each language.

Table 9.1. Complexity analysis and speech community sizes

Language	Strategies used	Type	Population
Adang	DM (limited)	D	7,000
Alawa	HM; DM	E	30
Arapesh	WO; HM	E	5,000
Babungo	WO (limited); DM (some pronouns only)	D	14,000
Berber (Middle Atlas)*	WO; DM	E	3,000,000
Cora*	WO; HM; DM	E	8,000
Cree (Plains)*	HM	A	34,100
Daga*	HM	D	6,000
Georgian	DM; HM	E	2,734,393
Gooniyandi*	DM; HM	E	100
Greenlandic (West)	WO and DM (complementary); HM	E	43,000
Hixkaryana	WO; HM	E	350
Hungarian	DM; HM	E	13,150,000
Iau	DM (limited)	D	400
Ika	DM; HM	E	7,000
Indonesian*	WO; DM (opt. for 3rd singular pronoun)	A	23,143,354
Jaqaru	DM; HM	E	1,500
Kannada	WO and DM (complementary)	A	25,000,000
Khoekhoe*	DM	A	233,701
Kisi	WO; DM	E	500,000
Koasati	DM; HM	E	400
Kombai	WO	A	4,000
Kuot	WO; HM	E	1,500
Lakhota*	HM	A	6,000
Lavukaleve	WO; HM	E	1,700
Maricopa*	DM; HM	E	181
Maybrat	WO	A	22,000
Mien*	WO	A	8,186,685
Miwok (Southern Sierra)	DM; HM	E	20
Namia	DM (pronouns only)	D	3,500
Ngiti	WO	A	100,000
North Slave*	WO; HM	E	790
Nubian (Dongolese)*	DM	A	280,000
Nuuchahnulth*	(HM only for A)	D	200
Pirahã	WO	A	110
Pitjantjatjara	DM	A	3,500
Qiang	DM; HM	E	70,000

(Continued)

Table 9.1. (Continued)

Language	Strategies used	Type	Population
Quechua (Imbabura)	DM	A	40,000
Semelai	DM (limited)	D	4,103
Shipibo-Konibo	DM	A	23,000
Sko	WO; DM	E	700
Somali*	DM; HM	E	12,653,480
Thai*	WO	A	20,229,987
Trumai	WO; DM	E	51
Tzutujil	HM	A	50,000
Urubú-Kaapor	DM (optional)	D	500
Warao	DM (pronouns only)	D	15,000
Welsh*	WO; DM	E	536,258
Yagua	WO; HM	E	3,000
Yimas*	HM	D	300

* No. of speakers taken from the Ethnologue (R. Gordon 2005).
WO = word order; DM = dependent marking; HM = head marking; A = adherence to the principle of one-meaning–
one-form; D = violation of distinctiveness; E = violation of economy.

4 Results

To begin with, Table 9.2 shows the distribution of adherences to versus deviations from the principle of one-meaning–one-form across different speech community sizes. Two general tendencies can be observed from the figures. First, the number of languages adhering to the principle increases as the number of speakers increases, and most of these languages ($N = 12$, 75 per cent) are larger than 10,000. Secondly, languages spoken by 10,000 speakers or fewer tend to violate either economy or distinctiveness ($N = 24$, 71 per cent) and the number of these languages decreases as the number of speakers increases. However, the number of languages violating economy jumps up again for languages spoken by more than 100,000 speakers; but all of these are spoken in the Old World.[3] These observations suggest greater support for hypothesis (i) than for hypothesis (ii) on p. 130 above.

Since it is very difficult to determine what constitutes a "small" or "large" speech community, several different community size thresholds were used (following Pericliev 2004), beginning from 250 and doubling the threshold size for each consecutive test. The hypotheses were rewritten for each threshold size accordingly:

---

[3] Old World covers Africa, Eurasia, and Southeast Asia, whereas New World covers the Pacific (Australia, New Guinea, Melanesia, Micronesia, and Polynesia) and the Americas (cf. Nichols 1992: 12–13, 25–8).

Table 9.2. Distribution of complexity values across different community sizes

	<=1000	1001–10,000	10,001–100,000	>100,001	Total
Violate distinctiveness	4	4	2	0	10
Adhere	1	3	6	6	16
Violate economy	9	7	2	6	24
Total	14	14	10	12	50

Table 9.3. Contingency table for the statistical tests

	Threshold size	
	<=	>
Adherence to 1M:1F	A	B
Violation of 1M:1F	C	D

(i′) Languages spoken by speech communities smaller than or equal to the threshold size are likely to violate distinctiveness or economy (cell C in Table 9.3).

(ii′) Languages spoken by speech communities larger than the threshold size are likely to adhere to the principle of one-meaning–one-form (cell B).

The hypotheses were tested in the open-source statistical computing environment R (R Development Core Team 2007) with chi-square, and with Fisher's Exact Test where chi-square was not a valid test due to low expected counts. Table 9.3 shows the contingency table and Table 9.4 the results.

The test was statistically significant for a number of threshold sizes, from 1,000 up to 32,000 speakers. Since the median of the sample was 6,500 (7,000 in the Ethnologue), these threshold sizes grouped around it rather evenly. The strongest association between the variables was for threshold size 16,000 ($\chi^2 \approx 12 \cdot 0$, $p = \cdot 00053$, d.f. $= 1$). Two follow-up tests were further performed to assess the reliability of the result. First, the reliability of the association was tested by observing the contribution of individual cells to the chi-value (Arppe forthcoming). If the contribution of an individual cell by itself exceeds the critical value which makes a table with the same degrees of freedom statistically significant ($\chi^2 = 3.84$; $p = \cdot 05$; d.f. $= 1$), this confirms the reliability of the result but also shows the locus of greatest deviation. For threshold size 16,000, the contribution of the expected value of languages larger than 16,000 speakers that adhere to the principle of one-meaning–one-form was $4 \cdot 9$, which by itself exceeds the minimum of the critical value. This confirms the reliability of the result and provides evidence especially for hypothesis (ii).

Table 9.4. Results for different threshold sizes

Threshold	χ^2	p
250		·41
500		·07
1,000		·02
2,000	8·1	·0045
4,000	5·2	·022
8,000	9·2	·0025
16,000	12·0	·00053
32,000	5·2	·023
64,000		·105
128,000		·163
256,000		·297

Secondly, the vulnerability of the association to potential misclassifications was tested by following the procedure in Janssen et al. (2006: 435–7). Keeping the sample size fixed, the margins (the sums of columns and rows) are altered until the *p*-value is no longer statistically significant. If statistical significance is lost by altering the values by one case, one should be careful in interpreting the results. The association for threshold size 16,000 loses significance when four languages at a minimum were misclassified. Consequently, the result seems relatively resistant to potential misclassifications.

As a preliminary conclusion, a statistically significant association occurred between speech community size and structural complexity of core argument marking for many different threshold sizes, corroborated by the follow-up tests. The high number of large Old World languages which violate economy (Table 9.2) indicates that hypothesis (i) is better supported than hypothesis (ii), while the size of deviations from expected values suggests greater support for hypothesis (ii). As indicated by the data in Table 9.2, the distributions of adherences versus deviations from the principle of one-meaning–one-form across different speech community sizes largely conform to our hypotheses, except for the high number of large languages violating economy. Since it is plausible that there are differences between languages violating distinctiveness versus economy, one further test was performed in which the effect of large languages violating economy was bypassed: languages which adhere to the principle of one-meaning–one-form were compared to those that violate distinctiveness. The association was statistically very significant for threshold size 16,000 ($p = ·0002$, Fisher's Exact Test). Since the association was resistant to three misclassifications at a minimum, its reliability is also confirmed. Consequently, when languages violating economy are discarded, there is rather strong support for both hypotheses (i) and (ii). These results suggest that large languages tend to avoid violations of distinctiveness, but do not mind violations of economy.

5 Discussion

There is a statistically relatively strong association between community size and complexity in core argument marking, measured as adherence to versus deviation from the principle of one-meaning–one-form. That there should be such an association is unexpected, and calls for an explanation.

One might claim on methodological grounds that this association is due to chance, insisting that an absolute definition of "small" and "large" ought to be used. According to this objection, rather than defining "small" and "large" relative to various threshold sizes, they should be defined, for example, relative to the world median or perhaps to some upper limit of community size which a community with tight network structure could still have. However, this would not necessarily be helpful, since the definitions of "small" and "large" depend to some extent on geographical areas (cf. Johanna Nichols, p. 119 above): a language spoken by, for instance, 10,000 people is small in Europe but already relatively large in the Pacific (the respective medians are 220,000 and 800 according to the Ethnologue). Moreover, the association was statistically significant ($\chi^2 = 8 \cdot 0$; $p = \cdot 0048$; d.f. $= 1$) even when using e.g. the world median (7,000) as the threshold size.

On the other hand, one could argue that the association is due to chance because of the uneven geographical distribution of small/large languages across the globe. One way of answering this is to consider geographical areas independently of one another, e.g. Old and New World separately. For the sixteen Old World languages in the sample, the association was not statistically significant with any threshold size (Fisher's Exact Test, $p > \cdot 05$). For the New World, however, the association was statistically significant for the median (2,300 speakers) as threshold size (Fisher's Exact Test, $p = \cdot 017$) and even more significant for 16,000 speakers as threshold size ($p = \cdot 0024$). The association for threshold size 16,000 loses significance when two languages at a minimum were misclassified. Since the result was resistant to at least one misclassification, its reliability is tentatively confirmed. According to these results, the association does not seem to have arisen by chance; but it does seem areally confined, which somewhat undermines the generality of the association.

However, the lack of association in the Old World might be a consequence of large languages tolerating different kinds of violation of the one-meaning–one-form principle compared to small languages. The data suggest that adherence to distinctiveness may be more important than adherence to economy in languages with more than 16,000 speakers, most of which are spoken in the Old World. Consequently, the data for the 16,000 threshold were scrutinized areally. According to the results, there was a statistically significant association in both Old and New Worlds ($p = \cdot028$ and $p = \cdot029$ respectively, Fisher's Exact Test). This suggests that large languages in both Old and New Worlds tend to avoid violations of distinctiveness but do not mind violations of economy. But why should large languages tolerate violations of economy more than violations of distinctiveness? One reason might be that because speakers of large languages generally have little shared background information, transparency and distinctiveness are especially needed for mutual understanding. Redundancy can be beneficial in these situations as well, because it can increase distinctiveness. But because the transparency of morphosyntactic strategies varies across languages, languages probably differ in how affordable redundancy is for them in these situations.

In section 2.1 I proposed that the criteria used by Trudgill (2004a) – size of speech community, amount of adult language learning by outsiders, and tightness of network structure – may be more or less intertwined. Although the matter has not been studied in great detail, it is not totally implausible to assume that small community size would tend to combine with tight network structure and little or no adult language learning by outsiders, rather than with loose network structure and/or large amount of adult language learning by outsiders. In case of large community size, it seems even more plausible that one particular combination of the criteria, namely that which combines loose network structure and large amount of adult language learning by outsiders, would represent a prototypical combination of the three criteria (cf. section 2.1).

If these generalizations are correct, the present results could be seen as an attempt to single out one variable from a multivariate phenomenon and to study its effect in isolation – but maybe, also, as an attempt to approximate the multivariate phenomenon. Interpreted in this way, Trudgill's (2004a) adapted model could provide an explanation here as well: small and isolated languages with tight networks can afford and preserve complexities thanks to great amounts of shared background information, whereas large languages with loose network structure and much adult language learning by outsiders tend towards greater transparency.

By and large, the present chapter indicates that language complexity is not necessarily independent of sociolinguistic properties such as speech community size. Future research should study the phenomenon with a multivariate cross-linguistic approach, paying more attention to geographical areas as well as to neighbouring languages with different sociolinguistic and typological profiles.

Appendix. The language sample

Africa

Babungo (Bantoid; Schaub 1985), Dongolese Nubian (Nubian; Armbruster 1960), Khoekhoe (Central Khoisan; Hagman 1977), Kisi (Southern Atlantic; Childs 1995), Middle Atlas Berber (Berber; Penchoen 1973), Ngiti (Lendu; Kutsch Lojenga 1994), Somali (Eastern Cushitic; Saeed 1999).

Eurasia

Georgian (Kartvelian; A. Harris 1981, Hewitt 1996), Hungarian (Ugric; Rounds 2001, Kiss 2002), Kannada (Southern Dravidian; Sridhar 1990), Welsh (Celtic; King 1993).

Southeast Asia–Oceania

Indonesian (Sundic; Sneddon 1996), Mien (Hmong-Mien; Court 1985), Qiang (Qiangic; LaPolla 2003), Semelai (Aslian; Kruspe 1999), Thai (Kam-Tai; Iwasaki and Ingka-phirom 2005).

Australia–New Guinea

Adang (Timor-Alor-Pantar; Haan 2001), Alawa (Maran; Sharpe 1972), Arapesh (Kombio-Arapesh; Conrad and Wogiga 1991), Daga (Dagan; Murane 1974), Gooniyandi (Bunuban; McGregor 1990), Iau (Lakes Plain; Bateman 1986), Kombai (Awju-Dumut; de Vries 1993), Kuot (Kuot; Lindström 2002), Lavukaleve (Solomons East Papuan; Terrill 2003), Maybrat (North-Central Bird's Head; Dol 1999), Namia (Yellow River; Feldpausch and Feldpausch 1992), Pitjantjatjara (Pama-Nyungan; Bowe 1990), Sko (Western Sko; Donohue 2004), Yimas (Lower Sepik; Foley 1991).

North America

Cora (Corachol; Casad 1984), Koasati (Muskogean; Kimball 1991), Lakhota (Siouan; van Valin 1977), Maricopa (Yuman; L. Gordon 1986), Nuuchahnulth (Southern Wakashan; Nakayama 2001), Plains Cree (Algonquian; Dahlstrom 1991), Slave (Athapaskan; Rice 1989), Southern Sierra Miwok (Miwok; Broadbent 1964), Tzutujil (Mayan; Dayley 1985), West Greenlandic (Eskimo-Aleut; Fortescue 1984).

South America

Hixkaryana (Cariban; Derbyshire 1979), Ika (Aruak; P. Frank 1990), Imbabura Quechua (Quechuan; Cole 1985), Jaqaru (Aymaran; Hardman 2000), Pirahã (Mura; Everett 1986), Shipibo-Konibo (Panoan; Valenzuela 1997), Trumai (Trumai; Guirardello 1999), Urubú-Kaapor (Tupi-Guaraní; Kakumasu 1986), Warao (Warao; Romero-Figueroa 1997), Yagua (Peba-Yaguan; Payne and Payne 1990).

10

Oh nɔ́ɔ!: a bewilderingly multifunctional Saramaccan word teaches us how a creole language develops complexity[1]

JOHN McWHORTER

1 Introduction

I have argued (cf. McWhorter 2005)[2] that creole language grammars exhibit less complexity than grammars of older languages, as the result of creoles' origins as radically reduced pidgin varieties. It is natural to human languages to accrete complexity as a matter of course over the millennia. Creoles, born as radically reduced pidgins and having existed as full languages for only a few centuries, have not had time to accrete the volume of complexity that Russian or Navajo has.

Arends (2001) has argued that creole grammars have not been sufficiently examined for it to be certain that they lack the complexity of older languages – this is a frequent objection to my thesis. But that point leads one to ask why even relatively brief grammatical descriptions of older languages reveal obvious complexity with respect to features such as inflectional paradigms, heterogenous word order, ample irregularity, multiple tones indicating lexical and grammatical contrasts, and the like. The complexity of Polish or Chinese is evident immediately, after all, in a Berlitz phrasebook.

However, that question left aside, Arends was correct that for too many creoles over which great quantities of rhetorical ink have been spilt over the years, the degree to which their grammars have been described is modest

---

[1] Title in salute to my erstwhile colleague Jim Matisoff's fabulous title for his paper on a distinctly analysis-resistant marker *ve* in Lahu (Matisoff 1972).

[2] McWhorter (2005) is a collection of various articles first published in journals and anthologies. I will cite this source in reference to those publications, in view of its more convenient accessibility.

enough that complexity may well reveal itself with further research. In this paper, I will show that this is indeed true in the case of the development in Saramaccan (a Creole English of Surinam) of a conventionalized system for marking new information, conditioned according to position, tense, and aspect.

My presentation will also demonstrate, however, that this feature – like so many complexities in creole grammars – was not present in the language at its emergence, and hence does not support any simple thesis that the immediate product of the creolization of a language is a grammar indistinguishable in complexity from, say, Korean. Rather, as I have often noted, complexity in creoles grows over time from an original state in which the language had much less. Moreover, as the growth process has occurred over a few centuries rather than millennia, creoles' complexities are not *maximally* elaborated relative to comparable features in older languages.

Finally, the discussion will also serve as a corrective to a tendency in studies of grammatical complexity – in creoles and beyond – to conceive of complexity as essentially a shorthand for inflectional morphology. A great many of the world's languages have little or no inflectional morphology, and yet display complexity in various other aspects of their grammars. In focusing on incipient inflectional morphology in creoles as evidence of their accretion of complexity, we miss much.

The Saramaccan data in this paper were gathered by myself and graduate student assistants at the University of California at Berkeley from native speakers unless otherwise noted.

2 Emergent versus original complexity

I must make clear at the outset that the claim is not that, at their emergence, creoles entirely lack complexity. They emerge with a certain degree of complexity already (albeit much less than in older languages; cf. McWhorter 2005: 102–41).

A great deal of this complexity is due to the tranfer of a feature from a source language. For example, Saramaccan tone sandhi is sensitive to syntax, breaking at the left edge of maximal projections (e.g. before objects and prepositional phrases):

(1) /mi wási koósu butá a dí sónu/ → [mi wásí # koósu bútá #
                                                          a dí sónu]

      I   wash   clothes   put   in   the sun
      "I washed my clothes and put them in the sun." (Rountree 1972: 325)

The principal creators of Saramaccan spoke the Niger–Congo language Fongbe, in which there is a similar tone sandhi system:

(2) /é   sà   àsɔ́n   wè/ →   [é   sâ̠   #   àsɔ́nc   wê̠]
  he   sell   crab   two   (Wiesemann 1991: 77)

Thus this feature can be assumed to have existed in Saramaccan from the beginning of its history.

However, most features in Saramaccan that are markedly complex were not modelled on Fongbe, and have arisen grammar-internally.

3 New information marking in Saramaccan: synchrony

The word *nɔ́ɔ* in Saramaccan is used clause-initially with great frequency, often translated as "then":[3]

(3) *Nɔ́ɔ   mi   ó   kándi   a   míndi   wósu.   Nɔ́ɔ   i   butá*
  NI   1S   FUT   lie_down   LOC   middle   house   NI   2S   put

  wã́   kódjo,   wã́   kódjo   a   bándja,   wã́   kódjo   a   bándja.
  a   cudgel   a   cudgel   LOC   side   a   cudgel   LOC   side

  Nɔ́ɔ   i   kái   woló,   kɛɛ́!...
  NI   2S   call   alas   cry

  "I'm going to lie down in the middle of the house. Then you put a stick, a stick off to the side. Then you wail out 'Alas'!..."

However, the "then" translation is inexact. In the first sentence of the example below, *hɛ̃́* "then" already conveys sequentiality (more precisely the collocation *hɛ̃́ wɛ* which includes focus marker *wɛ* and is the closest Saramaccan equivalent to English "then" in the sequential sense), such that at best, a "then" meaning for *nɔ́ɔ* would be redundant.

(4) *Nɔ́ɔ   hɛ̃́   wɛ   wã́   mujɛ́ɛ   bì   dɛ́   a   dí   kɔndé   naándé.*
  NI   then   FOC   a   woman   PST   be   LOC   DEF   village   there
  Nɔ́ɔ   dí   mujɛ́ɛ,   a   palí   dí   míi   wã́   dáka.
  NI   DEF   woman   3S   bear   DEF   child   one   day

  "So, then [in the wake of certain events described]: there was a woman in the village there. The woman, she bore a child one day."

---

[3] Interlinear glosses in this chapter use 1P, 3S, etc. for pronouns unmarked as subject or object, and 3SO for third person singular oblique pronoun. The new-information markers which are the topic of the chapter are glossed NI.

Of course, no language lacks redundancy. However, *nɔ́ɔ* is used with such frequency in spoken Saramaccan that a "then" meaning would imply a usage rate of "then" so peculiarly high as to seem an almost compulsive dedication to overtly marking chronological posteriority despite context and utterance order almost always making it quite clear.

Nɔ́ɔ has a more specific function than this, gracefully demonstrated by the following contrast. An informant once said to me, in reference to a planned conversation in the near future:

(5) A   búnu.   Nɔ́ɔ   mi   ó   tá   háika   i.
     3S   good   NI   3S   FUT   IPFV   listen   2S
     "Good. So I'll be listening for you (waiting for your answer)."

He prefaced the second assertion with *nɔ́ɔ*. Shortly thereafter, he repeated:

(6) A   búnu,   mi   ó   tá   háika   dí   kái   fii   tidé   néti.
     3S   good   1S   FUT   IPFV   listen   DEF   call   POSS.2S   today   night
     "Good, I'll be listening (waiting) for your call tonight."

but this time, without the *nɔ́ɔ*. This was because the impending phone call was now no longer new information within our discourse.

The function of *nɔ́ɔ* is marking new information. Saramaccan speakers use it as a foregrounding strategy, to point to shifts in a narrative. Each *nɔ́ɔ* indicates, so to speak, a new camera angle in the "film" of the utterance.

The foregrounding function of *nɔ́ɔ* is clear when we revisit citation (3) above, shown again in (7) below with the context of preceding material. The animal subject of the folk tale is talking to his wife about a famine they are suffering under, and starts using *nɔ́ɔ* to foreground his plan for getting food (which is to play dead, wait for the animals of the area to come and mourn him, and then wake up and club them to death):

(7) Já   sí   hángi   dé   ku   u?   Wá   sondí
     2S.NEG   see   hunger   be   with   1P   1P.NEG   thing

     u   njá.   Mi   ó   pɛέ   wǎ   kɔ́ni,   mi
     for   eat   1S   FUT   play   a   trick   1S

     ó   pɛέ,   mi   ó   ganjǎ   dɛ́dɛ. Nɔ́ɔ   mi
     FUT   play   1S   FUT   pretend dead   NI   1S

     ó   kándi   a   míndi   wósu.   Nɔ́ɔ i   butá
     FUT   lie_down LOC   middle house   NI   2S   put

     wǎ   kódjo,   wǎ   kódjo   a   bándja, wǎ   kódjo
     a   cudgel   a   cudgel LOC   side   a   cudgel

a   bándja. Nɔ́ɔ i   kái woló,   kɛέ...
LOC side   NI   2S   call alas   cry

"You see the hunger we are suffering from? We don't have anything to eat. I'm going to play a trick, I'm going to play... I'm going to pretend I'm dead. I'll lay down in the middle of the house. You put a stick, a stick to the side, a stick to the side. Then you call 'Alas!', you cry..."

Nɔ́ɔ comes in when the speaker starts describing what he is going to do, i.e. presenting a new "camera shot" within the utterance. In a film, one could imagine his description depicted in the hypothetical as a vignette while he narrated on the soundtrack.

Nɔ́ɔ is especially conventionalized in marking matrix clauses that occur after preceding adverbial complements, the matrix clause containing the new information. This is the case with temporal complements:

(8) *Té   mujéɛ sí   Kobí, nɔ́ɔ de   tá   kulé.*
     When woman see   Kobi   NI   3P   IPFV run
     "When women see Kobi, they run."

(9) *Dí   mi bì   ko   lúku de,   nɔ́ɔ de   bì   duúmi kaa.*
     when I   PST come look them then they PST sleep   already
     "When I came to see them, they were asleep."

and concessive ones:

(10) *Ée dí   míi   á   du   έ,   nɔ́ɔ dí   m'má ó   náki ɛ̃.*
      If   DEF child NEG do   3SO NI   DEF Mom   FUT hit   3SO
      "If the child doesn't do it, then the Mom will hit him."

New-information marking is sensitive to tense when occurring on matrix clauses after temporal adverbial complements. In the past tense, *nɔ́ɔ* is superseded as a new-information marker by *hέ*:

(11) *Dí   a   bì   ta   duúmi, hέ mi gó kumútu dé.*
      when he PST IPFV sleep   NI I   go leave   there
      "When he was sleeping, I left."

(12) *Dí   mi bì   jabí di   dɔ́ɔ, hέ mi sí   di   gɔ̃́ɔ́   munjá.*
      When I   PST open DEF door NI I   see DEF ground wet
      "When I opened the door, I saw the ground wet."

This word is derived etymologically from "then" and is usually translated as such. However, more precisely, "then" in the sequential sense is usually rendered, as noted above, by *hέ* in conjunction with focus marker *wɛ* as *hέ wɛ*:

(13) Dí   mujéɛ-míi   tá   fɔ́   pindá,   tá   fɔ́   pindá
     DEF   woman-child IPFV beat peanut   IPFV beat peanut

ku   táti   a   máta.   Hɛ́   wɛ   Anási   wáka
with pestle LOC   mortar   Then   FOC   Anansi   walk

dóu   dɛ́.
arrive there

"So one day, the girl was beating peanuts, beating peanuts with a mortar-and-pestle. Then Anansi approached."

Hɛ́ in isolation is a foregrounder (although there is also a homonym, the tonic third person pronoun: *A táa "Hɛ́!"* "He said, 'Him!'"). It could be translated in this function as "then", but in my view that translation obscures its actual function, an abstract pragmatic one.

Nɔ́ɔ, as the marker of new information applying most widely in the grammar, co-occurs optionally with *hɛ́* in the configuration *nɔ́ɔ hɛ́*.

(14) Mi   dé   a   dí   wósu   báka,   nɔ́ɔ   hɛ́   mi
     1s   be   LOC   DEF   house   back   NI   NI   1s

sí   wɛ̃́   mujéɛ,   hɛ́   mi   sí   dí   wómi   náki
see   a   woman   then   1s   see   DEF   man   hit

dí   mujéɛ.
DEF   woman

"I was behind the house, then I saw a woman and saw the man hit the woman."

(15) Dí   a   boóko   dí   báta   kaa,   nɔ́ɔ   hɛ́   a
     when   3s   break   DEF   bottle COMPL   NI   then   3s

léi   mi.
show   1s

"When he broke the bottle, he showed it to me."

The order of occurrence between these two markers is fixed: *hɛ́ nɔ́ɔ.

Only when applying to full clauses does new-information marker *nɔ́ɔ* occur clause-initially. Otherwise, it is postposed, as to dependent clauses:

(16) Té   wɛ̃́   óto   pási   báka   nɔ́ɔ,   i   tá̃   búnu.
     Until   a   other   time   again   NI   2s   stay good

"Till another time, be well."

and to arguments and adjuncts:

(17) A búnu   e –   amanjã   nɔ́ɔ mi ó   jéi   fii.
     3S good INTERJECTION tomorrow NI   1S FUT hear for.2S
     "So very good – tomorrow I'll listen for you (wait for your call)."

The following sentence usefully shows *nɔ́ɔ* used in both positions while also nicely exemplifying the essence of the foregrounding function. *Nɔ́ɔ u nɔ́ɔ* is a fronted nonverbal predicate (connoting "Us, this is" – in certain contexts, in Saramaccan the copula is deleted when the predicate is fronted):

(18) *Nɔ́ɔ*   u   *nɔ́ɔ,*   dísi   kaa.
      NI   1P   NI   this   compl
     "This is *us.*" (This is the way we are.)

The first *nɔ́ɔ* foregrounds the whole proposition amidst a larger discourse. The second, postposed because it modifies an argument rather than a clause, presents as new information the "us" whose traits have just been described. The meaning of the sentence within the context is "Consider the *new* realization that what I have just described constitutes not a random assortment of traits, but the essence of 'us', *new* to your knowledge."

Sentences without overt new-information marking via *nɔ́ɔ* or *hɛ́* are not ungrammatical:

(19) *Ée*   i   *bì*   *láfu*   *mi,*   mi   bì   ó   féti   ku   i.
     if   2S   PST   laugh   1S   1S   PST FUT fight with 2S
     "If you'd laughed at me, I'd have fought with you."

However, the markers are used much more frequently than not. Informants asked for translations of English sentences use them most of the time in their answers; spontaneous utterances are replete with them. They are considerably *entrenched,* in the terms of Langacker (1987), if not strictly *obligatorified,* in the terminology of C. Lehmann (1985) on grammaticalization.

Certainly *nɔ́ɔ* and *hɛ́* have been acknowledged and translated. However, they have not been parsed as marking, in systematic fashion, an aspect of grammar common to all languages but marked overtly by only a subset. In its use of two markers conditioned by tense, aspect and position, the marking of new information in Saramaccan is more complex than in, for example, English.

An indication of the "evolved" nature of this new-information marking is that the main marker *nɔ́ɔ* no longer has lexical content; it is a pure function word just as, for example, imperfective marker *tá* and focus marker *wɛ* are. Anglophone students of linguistics must be taught the concept of new versus old information via illustrations of topicalization, clefting, and intonation.

Saramaccan students of linguistics could simply be taught that "new information" is that which is marked by *nɔ́ɔ*.

4 New-information marking in Saramaccan: diachrony

4.1 *From* no more *to new-information marker*

Saramaccan has wrested its principal foregrounding marker from, rather counterintuitively, the adverb *nɔ́ɔmɔ*, derived from *no more*.

Nɔ́ɔmɔ lives elsewhere in the grammar in clause-final usage, having drifted semantically from the compositional meaning of *no more* into connoting, first, the pragmatic assertion "definitely":

(20) *Mi   ó   gó   téi   ɛ̃   nɔ́ɔmɔ.*
      1S   FUT go   take 3SO definitely
      "I'm definitely going to get her (romantically)."

(21) *Mi   ó   du   ɛ̃   nɔ́ɔmɔ.*
      1S   FUT do   3SO definitely
      "I'm definitely going to do it."

Presumably, the semantic derivation is based on a usage of *no more* to assert "That's all (and no more)", "That's all there is to it".

In a further semantic extension, *nɔ́ɔmɔ* also can connote "always", "continuously":

(22) *Nɔ́ɔ   léti   fuu   u   mú'   súku   nɔ́ɔmɔ.*
      NI   right POSS.1P   1P   must   look_for   always
      "We must always look for the right way for us to be."

The "definitely" meaning, intensifying an assertion, has been extended into an intensification of a durational nature. (*Nɔ́ɔmɔ* cannot, in the modern language, express its original compositional meaning of "no more".)

Neither of these meanings appear on their face relevant to a foregrounding marker. However, the source of new-information marker *nɔ́ɔ* as *nɔ́ɔmɔ* is supported by various facts. For one, the phonetic derivation is supported by the fact that *nɔ́ɔmɔ* was also the source for a homonym of new-information marker *nɔ́ɔ*, which means "only" – a sense which naturally derives from *no more*, given its restrictive connotation. This homonym occurs clause-finally, unlike the new-information marker. This difference in position, in fact, determines which meaning is conveyed: when *nɔ́ɔ* occurs clause-finally rather than clause-initially or after an argument, it connotes "only":

(23) Mi   lési   téni baáti u   dí   búku   nɔ́ɔ.
      1s   read   ten   page   of DEF   book   just
      "I've only read ten pages of the book."

(24) Mɛ́   sá'   fá   u   táki   ɛ̃   nɔ́ɔ.
      1s.NEG know how   1P   talk   3sO just
      "I just don't know how we say it...!"

Confirming that *nɔ́ɔ* as "only" is derived from *nɔ́ɔmɔ* is that the "only" usage still occurs occasionally as *nɔ́ɔmɔ*:

(25) A   táa   téi   dí   pási   akí   nángó   nɔ́ɔmɔ.
      3s   say   take DEF   road   here IPFV.go   only
      "He said 'Just go down this road'." (Price and Price n.d.: 170)

The derivation of "only" from *no more* is semantically obvious, but crucially, this diachronic pathway shows that the source of the *nɔ́ɔ* new-information marker in *nɔ́ɔmɔ* is phonetically plausible.

Yet while the *nɔ́ɔmɔ* > *nɔ́ɔ* evolution is phonetically plausible, a semantic evolution from "definitely" or "continuously" to a new-information marker is distinctly less graceful. One tempting solution is to suppose that the new-information marker has a different etymological source, such as "now". This account beckons in Saramaccan especially considering that the word for "now," *nɔ́unɔ́u* (reduplicated from an original *nɔ́u*), has the lax vowel that *nɔ́ɔ* has.

However, one problem with this account is that *nɔ́unɔ́u* does not occur in a clause-initial sequential or foregrounding usage. And in any case, comparative data indicate that the source of the new-information marker was indeed *nɔ́ɔmɔ*, its original compositional "no more" meaning drifting differently than it did in the clause-final usages of *nɔ́ɔmɔ*.

Crucial evidence that this was the case occurs in the sister languages of Saramaccan, namely Sranan and Ndjuka. A proto-creole in late seventeenth century, Surinam yielded three main present-day creoles: Sranan, Surinam's lingua franca; Ndjuka, a direct offshoot of Sranan spoken by descendants of slaves who established communities in the interior, about as similar to Sranan as Swedish is to Norwegian; and Saramaccan, also spoken in the interior by descendants of escaped slaves, which retains most of the grammar of Sranan and Ndjuka but has a vast amount of relexification from Portuguese and a higher component of lexical items from Fongbe and Kikongo.

In modern Sranan and Ndjuka, for example, the etymon from *no more* is used both in the clause-final semantic derivates in Saramaccan and in a function clearly similar to that of Saramaccan's clause-initial new-information marker *nɔɔ*. Here, for example, is Ndjuka's usage of its *naamo* to mean "continuously":

(26) *Ai*   *fufuu*   *naamo.*
      3S.IPFV   steal   continuously
      "He keeps stealing." (Shanks 1994: 137)

And here is Sranan's cognate, *nomo*, used as "only":

(27) *Mi*   *go*   *wan*   *leisi*   *nomo*   *na*   *Nickerie.*
      1S   go   one   time   only   LOC   Nickerie
      "I've only been to Nickerie one time." (Languages of Suriname Sranan–English dictionary)

Then, note that Sranan uses the same etymon clause-initially, not in a "continuously", "only", or "definitely" meaning:

(28) *M*   *tek*   *ontslag*   *a*   *bas,*   *a*   *no*   *wan*   *pai*   *moro,*
      1S   take   dismissal   LOC   boss   3S   NEG   want   pay   more

      da   *m*   *n*   *e-wroko*   *dj*   *ên*   *moro.*   *Nomo*   *den*
      then   1S   NEG   IPFV-work   give   3SO   more   then   DEF.PL

      sma   *tai*   *mi*   *tak:*   *W*   *a*   *no*   *sraften,*   *j*
      person   talk   1S   COMP   Well   3S   NEG   slavery_time   2S

      a   *leti.*
      have   right

      "So I let the boss fire me; he didn't want to pay me anymore, so I didn't work for him anymore. The people told me 'It's not slavery time anymore; you're right.'" (Voorhoeve 1962: 71; running translation mine [Voorhoeve did not give one])

Voorhoeve translates *nomo* here as "then", but in fact *nomo* is a rare rendition of "then" in his data, in which "then" is almost always expressed as *da(n)* (from Dutch *dan* "then") or *ne* (from English *then*, as will be discussed below). Note the *da* in the first sentence of the above passage, or the *da* and *ne* in this one which also includes a *nomo* usage:

(29) *Da*   *m*   *gw*   *a*   *masra*   *Engels,*   *go*
      then   1S   go   LOC   Mister   Engels   go

      aksi   *masra*   *Engels*   *tak:*   *M*   *wan*   *moro*
      ask   Mister   Engels   COMP   1S   want   more

      moni.   *Mi*   *no*   *kan*   *wroko*   *f*   *â*
      money   1S   NEG   can   work   for   DEF

mon	*dati.*	*Nomo*	*masra*	*Engels*	*e-ko*	*tak,*
money	that	then	Mister	Engels	IPFV-come	say

mj	*om*	*go*	*tai*	*mi*	*brada.*	*Ne*
1s	must	go	talk	my	brother	then

m	*taki:*	*M*	*n*	*a*	*neks*	*te*
1s	say	1s	NEG	have	nothing	until

make	*nanga*	*m*	*brada.*
make	with	my	brother

"Then I went to Mr Engels, went and asked him 'I want more money. I can't work for that money.' Then Mr Engels was up and saying I have to talk to my brother. Then I said 'I don't have anything to do with my brother.'" (Voorhoeve 1962: 70; running translation mine)

In Voorhoeve's data, *nomo* is not merely a chance variant used to mean "then". Instead, it is used to draw attention to an event of especial, decisive dramatic prominence: above, Mr Engels' condition for a raise in salary, or in the example before that, the speaker's friends' approval of his quitting. While Voorhoeve had no reason to attend to this nuance in his translations, it is *da(n)* and *ne* that are mere markers of the sequential; *nomo* has a different function, foregrounding new information.

Because English provides no single word serving to mark new information, predictably translations of this usage of *nomo* in Sranan and its cognate *na(a)mo* in Ndjuka are various (whereas translations of *da(n)* and *ne* as "then" are more consistent among sources). Voorhoeve (1962) prefers "then", while the Languages of Suriname Sranan–English dictionary translates it as "however" or "but":

(30)   *Nomo*   *di*   *a*   *bigin* *taki,*   *a*   *trawan* *ati*   *bron.*
        but   when 3s begin speak DEF other   heart burn
        "But when he began to speak, the other one got mad."

Then, Shanks (1994) translates the Ndjuka cognate as "meanwhile":

(31)   *Namo,*   *ne*   *a*   *si*   *wan*   *olo.*
        meanwhile then 3s see a   hole
        "Meanwhile, he saw a hole." (Shanks 1994: 137)

I suggest that the variation in these translations reflects the fact that this usage of the item has no true equivalent in English, and in fact has no semantic meaning at all, but a pragmatic one of flagging the information structure of running discourse. These usages of *nomo* (in Ndjuka *na(a)mo*) are, under a more graceful analysis than that indicated by the multifarious translations, new-information markers.

Their foregrounding function is not as conventionalized in Sranan and Ndjuka as *nɔ́ɔ* is in Saramaccan, classifying as sentential adverbs rather than the pragmatic particle that Saramaccan *nɔ́ɔ* is. Moreover, there is no tense-sensitive division of labour in Sranan and Ndjuka between *nomo/namo* and the *then*-derived forms (*ne* in both, with *neen* as an alternate in Ndjuka). *Nomo* and *namo* can be assumed to reflect an earlier stage in the process that yielded, in Saramaccan, a phonetically abbreviated and grammatically conventionalized new-information marker. In the terminology of Dahl (2004), the marking of foregrounding is more *mature* in Saramaccan, albeit not entailing the increased phonetic boundedness that Dahl's argument stresses.

Thus we can assume that the Saramaccan new-information marker *nɔ́ɔ* is derived from an earlier usage of *nɔ́ɔmɔ* in clause-initial position, confirmed by the fact that the full form *nɔ́ɔmɔ* does occur as a new-information marker on occasion, both clause-initially and after arguments:

(32) *Nɔ́ɔmɔ   déé   mbétimbéti   túu   kái   ɛ̃.*
     NI   DEF.PL   animal~animal   all   call   3SO
     "So all of the various animals called him." (Price and Price n.d.: 120)

(33) *Nɔ́ɔ   de   tá   píki   táa   ná   panyã́   mi,   hɛ̃*
     NI   3P   IPFV   answer   COMP   NEG   grab   1S   3SO

     nɔ́ɔmɔ   i   músu téi.
     NI   2S   must take

     "Then they were answering 'Don't grab me, it's him you should take'."
     (Price and Price n.d.: 148)

For *no more* to evolve into a marker of new information sounds, on its face, slightly absurd. However, in fact, the connotation inherent in the semantics of *no more* of drawing a boundary is a plausible source for a marker setting off what has come before as separate, and thus foregrounding the subsequent material.

That is, a clause-initial discourse marker with negative semantics does not necessarily connote a negative meaning. Mendoza-Denton (1999) has documented how, in the speech of many modern American English speakers, the use of *no* as a turn-initial discourse marker can convey agreement rather than denial:

A: Why don't you do it like this, it's better that way.
S: No, yeah, you're right. (Mendoza-Denton 1999: 282)

In the same way, it is common in many current dialects of English for turn-initial *no* to serve as a way of introducing novel observations, such that there is a *no* with each new "camera shot", as in this recent exchange the author was in:

> J: So you spent six years in New York, nine in L.A., and then . . . Toledo.
> T: (laughter) No, it was really hard at first, but after a while the low cost of living starts to become really attractive.

Nɔ́ɔmɔ can be assumed to have become a new-information marker in like fashion, the negative semantics of *no more* bleaching into a pragmatic guide-post marking a new development in a narrative or conversation.

4.2 *New-information marker nɔ́ɔ as a post-emergence development*

Our question at this point is whether new-information marker *nɔ́ɔ* was present in Saramaccan at its origins; if so, that would support an idea that creolization alone can yield deeply conventionalized marking of pragmatic nuance, and that increasing complexity is not a significant aspect of the morphing of creoles over time.

First, because a *no more* derivate has a foregrounding function in all three creoles today, we assume that this feature was present in their parent: the usage of *no more* in this particular function is too idiosyncratic (i.e. found in no other creole language or even older language known to me) to suppose that it emerged independently in all three.

This assumption is supported by the fact that *no more* already has this function in our earliest detailed description of Sranan, a dictionary of 1783 (Schumann 1783). Alongside citations showing that the clause-final usages of *no more* have already lexicalized into their current functions:

"definitely":

(34) *killi-man   musse   dedde,   <u>no morro</u>.*
     kill-man   must   die   no more
     "A murderer has to die, no questions asked." (trans. from German: *ein Mörder muss partout sterben, da hilft nichts davor*)

"only":

(35) <u>*no morro*</u>   *tu   jari,*   <u>*no morro*</u>   *passa,   sinse   mi   kommotto*
     no more   two   years   no more   pass   since   1s   exit

     janda   wantron.
     there   one_time

     "It's only two years so far since I left there." (trans. from German: *es sind nur erst 2 Jahr, es ist noch nicht über 2 Jahr, seitdem ich von dort weg bin*)

We find the citation below. The clause-initial *no more* has no ready translation (i.e. is left untranslated into German). To translate it as "definitely" or "only" would lead to incoherence. This suggests, given the foregrounding function of *nomo* in this very position in the modern language, that this usage of *no morro* was a foregrounding one. Thus, I include in the English translation an initial *so* marking the utterance as new information:

new information:

(36) *no morro   hulanga   tem   ju   sa   libi   dea?*
      no more   how_long   time   2S   FUT   live   there
      "So how long are you going to live hereabouts?" (trans. from German:
      wie lange wirst du dich hier aufhalten?)

In Saramaccan sources of the same period, there is no indication of a foregrounding function of *no more*. However, its modern clause-final usages are already in place, as in these sentences from Johannes Riemer's 1779 dictionary (Arends and Perl 1995: 326):

"definitely":

(37) *A   tann   go   kai   no morro.*
      3S   IPFV   go   fall   no more
      "He definitely will fall."

"always":

(38) *Ju   tann   siki   no morro.*
      2S   IPFV   sick   no more
      "You are constantly ill."

"only":

(39) *Mi   killi   wan   pingo,   no morro.*
      1S   kill   one   pig   no more
      "I only shot one pig."

This means that the grammaticalization of *no more* had proceeded apace clause-finally, and it is reasonable to assume that it had also done so clause-initially. Given that the sources for Saramaccan in the eighteenth century consist only of two rather brief dictionaries (one of which was modelled on the other), it is reasonable to suppose that the absence in them of examples of a foregrounding usage of *no more* is merely accidental.

Yet at this point we could theoretically surmise that early Sranan, the parent creole to all three present-day creoles, might have had a new-information marker *no morro* at its outset, when it formed after the English settled Surinam in 1651. Two things speak against this.

First, the usage of *no more* as a new-information marker is hardly compositional, and in fact appears at first glance counterintuitive. This means that its use in such an abstract, pragmatic function would have been the product of reinterpretation over a long period of time, such as the period between 1651 and the late eighteenth century when substantial attestations first appear.

Second, the only way around the time requirement of grammaticalization would be if this usage of *no more* were, like the Saramaccan tone sandhi patterns, inherited from Fongbe at the language's birth. However, despite the rich contribution from Fongbe to the grammars of these creoles, there is no evidence that the foregrounding system is a Fongbe inheritance – neither in its incipient form in Sranan and Ndjuka nor in its more developed form in Saramaccan.

There is no item in Fongbe cognate to *nɔ́ɔmɔ* used both as a marker of new information and as an adverb expressing conviction and/or duration (e.g. Höftmann 2003; Lefebvre and Brousseau 2001; Anne-Marie Brousseau, pers. comm. May 2007). Fongbe does not mark foregrounding overtly in any fashion as conventionalized as in Saramaccan or even in Sranan and Ndjuka. For example, the spoken Fongbe text in Lefebvre and Brousseau (2001: 539–42) indicates none such, whereas even in brief sequences of spoken Saramaccan *nɔ́ɔ* often occurs with great frequency.

Thus the process most fully realized in Saramaccan has its roots in a grammar-internal morphing that began in the creole spoken on Surinamese plantations in the late seventeenth century, before the slaves escaped who went on to develop the offshoot creoles Saramaccan and Ndjuka. In view of the argument that all the Atlantic English-based creoles, including the Surinam trio, trace back to a single creole born in West Africa, St Kitts, or Barbados (Baker 1999; McWhorter 2000), we can assume that the new-information marking described here began in Surinam rather than deriving from an earlier stage of the creole spoken elsewhere: the other Atlantic English-based creoles contain no comparable mechanism (although the clause-final usage of *no more* as "only" is a shared feature among them all).

4.3 *Nɔ́ɔ and multifunctionality*

In a broader sense, in Saramaccan *no more* has made an awesomely multifarious contribution to both the grammar and lexicon of the language. There is even one further development from *nɔ́ɔmɔ*, presumably via the "only" homonym of *nɔ́ɔ*: the "soft" member of a pair of interrogative markers. The neutral member is *ɔ*:

(40) I   ábi   tjiká   ɔ?
      2s   have   suffice Q
      "Do you have enough?"

Nɔ, however, lends a gentler tone to an interrogation:

(41) Tío   dédɛ   nɔ?
      Uncle   dead   Q
      "Oh dear, is Uncle dead?"

A minimal pair:

(42) I   kɛ́   baláki   ɔ?
      2s   want   vomit   Q
      "Do you want to throw up?"

(43) I   kɛ́   baláki   nɔ?
      2s   want   vomit   Q
      "Now, is it that you need to throw up, sweetie?"

In sum, then, *no more* has yielded a new-information marker, an intensifying pragmatic adverb "definitely", another adverb "continuously", an adverb "only", and an interrogative marker. This is a useful demonstration of how creole languages wrest the full, nuanced lexical and grammatical equipment of a natural human language from the limited lexicon resulting from pidginization, given that the Surinam creoles are based on a mere 600 English words (Koefoed and Taranskeen 1996: 120).

$$nɔ́ɔmɔ \text{ "no more"} > \begin{cases} nɔ́ɔ \text{ new-information marker} \\ nɔ́ɔmɔ \text{ "definitely"} > nɔ́ɔmɔ > \text{"continuously"} \\ nɔ́ɔ \text{ "only"} > nɔ \text{ interrogative marker} \end{cases}$$

4.4 *The diachrony of hɛ̃́*

The usage of *hɛ̃́* as a new-information marker in the past tense also emerged independently of the languages spoken by the creators of Saramaccan. There has been a suggestion otherwise, which does not stand up to scrutiny.

In its phonetic aspect, *hɛ̃́*, albeit traditionally translated as "then", is not a predictable reflex of English [ðɛn]. According to the regular rendition of English words in Saramaccan, one would expect [d] rather than [h] (e.g. *dísi* < "this"). Meanwhile, it happens that *hɛ̃́* is identical phonetically to the tonic form of the third person singular pronoun. Boretzky (1983: 110–11) suggested a reason for this that would explain the anomalous [h]: namely that *hɛ̃́* is not a reflex of *then* at all. He suggested that the homonymy between the pronoun and the "then" word is modelled on a similar likeness between the words for "he" and "and then" in Ewe (*éyé*) and Yoruba (*òun*).

However, Boretzky wrote at a time when research on slave shipments and correspondences between creoles and individual African languages were not as advanced as they have since become. It was once thought, for example, that the grammar of Saramaccan had been created by speakers of as many as a dozen West African languages (cf. Byrne 1987). However, subsequently neither historical research on the provenance of slaves in Surinam, etymological study of the Saramaccan lexicon, nor examination of which African languages Saramaccan grammar corresponds with most closely, have identified Ewe and Yoruba speakers as having played a significant part in the development of Saramaccan. Rather, all indications have been that Fongbe was the primary model; and there is no homonymy between "him" and "and then" in Fongbe.

In fact, the Ewe and Yoruba accounts are not necessary. *Hέ* is a plausible development from [ðɛn], albeit not following the more general *Lautgesetze*. The steps would have been the following:

1. [ðɛn] > [dɛn] (*this* > [disi])
2. [dɛn] > [nɛn] (In Sranan and Ndjuka, copula *da* > *na*; also, in Ndjuka, "then" is *neen* from original [den]; a short form is *ne*, which we have seen in Sranan, where it is the only form.)
3. [nɛn] > [ɛn] (In Saramaccan, heavily used grammatical items can lose initial alveolar consonants; e.g. original locative marker *na* > *a*, *na* now surviving largely as a morphophonemic alternative; copula *da* > *a* in sentences with a fronted possessive *U mí a̱ dí búku* 'POSS 1S COP DEF book' "The book is mine".)
4. [ɛn] > [hɛn] (analogously to a prothetic [h] in various vowel-initial English words as rendered in Saramaccan: *hánsi* "ant" < *ants*, *hógi* "evil" < *ugly*).

(This analysis leaves to speculation at which point in Saramaccan word-final nasal consonants eroded and left behind nasality on the preceding vowel as phonemic, a phenomenon the timing of which is obscured in documentation by orthographic conventions.)

Thus *hέ* is not, as the Boretzky analysis suggested, a sequential marker that Saramaccan got "for free" because speakers of West African languages were inclined to use the phonetic shape of the third person pronoun as a word meaning "then" as well. *Hέ* developed independently of West African influence as a natural phonetic evolution from English *then*, and took its place as a

tense-specific new-information marker unknown in English or Fongbe. *Hέ*
was part of the Saramaccan grammar-internal development of complexity.[4]

4.5 *But* how *complex?*

Although new-information marking in Saramaccan is certainly an interesting,
hitherto unacknowledged complexity in its grammar, it also teaches us that
just as creoles do not initially emerge with the mass of complexity typical of
millennia-old grammars, so too they do not accrete such a mass in the course of
just a few centuries. Where creoles do exhibit complexity, this does not reach a
superlative degree on a cross-linguistic scale. That is not an accident: it is
a symptom of youth.

For example, the overt tracking of information structure in Saramaccan is
analogous to the obligatory focus tracking in Philippine languages like Tagalog, which obligatorily marks focus on a sentential constituent with both a
trigger particle *ang* and affixal markers that vary according to the constituent
in focus (Schachter 1987: 941), as in (44). (In the glosses here, AT = agent
trigger, PT = patient trigger, DT = dative trigger, BT = benefactive trigger,
TG = trigger marker, AC = actor, DR = directional.)

(44) a. actor:

    <u>Mag-aalis</u> ang tindero ng bigas sa sako
    AT.PROG-take_out TG storekeeper PT rice DR sack

    para sa babae.
    BEN woman

    "The storekeeper will take some rice out of a/the sack for a/the woman."

  b. patient:

    Aalis-<u>in</u> ng tindero *ang bigas* sa sako
    PROG.take_out-PT AC storekeeper TG rice DR sack

    para sa babae.
    BEN woman

    "A/the storekeeper will take the rice out of a/the sack for a/the woman."

  c. directional:

    Aalis-<u>an</u> ng tindero ng bigas *ang sako*
    PROG.take_out-DT AC storekeeper PT rice TG sack

---

[4] This is a revision of my cautious willingness to accept the Ewe derivation in McWhorter
(2005: 374).

para sa   babae.
BEN   woman
"A/the storekeeper will take some rice out of the sack for a/the woman."

d. benefactive:

Ipag-aalis		*ng*	*tindero*	*ng*	*bigas*	*sa*	*sako*
PROG.take_out-DT		AC	storekeeper	PT	rice	TG	sack

ang   *babae.*
TG   woman

"A/the storekeeper will take some rice out of the sack for a/the woman."

However, the Tagalog system includes allomorphic variation of the affix according to grammatical relation, and involves marking the focus with two morphemes. The system is, therefore, more complex than that of Saramaccan. Foregrounding is also more obligatory in Tagalog than in Saramaccan: in Tagalog it is completely grammaticalized, whereas in Saramaccan it is better described as pragmaticized. This is to be expected, given that Tagalog has existed for countless centuries longer than Saramaccan, and emerges from the presumably unbroken transmission of an ancient language over tens of thousands of years.

Similarly, other features that have arisen in Saramaccan over time do show that the language "has grammar", without doing much to suggest that the grammar of a creole is indistinguishable in overall complexity from that of (say) Yoruba or Bengali. For example, the two Saramaccan copulas can subdivide the semantic domain of nonverbal predication more finely than Fongbe does – but at present only optionally, and other languages can subdivide the same domain among more morphemes than two (McWhorter 2005: 117–18, 125–6). The original Saramaccan predicate negator *ná* has split into two which subdivide the domain of negation differently, but not in more *complex* fashion, than Fongbe's two negators, while, again, many languages subdivide the negation domain between many more morphemes. The Austronesian language Muna of Sulawesi has an equative negator, a general predicate negator, a predicate negator used for the future, one used with participles, and a negative imperative marker:

(45) a. *Anoa   suano-mo   guru-mani.*
          he   NEG-PRF   teacher-1P.EXCL
          "He is no longer our teacher." (van den Berg 1989: 212)

      b. *A   Ntaapo-apo   miina   na-sumampu.*
          ART   Ntaapo-apo   NEG   3s-go_down
          "Ntaapoapo did not come down." (p. 207)

c. *Pa*   *a-kumala*   *we*   *sikola*   *naewine.*
   FUT.NEG 1S-go   LOC   school   tomorrow
   "I will not go to school tomorrow." (p. 210)

d. *Foo*   *aini*   *pata*   *ni-uta-ku.*
   mango this   NEG   PAP-pick-my
   "This is not a mango that I have picked." (p. 211)

e. *Ko*   *mo-limpu*   *itu.*
   NEG   IMP-forget that
   "Don't forget that." (p. 229)

Or again, Saramaccan has morphed into a language possessing a modest assortment of morphophonemic rules – but they are not only modest in tally but phonetically shallow (McWhorter 2005: 116–21).

However, it is hardly impossible that in several centuries to come, *nɔ́ɔ* may become a suffix (perhaps [-*na*]) obligatorily appended to foregrounded arguments. Meanwhile, *hɛ́* could easily lose its initial consonant and nasalize the vowel in the pronominal following it, perhaps yielding a paradigm of subject pronouns phonetically coloured by nasalization used exclusively in matrix clauses after adverbial subordinate clauses. The *nɔ́ɔ hɛ́* configuration could become frequent enough that in a future stage of Saramaccan, the past-tense new-information marker could be perhaps [nɛ́] or [nwɛ́] contrasting with nonpast *nɔ́ɔ*, and perhaps constituting the beginnings of a paradigm of foregrounding morphemes indexed to tense or aspect or other grammatical contrasts.

These are, of course, speculations. The main point is that Saramaccan is well positioned to morph into such directions, and already has an overt marking of a feature which is left largely to intonation and context in its source languages – as well as countless other languages of the world.

5 Complexity is more than inflection

This Saramaccan feature also demonstrates that grammatical complexity involves much more than inflectional affixation. Surely this is known to all linguists in the intellectual sense. However, there is a habit of mind that encourages linguists to think first of inflections when the topic of complexity is at hand.

This is partly because inflectional affixation is so readily documented even in brief grammars, is subject to the tidiness of counting, and has been so amply analysed in linguistic science (hence inflection is the topic in Kusters' 2003 foundational monograph on comparative complexity in grammars).

The focus on inflection is also a conditioned reflex driven by our familiarity with highly inflected European languages. The problem is that this focus can distract us from the nature of grammatical complexity in a broader sense. For example, if the new-information markers in Saramaccan actually were already inflections, they would long ago have been highlighted as evidence that creole languages "have grammar".

An inflection-free language like the Chinese variety Xiang marks at least eleven tense and aspect categories overtly (Mandarin marks five):

(46)   Aspect markers in Xiang

da	past
ga	perfective
gada	perfect
kelai	experiential
zai(goli)	progressive
da	durative stative
ji	durative as continuative background
can	durative as "vivid" continuative background
reduplication	brief delimitative
can	delimitative compared to another event
(da)zhe	trial or "for just a little while" delimitative

This paradigm encodes subtle differences such as that between simultaneous events whose conjunction is unremarkable versus those whose conjunction is pragmatically unexpected (aspect markers glossed ASP):

(47)   (a)   *Zhan¹San¹   da²   ji   kou³sau⁴   zou³lou⁴.*
             John   make   ASP   whistle   walk
             "John walked while whistling."

       (b)   *Zhan¹San¹   kan⁵   can   (kan⁵   can)   ku²   gada.*
             John   watch   ASP   watch   ASP   cry   ASP
             "John cried while watching." (Zhou 1998: 12–13)

Ngadha, an affixless Austronesian language of Flores, makes ample use of modal particles to convey pragmatic meanings, in a fashion similar to German. Certainly all natural languages can convey such pragmatic meanings using mechanisms of intonation or phrasal collocation; but where grammars develop entrenched monomorphemic indications of such meanings, it qualifies as added complexity. For example, here is *dzaö laä* "I go" modified with just a few of the particles:

(48)   Some Nghada modal particles (Arndt 1933: 27; my translation from
        German)

dzaö <u>mu</u> laä   "I'm going, whatever happens."
dzaö <u>mu</u> le laä   "I'm keeping on walking along, whatever happens."
dzaö <u>mu mara</u> laä   "I'm going whatever happens, and I'll deal with the
                            circumstances."

Cases like these need to be kept in mind when assessing development of
complexity in creoles. The current tendency is to operate under a tacit
assumption that the complexity to watch out for in creoles is the development
of inflectional affixation and/or marking of the categories typically associated
with it.

The problem is that this has often yielded less than promising results. For
example, DeGraff's (1993) argument that subject pronouns in Haitian Creole
are actually null-subject syntactic clitics (i.e. close to being inflections) was
intended to imply that Haitian was a step away from displaying subject
prefixes like, for example, Bantu languages. Yet Déprez (1992), Cadely
(1994), and Roberts (1999) have conclusively refuted this argument.

Another example of an attempt to identify inflectional complexity in
creoles that has not been successful has referred to Nubi Creole Arabic. Arabic
assigns nouns arbitrarily to a proliferation of "broken plural" patterns. In
Nubi Creole Arabic, plurality is indicated instead via a suffix *-à*. This would
appear to suggest that pluralization is less complex in Nubi than in older
Arabic; but Kihm (2003: 355–7) claims, on the basis of scattered fossilizations
in Nubi of the broken plural and some other pluralization strategies, that the
Nubi system is actually less predictable – i.e. more complex – than that of
older Arabic. Clearly, however, the fact that the suffixation of *-à* is the
productive strategy while the other cases are compact sets of exceptions
learned by rote cannot qualify as more complex (or irregular) than the living
system in Arabic itself exemplified in Table 10.1.

The development of inflectional affixation is only one of many directions in
which a grammar may move over time. There is certainly no general tendency
for analytic languages to show signs of developing inflections in the near
future – the Chinese languages, and many other Sino–Tibetan languages as
well as Mon–Khmer, Thai, and Niger–Congo languages, would contradict
that. Creoles tend strongly to be analytic, and there is no a priori reason to see
inflectional affixation as the most likely or interesting complexity that they
may develop. Other types of complexity which are common in analytic
languages include ergativity (e.g. in many Polynesian languages, indicated
via particles), alienability distinction in possession (which is also incipient in

Table 10.1. Broken plural patterns in Modern Standard Arabic

Singular	Plural	
qalam	*ʿaqlām*	"pen"
bayt	*buyūt*	"house"
kalb	*kilāb*	"dog"
kitāb	*kutub*	"book"
dawla	*duwal*	"country"
šahr	*ʿašhur*	"month"
wazīr	*wuzarāʿ*	"minister"
ṣadīq	*ʿaṣdiqāʿ*	"friend"

Saramaccan: McWhorter 2005: 116–17), evidential marking, and numeral classifiers (which can be analysed as a kind of grammatical gender marking).

Here, for example, is a sentence from an analytic language, Akha, a Sino-Tibetan language of Southeast Asia:

(49) ŋà <u>nɛ</u> àjɔq <u>áŋ</u> áshì thì <u>shì</u> bìq <u>ma.</u>
      1S ERG   3S   ABS fruit one CLF give EVIDENTIAL-MARKER
      "I gave him one fruit." (Hansson 2003: 243)

There are no inflectional affixes in Akha. Yet in the sentence above, we see ergative and absolutive marking, a numeral classifier (one of an entire paradigm in Akha), and an evidential marker, this one used to mark conviction exclusively in the first person (evidential markers often occur in first and non-first person shapes in Akha). Russian, to take an example of a highly inflected language, marks none of these distinctions overtly.

It is in this light that we must view the emergence of a system of new-information marking via particles in Saramaccan. This system is distinctly un-Indo-European, and yet in the cross-linguistic sense it counts as an accreted complexity. Tacitly to suppose that future stages of Saramaccan – or of other creoles – will be forms of language more like English or Dutch is arbitrary. Rather than becoming a European-type language, Saramaccan could just as easily morph into a language like Akha.

11

Orality versus literacy as a dimension of complexity

UTZ MAAS

1 Complexity of a language or complexity of a register

In this chapter,[1] I will look at complexity of language from a functional perspective, taking the full array of linguistic practices into account:

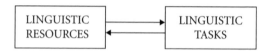

There are differences within the various tasks, usually defined by different *domains* of language practice, and there are differences between the linguistic resources employed to cope with these domains. A cover term for this is *register*. In all linguistic communities, we must differentiate between at least three different registers:

- an *intimate* register, calibrated to face-to-face communication with familiars;
- an *informal* register, calibrated to communication with unknown persons in a more public sphere;
- a *formal* register, defined by situation-independent criteria for the linguistic form. In societies making use of writing, writing is calibrated to the formal register (or better: it is founded on it).

Register differences have consequences for their structural articulation: in an intimate register, say in the daily cooperation between members of a family or a clan, mutual knowledge of the actors and the evident situational definition of the communicative aims can dispense with much structural elaboration in

[1] I am grateful to participants at the Leipzig workshop for comments. Geoffrey Sampson, John McWhorter, N. Himmelmann, and John Peterson made most helpful comments on an earlier draft of the paper, and John Peterson did his best to improve my English.

the utterances. Differentiated structural resources only become necessary when the context of interpretation itself must be produced by symbolic means. Thus, structural complexity depends on what developmental psychologists call the *decentring* of the conceptualization implied by differentiated human activity.

In a functional perspective, we compare linguistic registers with respect to their structural resources. Thus, language becomes a dependent variable: in many societies the different registers (or linguistic domains) are articulated by different languages – which *a fortiori* are structured in regard to the tasks they must cope with. This must also be the yardstick for comparing the structure of secondary "vehicular" languages (pidgins or the recently much discussed *basic varieties* of immigrants), with fully-fledged languages, which are made use of in formal registers (and which are also used as a second language by most bilingual speakers of the vehicular languages).

After some preliminary definitions of terms (in section 2), I shall illustrate the non-homogeneity of linguistic resources made use of in linguistic practice with data from research areas in which I have some experience:

- the historical development of literate languages (section 3);
- literate practices, i.e. linguistic editing when speech is transposed to writing, especially with immigrant children (section 4);
- constraints of linguistic elaboration, with regard to Bible translations (section 5).

2 Some preliminary definitions: literacy and writing

To a rough approximation I shall distinguish three levels of analysis:

- *scribal* practice, i.e. writing in a mechanical sense;
- *literate* structures (functionally defined) – I shall call structures calibrated to the other functional extreme, i.e. face-to-face communication, *orate*;
- *normative* aspects (especially orthography in a narrower sense).

Writing is distinguished from speech by medium. This refers to the material act, the *scribal* activity. Technical aspects of literacy can be included, i.e. representing phonetic/phonological forms by graphic ones. This presupposes mapping sounds onto some idealized word forms (much of what is dealt with in phonology is presupposed here). The scribal aspect of literacy is independent of the textual structure. In this sense, the act of writing does not change the textual structure, which is the domain of *literate* activities. These are adapted to the task of addressing a generalized "other": e.g. not presupposing a cooperative other for making sense of what is said, not relying on the situational context, and ignoring the physical constraints of the face-to-face communication (restrictions on short-term memory, the linear dimensionality of speech, etc.). Writing is learned in an institutional context where functional aspects are overlaid by normative traditional tasks. Writing is usually not learned to convey a message but to reproduce (written) cultural patterns (often in a religious context). These normative patterns can disguise the functional structures – and are often conflated with them, for example in much of the debate about writing focusing on orthography. The distinction between these three aspects is an analytical task.

The critical literate threshold is crossed when linguistic structures are produced in writing that do not exist in spoken language, i.e. when writing is not the transcription of a spoken text. There are two aspects of this threshold I will further comment on:

- the formal structures made use of, where I shall focus on the resources for integrating propositional content into a sentence;
- the language(s) that make these structures available.

The formal aspect highlights what is usually focused on in discussing literate *cultures*. The critical question is whether cultural complexity can be transferred to the linguistic resources employed. The aim of my chapter is to explore the interdependency of the relations in this field. This is in line with recent linguistic research in register variation that takes into account written language as well, such as the work of Wallace Chafe (summarized in Chafe 1994) and especially Douglas Biber, who has developed a detailed grid for analysis (Biber 1988; Biber et al. 1999). In keeping with this tradition, I will differentiate between *orate* and *literate structures*.

3 Adapting vernacular languages to literacy: the case of medieval German

The literate threshold becomes visible when we look at the historical development of our modern languages. In early medieval times they were exclusively spoken languages, the formal register and especially writing being reserved for Latin in Western societies. What we do have in the way of early documents in these vernacular languages shows casual transpositions of pre-existing oral texts: riddles, jokes, and the like, with which the medieval scribes amused themselves, scribbling them on the margins of their Latin texts. In these cases, the task is limited to *scribal* activities. This is true of longer literary texts as well, especially epics, that originated in oral practices. Even where literary texts were (later) composed in written form, such as longer historical texts, they could also make use of structures present in oral narratives. In narratives, a scenario of events is presented, with a temporal (chronological) dimension, more or less conflated with the causal state of affairs and/or motivations of the protagonists. Of course, narrations can be complex: by shifting the perspective, by the interplay of foregrounding and backgrounding, etc. But all this is present in oral narratives as well, although filtered by the constraints of on-line processing.

On the other hand, the structure is quite different in other genres that are tied to the written form, as e.g. legal instruments (contracts etc.). In earlier times, they were not only articulated in Latin, but also made use of sophisticated literate techniques to package the propositional content. These resources were not available in the vernacular languages, since they were not needed there as long as legal texts were the exclusive domain of professionals. The situation was different, however, when at least one of the parties concerned did not understand Latin, as was usual in later feudal societies where most of the gentry had no Latin education. The consequences can be seen in bilingual charters from the epoch: there is a plain Latin version which remained authoritative in case a conflict later arose, but a vernacular translation was also given to the non-literate party. An extract from such a bilingual charter will illustrate this situation: a contract from 1251 between the bishop of Cologne and the local count of Jülich (Neuß).[2]

The Latin text does not cause any problems of interpretation. In the following extract, its words are numbered to serve as reference for the vernacular version (to be discussed later). Word forms are glossed for grammatical categories, expressed by the underlined suffixes:[3]

1	2	3	4	5	6	7
[*Insuper*	*ordinatum*	*est*]	[*quod*	*litteram*	*dudum*	[*inter*
above	lay_down:PAP.ASE	be:PRS.3S	that	letter:AS(F)	before	between

8	9	10	11	12	13
archiep<iscopu>m	*et*	*comitem*	*memoratos*]	[*pro*	*sinceritate*
archbishop:AS(M)	and	count:AS(M)	mention:PAP.APM	for	sincerity:BS(F)

14	15	16	17	18	19	20
amicicie	*conseruanda*]	*sex*	*viri*	[*de*	*quibus*	*in*
friendship:GS(F)	maintaining:GV.BSF	six	men:NP(M)	of	whom:BP	in

---

[2] The documents can be found in Wilhelm (1932–63); our example is from vol. 1, p. 31. A groundbreaking work is Schulze (1975), which discusses this example on pp. 105–8.

[3] Nominal and adjectival inflections are coded here as combinations of the following codes: N nominative, A accusative, G genitive, D dative, B ablative; S singular, P plural; M masculine, F feminine, E (rather than N) neuter. Abbreviations for grammatical categories not on the standard list (pp. ix–xi) are FUTEX future perfect and GV gerundive.

21	22	23	24	25	26	27
ipsa	littera	mencio_	fit]	[si	eis	non
same:BSF	letter:BS(F)	mention:[NS](F)	make:PASS.PRS.3S	if	them:DP	not

28	29	30	31	32
[sufficiens	visa]	fuerit]	emendabunt]	[assumptis
suffice:PRP.NS	see:PAP.NSF	be:FUTEX.3S	amend:FUT.3P	take_up:PAP.BP

33	34	35	36	37	38	39
ad	hoc	sibi	aliis]	[[quod	duxerint	assumendos]
to	this	self	other:BP	that	lead:FUTEX.3P	take_up:GV.APM

40	41	42	43	44
ijdem	sex	viri	potestatem	habebunt]
same:NPM	six	men.NP(M)	power:AS(F)	have:FUT.3P

A somewhat free translation would be: "Above is laid down (1–3) that the six men (16–17) who are mentioned in this instrument ["letter"] (18–24) can amend (31) the former contract (5–6) between the aforementioned archbishop and count (7–11) with the aim of maintaining sincerity of friendship (12–15), if it seems to them not adequate (25–30), by calling in other [persons] (32–6); these six men (40–42) shall have the power (43–4) to call [them] in to accomplish [this] (37–9)."

The parsing of such involved *periods*[4] is well defined by the morphological markers of Latin. In this case, where ten propositions (indicated by the square brackets) are packaged into a single sentence, subordination is marked by subordinating conjunctions (*quod*, 4, 37) or by specialized nonfinite predicates: converbal (32), specialized nominal, as the complement of a verbal predicate (39) or a preposition (15), or as an attribute, where cohesion is secured by agreement marking (11, 28, 32).

How difficult it was at the time to replicate this structure in the vernacular language is shown by the German translation (in this case in a Ripuarian variety). I give only an interlinear translation into English, with figures referring to the words of the Latin original:

Den	brief	de	gemachit	ist	tuschin	deme	bischowe	inde	deme	greuin
the	instrument	that	made	is	between	the	bishop	and	the	count
	5			7		8	9		10	

---

[4] *Period* is the leading concept of contemporary grammar for (complex) sentence formation; cf. p. 199 of chapter 13, below.

van	*uruntschaffe*	*inde*	*uan*	*minnin*	*zehaldinne*	*die*	*seisse*	*die*	*da*	*inne*
of	friendship	and	of	love	to.hold	the	six	who	there	in
12	14			13	15		16	19	(20–22)	

benant	*sent*	*den*	*sulin*	*si*	*bezerin*	*inde*	*baz*	*ordinierin*	*owe*
mentioned	are	that	shall	they	improve	and	better	arrange	if
23	24				31				25

dir	*brief*	*on*	*niet*	*wale*	*inbehait*	*inde*	*dat*	*zedune*	*sulin*	*si*	*gewalt*
this	instrument	them	not	well	pleases	and	that	to.do	shall	they	power
—		26	27	28	29–30		(37 – 39)				43

hauin	*ze*	*nemene*	*zu*	*in*	*die*	*Giene*	*die*	*on*	*dar*	*zu*	*wgin*
have	to	take	to	them	the	ones	who	them	this	to	deserve
44	38				36 (?)				(39 ?)		

Even in modern German it is not easy to reproduce the period formation of the Latin original. By itself, the medieval German text will not have been comprehensible to a contemporary reader who did not know its content beforehand, just as it is incomprehensible to a modern reader.

There are of course some necessary formal changes: unlike in Latin, a NP in German requires a determiner, the subject of a finite clause must be represented at least by a pronoun, etc. But the contemporary translation did more than just implement these formal adaptations: it replicated the complex sentence formation by calquing Latin constructions (gerundival, 15) on the one hand, and broke up overly compact constructions by anaphoric elements on the other (*dir brief* in the conditional clause, 25ff.). Present-day German does not possess the differentiated grammatical resources to bring about cohesion in a complex period like this one (i.e. marking the government relation on the dependent element, marking complex constituents by agreement, etc.) any more than the medieval language did. Thus, the translator sometimes had to capitulate; for example, he did not translate the complex structure in 32–9.

It took a long time to elaborate the vernacular languages so that they could articulate complex literate texts, and Latin served as the model: Latin texts were "sparring partners" for writers struggling to cope with these tasks. They had to calque Latin structures until a flexible literate grammar was also available in languages like German. This process continued until the seventeenth and eighteenth centuries, when the modern syntactic structure had been established (for a good summary, see Admoni 1970, 1990):

- having a strict differentiation of main and subordinate clauses by word order, marking the main clause by the "verbal frame" (*Satzklammer*), with the discontinous arrangement of complex predicates, in which the finite element of the predicate appeared in second position and the nonfinite element in final position (see section 4 for an example);
- having the syntactic field of a clause polarized with respect to verbal (predicative) and nominal elements with a tendency to group inflection (phrasal marking); e.g. adjectives are only inflected in an NP, not in a VP (as adverbs or as predicative adjectives);
- having reduced case marking; e.g. genitive marking is only used adnominally, no longer adverbally, etc.

So long as German could not draw on these resources for the literate register, it could not oust Latin as the dominant written language: until the early seventeenth century the majority of books printed in Germany were printed in Latin. Thus, when looking for the formation of a literate German language, we have to reckon with a long bilingual phase: vernacular writing began with scribal activities in the eighth century, but only in the seventeenth century was German fit to replace Latin in all linguistic domains.

Orthography has been an important tool in this long process of structural elaboration in the literate register. Orthography is a means of helping the reader access complex literate texts. The printers, all of them formally trained in Latin and used to putting into print texts with involved Latin periods, knew of the difficulites of parsing texts without the differentiated grammatical markers of Latin. They attempted to remedy this by experimenting with additional grammatical orthographic markers. However, this was of course not necessary when the printed text reproduced a text which already existed in an oral form (say a poem or an epic). But when in the sixteenth century the demand for printed texts of a more abstract nature dramatically increased in the wake of religious strife and civil wars throughout Europe, the printers tried to make these texts accessible to a lay public that could not read the Latin originals. The printers found a means to compensate for the lack of government marking in the modern languages such as German, English, French, or Danish by recycling the older habit of capitalization for all kind of emphasis into a grammatical means of parsing literate sentences: marking the head of every expanded nominal group in a sentence by a capital letter, thereby marking also the right border of the syntactic group (NP) in the Germanic languages.

This orthographic practice was established all over Europe until the eighteenth century, but only Gemany has retained it (see Maas 2007). Most linguists would agree that orthography, especially sentence-internal capitalization, is only a superfluous complication of writing. When using a one-dimensional model of language, ignoring register differentiation, this is understandable. There is no need to capitalize texts with an orate structure, e.g., the medieval literary texts. But grammatical capitalization makes sense when readers are to be given access to the complex argumentation in political, religious, or scientific texts. Although it represents a "complication" of writing, it also facilitates the task of reading these kinds of text, i.e. texts with a literate structure.

It is evident that a language such as German was simpler before it was put into literate use, especially when we take into account literate structures such as orthography. But the linguistic tasks of German speakers who had to cope with literate practices during this time were more complex: they had to master both German and Latin. By integrating literate structures into one language (i.e. German), the array of language resources was optimized.

A comprehensive study of linguistic complexity should take account of this concept of resource arrays. What I have illustrated here with an example from German is a general scheme of elaboration of linguistic resources within a language community. In all linguistic states of affairs where we can trace this development, a similarly long initial phase of bilingualism, making use of different languages for different registers, is evident:

- In the Babylonian empire, Sumerian was used for writing until Akkadian had developed grammatical structures adapted to literate tasks on the Sumerian model.
- Latin literacy was calqued on Greek, which remained the language of culture and scientific writing during the Roman Empire.
- All modern Western literate languages were elaborated within the matrix of the Latin literate culture (as Eastern European languages, beginning with Gothic, were elaborated within the matrix of Greek).

In all these developments, the critical stage was reached when formal literate tasks could be articulated by the same language that articulated the intimate register – which in all of these cases took a very long time. How long it takes to reach this point depends on factors which are still not entirely clear: a relatively short development (nevertheless taking several centuries) was needed in ancient (monolingual) Greece, where literate culture to a certain extent took the structure of orate texts (e.g. with the Homeric epics as their model). Thus societal bilingualism can be a retarding factor, as can be seen in medieval European societies – but it can also be a factor of tremendous acceleration, as can be seen in modern Third World societies. In any case, no conclusive results can be attained without analysing the societal constellation where linguistic structures are employed – where a more detailed analysis has been done, societal bilingualism proves to be a decisive factor of development.

4 Ontogenesis: the literate follow-up to language acquisition

The language situation in a society such as Germany is defined by a language that allows one to articulate all registers. This makes the language more complex, compared to what it would be if it could only articulate the intimate register – but it makes linguistic competence less complex than in cases where different languages are needed for the different registers. Linguistic complexity is the price for linguistic integration of different registers. In this case it has a correlate in the family relation between the linguistic structures that articulate intimate communication as well as formal practices. Children that grow up under these conditions not only learn a language, but by learning to shift between registers they learn to *abduce*, as Peirce would have called it, the structural differences between them.

Children socialized into a Western society cannot help but conform to this process. This is true even of children growing up in families living at a certain distance from the literary culture, as shown by our research over the last twenty years in Osnabrück on the acquisition of literate practice by immigrant children in Germany. The research design is simple: we record oral narratives by these children, which they then later listen to and write down. The instructions they receive ask simply for a transcription of what is on the tape. The first example is one I have already quoted many times, an extract of a narrative by Tülay, a ten-year-old Turkish girl:

Orally:

1	2	3	4	5	6	7	8
un	ḍa	maɪnə	'mʊtɒ	ʊnt	maɪnə	ʃvɛstɐ	di:
and	then	my	mother	and	my	sister	TOPIC

9	10	11	12	13	14
vɑ:n	'glaʊb	ɪç	bɪs	ʊm	tsvœlf
were	believe	I	until	at	twelve

Written:

1'	2'	2a'	3	4	5	6	7
und	*dann*	*ist*	*meine*	*Mutter*	*und*	*meine*	*Schwester*
and	then	is	my	mother	and	my	sister

12′	14′	14a′	14b′
bis	*12.00*	*Uhr*	*geblieben.*
until	twelve	o'clock	stayed

The written version shows that Tülay has edited her spoken text while putting it into writing, thereby turning an orate text into a more literate one. The traces of a centred, addressee-oriented practice are thereby eliminated:

- The focus marking by postponed *di:* (8) is such an orienting device that is left out (this is quite typical of such texts).
- Attitudinal expressions, also used for disguising planning problems, such as 'glaʊb ɪç (10–11), are eliminated.

On the other hand, the literate structure is also augmented:

- The descriptive content of the words used is enriched, also of non-rhematic words, e.g. the predicate is lexically elaborated (*sein* "to be" [9] > *bleiben* "to stay" [14b]).
- The syntax is more compact, making use of the "verbal frame" of modern German, with the functional element that articulates semantic finiteness in second position and the propositional predicate (the lexical verb) in final position, i.e. discontinuous *ist* (2a′) … *geblieben* (14b′).

There is a problem with analyses of such examples that I can only allude to here: a literate bias is almost unavoidable in the syntactic analysis of orate texts. We are used to projecting literate structure (sentences) onto the textual chunks in the oral version, where the utterances show only the juxtaposition of intonational units with minimal internal morphosyntactic structure and integrated in a binary structure of an opening *thematic* (presentative) element and a closing *rhematic* (focal) element. Current research has established at least some elements of this basic orate structure: the textual structure as an aggregate of propositional chunks with only one content element per intonation unit (Chafe 1994; J. Miller and Weinert 1998; J. Miller and Fernandez-Vest 2006).

This defines *ex negativo* literate structures as well. It corresponds to the constraints of oral ("online") speech production where cognitive resources are limited and bound by a myriad of simultaneous tasks in communication. In consequence, presenting a text with an orate structure to a reader, who is not in the stressed situation of orate communication, would be treating him as someone who has not mastered literate competence – an extremely impolite attitude. Giving someone *a text to read* implies addressing him as someone who is competent in decoding a literate text (not just mastering its scribal aspects, as first-graders do).

One difficulty for research is the superimposed layers of functional and normative structures. Literate structures are learned by replicating textual models. By necessity, this modelization has a normative impact – in the usual case, enhanced by the sanctioning activities of teachers. But that is not the explanation for what Tülay did, who, by the way, was seen by her teachers as a weak pupil who would not succeed in school. Yet even she could not avoid learning register variation, editing her orate text production. In our ongoing research we are currently looking for this kind of register differentiation practised by pre-schoolers without scribal know-how. To do so, we ask them to *dictate* their story after having told it, so that the adult in front of them can write it down. In this situation, most of them shift the register – dictating in a proto-literate style, editing their spontaneous narrative in a similar way.

The cultural context is an important factor here. We conducted comparative research with Moroccan children, comparing the practice of immigrant children in Germany with that of their peers in Morocco (in the region of origin), comparing the practice in all languages available (on the one side Berber, Moroccan Arabic, perhaps Standard Arabic, and on the other side German and/or French: cf. Maas and Mehlem 2003, 2005). What was most interesting was what they did with spoken varieties that they believed beforehand could not be written (not only Berber but Moroccan Arabic as well). In general they enjoyed the experiment and showed most creativity when no normative model interfered (in Berber). On the average, immigrant children achieved more orthographic consistency. In Morocco, literate culture remains the artisanal practice of specialists for a large portion of the population: they go to a professional writer (or a literate neighbour) if a letter has to be written or something written (say, a bill or a medical prescription) has to be read. Correspondingly, there were many children in Morocco, but not in our German sample, who had learned the scribal practices without mastering the differentiation of orate and literate structure – in writing they simply tried to reproduce something written they had already seen in written form (i.e. they adhered to the normative but not the functional side of literacy).

5 Social and structural constraints of linguistic elaboration: the example of Bible translations

Translations make the structural constraints of languages visible, and Bible translations are an easily accessible corpus. A good resource for examining the problems of translating the New Testament into diverse languages is Bible-Works 5 (2001). Here we can study the writers' dilemma mentioned in the discussion of the example in section 3: on the one hand, adhering to the authoritative text, calquing the period formation of Greek and Latin, and on the other adapting the translation to the "natural" patterns of the target language, elaborating them at the same time. As space does not permit an extensive discussion of textual examples, I will present only a few summary comments.

The Greek original has complex period formation even in narrative passages. Period elaboration by semantically and morphologically nonfinite secondary propositions is possible, as Greek has a rich array of specialized participial and converbal forms in combination with a rather free constituent order. The Latin version can replicate this structure, as Latin has a rather similar structure. But as far as I can see, all later versions break up the periods into sentences: although older versions even in West European languages tried to replicate the nonfinite syntax, most modern versions have revised this, transforming them into finite predicates, with interesting differences between the languages. The extreme case in the BibleWorks corpus is Haitian Creole, which presents an independent (finite) sentence for almost every predicate (finite or nonfinite) in the original.

This fits well with our expectation of a creole text – and could be seen as a confirmation of McWhorter's claim that "the world's simplest grammars are creole grammars" (McWhorter 2001a). But, given the premises of my argument, I would not see it as the reflex of shorter time depth in the development of linguistic structures in Haitian Creole, but rather as the reflex of a linguistic structure which is less used for (and *a fortiori* less adapted to) complex literate tasks. In fact, as far as I know, except for special contexts (such as evangelization), reading and writing is done in French in Haiti – if it is done at all: literacy statistics give a figure of only 42 per cent literacy.

But things are not quite that simple: we cannot deduce structural linguistic facts from societal conditions. Among other things, what makes the building of periods on the Greek and Latin models difficult in languages such as English, German, French, or Haitian Creole is the verb-second constraint in word order. Where languages do not have such a constraint, the situation is different, as in the Mongolian or Chinese translations I had analysed.[5] Mongolian is a verb-final language with a rich series of converbal secondary predicates that in principle may appear in any number before the main predicate, each operating as the predicate of the preceding clause unless otherwise marked. Thus Mongolian can replicate the period structure of the Greek original; but in doing so, it makes use of structures that articulate oral

---

[5] I thank P. Nyamaa for helping me with Mongolian and Y. Hong for helping me with Chinese.

Mongolian texts as well – the difference between them being apparently a question of online processing. Access to literate texts must be very different in Mongolian vis-à-vis Haitian: apparently no special grammatical means have to be acquired (which, however, is not to say that there are not other, more "global" means of organizing literate texts in Mongolian).

The case of Mandarin Chinese is somewhat different, although leading to a superficially similar packaging of the text. The concept of sentence is notoriously problematic in Chinese linguistics, as the categorization as main or secondary predicate does not depend on the presence of morphological markings (e.g. no overt subordination by specialized subordinating particles, no specialized verbal morphology, whether for primary or secondary predicates). The integration of longer periods is apparently a matter of packaging the propositional constituents by what might be called a kind of syntactic "clitization": dependent propositions are reduced and require information from the main proposition. In other cases, "hypotactic" binding is accomplished by a pivot in the construction. Apparently, these resources are available in spoken Mandarin as well. Again, the difference between literate and orate structures is probably a question of constraints of online production. Thus, linguistic structure does make a difference that cannot be ignored even in a functional perspective.

This cursory glimpse at different language structures provides us with at least one further aspect of linguistic complexity: the integration of different register varieties in languages such as Mongolian or Mandarin does not presuppose the "invention" of special structural means to put complex texts into writing. There is apparently no structural criterion to distinguish orate from literate texts in Mongolian and Chinese, whereas in modern German (for example) we must learn different structures, and must perhaps edit orate texts when writing them (as Tülay did in the example presented in section 4). However, we have only to learn one language for these different purposes, and

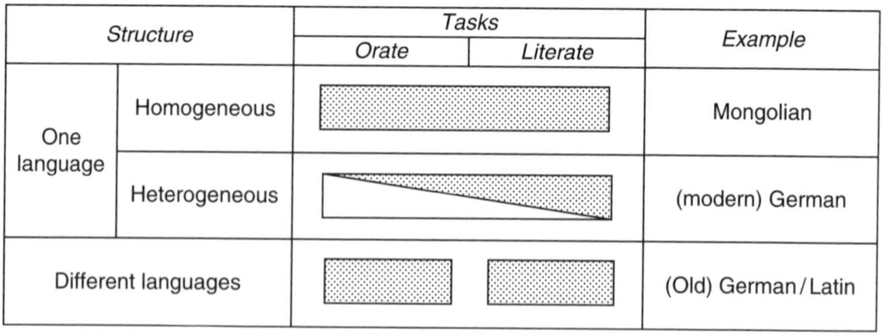

Structure		Tasks		Example
		Orate	Literate	
One language	Homogeneous			Mongolian
	Heterogeneous			(modern) German
Different languages				(Old) German / Latin

FIG. 11.1 Diverse oracy–literacy relationships

Structure	Tasks		Example
	Orate	Literate	
Different languages	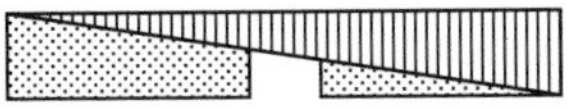		Haitian Creole / French

FIG. 11.2 A language difference evolves into a register difference

the different register structures are all in a family relationship to one another – we need not learn two languages, as was the case in medieval times (i.e. German and Latin). Of course, competent literate practices in Mongolian or Mandarin will be more than just scribal practices, representing orate texts. This results in the typological classification shown in Fig. 11.1.

Of course, the typology is not complete. In a certain sense, Mongolian (and Chinese) represent the simplest case. But the Haitian example is more complex. If we take into account the possible (but probably for the native speakers not entirely evident) family relationship between Haitian Creole and French, we can postulate a rudimentary structure (Fig. 11.2), similar to the beginnings of literarization of German.

This is in fact a complex picture, but one that is at least adequate for a situation such as in Morocco, where the spoken language (Moroccan Arabic) and the written language (Standard Arabic) are in a similarly close relationship. But they are not perceived as such: Standard Arabic is learned as a foreign language, thus exemplifying in the same way a borderline case, whereas for the vernacular language even restricted literacy (in a literary and evangelization context), as in Haiti, is lacking.

By way of conclusion, I should like to modify McWhorter's statement: the world's simplest grammars are orate grammars. There are evidently structural differences between different languages that can be mapped onto a convenient complexity scale; but even if these differences influence the pacing of the acquisition process, they do not make a crucial difference to its outcome: in all languages children master the language of their family by puberty, whatever its grammatical structure may be. Things become more complicated when grammar has to cope with literate tasks. In doing so, it has to exploit the resources of the available linguistic structures – which can mean quite different things in languages such as Mongolian and English. And of course, all this is overlaid by non-functional, but often rigid, normative patterns established in the relevant culture and, in some cases, foreign models used as sparring partners in elaborating literate structures. As Bible translations show, there is a limit to syntactic homogenization in interlingual structural elaboration – *pace* David Gil (2001). The question of linguistic complexity is a complex one, indeed.

12

Individual differences in processing complex grammatical structures

NGONI CHIPERE

1 Introduction

Other contributions in this volume have addressed the widespread assumption that all natural languages possess uniform grammatical complexity. My contribution addresses the equally widespread assumption that all native speakers possess a uniform underlying competence to process complex grammatical structures. I argue that this assumption is false. I develop the argument over three sections. In the first section, I present empirical evidence, drawn from fifty years of experimental research, that shows that native speakers vary extensively in grammatical ability. In the second section I note, however, that it has been argued that native speakers do not vary in grammatical competence but in the performance factor of working memory. Variations in working memory capacity, so the argument goes, lead to variable expression of an otherwise uniform underlying grammatical competence.

Thus we have two candidate sources of native speaker variation in grammatical ability: grammatical competence or the performance factor of working memory. I propose, in section 3, that the true source of native speaker variation can be determined by providing one group of experimental subjects with memory training and another group with grammar training. The effects of the two types of training on the subjects' ability to comprehend complex sentences can then be measured. If the experimental subjects possess complete grammatical competence but lack the memory capacity needed to express it, then memory training should cause an increase in comprehension scores. Grammar training, however, should have no effect, given that one cannot logically improve on complete competence. If, on the other hand, the subjects lack grammatical competence, then one would not expect memory training to affect their comprehension scores. Grammar training, on the other hand, ought to cause an increase in comprehension scores. Thus, by comparing the effects of memory and grammar training on comprehension scores, it should be possible to decide between the two candidate sources of native speaker variation.

I will present results in section 4 from a series of experiments that I carried out using the experimental design described above. In line with previous studies, I found that native speakers vary widely in their ability to comprehend complex grammatical structures. Memory training led to improvements in memory capacity but not to improvements in sentence comprehension. Grammar training, on the other hand, led to increases in *both* comprehension and working memory capacity. I therefore concluded that grammatical competence, and not working memory capacity, was the source of the subjects' variations in ability to comprehend complex sentences.

In the fifth and final section of the chapter, I will consider some implications of the findings for linguistic theory. I now begin the discussion by presenting evidence of native speaker variations in various forms of grammatical ability.

2 Evidence for individual variation

2.1 *Individual differences in grammatical performance*

In this section, I present evidence to show that native speakers vary in almost every aspect of grammatical performance: in phonology, morphology, the lexicon, and syntax. These differences appear to derive from differences in the use of storage-based versus computation-based language processing strategies. In computer science, there are certain kinds of computing problem for which ready-made solutions exist. In such cases, a solution can be obtained from a look-up table (storage) when required. There are certain other kinds of problem, however, for which no ready-made solutions exist (or, if they did, would be too expensive to store). In such cases, the problems can be solved by following a general algorithm (computation) whenever the need arises. The storage strategy is fast in the case of solved problems but is of no use in the case of unsolved problems. The computation strategy may be slower, but it works equally well with both solved and unsolved problems. As the review below indicates, some native speakers appear to adopt a storage-based strategy while others adopt a computation-based strategy towards language processing.

2.2 *Individual differences in phonology*

Ferguson (1979) reports an informal experiment that uncovered wide variations in knowledge of phonological rules among child and adult native speakers of English. He also reviews formal studies that indicate that some children tend to build up their phonological representations in a more systematic manner than other children. A more extensive review of this research is undertaken by Bates et al. (1988). The research that they review indicates the existence of two language learning styles: holistic and analytic. According to the research, holistic learners attend primarily to suprasegmental phonology, while analytic learners attend primarily to segmental phonology. Holistic learners also tend to produce fluent, adult-sounding speech, but their pronunciation is context-dependent and inconsistent across word tokens. Analytic learners produce halting "telegraphic" speech, but their pronunciation is context-independent and consistent across word tokens. Analytic learners also display a greater ability to generate new utterances.

The difference between holistic and analytic learners can be understood in terms of the storage and computation strategies referred to above. One could say that holistic learners have adopted a storage strategy to address the problem of using language while the analytic learners have adopted a computation strategy. Having rote-learned familiar chunks of speech, holistic learners are able to sound fluent and adult-like when reproducing familiar utterances, but they have difficulty in producing novel utterances. Analytic learners, on the other hand, have learned more basic units of speech and the rules for combining them. While they may not be as fluent as holistic learners, they can produce both familiar and novel utterances with equal facility.

Individual differences in phonology have also been discovered independently in the psychology of reading. The interest in phonology within this field arises from the fact that phonological competence is a key prerequisite for the development of reading. It has been found that children who are native speakers of the same language vary widely in phonological awareness – the understanding that sentences are constructed from words, words from syllables, and syllables from phonemes (see Snow et al. 1998; Morais et al. 1998; Stahl and Murray 1994; Goswami and Bryant 1992).

Children also vary widely in a subset of phonological awareness skills called phonemic awareness, which involves the ability to detect and manipulate phonemes (Langenberg 2000; Muter et al. 1997; Naslund and Schneider 1996). Some children apparently fail to develop phonemic awareness (Torgesen et al. 1994; Holligan and Johnston 1991; Olson et al. 1990; Bryant et al. 1990). It is interesting to note that, while many linguists generally assume that phonological acquisition is completed early in life, and with no instruction, research in the psychology of reading shows that most children do not develop full phonological awareness in the absence of explicit instruction (Morais et al. 1998; Torgesen et al. 1994; van Kleeck 1990; Dickinson and Snow 1987).

2.3 *Morphology*

By the time children attend school, they ought, according to the predictions of generative grammar, to have acquired full competence in the morphology of their native language. However, evidence of individual variations in morphological knowledge among school-aged children has been widely reported. The general pattern of individual differences found is that some children treat morphologically complex words as unitary wholes, while other children can analyse such words in terms of their constituent morphemes (see Larsen and Nippold 2007; Carlisle 2000; Mahony et al. 2000; Singson et al. 2000; Leong 2000; Anglin 1993; Freyd and Baron 1982). Schnitzer (1993) also reports native speaker variation in morphological competence from a study involving both children and adults who are native speakers of Spanish.

It is noteworthy that the storage and computational strategies appear to be also active in the processing of morphological structure. The children who treat words as unitary wholes appear to learn whole words by rote, whereas the children who can analyse words into their constituent morphemes appear to be capable of deriving new words by computation. As noted later in this chapter, the ability to derive new words using morphological rules appears to be responsible for much of the growth of vocabulary during the school years. This means that children who adopt a computation-based strategy towards morphology enjoy faster vocabulary growth than those who adopt a storage-based strategy.

2.4 *Lexical knowledge*

One hardly needs to refer to any research in order to appreciate how widely native speakers vary in lexical knowledge. The research is still instructive, however. For instance, some first graders are said to have half the vocabulary of other first graders (White et al. 1990). These differences widen as children grow older, with some children learning about seven words a day, while others learn just one or two (Beck and McKeown 1991). Among adult native speakers, differences in vocabulary size are likely to be very wide. Difficulties in measuring vocabulary size reliably, however, make it difficult to cite figures with any degree of confidence. The more important issue is that differences in lexical knowledge should lead logically to differences in syntactic ability, given that considerable grammatical information is attached to individual lexical items. Cupples and Holmes (1992) found that adult native English speakers who were also poor readers appeared to have incomplete lexical entries, causing them to perform poorly in syntactic tasks. Maratsos (1976) found that about half of the children and half of the adults in his study were unable to use definite and indefinite articles appropriately.

The storage and computation strategies thus appear to operate also in the development of lexical knowledge. As indicated earlier, children differ in their knowledge and application of derivational rules, with some children treating words as unitary wholes that simply have to be memorized while others treat them as morphological complexes that are built up via computation. One would expect children who treat words as unitary wholes to experience slower vocabulary growth than those who can derive new words through computation. This is precisely what Anglin (1993) found: different rates of vocabulary growth during the school years could be accounted for in terms of individual differences in the use of derivational rules.

2.5 *Syntax*

The storage and computation strategies also appear to give rise to individual differences in syntactic ability. Gleitman and Gleitman (1970) and Geer et al. (1972) found that university students and individuals educated only up to high school level understood familiar compounds, such as *dog house*, equally well. However, university students were significantly better at paraphrasing novel compounds, such as *bird house thin* (i.e. thin like a bird house). It appears that the less educated speakers could understand known compounds via the storage strategy but were unable to compute the meanings of novel compounds, which required syntactic rule application.

Many other studies have produced evidence of native speaker variation in syntactic competence: for example, in the making of grammaticality judgements (Hill 1961; N. J. Spencer 1973); in the making of acceptability judgements (Greenbaum and Quirk 1970; Mills and Hemsley 1976); in the ability to cope with syntactic ambiguity (Lefever and Ehri 1976; Cupples and Holmes 1992; Pearlmutter and McDonald 1995); in the ability to cope with decreases in syntactic predictability (Graesser et al. 1980); in brain wave responses to syntactic anomaly (Osterhout 1997); in parsing exceptional constructions (C. Chomsky 1969; Kramer et al. 1972; Sanders 1971); in assigning constituent structure (Huey 1968; Levin and Kaplan 1970, and Dearborn and Anderson 1973, both papers cited in Cupples and Holmes 1987; Cromer 1970; Baruzzi 1982; Muncer and Bever 1984; Cupples and Holmes 1987; Dąbrowska 1997); and in assigning thematic roles (Dąbrowska and Street 2006; Bates et al. 1982; Wulfeck et al. 1986; Kilborn and Cooreman 1987; Harrington 1987; Kail 1989; McDonald 1989; Kilborn and Ito 1989; Sasaki 1997). These studies are too numerous for me to discuss in any detail. I will, however, discuss studies relating to native speaker variation in understanding complex grammatical structures, as this is the main topic of the chapter.

Ewa Dąbrowska (1997) carried out a study to find out how well native English speakers with different levels of education could understand various kinds of complex sentence. She used *tough*-movement sentences, for instance *Sandy will be easy to get the president to vote for;* complex NP sentences, for instance *The manager knew that the fact that taking good care of herself was essential upset Alice;* and parasitic gap sentences, for instance *It was King Louis who the general convinced that this slave might speak to.* She found that university lecturers understood such sentences better than undergraduates, who in turn understood them better than porters and cleaners.

I carried out a similar study (Chipere 1997), only this time I also tested non-native graduate speakers of English. I obtained the same pattern of results as Dąbrowska, with the difference that the non-native graduates performed better than native speaker graduates and native speaker non-graduates. I interpreted this result as a consequence of the fact that non-native speakers often undergo explicit instruction in English grammar, whereas native speakers generally do not. If being a native speaker does not automatically lead to full competence in the grammar of one's language, then it is not surprising that highly educated non-native speakers who have been explicitly instructed in the grammar of that language should be able to outperform native speakers in tests of syntactic ability.

It appears from the two studies just described that native English speakers vary in their ability to process sentences that involve self-embedding. Indeed, previous studies from the 1960s and 1970s show that self-embedding, or recursion, causes serious difficulty for some native speakers of English. G. A. Miller and Isard (1964) discovered that some individuals could process sentences with at most one level of self-embedding, whereas other individuals could process sentences with two levels of self-embedding. The investigators were unable to explain this result. Stolz (1967) also obtained evidence of individual differences in the processing of sentences with two levels of self-embedding. He found, in addition, that many subjects could understand self-embedded sentences only if they were provided with training. The fact that subjects had to be trained in order to be able to process recursive structures is problematic for generative grammar, which characterizes native speakers as fully competent in the grammar of their native language.

Even with training, however, Stolz found that subjects had difficulty grasping the notion of recursion as an autonomous device that can be used to produce sentences of arbitrary complexity. Freedle and Craun (1969) replicated Stolz's findings, and they also found that many subjects failed to generalize the notion of recursion to levels of self-embedding greater than two. This observation suggests that subjects learned to process self-embedded sentences in a highly structure-specific way, without having acquired a true understanding of recursion. Subjects appear to rote-learn syntactic construc-tions (using "construction" here in the sense of Construction Grammar), as opposed to learning an abstract grammatical principle that could be used to compute more complex, novel sentences. This second observation presents yet another problem for generative grammar, which characterizes grammat-ical knowledge as rule-governed and not structure-specific.

I should note, however, that Blaubergs and Braine (1974) were able to train their subjects to comprehend sentences with up to five levels of self-embedding. Presumably, the training procedure that they provided was able to push subjects beyond structure-specificity and enable them to grasp an abstract notion of recursion that could be generalized to an arbitrary degree of complexity. This study shows that subjects do have the potential to grasp the concept of recursion as an abstract generative device. Incidentally, this training study provides a methodological precedent for the training studies reported later in this article.

2.6　*Section summary*

A clear pattern of individual differences arises from much of the literature reviewed above. There are some native speakers who, from childhood, adopt a storage-based strategy in order to deal with the problem of producing and understanding language. Other individuals tend towards computation. It seems to me that explaining individual differences in terms of storage-based versus computation-based strategies is the simplest way of accounting for the experimental data presented above.

However, a more complex account has been proposed. It has been sug-gested that native speaker variations in performance do not signify variations in the underlying grammatical competence. Instead, it has been argued that individuals vary in the performance factor of working memory capacity (Just and Carpenter 1992). Individuals with low working memory capacity are said to be unable to build complex grammatical representations, unlike those with a high working memory capacity. This working memory account is highly influential, and needs to be addressed fully.

3　Variable competence or variable memory?

3.1　*The competence/performance distinction*

When G. A. Miller and Isard (1964) found that native speakers were unable to process recursive sentences with more than one degree of self-embedding, they proposed "a distinction between knowing a rule and obeying it" (p. 294).

By this they meant that, while human beings have the grammatical potential to process recursive structures to arbitrary degrees of self-embedding, memory limitations prevent them from doing so. Noam Chomsky (1965) later expressed the same notion in terms of his competence/performance distinction.

At the time that Miller and Isard and Chomsky proposed the competence/performance distinction, it was believed that working memory capacity (referred to then as short-term memory capacity) was uniform across all human beings (with a size of seven plus or minus two items, Miller 1956). The model of human memory in vogue then was the one described in Atkinson and Schiffrin (1968). The concept of working memory has undergone substantial revisions since then, and these revisions have implications for models of sentence comprehension. Below, I describe two contemporary models and discuss their treatment of the competence/performance distinction. One model was proposed by Just and Carpenter (1992), and the other by Ericsson and Kintsch (1995).

3.2 *Short-term working memory capacity*

Just and Carpenter define working memory as a kind of mental energy or "activation" that fuels mental processes. This activation can be used to store information as well as to process it. Depending on the needs of the task, automatic memory management mechanisms allocate memory dynamically to processing or storage functions. Just and Carpenter propose that individual differences in working memory capacity impinge on syntactic performance, so that individuals with low working memory capacity are unable to construct complex syntactic representations whereas individuals with high working memory do not suffer from this constraint. Just and Carpenter retain the assumption that native speakers possess a uniform grammatical competence. They do not, however, provide any justification for the assumption, and thus perpetuate the tradition of treating uniform competence as axiomatic.

3.3 *Long-term working memory capacity*

Ericsson and Kintsch accept that there exists a limited-capacity and domain-independent working memory, which they call *short-term working memory*. However, they argue that skilled individuals recruit long-term memory for online cognitive processing by effectively creating a *long-term working memory*. Individuals differ only in terms of this long-term working memory capacity, depending on their degree of expertise in a given domain. Ericsson and Kintsch provide an extensive review of studies which show that the development of expertise in any domain is accompanied by dramatic increases in working memory capacity for that domain. Hence a chess grand master may have high long-term working memory for chess, but not for other domains in which he or she is not expert. Ericsson and Kintsch attribute individual differences in language comprehension to individual differences in linguistic expertise (competence), rather than to any inherent individual differences in a domain-neutral short-term working memory.

3.4 *Training studies*

It is fairly easy to design a test to decide between these two models of memory and language comprehension. Such a test would involve training subjects in either memory or grammar. There are precedents for such a training study. G. A. Miller (1956) showed that short-term memory capacity can be boosted through training. Blaubergs and Braine (1974), on the other hand, showed that the ability to process self-embedded sentences can also be improved through training. It should therefore be possible to design a series of experiments that involve providing memory training to one group of subjects and grammar training to another. The predictions of either model regarding the relationship between memory and comprehension can then be checked against the results.

The two models make the following predictions. First, with regard to the effects of memory training, Just and Carpenter's model predicts that boosting subjects' short-term memory should free up extra working memory capacity for processing functions. The result should be an improvement in comprehension. Ericsson and Kintsch's theory, on the other hand, does not predict any effect of memory training on comprehension.

Secondly, with regard to comprehension training, Just and Carpenter's model predicts no effect on comprehension, given that subjects who are perfectly competent in grammar cannot, logically, improve upon that competence. On the other hand, Ericsson and Kintsch's model predicts that grammar training will improve comprehension, given that comprehension failure arises from inadequate linguistic expertise. Ericsson and Kintsch's model also makes a secondary prediction. In their model, accurate sentence encoding processes create long-term memory traces that facilitate recall. Therefore comprehension training ought also to improve sentence recall.

The two models therefore make opposing and testable predictions about the effects of memory and grammar training on recall and comprehension. These predictions were tested in the experiments reported in the next section.

4 Experimental tests

4.1 *Individual differences in grammatical competence*

I carried out a series of experiments designed to determine if native speaker variations in understanding complex sentences arise from variations in working memory capacity or from variations in grammatical competence. Full experimental reports are available in Chipere (2001, 2003). Only an overview of the methodology and results is presented here.

4.2 *Materials*

In the experiments, I used complex NP sentences that I adapted from Dąbrowska (1997). For example:

Tom knows that the fact that flying planes low is dangerous excites the pilot.

Some commentators have suggested that such sentences would be unacceptable to many native speakers and are therefore inappropriate as experimental stimuli. However, the sentences used in the experiments are perfectly grammatical and ought to be comprehensible to competent native speakers of English. Their structure is only moderately complex, and is in fact simpler than that of some sentences that occur naturally. Here are some examples from the British National Corpus:

Bourne, creator of the original Unix Bourne shell command interpreter, believes that the fact that development of Unix operating systems is generally done in a handcrafted manner is not a function of the inherent diversity of Unix itself, but is a long-term software engineering problem.

But one may also say, from the fact that this has needed to be discussed – and from the fact that, as I say, throughout the greater part of Christendom women have not been ordained – it would be difficult to argue that the fact that this religion has had at its centre a male figure has been of little significance.

Consequently, the answer to be given to the national court must be that the fact that the competent minister of a member state has the power to dispense with the nationality requirement in respect of an individual in view of the length of time such individual has resided in that member state and has been involved in the fishing industry of that member state cannot justify, in regard to Community law, the rule under which registration of a fishing vessel is subject to a nationality requirement and a requirement as to residence and domicile.

Clearly, sentences that occur naturally can be highly complex, and the objection to the test sentences on the basis of unnaturalness can be put aside.

4.3 *Participants*

Thirty-nine native speakers of English with an average age of eighteen years participated in the study. All were students in a further education college who had undertaken their GCSE examinations in the previous year. Pilot experiments had shown a close correlation between the ability to understand complex NP sentences and performance in the GCSE examinations. Students at the highest end of academic ability were almost always able to comprehend the test sentences, whereas students of average to low academic ability were almost always unable to comprehend the test sentences. An examination of the academic profiles of the participants showed that those with an A grade in English and A grades in at least four other subjects could reliably comprehend the test sentences. Those with at most a B in English and B grades in all other subjects consistently failed to comprehend the test sentences. Students falling between these two subsets behaved inconsistently.

The basis of the correlation between academic ability and sentence comprehension skill is not clear. Note that, since they were native speakers of English, there should have been no differences between these students in terms of grammatical competence, if the claims of generative grammar are correct. It was not the aim of the experiment to explain the correlation between academic ability and comprehension scores. Rather, the experiment used academic ability purely as a means of grouping participants into those who could comprehend the test sentences and those who could not, in order to create the conditions for the training study.

The following criteria were used to group the students. Students who had obtained Grade A in English and in at least four other subjects were assigned to the High Academic Ability (HAA) group. Students who had obtained Grades B or less in English and all other subjects were assigned to the Low Academic Ability (LAA) group. Intermediate students, for example students with an A in English and Bs in four other subjects, were left out of the sample. Note that the LAA group would have included students spanning the range of average to low academic ability; for example, this group could have included students who received five Bs and students who received five Ds.

4.4 *Procedures and results*

In the first experiment, I compared the performance of an HAA group to that of two LAA groups on two tasks. In the first task, participants were asked to recall each test sentence immediately after it was presented to them. In the second task, participants were asked basic comprehension questions such as:

Tom knows that the fact that flying planes low is dangerous excites the pilot.

What does Tom know? – the fact that flying planes low is dangerous excites the pilot.

What excites the pilot? – the fact that flying planes low is dangerous.

The HAA group scored significantly higher than one LAA group in both recall, $F1(1,27) = 26·27$, $p < ·001$, $F2(1·29) = 186·96$, $p < ·001$, and comprehension, $F1 (1,27) = 44·37$, $p < ·001$, $F2(1,29) = 199·79$, $p < ·001$. In fact, most participants in the LAA group completely failed to answer the comprehension questions correctly.

In the second experiment, a subset of the LAA group was given memory training in order to boost working memory capacity. Training was successful and the LAA group achieved recall scores that were approximately equal to those of the HAA group. A comparison of HAA recall scores and LAA recall scores after memory training showed no significant difference between the two groups. The LAA group was then asked to perform a comprehension task, in order to see if the boost in working memory capacity had improved their comprehension. Results showed that memory training had no effect on comprehension scores, which remained approximately the same as those that the group had obtained prior to training.

In the third experiment, the second subset of the LAA group was provided with comprehension training. Training was successful and participants achieved comprehension scores of nearly 100 per cent. These scores were in fact higher than those of the HAA group, but not significantly higher. This LAA group was also asked to perform a recall task in order to find out if comprehension training had an effect on working memory capacity. Results showed that the second LAA group achieved very high recall scores – roughly equal to those of the HAA group. The difference between the two sets of scores was not significant.

4.5 *Discussion*

Memory training caused increases in recall scores (a measure of working memory capacity) but not in comprehension scores. Comprehension training, on the other hand, caused increases in both comprehension and recall scores. It can therefore be concluded that the differences between the HAA and the LAA groups were caused by differences in grammatical competence and not by differences in working memory capacity. It is also notable that comprehension training led to improvements in working memory capacity. This is exactly what the Ericsson and Kintsch model predicts.

In the next section, I summarize the discussion and consider some implications of native speaker variations in grammatical competence.

5 Conclusion

There is a common assumption, underlying much of linguistic theory, that native speakers have a uniform grammatical competence. This assumption has been shown here to be false. The experimental literature shows that native speakers vary widely in phonology, morphology, the lexicon, and syntax. There appears to be a pattern in the variation. Some native speakers appear to have adopted a storage-based strategy with respect to language use while others appear to have adopted a computation-based strategy, with the result that the latter group possesses a greater generative potential than the former.

These individual differences cannot be accounted for in terms of the competence/performance distinction, whereby variations in working memory capacity cause variable expression of an otherwise uniform grammatical competence. The training studies reported here show instead that native speaker variations in understanding complex sentences arise from differences in grammatical competence and not in working memory capacity. Furthermore, the results show that variations in competence cause variations in working memory capacity. This finding turns the competence/performance distinction on its head.

It has always been assumed that working memory is a linguistically extrinsic constraint on the expression of grammatical competence. It now turns out that grammatical competence is intimately related to working memory, and actually determines its size. This outcome is entirely consistent with Ericsson and Kintsch's model, in which long-term memory contributes to a domain-specific working memory. The model suggests that, as in other domains of expertise, human beings actively construct systems of representation (grammars, in the case of language) and that, as in other domains of expertise, their creative efforts produce different results.

The fact that native speakers vary in grammatical competence has deep implications for linguistics and related disciplines. It is not within the scope of this chapter to explore these implications in any detail. I will confine myself to mentioning one major implication, from which other implications flow. In order to appreciate this implication, it is important to consider why the assumption of uniform native speaker competence has enjoyed axiomatic status in linguistics, as discussed by Geoffrey Sampson in Chapter 1. In Chipere (2003), I suggest that many linguists have an ideological objection to native speaker variations in grammatical competence, which they regard as socially dangerous, in that they can be used to justify social discrimination based on class and race. I also suggest that generative grammarians have a theoretical objection to individual differences. They are committed to the notion of an innate universal grammar, and individual differences are fundamentally incompatible with this notion.

The findings reported here suggest that linguists, whether they have been driven by ideological or theoretical considerations, have been working at the wrong level of abstraction. They have focused on what native speakers know about their language, and sought to argue that this knowledge is universal. As this chapter has shown, the assumption of universality is incorrect. The chapter has also shown, however, that native speakers who do not possess the competence to process certain kinds of sentences have the potential to learn how to process these sentences successfully. The implication is that linguists need to focus on this abstract potential to make grammatical generalizations.

According to Saussure, "it is not spoken language which is natural to man, but the faculty of constructing a language" ([1916] 1983: 10). From the existence of such a faculty, we can draw the following conclusions. From an ideological point of view, we can say that native speakers vary in grammatical competence but that they have an equal potential to acquire full grammatical competence. Thus egalitarianism is not really given up – it simply shifts its locus to a more abstract level of mental functioning. From the point of view of linguistic theory, we could say that what is universal to humanity is not a universal grammar as such, but the mental capacity for constructing grammars. Thus the search for universal mechanisms in language need not be given up either, but simply refocused towards a more abstract mental capacity.

13

Origin and maintenance of clausal embedding complexity

FRED KARLSSON

1 Introduction

There are many well-known parameters of grammatical complexity: number of terms (e.g. cases or genders) in a grammatical subsystem; more or less intricate elaboration of phrases by premodification and postmodification; restricted versus repeatable nominalization processes; number of affixes in word forms; simplex versus iterative compound formation; number and depth of embedding of clauses in sentences, etc.[1]

The purpose of this chapter is to analyse one aspect of grammatical complexity, that of clausal embedding complexity, by which we mean the possibilities of repeatedly embedding subordinate clauses in various positions in their main clauses. After a presentation of some clausal embedding complexity constraints recently established for "Standard Average European" (SAE) languages like English, German, Swedish, and Finnish, we shall inquire what the origin of these constraints is and whether they have been stable or fluctuating over time. Particular attention will be paid to centre-embeddings, the theoretically most interesting type of clausal embedding.

2 Constraints on clausal embedding complexity

Clausal embedding complexity increases with repeated embedding of clauses in initial, central, or final position. Initially embedded clauses (IEs) have either nothing to their left, or at most a subordinating conjunction belonging to the superordinate clause (cf. Dryer 1980: 154–5; Quirk et al. 1989: 1037). Centre-embedded clauses (CEs) have superordinate clause constituents both to their left

---

[1] Valuable help and advice have been provided by Guy Deutscher, John W. Du Bois, Simo Parpola, and Geoffrey Sampson.

(other than conjunctions) and to their right. Final embeddings (FEs) have no material to their right that belongs to the immediately superordinate clause.

Karlsson (2007a, b, c) empirically established constraints, i.e. quantitative limits and qualitative restrictions, on clausal embedding complexity in many European languages. The data were (i) complex sentences in the British National Corpus (BNC), the Brown corpus, and the LOB corpus, (ii) computerized extraction of complex embedding patterns in Finnish, German, and Swedish, and (iii) consultation of more than one hundred corpus-based syntactic and stylistic descriptions of European languages, especially Latin and older variants of German, both well known for being syntactically complex.

Examples (1–5) below are some constraints operational in Standard Average European languages. 'I' stands for initial clausal embedding, 'C' for clausal centre-embedding, 'F' for final clausal embedding, and the raised exponent expresses the maximal degree of embedding of a sentence, e. g. I^2 is double initial embedding as in sentence (6). Expressions like C-2 indicate type and embedding depth of individual clauses; e.g. C-2 is a centre-embedded clause at depth 2.

(1) I^2max: the maximal degree of initial embedding is two (some 100 instances found, as in (6) below).

(2) Qualitative I^2-constraints: Double initial embedding strongly prefers (a) written language, (b) an *if*-clause as higher embedding, (c) a sentential subject, e.g. a *what*-clause as lower embedding, and (d) finiteness. Cf. (6).

(3) C^3max-w: in written language, the maximal (utterly rare) degree of multiple centre-embedding is three (thirteen instances retrieved, (7)).

(4) C^2max-s: in spoken language, the maximal (utterly rare) degree of multiple centre-embedding is two (a handful of instances retrieved, (8)).

(5) Only-postmodifying-self-embedding: only postmodifying (i.e. typically relative) clauses allow self-embedding (7, 8), i.e. repeated embedding of precisely the same type of clause.

Examples:

(6) [Main [I-1 If [I-2 what he saw through security] did not impress him] Tammuz...] (BNC)

(7) [Main Der Ritter von Malzahn, [C-1 dem der Junker sich als einen Fremden, [C-2 der bei seiner Durchreise den seltsamen Mann, [C-3 den er mit sich führe,] in Augenschein zu nehmen wünschte,] vorstellte,] nötigte ihn...] (Kleist, *Michael Kohlhaas*)

(8)   [Main A lot of the housing [C-1 that the people [C-2 that worked in New Haven] lived in] was back that way.]

No genuine triple initial embeddings nor any quadruple centre-embeddings are on record ("genuine" here means sentences produced in natural non-linguistic contexts, not sentences produced by professional linguists in the course of their theoretical argumentation). Only some 130 double CEs were retrieved among the tens of millions of words checked, indicating that even C^2 is a rarely used structural option. Here are three more of these genuine double CEs (see Karlsson 2007c for details):

(9)   a. [Main A number of speeches [C-1 into which a great deal of thought and preparation on a level a great deal higher [C-2 than is common in modern politics] have gone] are not reported at all...]

    b. [Main ...for that matter, [C-1 when one compares *Swann* and *Jeunes filles*, [C-2 – in which the theme of homosexuality remains latent –] with the shoddiness of the later volumes,] one is inclined to wonder...]

    c. [Main It was not [F-1 until he was an old man [F-2 that one day his son, [C-3 who, [C-4 as was the way of the world,] had left the shamba] explained to him [F-3 that...]]]]

The overall rarity and the numerous constraints on multiple IE and CE prompt the conclusion that multiple clausal initial and centre-embeddings are not fully recursive in SAE. Particularly important is the observation (cf. (4) above) that multiple centre-embedding, i.e. multiply nested clausal recursion, is practically absent from ordinary spoken language. Only a handful of genuine spoken C^2s like (8) are on record.

Note that C^3max-w and Only-postmodifying-self-embedding taken together license triple relative self-embedding, which does indeed occur (e.g. (7)).

Final clausal embedding is less constrained but not totally unregimented. In an extensive unpublished empirical study, Kaius Sinnemäki and I have found evidence in SAE languages for a tendency we call F^{3-5}max:

(10) F^{3-5}max: Syntactically simple genres (such as spoken language) avoid final clausal embedding in excess of degree three, complex genres in excess of degree five.

As sentence (11) from the Brown Corpus with eight finally embedded clauses shows, F^{3-5}max may be overstepped, but such sentences are perceived as complex. F^{3-5}max thus is a stylistic preference. In what follows, written language only will be treated, and therefore we refer to (10) by the abbreviation F^5max-w.

(11) [...it seems... [that...it is unlikely [to bear much relation...to
      the...need of [ensuring... [that there may be adequate opportunity
      given to the staff [to do [what they can [to get the man [to stand
      again...]]]]]]]]]]

3 Origin of clausal subordination

Typical everyday spoken language consists of brief utterances containing few
constituents and fewer than ten words. The utterances of early spoken language or "protolanguage" must have been even briefer. Formally marked
embedding of finite subclauses – hypotaxis – arose much later than such
simple protoclauses, but also later than clausal coordination (parataxis) and
later than nonfinite constructions based on infinitives, participles, and ger-
unds, all of which presuppose the existence of a (finite) main clause verb.
Deutscher (2000) substantiates this claim for Akkadian, Itkonen (1966) for
Finno-Ugric.

Before the advent of writing in the third millennium BC, the major exposi-
tory genre was oral narrative, which has been shown to be aggregative and
paratactic rather than subordinating. Phrases are strung together into loosely
conjoined shallow sequences (Lord 1960). This pattern of ancient additive
structure is found across the world. As a case in point, Leino (1975) analysed a
section of the *Kalevala* (402 lines of verse, some 1,300 words) and found only
three subordinate clauses, all "when"-clauses embedded at depth 1 immediately below the main clause. For comparison, 1,300 words of current written
Finnish would typically contain some sixty finite subordinate clauses (Hakulinen et al. 1980).

Nonfinite clausal embedding, especially final embedding such as the in-
finitive constructions in (11), certainly dates back to preliterate times in
many languages. As for the origin of finite clausal embedding, there are
preliterate languages lacking finite subordinate clauses: Inuktitut, for example, is in the very process of acquiring clausal embedding along with the
development of the native press (Kalmár 1985). But finite subordinate clauses
do occur in some preliterate languages. Mithun (1984) notes the existence of
such clauses in oral texts in Mohawk, Gungwingu (Australian), Kathlamet
(Chinookan), and Tlingit (Na-Dené). However, their incidence is much lower
than in English.

Even if some basic finite embedding patterns date to preliterate times, there
is ample evidence, for example from Semitic, Indo-European, and Finno-
Ugric languages, that the emergence of more elaborate grammaticalized

patterns of finite clausal subordination is related to the advent of written language, especially to the conventionalization of various written registers. Proof of this development is provided for instance by Deutscher (2000) for Akkadian, by W. P. Lehmann (1974) for subordinate clauses in Vedic, by O'Neil (1976) for subordinate clauses in Old English, by M. Harris (1988) for concessive clauses in English and Romance, and by König and van der Auwera (1988) for subordinate clauses in Dutch and German.

4 Origin and development of I²max

In view of what was said in section 3 concerning the overall emergence of embedding, it is clear that the appearance of multiple clausal embeddings (especially finite ones) must be sought in the realm of written language. The age of this phenomenon can be no more than 5,000 years, because Sumerian became the first written language around 3000 BC.

As already noted, no genuine triple (or deeper) initial clausal embeddings have been attested from any period. Interestingly, the oldest genuine instance of I² we have found dates to as far back as Hammurabi's Code of Law (Middle Babylonian, 1800 BC). The sentence starts with the subordinating conjunctions *šumma ištu* "if after", and here is its (somewhat shortened) literal gloss (Roth 1997: 92):

(12) [$_{Main}$ [$_{I-1}$ If [$_{I-2}$ after the sheep and goats come up from the common irrigated area [$_{F-3}$ when the pennants [$_{c-4}$ announcing the termination of pasturing] are wound around the main city gate]] the shepherd releases the sheep and goats into a field ...] the shepherd shall guard the field ...]

Another notable fact about (12) is that the lower clause I-2 in the double initial embedding contains a further final finite embedding F-3, which contains a further nonfinite centre-embedding c-4 (nonfiniteness indicated by lower-case "c" while upper case signals finiteness). The complex initial embeddings typical of law language ever since are likely to have their origin in Hammurabi's Code of Law (Simo Parpola, pers. comm.). Thus, the border of constraint I²max ((1) above), still operational today, was already reached in Akkadian when the Akkadian tradition of writing was at most 500 years old.

5 Origin and development of C³max-w

As for the origin of multiple centre-embedding, Thomsen (1984: 244) and Frayne (1993: 285) provide a most interesting Sumerian instance from *c.* 2000 BC of triple centre-embedding (here kindly glossed by Simo Parpola; the glossing code SUBORD stands for a Sumerian form which functioned as a general subordination and nominalization marker):

(13) *lú*   *Dabrum-ak-e*   *Utu-Hegal*   Main
     people   Dabrum-GEN-ERG   Utu-Hegal

  bar   C-1
  account

    lugal   C-2
    king

      Enlil-e   *á*   *šúm-a*   C-3
      Enlil-ERG   strength   give-SUBORD

    ì-me-a
    PREF-be-SUBORD

    ì-zu-a-ak-eš
    PREF-know-SUBORD-GEN-DIR

  Tirigan-ra   *šu*   *nu-ni-ba*
  Tirigan-DAT   care   NEG-he-LOC.grant

"The people of Dabrum did not give security to Tirigan, because they knew that Utu-hegal was a king to whom Enlil had given strength."

This means that C³max-w was reached already in Sumerian, at a time when written language had existed at most one thousand years.

Here is a Latin C³ from Cicero's *De haruspicum responsis*, pointed out by von Nägelsbach ([1846] 1963: 645) to "stretch the limits of Latin grammar to the extreme":

(14) *Postea*   *vos,*   *patres conscripti,*...   M
     then   you   Senators

    huic   *furiae,*   C-1
    from this   madman

      si   *diutius*   *in*   *hac*   *urbe,*   C-2
      if   longer   in   this   city

        quam   *delere*   i-4
        which   destroy

> *cuperet,*   C-3
> wanted
>
> *maneret,*
> would stay
>
> *vox   interdiceretur,*
> vote   cancel
>
> *decrevistis...*
> decided

"After this you, Senators, decided to cancel this man's right to vote if he would stay longer in this city which he wanted to destroy."

Sentence (14) is close to falsifying our empirical generalization C³max-w (3) because the C-3 of (14) contains a fourth level of embedding, *quam delere*. But this clause is initially embedded (i-4) in its matrix clause C-3.

A sum total of thirteen examples of C³ from all periods are at hand in our corpus. This tiny amount certainly indicates that the construction is a marginal one. Here is a C³ from the twentieth century (pointed out by Geoffrey Sampson, pers. comm.):

(15) [Main In an excellent article... Salvini draws a parallel between the way [C-1 in which the spoken Latin of the men [C-2 with whom Gregory of Tours, [C-3 whom he has no reason [f-4 to mention,]] must have mixed] eventually became Old French...,] and the comparable direct development of pre-Romanesque painting...] (L. Thorpe, *Gregory of Tours: the history of the Franks*, Penguin, 1974: 39)

Even if the existence of C³s is incontestable, it must be stressed that many of the attested examples (see Karlsson 2007c for the whole material) are so convoluted as to be almost incomprehensible. They overload the short-term memory resources by having (too) many unresolved syntactic dependencies pending, and by stretching these unresolved dependencies over the introduction of (too) many new referents, which also drains available memory resources. In this regard, note that the deepest embedding C-3 of both (7) and (15) contains only pronouns referring to already introduced referents, thereby considerably easing the processing load.

Archaic Latin syntax before 300 BC was basically paratactic (Devoto 1968: 92). Clausal embedding below depth 1 was not established in Latin before 100 BC (Lindskog 1896). Relative centre-embedding next to the antecedent was consolidated by Cicero, who discussed centre-embedding from a stylistic and rhetorical point of view in *De oratore* (55 BC). If Cicero was the first Latin writer to use C^3, the time extension from the earliest beginnings of Latin writing to (14) is some 500 years, a magnitude similar to that of reaching I^2max in Akkadian and C^3max-w in Sumerian.

By laying down rules for sentential composition Cicero completed the doctrine of *periods*, a cornerstone of Western rhetoric and stylistics initiated by Aristotle, which has greatly affected the later development of sentence composition, especially the use of multiply centre-embedded clauses, in Ancient Greek, Latin, and later European languages. Here is a direct quotation from the relevant section in Aristotle's *Rhetoric*, translated by Fowler (1984):

(16) By a period I mean a portion of speech that has in itself a beginning and an end, being at the same time not too big to be taken in at a glance. Language of this kind is satisfying and easy to follow. It is satisfying, because it is just the reverse of indefinite; and moreover, the hearer always feels that he is grasping something and has reached some definite conclusion; whereas it is unsatisfactory to see nothing in front of you and get nowhere. It is easy to follow, because it can easily be remembered; and this because language when in periodic form can be numbered, and number is the easiest of all things to remember. That is why verse, which is measured, is always more easily remembered than prose, which is not: the measures of verse can be numbered. The period must, further, not be completed until the sense is complete: it must not be capable of breaking off abruptly…

A typical periodic sentence contains at least one centre-embedding, a detour from the overriding sentence scheme, brought to structural completion and the satisfaction of "full meaning" by the latter part of the main clause. The master of periodic sentences was Livy (59/64 BC–13 AD), along with Cicero a stylistic icon for centuries. Cicero and Livy were the ones who set the model for the use of multiple centre-embeddings in written language. W. Kriebel described the principles of their sentence composition in his doctoral dissertation "Der Periodenbau bei Cicero und Livius", defended at the University of Rostock in 1873. Here is a typical example of a C^2 by Livy (from his *Ab urbe condita*; see Kriebel 1873: 15):[2]

(17) [$_{Main}$*Nunc,* [$_{C-1}$*quod temeritatem temeritate alia luerit,*] [$_{\&C-1}$*tristioremque rem,* [$_{C-2}$*quam necesse fuerit,*] *fecerit,*] *leniter castigat.*]

"(M) Now, (C-1) as he [Masinissa] had paid one thoughtlessness with another, (&C-1) and worse the situation (C-2) than was necessary (&C-1) had made, (M) he [Scipio] mildly criticized [Masinissa]."

---

2 The character "&" in a tag like &C-1 indicates a coordinated clause.

Cicero's orations are known to have been carefully rehearsed and imprinted in long-term memory by ingenious retrieval techniques (van Dijk and Kintsch 1983: 368), thus differing from the conditions of natural everyday discourse. This underlines the special nature of these unusually complex constructions.

From the Renaissance to the twentieth century there are hundreds of grammars, stylistic manuals, and scholarly monographs treating periodic sentence structure, e.g. Boivie's (1834: 99–102) Swedish and K. F. Becker's (1870: 418–23) German grammars. This is the historical source of the fairly uniform patterns of clausal subordination in present-day Standard Average European. In the words of Blatt (1957: 49): "Above all the limpidity and transparence [*sic*] of the Latin period was the big model."

Over the centuries one can spot occasional uses of C^2s, and every now and then of C^3s, in written European languages. Kracke (1911) studied the development of centre-embedding in German texts from the ninth to the late eighteenth century, with no fewer than fifty-eight authors in his corpus. He spotted twenty C^2s, the earliest occurring in the *Heliand* from around 830. Erman (1913: 43–4) found four C^2s in his large Old High German corpus. Admoni (1980) conducted an extensive study of the syntactic development of New High German literary language from the period 1470–1730. In his material containing more than 500 particularly complex sentences, there are one C^3 and some fifty C^2s.

In the Romance languages, the first complex periodic sentences did not appear until Dante in the 1300s (Blatt 1957: 37).

6 Origin and development of F^5max-w

As for the emergence of multiple final embedding, the earliest relevant data known to us concern Ancient Greek. Webster (1941) studied the development of sentence complexity in Ancient Greek, especially of FE. F^3 was used already by Homer around 700 BC, but he has only one instance of it. This shallow syntactic depth of the *Iliad* and *Odyssey* is in keeping with current theories of their origin in oral narrative. F^4 was first used by Herodotus, Sophocles, and Thucydides around 450 BC, and F^5 by Xenophon a century later. Demosthenes and Plato both have one F^6 and, as an extreme, Dinarchus (360–292 BC) one F^9. Overall, even F^3 was rare in Ancient Greek (Schwyzer 1950: 710). One may conclude that F^5max-w (10) of final embedding in written Ancient Greek was reached in less than 500 years from the introduction of the alphabet.

Meader (1905: 39) and Otto (1928: 810) found F^6 in Classical Latin (Plautus, Cicero, Tacitus), just as in Classical Greek. Erman (1913) analysed the embedding depths of 3,302 Old High German sentences with at least two subclauses (see Table 13.1), demonstrating that F^{5}max for written language had been reached and even surpassed in three instances (p. 474).

Holm (1967) investigated the development of written style in Swedish. The medieval Icelandic Sagas contain subclauses, preferably in final position and normally just one. Due to Latin influence, Renaissance Swedish contained F^4 and a growing share of centre-embedding. The hundreds of texts from 1100–1960 analysed by Holm contain one C^2, several instances of F^4, a few of F^5, and one of F^6. In his history of Swedish, Bergman (1968: 123) gives, as an extreme example of Latin-inspired periodic sentence structure, one F^7 from 1712.

Hiltunen (1990) studied the development of the syntactic structure of English law language from Anglo-Saxon in the seventh century, finding that sentences became more complex towards the eleventh century. F^5 occurred.

7 Conclusion

Evidence from many language families indicates that nonfinite clausal subordination and initial stages of finite clausal subordination existed already in preliterate languages. The more complex forms of (especially finite) clausal embedding arose as part of large-scale grammaticalization, along with the advent of written language and the consequent gradual conventionalization of written registers (Givón 1979: ch. 5). Of course there is a well-known underlying reason for the greater embedding complexity of written language: it enables more extensive and time-consuming processing in short-term memory of longer syntactic dependencies and more simultaneous discourse referents than in spoken language. This new property gradually pushed the complexity limits of clausal embedding to I^{2}max, C^{3}max-w, and F^{5}max-w which, as we have demonstrated, were already reached in the ancient languages and have not since been surpassed. The complexity maxima set by

Table 13.1. Frequency of clausal embedding depths (>1) in Old High German

Depth	N
2	2,747
3	478
4	70
5	4
6	2
7	1
Total	3,302

these three constraints were reached over a period of at most 500 years for I^2max in Akkadian, for C^3max-w in Latin, for F^5max-w in Ancient Greek and Latin, and over at most 1,000 years for C^3max-w in Sumerian. Available data for older forms of English and German similarly indicate that it took some 500 years from the introduction of writing to reach these maxima. This seems to confirm Comrie's (1992: 202) hypothesis that the languages of 4,500 to 6,500 years ago might not have been noticeably different in complexity from those today, at least as regards this particular aspect of syntactic complexity.

It goes almost without saying that these developmental times limits are provisional, and set the upper time limit on the basis of currently available documentation.

Latin syntax was affected by Greek, and both of these by ancient Near Eastern languages, especially Akkadian. Latin strongly influenced other written Western languages, especially as concerns periodic sentence structure, for more than 1,500 years, and imposed common embedding limits on them. These limits must, of course, have roots in biological properties of the human organism, especially restrictions on syntactic and discourse management in short-term memory.

It is a well-known fact that, mainly due to Latin influences, German and English were syntactically most complex in the seventeenth century and Swedish in the nineteenth century (Admoni 1974: 30–55; Jespersen [1905] 1967: 118; Lindstedt 1927; Engdahl 1962). Since the gradual disappearance of the Latin-based school system in the nineteenth century, patterns of clausal embedding have become successively simpler, especially in the twentieth century, as a result of systematic language planning in schoolteaching and phenomena like the Plain English movement.

But the upper limits of clausal embedding complexity have remained the same since the advent of written language.

14

Layering of grammar: vestiges of protosyntax in present-day languages

LJILJANA PROGOVAC

1 Some (Mad) clauses and compounds

In this section I identify two sets of data available in present-day languages, which clearly defy the rules and principles of present-day morphosyntax: Root Small Clauses (RootSCs), and verb-complement exocentric compounds (ExCs).[1] In section 2 I show that these data instantiate a grammar/syntax measurably simpler than that of more typical sentential speech, leading to the proposal in section 3 that they can be seen as vestiges/"living fossils" of a protosyntax stage in language evolution. This (evolutionary) approach starts to shed light on the very nature of clausal derivation: modern syntax analyses even finite clauses/sentences as being built upon the layer of the small clause. Metaphors of evolutionary layering have been invoked in various other domains, as discussed in section 4. Section 5 offers some corroborating evidence for the proposal, including language acquisition.

Consider the following three types of (marginal) RootSCs (i.e. small clauses used in root/unembedded contexts): (1) the so-called "Mad Magazine"/incredulity clauses (Akmajian 1984), (3) imperative/optative clauses, and (5) RootSCs anchored in pragmatic context (e. g. here-and-now, photograph captions, etc.). While (2), (4), and (6) can be considered their respective sentential counterparts, no sentential paraphrase completely captures the

[1] For travel support, I am grateful for the WSU Humanities Grant for Innovative Projects. For many good comments and discussions regarding various ideas in this paper, I am grateful to: Martha Ratliff, Natasha Kondrashova, Relja Vulanović, Eugenia Casielles, Ellen Barton, Kate Paesani, Pat Siple, Dan Seeley, as well as the audiences at 2006 SLS, 2006 MLS, 2007 GURT, 2007 ILA, 2007 Max Planck Workshop on Complexity in Leipzig, 2007 ISU Conference on Recursion, and 2007 FASL, especially, David Gil, Geoffrey Sampson, John McWhorter, Dan Everett, Tecumseh Fitch, Stephanie Harves, Richard Kayne, John Locke, Eric Reuland, Ken Safir, and Rafaella Zanuttini. All errors are mine.

expressive power of RootSCs. This is just one indication that RootSCs are not simply elliptical versions of full sentences (see section 2).

(1)   Him retire!?   John a doctor?!   Her happy?!
(2)   Is he going to retire?   Is John a doctor?   Is she happy?
(3)   Me first!   Family first!   Everybody out!
(4)   I want to be first!   Family should be first!   Everybody must go out!
(5)   Class in session.   Problem solved.   Case closed.   Me in Rome.
(6)   The class is in session.   The problem has been solved.   The case is closed. I am in Rome.

These marginal clauses involve at least one application of the combinatorial principle (Merge), which combines a noun/pronoun with a predicate (not necessarily verb), the semantic import of which can be characterized as predication. When it comes to embedded small clauses, they are sometimes considered to be projections of the predicate, for example VPs, APs, PPs (cf. Stowell 1981, 1983; see section 2 below), while at other times they are simply labelled as SCs, suggesting hesitation about determining their nature/headedness.

Verb-Noun (VN) "exocentric" compounds, illustrated below for English and Serbian, are the clearest examples of unheaded structures (hence the term "exocentric"): neither of the morphological elements in these compounds determines their semantic or morphosyntactic nature:[2]

(7)   *daredevil, killjoy, Lovelady* [surname for a philanderer], *pickpocket, sawbones, scarecrow, Shakespeare, turncoat*

(8)   *cepi-dlaka*   "split-hair = hairsplitter"
      ispi-čutura   "empty-flask = drunkard"
      jebi-vetar   vulgar: "screw-wind = charlatan"
      kljuj-drvo   "peck-wood = wood-pecker"
      muti-voda   "muddy-water = trouble-maker"
      seci-kesa   "cut-purse = pick-pocket"
      vrti-guz   "spin-bottom = fidget"

Adding to the curiosity (and madness), the verb in Serbian VN compounds surfaces with a distinct imperative ending *i/j* (as in the examples of (8)), reinforcing the syntactic/clausal derivation. Progovac (2006b, 2007a) has proposed that these compounds preserve ancient mood morphology, which in Serbian is best approximated as imperative.[3] While ExCs used to be plentiful

---

[2] In this respect, Jackendoff (1999, 2002) noted that the relatively flat (non-hierarchical) structure of adjuncts, as well as raw concatenation of compounds, still retain a bit of protolinguistic flavour.

[3] A fossilized imperative is also still used in some dialects of Serbian in narratives as "Historical Imperative" (Stevanović 1966: 412–13):   [footnote continues on opposite page]

in, for example, English (Weekley 1916) and Serbian (Mihajlović 1992), demonstrating striking metaphorical and expressive richness, thousands of them have been lost, partly due to their derogatory and/or vulgar nature.[4]

2 Measuring syntactic complexity

This section shows that one can establish syntactic measures of complexity even using the theoretical tools of Minimalism (e.g. N. Chomsky 1995), the framework most reluctant to embrace either graded syntactic complexity or gradual evolution of syntax (see e.g. N. Chomsky 2005 and references there).[5]

The rudimentary grammar of RootSCs and ExCs can be characterized as having the following salient properties (see also Roeper's (1999) notion of Default Grammar):

(9)   Rudimentary grammar properties:
   (i)   There is *(at least) one instance of the combinatorial syntactic principle Merge*, which combines two words into a single utterance, as in *Me retire?!, Family first!, scare-crow.*[6]
   (ii) In contrast to their sentential/finite counterparts, RootSCs ((1), (3), (5)) show *no tense or structural (nominative) case*: subject pronouns exhibit default accusative case (see e.g. Schütze 2001), and NPs need not have articles (5), suggesting that D(eterminer) P(hrase) is not obligatory (see also note 9 below). The sentence/clause is analysed in Minimalism as necessarily involving a TP layer (Tense Phrase), superimposed over the small clause layer. My argument is that *RootSCs project/involve no TP* layer.

(i) *A on ti skini motiku s ramena, zabij je u zemlju, ostavi fenjer kraj sebe i sedi na ladju.*
"And he take off.IMP the spade from his shoulder, dig.IMP it into the ground, leave.IMP the lantern by himself, and sit.IMP on the boat."

It is commonly held that the Slavonic imperative descended from the ancient Proto-Indo-European "injunctive," possibly via an optative sense (see e. g. Kiparsky 1968 for definition and discussion; see also Stevanović 1974). The injunctive at some point became specialized for non-indicative (irrealis) moods, expressing wishes, commands, and/or exclamations. Note that RootSCs are also predominantly interpreted as irrealis ((1), (3)); see section 2 for further discussion.

[4] ExCs are found not only across Indo-European languages, but also in non-Indo-European languages, exhibiting intriguing similarities in form and imagery (Progovac 2006b, 2007a). One example is Tashelhit Berber, spoken in Morocco (Dris Soulaimani, pers. comm.), whose *ssum-sitan* "suck-cow = insect" closely corresponds to Old English *burst-cow,* with the same meaning.

[5] The reader not versed in Minimalism will have no trouble following the arguments, given that I have avoided any unnecessary formalisms, as well as providing ample clarification. For a more technical and extensive background on clause structure in Minimalism, with special reference to RootSCs, the reader is referred to Progovac (2006a).

[6] I assume that transitivity involves an additional layer of structure, such as an additional VP shell. Since transitivity may be a later evolutionary development in clause building, I do not consider it here. While the issue deserves further consideration, I tentatively assume that passive-looking clauses (e.g. *Problem solved*) do not involve a transitivity layer or Move(ment) (see Progovac 2006a for some discussion).

(iii) Many of these RootSCs are verbless, and even where a verb is present, it shows no tense or agreement with the subject. The semantic conse-quence of no tense is arguably an *underdetermined illocutionary force*, which in RootSCs of today typically ranges over a variety of irrealis (non-indicative) interpretations (Akmajian 1984; Progovac 2006a).[7]

(iv) Furthermore, *neither RootSCs (SCs with default case subjects) nor ExCs are recursive*: neither can self-embed, which is expected if they lack functional projections that would facilitate embedding (see Progovac 2007c for details and implications).

This chapter raises the following questions, which also serve as themes in the other contributions to the present volume. First, are apparently simpler structures truly simpler, or do they in fact encode silent, hidden categories? Second, if they are truly simpler, can the degree of complexity be quantified? Third, can the degree of complexity be determined only for specific domains, or can there be a measure of overall complexity? Given the morphosyntactic and semantic makeup of RootSCs (e.g. their distinct default case, uninflected verb form, expressivity), RootSCs cannot be analysed as just elliptical/abbre-viated versions of full sentences, other than by resorting to brute force (see Progovac 2006a for discussion). Instead, RootSCs exhibit consistent and systematic properties of a different, simpler syntax. The rest of the section shows how the differences in complexity between RootSC grammar and finite sentential grammar can be quantified.

In fact, Minimalist syntactic theory (including N. Chomsky 1995) analyses every clause/sentence, including finite sentences, as deriving from a small clause (see e.g. Stowell 1981, 1983; Burzio 1981; Kitagawa 1986; Koopman and Sportiche 1991; Hale and Keyser 2002). This small clause core gets transformed into a full/finite clause only upon subsequent merger of a layer of e.g. Tense/ TP and the subsequent Move(ment) of the subject into TP:

(10)   a. $[_{SC/AP}$ John happy]
       b. $[_{TP}$ is $[_{SC/AP}$ John $[_{A'}$ happy]]] $\rightarrow$
       c. $[_{TP}$ John $[_{T'}$ is $[_{SC/AP}$ t $[_{A'}$ happy]]]]

(11)   a. $[_{SC/VP}$ John worry]
       b. $[_{TP}$ will $[_{SC/VP}$ John $[_{V'}$ worry]]] $\rightarrow$
       c. $[_{TP}$ John $[_{T'}$ will $[_{SC/VP}$ t $[_{V'}$ worry]]]]
       ("t" stands for the trace of the moved subject.)

---

[7] Importantly, such small clauses typically express statements in early child language. This shift in interpretation of RootSCs from childhood to adulthood arguably parallels the historical development of indicative from injunctive in pre-Indo-European, as discussed in section 5; see also note 3 for the nature of the irrealis verb form in exocentric compounds.

In contrast to the (a) examples, which only involve a small clause layer, the (c) examples, in addition, have a functional TP layer, more instances of Merge, at least one instance of Move, and structural (nominative) case, which is associated with TP. Given this derivation, as well as the discussion of RootSCs above, the following seems an obvious way to quantify/measure the differences in complexity between RootSCs and finite clauses:

(12)   Some preliminary measures of syntactic complexity:
   (i) All other things being equal, a grammar which operates with only one layer of clausal structure (small clause layer) is *syntactically* simpler than a grammar which, in addition to that, has a functional layer of tense/TP (or comparable functional projection) superimposed upon it.[8]
   (ii) Related to (i), all other things being equal, a grammar which involves only the principle of Merge is *syntactically* simpler than a grammar which also involves the principle of Move (which typically serves to connect different syntactic layers – see (i); see also discussion below).
   (iii) Also related to (i), all other things being equal, a grammar which involves structural case distinctions (associated with DP and TP in English) is more complex than the one which shows no such case distinctions.[9]

Thus, RootSC grammar is simpler than full sentential grammar on at least three measures of syntactic complexity, as proposed above. The simplest grammars in this regard would be the ones which involve one single instance of Merge, no Move, and no structural case. While at least some RootSCs can be analysed in this fashion, exocentric compounds arguably come closest to this kind of grammar.[10]

While exocentric compounds exhibit possibly basic VN order (e.g. *kill-joy*), arguably derived by a single instance of Merge, their endocentric counterparts

[8] TP is considered to be an "extended" projection typically of VP; on the other hand, DP is considered to be an extended projection typically of NP.

[9] Notice that only TP subjects can and must receive nominative case, while RootSC subjects necessarily appear in the default case, which coincides with accusative with English pronouns (examples (1–6)). Likewise, the article is only obligatory with TP subjects, but not with RootSC subjects (5, 6). For further discussion of Case, DP, and Tense correlations, as well as for a difference in this respect between embedded small clauses and RootSCs, see the discussion in Progovac (2006a), based on Longobardi (1994).

[10] As a working hypothesis, I assume that only certain morphemes are syntactically Merged, e.g. those that are associated with syntactic functional projections, such as Tense. In this respect, the accusative morpheme on default case pronouns would not involve syntactic Merge; rather, the whole accusative form should be seen as the closest approximation in English of a proto-syntactic caseless form.

(e.g. *joy-kill-er, mind-read-er*) involve not only additional morphemes (Merges), but also arguably an additional layer of structure (transitivity), as well as an instance of Move (see Progovac 2006b, 2007a).[11] Moreover, E. Clark et al. (1986) found that children initially produce compounds such as *grate-cheese/rip-paper* in lieu of *cheese-grater/paper-ripper*, attesting to the more complex nature of the latter.

If indeed grammars can vary in complexity in a measurable way, then it is possible to make an argument for the gradual evolution of syntax, and moreover it is possible to do so even using the tools of Minimalism. The measures of complexity discussed here pertain to syntax alone, and not to language complexity in general. However, seen in an evolutionary light, developing a more elaborate syntax may have contributed to redundancy and robustness with respect to other domains, such as prosody and pragmatics; according to Carroll (2005: 170–1), this situation creates the opportunity for the evolution of specialization through the division of labour, which in turn can lead to increased overall complexity (see also section 4 on the complex interaction between prosody and speech). However, measuring overall complexity would be a much more challenging task than what this chapter has attempted.

3 Evolutionary layers of clausal structure

Many syntacticians believe that it is inconceivable for there to exist, or to have ever existed, a human grammar which does not come complete with multiple Merges, Moves, structural case, and a series of functional projections. The following quotation from Berwick (1998: 338–9) summarizes this widespread view:

In this sense, there is no possibility of an "intermediate" *syntax* between a non-combinatorial one and full natural language – one either has Merge in all its generative glory, or one has no combinatorial syntax at all . . .

This stance has been challenged by e.g. Pinker and Bloom (1990) and Jackendoff (1999, 2002), specifically when it comes to evolution.

While I cannot produce physical proof that RootSCs and ExCs are illustrative of an early stage of grammar in language evolution, I can show, given such data, not only that gradual evolution of syntax is conceivable, but that there are many

---

[11] Given the discussion in notes 6 and 10, the morpheme *-er* should be subject to syntactic Merge, since it induces transitivity/agency, associated with a functional projection. For some early syntactic approaches to word formation, which include (equivalents of) Merge and Move, see e.g. Roeper and Siegel (1978), Fabb (1984), as well as references in A. Spencer (1991) and Progovac (2007a).

aspects of sentential grammar itself that can best be explained by invoking such gradual evolution. Furthermore, some support for this view can be found in language acquisition and grammaticalization processes (section 5).

My concrete proposal is that RootSCs and ExCs instantiate/approximate a grammar of an earlier stage of syntax, protosyntax, which was measurably simpler: while it exhibited the basic principle of Merge and basic predication, it operated with no Move, no Tense, no TP, and no structural case (see section 2). In this sense, RootSCs and ExCs can be seen as "living fossils" from this proto-syntax stage (see Progovac 2006b, 2007a).[12] The idea of language fossils is introduced in Bickerton (1990), and applied to syntax in Jackendoff (1999, 2002). Importantly, what I consider here to be preserved is the RootSC syntax, and our ability to tap into it, rather than these specific present-day realizations/approximations of such syntax.

The small clause is at the heart of syntax. Almost any full (simple) sentence has a RootSC counterpart, rendering RootSCs quite productive, even if marginal. Moreover, as pointed out in the previous section, full clauses/sentences are now analysed as involving (at least) two layers of structure: the inner small clause (SC) layer, and the outer TP layer, with the subject first merging in the small clause, and then moving to TP, as the following examples repeated from (10, 11) above illustrate:

(13) $[_{TP}$ John $[_{T'}$ is $[_{SC/AP}$ t $[_{A'}$ happy$]]]]$

(14) $[_{TP}$ John $[_{T'}$ will $[_{SC/VP}$ t $[_{V'}$ worry$]]]]$

Parker (2006: 285) raises the interesting question of why the Minimalist framework has to resort to the principle of Move, in addition to Merge. If the small clause layer of the sentence can be seen as a vestige of the evolutionary tinkering in building clausal/sentential structure, then Move can be seen (metaphorically) as a force which connects different layers of clausal derivation as determined by such evolutionary tinkering (almost as if sentence building retraces evolutionary steps) (see Progovac 2007b, c for more arguments along this line).

In this evolutionary view, Tense and TP did not emerge from scratch, but were added to/superimposed upon what was already there – the small clause layer – allowing small clauses to survive, but only in marginalized and subordinated roles. This gradual building of clausal structure is arguably also evident in language acquisition (section 5). The following section discusses metaphors of layering and dominance applied to other domains.

---

[12] "Living fossils" are species that have changed little from their fossil ancestors in the distant past, e.g. lungfish (Ridley 1993: 525).

4 Evolutionary strata in other domains

A rather concrete example of evolutionary layering and recency dominance comes from the adaptation that led to black coloration in leopards, which still preserves the previous layer of orange spots (Carroll 2005). Metaphorically speaking, the small clause grammar can be seen as orange spots still lurking through the layer of the more recent, dominant black coloration of sentential/ TP speech.

Stratification accounts have also been proposed for brain development in general, where newly emerged patterns become dominant and "rework" older patterns into conformity with them (e.g. Rolfe 1996; Vygotsky 1981). Vygotsky (pp. 155–6) states:

> Brain development proceeds in accordance with the laws of stratification of construction of new levels on old ones.... Instinct is not destroyed, but "copied" in conditioned reflexes as a function of the ancient brain, which is now to be found in the new one.

A repeated theme in Piaget's work is the inclusion of attainments of earlier stages in the structures of later stages (Gruber and Vonèche 1977: xxiii). In this perspective, RootSCs can be seen as the older/lower structures, which are retained in, and subordinated to, the newer/higher sentential TP structures.

The notion of the "triune brain" is also consistent with the idea of evolutionary layering/subordination (Dan Seeley, pers. comm.). According to Isaacson (1982: 1, 240), following Broca (e.g. 1878), the inner lobe of the brain is organized into two layers: the inner and phyletically oldest ring (allocortex) and the outer limbic ring (transitional cortex). The lowest, protoreptilian brain involves ancestral learning and memories, which are subjugated by the higher limbic brain, thus allowing forgetfulness and suppression of the protoreptilian habitual way of responding (MacLean 1949: 240–2, 247). In turn, rational decision-making is associated with the prefrontal cortex, or yet higher brain (Strickberger 2000: 506).

Deacon (1997: 300) argues that each higher-order form of a representational relationship must be constructed from, or decomposed into, lower levels of representation, in such a way that indexical reference depends upon iconic reference, and symbolic reference in turn depends upon indexical reference. Deacon (p. 453) concludes that a failure to appreciate the constitutive role of lower forms leads to a perspective that "kicks the ladder away after climbing up to the symbolic realm and then imagines that there never was a ladder in the first place".

In addition, according to Deacon (1997), speech prosody, which is recruited from ancestral call functions, is subordinated to speech. Like calls, prosodic features are primarily produced by the larynx and lungs, and not articulated by the mouth and tongue. But unlike calls of other species, prosodic vocal modification is continuous and highly correlated with the speech process (p. 418):

It is as though we haven't so much shifted control from visceral to voluntary means but superimposed intentional cortical motor behaviors over autonomous subcortical vocal behaviors. (Deacon 1997: 251)

When it comes to clause structure, it is as though we have not so much replaced small clause grammar with sentential grammar, but superimposed one upon the other, forcing them to adjust to each other, and creating syntactic quirks and complexities that only evolution can get away with.

5 Some corroborating evidence

An evolutionary path from a tenseless stage to a TP stage, such as the one explored here, is consistent with more recent grammaticalization processes. Kiparsky (1968), among others, has argued that once tense/indicative emerged in pre-Indo-European, the older unmarked tense/mood form, injunctive, began to specialize for non-indicative/irrealis (elsewhere) moods (see notes 3 and 7 above). It is thus conceivable that human grammars also proceeded from a protosyntax stage, characterized by RootSCs, to a stage with Tense/TP, abstracting away from any intermediate stages and properties.

Arguably, this is also the path along which language acquisition proceeds. Children's two-word stage is characterized by argument–predicate utterances, many of which can be analysed as RootSCs (see e.g. Radford 1988, 1990; Guilfoyle and Noonan 1992; Lebeaux 1989; Ouhalla 1991; Platzak 1990; Potts and Roeper 2006; but see e.g. Guasti 2002 for opposing views and references).[13]

Even though the issue is controversial, according to e.g. Rolfe (1996: 782) recent views permit the use of data from ontogeny (language acquisition) to corroborate other arguments regarding phylogeny/evolution. Burling (2005: 174) also makes use of the phylogeny/ontogeny connection, and so does Lieberman (e.g. 2000) in his discussion of the descent of the larynx (see also Strickberger 2000: 493–4). Ridley (1993: 551) considers the relationship to be a classic topic in evolutionary biology, which is again active today.[14]

---

[13] Agrammatic aphasic patients also often resort to RootSCs and other subsentential speech (e.g. Kolk 2006; Siple 2006; and references there).

[14] Additionally, the reader is referred to Fitch (1997), Carroll (2005), and Locke and Bogin (2006) for more recent perspectives regarding the relationship between what they call DEVO and EVO.

In his work on Riau Indonesian, Gil (2005a) also invokes the phylogeny–ontogeny connection. In particular, he argues that Riau comes close to being a perfect example of an IMA language (Isolating–Monocategorial–Associational), a language whose syntax can be characterized as exhibiting a simple combinatorial principle (call it Merge), the semantic effect of which is a loose associational relationship. According to Gil, IMA language may constitute a stage both in language acquisition and in language evolution. My own conclusions are consistent with the possibility that there exist languages spoken today which are characterized by a version of RootSC syntax, and such languages may indeed include Riau Indonesian, as described in Gil (2005a, and see Chapter 2 above), as well as Pirahã, as described in Everett (2005; see also Chapter 15 below).

6 Concluding remarks

The first goal of this chapter is to demonstrate that Root Small Clause (RootSC) syntax is measurably simpler than sentential TP syntax. Roughly speaking, in comparison to sentential grammar, RootSC grammar involves fewer layers of clausal structure, typically one (the small clause layer), lacking at least the Tense Phrase (TP), but also Move and structural (nominative) case, which are associated with TP. My second argument is that RootSCs (and exocentric compounds), which approximate this rudimentary grammar, can be seen as living fossils of a protosyntactic stage in language evolution.

Ultimately, the strongest arguments for gradual evolution of syntax will come from syntax itself, if indeed syntax still keeps the ladder along which it has been climbing (see section 4). It is thus significant that this evolutionary scenario sheds light on the very nature of present-day syntax, including why clausal structure is layered, and why the clause always begins to unfold at the bottom of the ladder, with the small clause.

15

An interview with Dan Everett

GEOFFREY SAMPSON

One of the most startling recent events in linguistics was the publication in 2005 of an article by Dan Everett (then of the University of Manchester, and since 2006 chairing the Department of Languages, Literatures, and Cultures of Illinois State University) on the language and culture of the Pirahãs, a tribe of a hundred or so people in a remote area of Amazonia. Pirahã, as Everett describes it in his *Current Anthropology* article, lacks many basic features often seen as essential to any human language. For instance, it is totally devoid of grammatical recursion, and it has no means of making precise statements about quantities – a forthcoming paper describes experiments which appear to establish that the Pirahã cannot distinguish even between "one" and "more than one".

Everett's account has naturally sparked intense controversy among academics; and his portrait of the remarkable Pirahã world-view has attracted great interest among the public at large. A new book, *Don't sleep, there are snakes: life and language in the Amazonian jungle*, is to be published simultaneously by Pantheon in the USA, Profile Books in Britain, DVA in Germany, and Flammarion in France. Film rights are under discussion.

In view of the fascinating and extremely controversial nature of Everett's work, the editors felt that rather than including a written version of his Leipzig talk here, it might advance our understanding of the overall workshop topic better to publish an interview challenging Everett on some of the points where linguists have felt sceptical. Happily, Everett was agreeable to this, and the "interview" was conducted via e-mail exchanges between Sampson and Everett after the close of the workshop.

GRS: Most of your critics appear to reject your portrayal of the Pirahã and their language on *a priori* grounds – because the Pirahã language as you describe it contradicts generative theories about language universals to which they are wedded, and/or because of political objections to the idea that one human culture might be simpler, cruder, or more primitive than another. I have no quarrel with your picture on either of those grounds. I share your belief that there is no evidence for innate language universals (Sampson 2005). And it strikes me as just daft to suggest that all human cultures are equally sophisticated. It seems obvious, for instance, that my own ancestors of fifteen centuries ago, the Anglo-Saxons of post-Roman, pre-Christian England, had a cruder culture than that of, say, their descendants and my recent ancestors in the nineteenth–twentieth centuries. Indeed it is really paradoxical for professional academics to deny the existence of such differences: if we ask what purpose the academic profession serves, a standard answer is that its function is to maintain and further refine the cultural heritage of society – which implies that societies can differ in levels of culture.

So I have no "ideological" differences with you. Still, I do wonder whether we are justified as seeing the Pirahã as so extremely distant from ourselves as you claim.

DLE: On the *a priori* objections, I find these troubling at various levels and it seems important that they be confronted head-on. First, there is the idea that if it is claimed that a culture is primitive in any sense, the claimant is thereby asserting that the people of this culture are inferior to other people. I deal with this at length in *Don't sleep, there are snakes*. Here is what I say in one of the later chapters:

Is it possible to live a life without these crutches of religion and Truth? The Pirahãs do so live. They share some of our concerns, of course, since many of our societal preoccupations derive from our biology, independent of our culture (our cultures attribute meanings to otherwise ineffable, but no less real, concerns). But they live most of their lives outside these concerns because they have independently discovered the usefulness of living one day at a time. The Pirahãs simply make the immediate their focus of concentration and thereby, at a single stroke, eliminate huge sources of worry, fear, and despair that plague so many of us in Western societies.

They have no fictional stories. They have no craving for "Truth" – indeed the concept has no place in their values. Does this make them primitive? Many anthropologists have suggested so, which is why they are so concerned about finding Pirahã fiction and creation stories.

But there is an interesting alternative way to think about things. That would be that it is the *presence* of these concerns that makes a culture primitive, if we want to think in terms of primitive v. non-primitive. It would then be their absence that renders a culture more sophisticated. If that were true, the Pirahãs would be a very sophisticated people. Does this sound far-fetched? Ask yourself whether you think it is more sophisticated to look at the universe with worry, concern, and a belief that we can understand it all, or to enjoy life as it comes, recognizing the likely futility in looking for Truth or God.

The Pirahãs' culturally constrained epistemology can only be evaluated in terms of the results that it gives the Pirahãs relative to their own values. Since it serves them very well, there is no sense in the idea that it is inferior. In terms of overall complexity, however, one can make a case that the lack of recursion, the lack of number, numerals, and counting and so on, is more primitive in the technical sense of revealing that there are living languages that correspond to what some theorists, such as Ken Hale (1976) and Tom Givón (2008), have argued to be earlier stages of language evolution, when they claim that, phylogenetically and historically, parataxis and adjunction precede embedding. And there will almost certainly turn out to be other languages like Pirahã in many respects as fieldwork continues.

GRS: One of the besetting problems of social anthropology is that the most exotic, and therefore most educative, phenomena relate to inaccessible societies. As a result there has been a history of tall tales being taken seriously. One of the founders of the discipline, Bronisław Malinowski, is best known for his claim, backed up with circumstantial evidence, that natives of the Trobriand (now called Kiriwina) Islands were unaware of the male role in conception of babies – they did not believe that a person's father was a blood relative. (In early writing Malinowski said the same was true for most Australian aboriginal tribes.) When a local District Officer of the colonial administration objected that the Trobrianders did know about fatherhood, Malinowski seems to have begun by blustering about non-scientists being unqualified to debate with professional anthropologists, and finally more or less conceded that he was wrong (Pulman 2004) – though I wonder if one person is aware of that, for every hundred that have read about and accepted Malinowski's claim. Then there was Margaret Mead, who on the basis of a nine-month stay on Samoa with an expatriate white family in her early twenties published a romantic account of the Samoans as a carefree society entirely devoid of the stresses familiar in European life (Mead 1928); this has turned out to be an absurd travesty of the truth, seemingly based in part on her informants amusing themselves by winding her up (Freeman 1983), yet for decades it was taken extremely seriously and I believe it was even influential in American policymaking.

I certainly do not mean to accuse you of sharing Malinowski's pomposity, or the innocence which was no doubt appropriate to a well-brought-up American girl in the 1920s. Nevertheless, you will appreciate that people are bound to wonder whether Everett's Pirahãs may be another case of the same syndrome. What considerations convince you that the more remarkable aspects of Pirahã culture as you describe it are actually correct, rather than a misinterpretation of some more humdrum reality? And if the answer is largely gut feeling from immersion in the culture, then what considerations ought to convince the rest of us, who have no realistic opportunity to share that immersion?

DLE: The Pirahãs are not inaccessible. I have taken over twenty researchers with me to the Pirahãs over the years, from Peter Ladefoged (UCLA) to Ted Gibson (MIT). Jeanette Sakel (University of the West of England) and Eugénie Stapert (University of Manchester)[1] are learning the Pirahãs' language. Gibson and I have submitted a proposal for funding to eventually publish all the data I have collected in thirty years of field research on Pirahã on the internet – to provide anyone access to a searchable data base of Pirahã sounds, stories, grammar, and videos of experiments. And there are three other Pirahã speakers that I have used to check my ideas for quite some time: Steve Sheldon, Keren Madora, and Arlo Heinrichs, all of the Summer Institute of Linguistics. Sheldon lived among the Pirahãs from 1967 to 1976 and speaks the language well. Heinrichs lived among the Pirahãs from 1959 to 1967 and still remembers a great deal of the language – he was the first one to work seriously on the language (there is a brief description of the conditions under which Heinrichs worked in William Samarin's book, *Field linguistics*). Keren Madora has lived among the Pirahãs since 1977, for long periods of time. None of them disagrees with the core facts of my claims about the Pirahãs' culture and language.

But of course, the examples of Malinowski and Mead do come to mind. I worried quite a bit in the early years that I could be "committing a Malinowski". And one of my favourite quotes on field research comes from Mead in a letter of 16 January 1926 to her thesis adviser, Franz Boas:

I have no idea whether I am doing the right thing or not, or how valuable my results will be. It all weighs rather heavily on my mind.

This is the angst of every honest field researcher, in my opinion. As I describe field research in Everett (2004):

The history of research in general and field research in particular, is the history of fallible humans, evolved creatures, struggling to understand nearly infinite complexity in an alien environment. No one person is up to the demands of fieldwork, requiring as it does an idealized character from Arthur Conan Doyle. The outputs of our fieldwork will necessarily be incomplete records of our progress in understanding parts of wholes that exceed our abilities. Thus, our research reports, whether gram-

---

[1] [Editorial note:] Since the date of this interview, Eugénie Stapert has moved to the Max Planck Institute, Lepizig.

mars or articles or talks or webpages are never more nor less than our efforts to communicate with interested interlocutors about the beliefs we have come to form and hold, based on our experiences and how these beliefs affect our actions in science and in life. This is our canopy of epistemic humility.

Could I be wrong about Pirahã? Yes, of course. I probably am in many ways. But is unlikely that I am wrong simply because the Pirahãs are inaccessible or because I am being hoaxed like Mead (if she indeed was – I am not all that sure that she was wrong, in spite of Derek Freeman's regular assertions to the contrary). Field researchers like Mead, Malinowski, and, in more recent times, Napoleon Chagnon, are often criticized after the fact for various reasons, many of them petty and personal.

I think that Chagnon, for example, is the best anthropologist ever to work in the Amazon. But many criticize him, accuse him of staging the things he described, ascribe evil motives to him, and so on, because he made the politically incorrect assertion that the Yanomami are a "fierce people". He has been accused of racism, of failing to help the Yanomami in times of need, of being disrespectful of the Yanomami's political aspirations and so on. So far as I have been able to tell, these assertions are all false and Chagnon has given us the best account of the Yanomami that we have to date. I have come to sympathize with him more and more as people have begun levelling many of the same accusations against me.

When I first realized that I was not finding numbers, recursion, quantifiers, and so on in the language, all I thought about it was that if I looked harder and could devise better methodologies, I would discover these things. I believed then that all languages had to have these things. I know that "absence of evidence is not evidence of absence". I thought that maybe I just missed these phenomena. That was my opinion for a couple of decades. But I am now a more experienced field researcher. I have worked on more than two dozen languages in Mexico and Brazil. I am convinced that we are not going to find these things in the Pirahã language. On the other hand, that kind of authoritative assertion is not going to, nor should it, convince other researchers. That is why there is now a team of researchers conducting experiments on all of these claims. On numerals and counting, for example, Mike Frank, Evelina Fedorenko, and Ted Gibson (of MIT's Brain and Cognitive Sciences Department) and I have just had a paper accepted in *Cognition* (pending revisions), where we provide strong empirical support for the absence of any numerals or counting in Pirahã. With regard to recursion in Pirahã, Jeanette Sakel and Eugénie Stapert have a paper to appear in a special issue of the *Linguistic Review* that I am guest-editing in which they argue that there is indeed no evidence for recursion in Pirahã, based on their own fieldwork and a series of experiments and surveys of all the data I have collected on the language. Other experiments have been conducted, and results are still being analysed on a wide range of cognitive and linguistic behaviours of the Pirahãs. So far, there is not only no counterevidence to my claims, but the data are all consistent with and/or supportive of my claims. The videos of our experiments are archived in web-accessible format in Ted Gibson's MIT laboratory.

Whatever errors I may have committed, they are not of the Mead type, nor because the Pirahãs are as inaccessible as the Trobriand Islanders were, so that my claims cannot be independently investigated.

In recent correspondence with William Poser, he makes the following points that seem relevant to this issue (e-mail dated 30 September 2007 to Everett):

... granting that there is a history of anthropological fieldworkers making serious errors that were not recognized for a long time because there was no one to contradict them, we need to recognize that a lot of linguistic and ethnographic claims about much better known and accessible languages and societies have been similarly flawed. Cultural blinders, personal biases, theoretical fads, and flawed methodology, especially, in the linguistic case, elicitation techniques, operate even when the language or culture is well known and accessible. Furthermore, many questions are studied only by a small number of scholars, even in well known languages, so that, unless and until something triggers careful investigation, a factual claim may remain unchallenged for a surprisingly long time. (A minor example is the claim found in almost all descriptions of Japanese phonology that all syllables contain either one or two moras – in fact, all speakers of Japanese have some tri-moraic syllables.)

This is not to say that claims about obscure, inaccessible languages and cultures should not be carefully scrutinized, but rather that we need to recognize that received views based on better known languages and cultures do not contrast with them as discretely as we might think.

GRS: In 1986 you published an extensive description of the Pirahã language which made it sound interesting but not extraordinary. In your recent publications, you have sometimes described some of the very same language forms in new ways which do now put them outside the spectrum of language phenomena familiar to most linguists. Your leading critics, Nevins et al. (2007), proceed largely by saying that they find 1980s-Everett more believable than twenty-first-century-Everett. You have explained (e.g. in Colapinto 2007) that in the 1980s you were a convinced generative linguist, who forced any observation into the Procrustean generative analytic framework (as members of that school commonly do), while deeper experience of Pirahã, and more willingness to allow observation to control theorizing rather than vice versa, have led you recently to a better interpretation of the workings of the language.

That is fair enough. But Nevins et al. do have a point, surely, when they complain that you do not justify your changes of mind? Your *Current Anthropology* piece contains only few references to Everett (1986), and so far as I have seen those references do not focus on differences between the two language descriptions. If someone publishes a full-dress document saying *X*, and twenty years later publishes others that say not-*X*, we usually look for material within the later writings that draws attention to the inconsistency and explains why the earlier account has proved to be in error. If readers do not find much of that, can they be blamed for saying: "They can't both be right, we are given a free choice so I choose *X*"?

DLE: When I published the *Current Anthropology* article, I knew full well that I would need to do a lot more work and publish a great deal more to convince the linguistic public. But that paper was never intended to be the final word. It was the opening salvo in what I hope will be a revolution in linguistics, a revolution in which linguists come to see field research as a fundamental part of their identities as linguists and in which culture's effects on language are seriously investigated. There is a widespread view that it was long ago shown that culture has no significant influence on grammar. Steve Pinker has made this claim to me in recent e-mails, and says pretty much the same thing in his book *The stuff of thought* (2007). I think that is just wrong. I knew that a linguistic journal would be unlikely to publish my culture–grammar paper for these very reasons. So I submitted the paper to the premier journal of cultural anthropology instead. I felt confident in my analysis, but I wanted the proposal out there, with rigorous testing of all the claims to follow. I don't see that this order of things is any different from what goes on in most linguistic theorizing or scientific research in general. And now the testing is under way.

But the contradictions between Everett (1986) and Everett (2005) are just not all that big in terms of the data discussed. The differences have been grossly exaggerated. I told Chomsky in 1984, when I was a Visiting Scholar at MIT, that I could find no evidence for embedding in Pirahã other than the *-sai* nominalizer (which was a focus of Nevins et al.'s discussion). It turns out that *-sai* has functions that overlap with nominalization but that this is not the best analysis of it. Experiments by Mike Frank and others, and the new paper by Sakel and Stapert, show this clearly. With that gone, there just is no evidence for recursion in Pirahã. As often happens in field research, a minor difference in the way this or that morpheme or construction is analysed can have profound effects on the grammar as a whole. One doesn't see all of this at first.

So Everett (1986) is a good study, I think. I am proud to have written it. And my opinions about the facts have changed really very little since then. I have found that some of the data were incomplete and so on, as I state in Everett (2007). But these are minor factual adjustments that turn out to have major theoretical consequences. What *has* really changed over the years is my analysis of how all the pieces fit in the grammar as a whole. That is natural. Some would call it progress, not contradiction.

And we know that if we look at, say, Chomsky's writings over the years, we get changes of a similar nature and even changes in the judgements on the grammaticality of English utterances. The difference is that the methodology of Chomskyan grammar is much poorer, much less likely to test claims by experimentation or to move beyond solipsistic grammars towards testable grammars subject to, say, the methods being developed by Josh Tenenbaum and his laboratory colleagues at MIT's Brain and Cognitive Sciences department. The methodology of descriptive linguistics or structuralist linguistics, as outlined in, say, Longacre (1964), Z. S. Harris (1947), Samarin (1967), or even my own field guide (Everett forthcoming b), is arguably superior to the introspective work characteristic of what I call "armchair linguistics". Couple field methodology with standard psychological experimentation and you begin to approach a much more scientific basis for a linguistics which is cautiously deductive, enthusiastically inductive, and mainly abductive – with the different types of reasoning appearing, of course, at different stages in the analytical process.

Another point worth reminding readers of is that although there is an increased burden of proof on claims like mine that go so against the grain, just about every point that is raised against the lack of replicability of my claims and differences in earlier and later claims can be raised (as I mention with regard to Chomsky) with regard to just about any linguist's body of work. But we generally are not as demanding on the factual claims that support our pre-existing ideas as we are on the claims that contradict them. So there are likely many "false positives" in published grammars for ideas popular in certain theories, but those go unchallenged because they are "comfortable" facts. The possibility of "false negatives" is what worries most of us. This is human nature.

GRS: Nevins et al. quote Anna Wierzbicka (2005) as saying that your recent writings gratuitously "exoticize" Pirahã, by describing morphologically complex words with simple meanings in terms of the etymological sense of the roots – as if a Frenchman were to argue that English speakers have a weird view of intellectual activity, because, instead of the simple concept *comprendre*, English-speakers say that people *se tiennent debout sous* (under-stand) an idea. In 1986 the Pirahã phrase *hi xogi* was treated as unproblematically meaning "all" or "everyone"; the two morphemes literally translate as "third person" and "big", and in 2005 you insist on translating *hi xogi* as "he big" as opposed to "all". I have not seen Anna Wierzbicka's commentary, but she has a real point, hasn't she? It has often struck me that if the French were a remote jungle tribe, English speakers who learned about the gender system of their language might conclude that they are animists who believe that every object embodies a male or female spirit. We know that the French are no such thing, but that is because many of them are eloquent intellectuals who tell us what they do and do not believe; we could not infer their rational world-view from the structure of their language.

In Everett (2007) you respond to Wierzbicka's objection by saying that translating *hi xogi* as "all" would be inaccurate "because... there is *no* word in Pirahã with the meaning of the English word 'all' ". That is circular: "Pirahã has no quantifiers, and if you doubt this and think you have found one you must have mistranslated it, because Pirahã has no quantifiers." What guarantees that it is your new treatment of *hi xogi* which is correct and your earlier treatment erroneous?

DLE: What I say about "all" (*hixogii*) is not circular. It is a simple point. When I asserted that it meant "all" in 1986 I didn't check the truth conditions. The truth conditions for universal quantification are not met by any Pirahã word, at least not by the word that I used to think meant "all". There is no situation in which the use of the expression *xogii/xogiaagao/etc.* would be rejected if there were an exception. "He ate meat *xogio*", for example, is acceptable to any Pirahã, any time, even if part of the meat is still uneaten, so long as a lot of the meat is eaten (not even "most" of it – just a lot). I answer Wierzbicka's objections, and those of Nevins et al., at length with similar reasoning in both my 2005 *Current Anthropology* article and in Everett (2007). I don't think that there is anything to add.

Of course it is easy to exoticize other languages and peoples. We do it all the time. And this can be a mistake. In *The language instinct* Pinker criticizes Whorf for doing exactly this with the Hopi language in order to make a point about language's effect on thought.

But the reverse mistake is just as bad – homogenizing languages and cultures so that they all fit the same assumptions about what languages can do and how they should sound. If one language has a word that doesn't have a counterpart in another language, then it can be and usually will be wrong and misleading to translate them as the same. True, if we don't do this, one language can look "exotic" to the speakers of another language (the Pirahãs could say that my translation of English "all" exoticizes English, if they cared about such things). My translations of Pirahã utterances in my writings on the language reflect my best judgement on what is meant. If it sounds like natural English, fine. If it sounds exotic that is because it doesn't mean exactly what any English word or utterance means.

I do not believe in Universal Translation. I don't believe that what can be said in one language can be said naturally (or even at all) in all other languages. I do not believe that all languages have the same expressive power. In fact, if I am right, some languages are nonfinite and others are finite.

This is one of the reasons why I am sceptical of any grammar that lacks a certain exotic flavour. I would bet that for any grammar in which all the sentences can be translated into idiomatic, natural English, the field researcher is probably missing something. But that is my view.

GRS: A point that is not a criticism but a request for clarification: I am not sure what you are saying about the history of Pirahã language and culture. We are told that the Pirahãs are closely related ethnically to a group called Mura, who used to speak various languages (or dialects) related to Pirahã but who have now assimilated to Portuguese-speaking Amazon culture, so that by 1986 (p. 200) you described the Mura language(s) as "(probably) extinct". Is enough known about those languages, and the pre-assimilation Mura culture, to say whether they shared the special features and "gaps" of Pirahã language and culture? (Comments you make in Everett (2005) referring to the work of Curt Nimuendaju suggest that they did not share some of them.)

In his critique of you, Richard Boast (2006) saw it as a potential refutation if one could show that Pirahã language/culture had decayed in the historical period from a more sophisticated earlier state. We know that material cultures do sometimes decay – the well-known example (Diamond 1998: 312–13) is the indigenous Tasmanians, who lost much of the culture they inherited from mainland Australia; so perhaps the same might happen with a language. Unlike Boast, I cannot see how that would go against anything you say. Surely it would be just as interesting to find that an "ordinary" language can fall so far down the scale of complexity, while still being the sole language of a community, as it would be to find languages which have been as strikingly simple as Pirahã throughout known history. But it would be good to know which it is in this case; or is the answer that we just do not know?

DLE: I also address this in the *Current Anthropology* article. First, there is no evidence for "decay" of Pirahã culture. Second, even if there were, this isn't relevant. We know that for more than 100 years, likely for 300 years, the Pirahã culture has been pretty much the way it is now. That is a stable system and needs to be described for what it is, not for what it was. If this description concludes that Pirahã lacks recursion or has an Immediacy of Experience Principle, etc., then it is just irrelevant that the language might have had recursion or no Immediacy of Experience Principle 500 years ago.

I wouldn't be mistaken describing current English culture without reference to Arthur and the Knights of the Round Table, whether or not the culture of that fable was ever the dominant culture. One might claim that English culture has "degenerated" since the days of chivalry, since degeneration in this sense is largely in the eye of the beholder and is not a scientific notion; but that would not entail that description of the current state of the culture is wrong because it fails to refer to earlier stages. This is the cultural equivalent of Saussure's diachronic v. synchronic distinction in the study of language.

As to the Mura, we know relatively little about them before their assimilation of Brazilian culture, other than that they had large villages, controlled the Amazon from Peru to modern-day Manaus, and were eventually nearly wiped out by the Mundurucùs who were armed by Brazilians for exactly that purpose. We do know that the Muras alive today, near Manaus, look very much like the Pirahãs, though they live as Brazilians. So one probable lesson we can draw from this is that – contrary to what many have claimed (never me!) – there is no genetic difference that "limits" the Pirahãs' grammar or culture: the Muras are doing fine speaking Portuguese, with recursion, numerals, and so on. Along this same line, Pirahãs that were kidnapped and then raised from an early age among Brazilians (there are some) speak Portuguese just fine, natively, and show no obvious cognitive or linguistic differences from the Brazilians that have raised them.

GRS: Much of your theorizing about Pirahã language and culture focuses on what you call the Immediacy of Experience Principle, which is central enough for you to reduce it to an acronym, IEP. You claim that this principle, that Pirahã assertions always relate directly to the moment of speech, predicts a range of quite diverse "gaps" in the language, from recursion to numerals to colour terms and more; it is often far from obvious how the IEP as you state it does entail all these consequences. But one thing it surely must entail is that the Pirahãs would not talk about hypothetical future events. Yet Anthea Fraser Gupta points out to me that Kate Douglas's (2006) account of your work quotes a group of Pirahãs on tape saying things like "When will we see you?", "When you come, bring us some matches", and so forth. Presumably these are translations of utterances in Pirahã, but how are they compatible with your "IEP"? Is this just a case of popular journalism getting the wrong end of the stick, or what?

DLE: Asking me when I am returning to the village is not *speculation* about future events. Counterfactuals, discussions of what to do in three years from now, hypothetical future events, do not occur so far as I can tell. These are speculations about future events. But the Pirahãs experience people coming and going from villages all the time. Comings and goings are part of their immediate experience. So asking me when I am coming is asking for an assertion relative to the moment of speech, well within their everyday experience, and is allowed by the Immediacy of Experience Principle as I state it.

GRS: I also wonder why it is important to you to derive diverse properties of Pirahã from a single, simple abstract principle such as Immediacy of Experience. That feels like the kind of intellectual move that is attractive to the true believers in innate knowledge of language. They hold that there is something in human DNA, we know not what, which leads to our already knowing most of what there is to know about the grammar of our mother tongue before we hear examples of it. If that is credible at all, it is more likely to be true provided what look superficially like many separate structural features all follow from a few basic principles; so the generativists postulate mathematical abstractions with names like "A-over-A", or "Move Alpha", and argue that large ranges of specific structural facts about particular languages follow as logical consequences of those abstractions. If one sees languages as cultural institutions, evolved step by step like other products of human culture, that picture becomes implausible. Products of evolution typically do not have that all-of-a-piece quality; they successively incorporate separate, unrelated structures, as the long-drawn-out process of evolution seizes on whatever solutions it happens to encounter to particular fitness issues. Evolutionary products are more like the imperial system of weights and measures in its full glory, with, I don't know, two units of length of the same order of magnitude for measuring horizontally (in yards) and vertically (in feet), or one complicated system for weighing most things and a loosely related complicated system for weighing gems, or weighing medicines, than they are like the metric system in which units for every possible physical quantity are derived logically from a few fundamentals. How does your rejection of innate Universal Grammar square with your wish to derive many separate facts about Pirahã from the IEP?

DLE: My rejection of Universal Grammar is based on my observations that culture can exert architectonic effects on grammar. And I also reject the methodology of Universal Grammar – the deductive reasoning from an assumption to facts. By and large I don't think that this is useful in linguistics.

Does the IEP sound like this? I suppose that it does in some narrow way. Maybe it is wrong or less than useful for the same reasons. That needs to be tested. But the IEP is fundamentally unlike UG on closer examination. It is the result of trying to understand or make sense of the number of "gaps" in *Pirahã* culture and grammar. Are these coincidences in the same language or do they all follow from a single principle? I think that the evidence suggests that they follow from a single principle.

The IEP is unlike UG because I doubt that it is found in any other language. I suspect that what we will find when we begin to research the interactions of culture and language more carefully is that we will have at least as many principles governing grammar–culture interactions as there are grammar–culture pairings. Probably many more, because it is less likely that each grammar–culture relation can be summarized by a single principle.

GRS: Again, Everett (2005) includes a passage about "parameterization" of a universal feature [R] (for "reference"), with a default value that can be reset by a child's language experience. This sounds as though you are assuming the kind of innate Language Acquisition Device, imposing specific properties on any humanly learnable language, which the bulk of your recent writing rejects. I am puzzled.

DLE: That is a citation from an earlier work of mine (Everett 1993) during the time that I believed in parameters. Now I would simply say that if we applied a neo-Reichenbachian model of tense to Pirahã, Pirahã's tense system lacks Reichenbach's "R-point".

GRS: At one point in your reply to Nevins et al. you push your rejection of the Universal Grammar idea further than your evidence seems to warrant, even if we accept your interpretation of Pirahã: you write: "I am claiming [that] every language is non-trivially different from other languages in ways incompatible with UG." It is a bit difficult to unpick the logic of the quantification here! You might be saying "for any language *L*, there is at least one member of the set of all other languages that is sufficiently different from *L* to disprove UG" – in which case all you need to do is point to one really strange language, such as Pirahã. But you *sound* as though you are saying something about all languages, rather than about one strange language. It sounds as though you are saying that for any plausible theory of Universal Grammar, English will refute it in some way(s), French in other way(s), Chinese in other way(s), and so on and on. Is this what you are saying? In that case, you might believe it but you would surely agree that no amount of discussion of Pirahã alone could substantiate it.

(To me it seems implausible. Because of intensive cultural interactions, the main present-day European languages, at least, seem to me pretty well wholly intertranslatable. What I find really offensive about generative linguists is that they observe this confluence of cultures and argue that it is not a contingent fact about the present-day world but a biological necessity, and hence they refuse to recognize the separateness of Third World cultures or those of our own ancestors; cf. Sampson (2007). That is robbing people of their patrimony, to my mind.)

DLE: I am claiming merely that I do not believe that Pirahã is unique. I hypothesize that all grammars are likely to show cultural effects. Role and Reference Grammar is unique among linguistic theories, it seems to me, for explicitly connecting pragmatics, syntax, semantics, and morphology in such a way that cultural constraints can in principle be easily fitted into the grammar. For example, one could say that cultural constraints restrict the types of syntactic template that an RRG grammar provides for a particular language. To a lesser degree, Construction Grammar also gives us a way of thinking about this connection (see especially Nick Enfield's *Ethnosyntax*, Enfield 2002). I do believe that every language will turn out to refute UG in some way. And theories are already around that give us a potentially useful tool for testing this as researchers turn to examine if or how constructions emerge from the cultures of their speakers. It is likely to me that we will discover evidence for this in every language. The chapters in Enfield's book point in this direction, it seems to me.

I have no evidence for this assertion other than Pirahã and studies such as those in the book just mentioned. But I need no evidence. That claim is a proposal for future research, not a statement of completed research. It simply asserts that this would be a useful way to reexamine languages and to conduct future field research.

On the other hand, I think that UG is too vague to be subject to testing or verification of predictions in any useful sense of the word. Even Chomsky, in personal correspondence with me, admits this, saying that UG is not a hypothesis. It makes no predictions. It is a field of study, like Biology, according to Chomsky. That is unlikely. I can't imagine scientists studying living creatures apart from Biology. But many psycholinguists and linguists study language and its acquisition just fine without the idea that there is a specific biological endowment for grammar.

GRS: In Everett (2007) you describe yourself as working in the Boas tradition. But what I think of as Boas's master idea is something which you are undermining as actively as you undermine the Chomsky tradition. Boas was pre-eminently the scholar who argued that there are no "primitive languages". If an indigenous Third World language lacked parallels to the structural features which give typical European languages their logical sophistication (Boas said), it did not follow that the former languages were unsophisticated; if you looked, you would often find that they had highly subtle structural features of their own for which European languages have no parallel (cf. Boas 1911: 39).

In the first half of the twentieth century, most Europeans and North Americans did take for granted that Third World languages were inferior as vehicles for thought and communication. I still have the 1956 edition of the *Guinness book of records*, which I was given as a boyhood birthday present: one of the records it includes is "most primitive language" – the answer was the Australian language Arunta (I believe the name is nowadays written Aranda) in which "Words are indeterminate in meaning and form". That was the received wisdom of the time, but linguists were people who thought they knew better; and the person who had taught them better was Boas. I appreciate that you make comments about certain features of Pirahã being unusually complex, but the overall balance of your account, as you would surely agree, is to portray Pirahã as a remarkably intellectually crude language. So why do you place yourself in the Boas tradition?

DLE: I am following Boas's research tradition by taking seriously the idea that grammars and cultures interact in significant ways and that each language should be described in its own terms. I believe that linguists too often fail to recognize that there were two parallel research traditions in American linguistics following Boas's initial crop of students, including Sapir. These were Bloomfieldian structuralism and Sapiran descriptivism.

The structuralists were concerned with finding the tagmemes and syntagmemes of each language's grammar, and assumed that these elements would come from a universal set of structures. This is found clearly in Bloomfield's *Language* of 1933. I have long thought that Chomsky's work fits in this tradition, and that in this sense Chomsky is the most sophisticated proponent of structuralism.

Descriptivists followed the Boasian tradition of describing languages "in their own terms". Kenneth Pike, Edward Sapir, and Boas were in this tradition, at least in my reading of their works. In my first linguistics class Kenneth Pike, my first linguistics teacher, began the lecture by saying: "Languages are extremely different from one another. Of course they're not *utterly* different or there would be no linguistics." The Boasian tradition to me is the inductive approach to the study of language and its interaction with culture, allowing that languages and their grammars may be more or less shaped by their cultures, at the same time that the cultures and the speakers' ways of thinking can also be affected by their language. The Boasian, according to this conception, sees language and culture as a complex symbiosis.

There is nothing in what I have written that should be interpreted as making the Pirahãs or their language seem intellectually crude. Rather, what should be concluded is that their language fits their culture and their culture fits their needs and their environment. This is another reason that it is so crucial to study endangered languages and cultures – not because they are all alike in some fundamental way, but because they are so different in interesting ways. Each culture–language pairing is unique in this sense (at least I am placing my bets on this expectation), and thus each pairing has something to teach us that no other does. In this sense, it becomes more urgent and imperative that linguists develop again a culture of field research so that field research is the norm, not the exception, for all linguists' careers, and that we document, describe, and theorize about all the language–culture pairs that are known. That is an ambitious goal, but a good one to have, I believe.

GRS: A specific point about the Boas tradition has to do with speech sounds. Most of what you say about Pirahã is about its grammar and semantics; but you also write about its phonology, commenting that it has an unusually tiny phoneme inventory and that the phoneme distinctions it does include are not always maintained – what you call the "sloppy phoneme effect". Boas wrote about phonology in connection with his arguments against the "primitive language" idea; he showed (1911: 12–14) that what Europeans took to be vagueness of sounds in exotic languages were really cases where allophone/phoneme relationships in those languages conflicted with corresponding relationships in European languages, so that the impression of vagueness was symmetrical – a Kwakiutl speaker would perceive English as having vague sounds.

I am curious whether you see the limited phonology of Pirahã as related to its simplicity of structure in other respects. To me, the two domains seem unrelated. The exotic language I know best is Chinese, which relative to most European languages has a strikingly limited phonological system (it is tonal, but the tones do not make up for the fewness of distinct consonants and vowels). Yet, until our Industrial Revolution, China was probably the most sophisticated culture on earth. Conversely, so far as I know there are primitive societies whose languages are phonologically highly complex. Does your discussion of sloppy phonemes mean that you see a connection with the main points you were making about Pirahã language and culture?

DLE: Yes, I do see a connection between culture and grammar even in Pirahã speech sounds. But not in the way you put it – I see no connection between the simplicity of a culture and its phonemic inventory.

I have written on this at length, and I published an account of this compatible with my current work back in 1985. The idea is that the segmental inventory and the process of "free variation" that I refer to as the "sloppy phoneme effect" are conditioned by Pirahã's "channels of discourse".

Pirahã can communicate with consonants and vowels, but it can also use whistle speech, hum speech, yell speech, and musical speech, as I describe in the 1985 paper and in the online appendix to my *Current Anthropology* paper. All channels of Pirahã discourse use prosody (tone, syllable length and boundaries, and stress), and each has its particular cultural function.

The culture, not the grammar, determines how and with what frequency the different channels are used. Because the consonant-vowel channel is used so rarely relative to other languages, I proposed the implications below as a way of accounting for the free variation and the small inventory:

Functional Load Principle
a. Greater dependence on the channel → greater contrast required.
b. Lesser dependence on the channel → less contrast required.

This just means that you need contrast to use a channel, a way of telling units apart. The greater your dependence on a channel, the more it is used across a variety of communicational contexts, the more contrast you need to be able to distinguish units in a variety of contexts. The less you use a channel, the less you need contrast. Notice that the lesser need of contrast doesn't imply that a language will lack contrast. Lalana Chinantec of Mexico, to take one example, has whistle speech every bit as functional as Pirahã's from what I can tell, but it also has a very complex segmental inventory. Pirahã's inventory is consistent with the principle above, but so is Chinantec's.

So in this case, what connects Pirahã's phonology and culture is different from what connects its syntax and culture. The morphology could turn out to be different yet. I am not claiming any single effect that accounts for all. But I am claiming that the effects of culture can be seen potentially in any component of the grammar.

GRS: Thank you, Dan; and good luck for *Don't sleep, there are snakes!*

16

Universals in language or cognition? Evidence from English language acquisition and from Pirahã

EUGÉNIE STAPERT

1 Introduction

One of the most intriguing issues every linguist sooner or later has to deal with is the relation between language and cognition. Are we to draw a clear distinction between the two, as is done by supporters of an autonomous language faculty, or is language just part of our general cognitive system? This question has gained particular relevance in the current discussion on language complexity and its connection to language universals. Most people agree that human languages have certain properties in common, which distinguish language from other communication systems. However, depending on one's view on the above question, these possible universals are seen either as part of the syntactic component in a language faculty or as part of general cognitive structures.

It is essential clearly to specify one's stance from the beginning, since the two viewpoints have different implications with respect to hypotheses about constraints on human syntax as well as to the kind of variation that is possible across languages. This is exemplified by the variety of opinions expressed with respect to language complexity. Are all languages equally complex, or is complexity rather a property of human cognition, which would leave room for variation in the level of complexity in syntax?

In this chapter I shall discuss one instance of how complexity can figure in cognition and language, and I shall argue that if complexity is a universal and distinctive feature of humans, it is a feature of human cognition rather than of syntax. I will compare mental verb constructions in English and Pirahã, and we shall see that the syntax of the sentences at issue seems very different at first sight. However, relating my findings to research by Diessel and Tomasello (2001) on the use and acquisition of those constructions in English, I shall argue that the difference is perhaps not as profound as it seems. Investigation of the acquisition process, and of the different ways mental verbs are used in discourse, leads Diessel and Tomasello to conclude that English mental verb constructions need not be analysed as complex structures in young children's speech. They propose an alternative analysis, which in many respects is similar to what we find in Pirahã.

Only later in development do the mental verb constructions get an additional interpretation as complex embedded sentences consisting of two propositions, in the way usually proposed. This hypothesis in turn would support the idea that language use must direct and guide our analysis of language form.

2 Mental verb constructions and language complexity

2.1 *Terminology*

Complexity in language is a large issue, and is certainly not restricted to the realm of syntax alone. Morphology and phonology vary equally in number of categories and phonemes across languages; and to fully assess complexity of a language as a whole, all levels should be taken into account. However, as long as there is no standardized way to quantify complexity (cf. Östen Dahl's Chapter 4, above), comparison of overall degrees of complexity between languages remains problematic.

In this chapter I shall restrict the discussion to syntax. A structure is complex when it represents a complex state of affairs consisting of more than one proposition, the one embedded in the other.

Mental verbs are verbs expressing illocutionary force, attitude towards the proposition, or source of information (Diessel and Tomasello 2001). Although there is a broad range of mental verbs, for the purpose of clarity and conciseness I shall stick to the verbs that figure in the corpus used by Diessel and Tomasello and to their division into semantic classes: epistemic markers (*think, guess, bet, mean, know*), what they call deontic modality markers (*wish, hope*), discourse directives (*see, look, remember*), and three verbs treated separately: *say, tell,* and *pretend*.

2.2 *Why mental verbs?*

The reason to investigate mental verb constructions in the context of language complexity is straightforward. According to traditional analysis, mental verb constructions conform to the definition given in section 2.1. By the principle of iconicity, the complex state of affairs is likely to be reflected by complex syntactic structures if they are available in the language, which make such constructions a good starting point in the search for complexity.

In the English example:

(1)   [s I think [s that he is ill]]

we see a complex sentence in which *I think* represents the first proposition and *he is ill* the second, which is embedded in the first as is overtly signalled by the presence of the complementizer *that.*

2.3 *Why Pirahã?*

In current discussion on language complexity, Pirahã, a Muran language spoken in the Brazilian Amazon, has become the focus of attention because of its alleged lack of sentential complexity (Everett 2005). Since we have just seen that mental verb constructions often involve complex syntactic structures, Pirahã is interesting to investigate for two reasons: to confirm or disconfirm the presence of complex structures in Pirahã in this context, and to see what structures are used instead.

Recently, syntactic complexity, in particular syntactic recursion, has been given major attention as a result of a chain of claims and counter-claims touching on core assumptions about human language and cognition.

Although the details of a definition of recursion have not been unequivocally agreed (as became apparent at the conference on Recursion in Human Languages, held in Illinois in April 2007), the essence of the concept is: an item (sentence, clause, constituent) that is defined in terms of itself (e.g. a sentence within a sentence, a clause within a clause), or in mathematical terms a function that calls itself.

This characteristic is said to account for discrete infinity, the alleged unique property of human language, which enables us to express and understand sentences we have never heard before and is thus the basis for creativity in language. Some scholars (Hauser et al. 2002) have even suggested that it might be a central, and maybe even the only defining, property distinguishing language from non-language, and humans from non-humans. In their theoretical framework this means that it would be the only content of the Language Acquisition Device.

This idea has initiated a chain of reactions. Pinker and Jackendoff (2005) provide evidence for the view that this kind of complexity is neither uniquely human – it can be found in animals as well (social cognition, navigation) – nor unique to language (it can be found in other cognitive domains). Nonetheless both objections acknowledge its presence in human language.

The strongest reaction has come from Everett (2005), who claimed that some human languages do not make use of recursive syntax at all, so that recursion cannot be the core property of human language. He presented examples from Pirahã, which according to his analysis uses non-embedded structures in all cases where, in theory, recursive syntax might be expected.

This caused a stir among linguists, and the claim is currently being sub-jected to further investigation (Stapert et al. in preparation). But if Everett's claim is confirmed, the implication would be that languages indeed can differ with respect to their degree of complexity, at least on a syntactic level.

To summarize: we have seen that, in accordance with the principle of iconicity, mental verb constructions are likely to be expressed by complex sentences cross-linguistically. Therefore these constructions seem a good starting point for further research on complex structures in Pirahã.

Pirahã is particularly interesting because (a) if it has complex sentences that would refute Everett's claims, and (b) if it encodes these meanings in some other way, it will be interesting to see how.

2.4 *Why English?*

English is one of many languages in which complex propositions can be expressed by complex syntactic structures. Since Diessel and Tomasello's work on mental verb constructions in English will play an important role in my argument, following them in their choice of language will make compari-son most transparent.

On the basis of data from children's language acquisition and the use of mental verbs in children's – but importantly also in adult – speech, they argue that, even in a language like English, mental verb constructions need not be analysed as complex sentences (see also Thompson 2002; Fox and Thompson 2007; Mithun 2007).

This raises the question to what extent the differences we notice on the surface are a consequence of our theoretical assumptions. The syntactic structures, whether analysed as simple or complex, fulfil the same functions; and it is not clear whether such a distinction is really there, or whether we are projecting relations that exist in cognition on to the syntax by assuming iconicity.

3 The traditional analysis of mental verb constructions in English

As was mentioned above, traditionally mental verb constructions in English are analysed as complex constructions consisting of two parts: a part contain-ing a mental verb and a part containing the embedded proposition. Noonan

(1985: 42) defines complement clauses as clauses that function as a subject or object of a predicate. This can be shown by replacing the subordinate clause with a noun:

(2)   The teacher noticed [s that Bill was not in class]
(3)   The teacher noticed [N Bill's absence]

The dependency relation between the two parts is used as an argument for embeddedness, and hence complexity of the construction. More formally, those structures can be called recursive, since theoretically the levels of embedding could be repeated infinitely (though see Karlsson (2007a, and Chapter 13 above) for practical constraints).

(4)   Mary believed [that Peter thought [that James said [that the teacher noticed [that Bill was not in class]]]]

   In this view, no distinction is made between sentences with or without an overt complementizer. In both situations the assumption is that we have to do with separate propositions, reflected by an equally complex syntactic structure; and presence versus absence of a complementizer would not alter that.

   This would contrast with sentences using sentential adverbials instead of mental verbs, which are said to consist of only one proposition, although the meaning can be very similar.

   Adverbs do not represent propositions in themselves, in the first place because they are not clauses with a subject and a predicate, but also because they are more loosely attached to the main clause in that they can be put into different positions.

(5)   a. Apparently, he is ill.
       b. He, apparently, is ill.
       c. He is ill, apparently.

However, (6) shows that the behaviour of certain uses of clauses like *I think* is very similar:

(6)   a. I think he is ill.
       b. He, I think, is ill.
       c. He is ill, I think.

Would this mean that either we have to analyse adverbials as propositions, or that in certain contexts clauses like *I think* do not actually constitute clauses and are better analysed as something similar to adverbials? We can at least say that there is reason to question the traditional analysis.

4 Mental verb constructions in Pirahã

If one investigates the way mental verb constructions are expressed in Pirahã, the first surprising finding is that there are no lexical mental verbs. The work of compiling a dictionary for Pirahã (Sakel, in preparation) has produced no grounds for creating entries corresponding to the English lexemes *think, guess, believe, bet, mean*, etc. One entry is translated as "know", but it equally translates "see", and refers to ability rather than to abstract knowledge.

Similarly, there is no entry for the deontic modality markers "wish" and "hope", although there is a word for "want", which lacks a counterfactual implication.

Furthermore, there is no entry for "tell" or "pretend". We do find an entry for "see/watch", but this verb is only used literally as a perception verb and not as an attention getter, as is frequent in English discourse (e.g. *See, it works on here!*, Diessel and Tomasello 2001: 120).

What does this tell us? One possibility is that the dictionary is incomplete. But given the fact that the verbs under consideration occur frequently in spontaneous speech (at least in our cultures), it is unlikely that they would have been overlooked completely if they did occur in Pirahã.

Another possibility is that the meaning of those verbs in English is in Pirahã expressed by elements other than lexical verbs. A closer look in the dictionary and at the language structure of Pirahã in general supports this possibility. Pirahã is a strongly agglutinating language, and verbs can be extended considerably by a wide variety of suffixes. Among all those suffixes, many can modify the verb with respect to the attitude of the speaker towards the denoted proposition. That might indicate that this function in Pirahã is fulfilled by suffixes instead of full lexical verbs or adverbs used in English. The different means of expression are summarized in Table 16.1.[1]

The following examples illustrate the use of the verbal suffixes in context. Most are my own fieldwork data, others are based on Everett (1986). Often the translation of the examples in Everett's grammar does not clearly reflect the function of the suffixes. Since the suffixes clearly have an effect on the meaning of the verb, I have provided alternative translations for those cases based on their description in the grammar, even if a different syntactic structure from the structure we see in Pirahã is needed to express the meaning.

---

[1] The categories of Table 16.1 will be abbreviated in glosses as UNCERT, REL_CERT, COMP_CERT, DESID, HSY, DEDUCT, OBSERV, EMPH. Other special grammatical codes used below are ASSOC associative, INGR ingressive, REM remote, FRUST_INIT frustrated initiative, DM discourse marker, EP epenthetic vowel.

Table 16.1. Pirahã suffixes representing speakers' attitudes to propositions

Verbal suffix	Category	Equivalent in English	
		Mental verb	Adverb
-áti	UNCERTAINTY	I doubt, I'm not sure	Maybe, perhaps
-haí	RELATIVE CERTAINTY	I think, I guess	Probably
-há	COMPLETE CERTAINTY	I know, I bet, I'm sure	Definitely, certainly
-sog	DESIDERATIVE	I wish, I want, I hope	Hopefully
-híai	HEARSAY	I heard	Apparently, allegedly
-sibiga	DEDUCTIVE	I understand, I suspect, I get the impression	Apparently, Seemingly
-xáagahá	OBSERVATIVE	I notice, I see (literal sense)	Clearly
-bai/-koí	EMPHASIS/INTENSIFIER	I bet, I mean (clarification)	Obviously, certainly, for sure

(7) *xigí-xaoaxái   xagaoa   xiga-hoag-a-áti* (Everett 1986: 360)
     ASSOC-UNCERT.INT   canoe   take-INGR-REM-UNCERT
     "Would it be possible for you to take the canoe?"

(8) *Hi   pi-ó   pibaí-haí   xagaoa* (informant: Kaaxáoi)
     3   river-LOC paddle-REL_CERT   canoe
     "He was paddling his canoe on the river."

(9) *Hi   kagáihiai   koabái-p-á-há*   (informant: Kaaxáoi)
     3   jaguar   kill-PERF-REM-COMP_CERT
     "He shot the jaguar."

All three cases can be translated as simple statements in English, but the function of the suffix closely matches the description given by Bloom et al. (1989) for the use of the mental verbs *think* and *know* in children's English. They say that children use those verbs "in order to qualify the degree of certainty-uncertainty of the complement proposition".

This fact, in addition to the finding that there are no lexical means to express mental attitude in Pirahã, leads to the idea that this function is carried out by suffixes instead, if we assume that all humans find it relevant to report on their attitude towards a proposition in some way. Alternative English translations could be:

(8) "I guess/probably he was paddling his canoe on the river."

(9) "I bet/I am sure he shot the jaguar."

The function of the other suffixes is more straightforward. DESID clearly expresses desire or wish (*I want, I wish, I hope, hopefully*):

(10) *ti kapiigakagakai-sog-abagai*   (informant: Bixí)
      1   study-DESID-FRUST_INIT
      "I want to study."
      Alternative: "I would like to study."

HSY indicates that the source of information was some other person (*I heard, allegedly*):

(11) *Hi gai-sai baíxi   xigío   xait-á-hoí-híai* (informant: Xibáihoá)
      3   say-DM   parent ASSOC   sleep-?-INGR-HSY
      "He says: the parent went to sleep."
      Alternative: "He said: I heard that the parent went to sleep."

DEDUCT tells us that the proposition can be derived from the (non-) linguistic circumstances (*I assume, bet, believe, guess* – those English verbs do not specify the basis on which the assumption is grounded):

(12) *Kaogiái xís   ibá-bo-í-sibiga*   (Everett 1986: 372)
      Kaogiái   animal   fish-come-EP-DEDUCT
      "Kaogiái must be going fishing."
      Alternative: "I deduce/I believe/I bet/I guess Kaogiái must be going fishing."

OBSERV reflects direct observation, which can be expressed in English *by I see* or *I'm sure*:

(13) *Piboi-bai   hi   kahápi-hiab-áagahá* (informant: Xibáihoá)
      Rain-EMPH   3   go-NEG-OBSERV
      "It's really raining; he is not going (to the forest)."
      Alternative: "It is raining; I see/clearly he is not going (to the forest)."

The two emphatic suffixes do not indicate source of information, but match the English *I'm sure, really* (emphasis), *I mean* (clarification):

(14) *Kagaihiai gáihi migí   kaobí-koí* (informant: Xaipipo)
      Jaguar   DEM   ground   fall-EMPH
      "(I'm sure) that jaguar really fell down."

Given the above facts, we must conclude at this stage that across languages we see different representations for concepts that are equally complex. For the expression of illocutionary force, attitude, or discourse directives, English has the option of using mental verbs, which entail embedded syntactic structures. Pirahã, on the other hand, achieves the same goal by attaching suffixes to the verb, which leaves the syntactic structure simple. Since in Pirahã this is the only possible way to express these concepts, one must conclude that in this respect the languages differ in syntactic complexity.

Dissimilarity becomes even more profound if we extend the difference to a cognitive level and assume (as traditionally) that mental verb constructions in English consist of two propositions. The implication of such an assumption is that English and Pirahã differ not only with respect to syntactic complexity but also in cognitive organization: the same concept is encoded in two propositions or one proposition in English and Pirahã respectively.

It would be odd to claim that, underlyingly, the structures in Pirahã also represent two propositions, encoded in a single verb. This would imply an extremely Anglocentric view of language: it takes the syntactic organization of English as the basis for cognitive organization in general. It would be comparable to an analysis of the English past tense *I went* as "it happens in the past that I go". Even though this is a common way to treat tense in logical terms and might clarify the elements semantically comprised in the expression, it splits apart something that in our brain is clearly stored as a unit.

Rather than presupposing English as underlying all cognitive organization, we might as well question the traditional analysis and ask whether the two-proposition interpretation for English is correct or whether this structure is imposed on the language by syntacticians.

5 Analysis of English revisited

This question was addressed by Diessel and Tomasello in 2001. They studied the acquisition of mental verb constructions in English children, and found that during the first years the use of mental verbs is very restricted. Until three years of age children only use invariable forms of the mental verbs, comparable to adverbs. Only later in development does this formulaic verb use evolve into the use of genuine verbs with variation in form and with their own argument structure. But the formulaic use continues to be very frequent with adults too. On the basis of these findings, Diessel and Tomasello argue that a one-proposition analysis represents the attested patterns much more naturally than a two-proposition analysis. What is more, they argue that such interpretation applies even to most instances of mental verbs in adult speech (cf. Thompson 2002).

A similar idea had earlier been proposed by Limber (1973), who examined twelve children aged from 1;6 to 3;0. He said that those children "use 'I think' parenthetically as a holistic formula without knowledge of its literal meaning" (Limber 1973: 185).

Likewise de Villiers (1999) did a study on WH-movement and tested sentences like:

(15)   What did the girl say she brought?

Children would always answer these sentence with what the girl really brought, rather than what she said she brought. De Villiers concluded that this happened because the *say* part did not constitute a real proposition. Only later on will children acquire the full syntax and semantics inherent in *say* and do the task correctly. A fully developed theory of mind and literacy play important roles in this process.

To explain this, Diessel and Tomasello propose that mental verbs have more than one use. They distinguish between assertive, performative, and formulaic uses.

In the assertive use, the complement-taking verb (CTV) clause expresses the main proposition of the composite structure (Diessel and Tomasello 2001: 102):

(16)   <u>Peter saw</u> that Mary was coming.

The sentence refers to the cognitive activity, and the complement clause is subordinated (formally and semantically) to this main verb.

In the performative use, the clause containing the complement-taking verb does not express the main proposition but "addresses a specific aspect of the interaction between the interlocutors" (Diessel and Tomasello 2001: 102). This can be shown by the fact that the performative mental verb can be omitted without changing the main proposition if the context is sufficiently determined by discourse, or it can be replaced by an adverb. This would not be possible in the assertive use.

(17)   I believe that this is a mistake. → Probably this is a mistake.

In the performative use, the clause containing the complement taking verb may indicate illocutionary force, propositional attitude of the speaker, or source of knowledge (Diessel and Tomasello 2001: 106), and thus operates on a speech act level that is different from the complement clause. This suggests that the two parts are less tightly integrated than in the assertive use, in which they are part of the same speech act. Diessel and Tomasello even go on to say that the complement clause is not conceptually embedded at all. According to this view, the "complement" clause is analysed as the main proposition, modified by the clause containing the mental verb.

This explains the similarity in distribution we saw in section 3 for adverbs and mental verbs in the performative use.

I believe that this is a mistake.	Probably this is a mistake.
This is, I believe, a mistake.	This is probably a mistake.
This is a mistake, I believe.	This is a mistake, probably.

Such flexibility is not possible in the assertive use:

Peter saw that Mary was coming.
?Mary, Peter saw, was coming.
?Mary was coming, Peter saw.

The third use distinguished by Diessel and Tomasello is the formulaic use, which according to them is historically related to the performative use and even forms a continuum with it. The formulaic complement-taking verb is not a fully-fledged main clause, but rather a "holistic formula functioning as an epistemic marker or attention getter that is only loosely adjoined to the [complement]-clause, which is really an independent utterance" (Diessel and Tomasello 2001: 106). Its similarity to adverbs is even more striking than the performative use.

This is supported by the following list of properties:

a. The CTV clauses are always short and formulaic.
b. The subject of the CTV clause is either not overtly expressed or it is first or second person.
c. The complement-taking verb itself occurs in the present indicative active.
d. There are no auxiliaries, modals, adverbs, or propositional phrases in the CTV clause.
e. The complement clause is non-embedded (both formally and conceptually); it does not include a *that*-complementizer.
f. The order of CTV clause and complement clause is variable: the CTV clause may precede or follow the complement clause or may even be inserted into it.

If Diessel and Tomasello are correct, a formal description of a verb and its argument structure alone might not be sufficient to determine its full character. Investigation of the *use* of a verb can lead to essential discoveries, reaching as far as differences in cognitive organization.

6 Discussion

At the end of section 4 we concluded that English mental verb constructions represent a complex state of affairs consisting of two propositions, iconically represented by an embedded sentence structure consisting of a mental verb and its complement.

For Piraha the same construction was analysed as a single proposition modified by a suffix indicating mental attitude, illocutionary force, or source of information.

However, reanalysis of English that takes into account different uses of mental verbs has narrowed the gap between the languages. Diessel and Tomasello suggest that in their performative and formulaic use, complement-taking verbs are more adequately analysed as single propositions in English too. And it is exactly this use that we find in mental verb constructions. The parenthetic character of the CTV is supported by its formulaic appearance and use, its flexibility of position, the fact that it can be omitted without affecting the proposition, and the fact that it does not take *that*-complementizers. Therefore the CTV is closer to an adverb and not conceived of as a full proposition.

Although the gap between the languages with respect to performative use may have been bridged, differences with respect to assertive use remain.

Rather than thinking in rigid categories such as simple and complex, a continuum approach seems more fruitful for describing complexity. Even within one language we have seen situations that clearly are embedded, situations that clearly are not, and situations in which it is difficult to decide. For this last category, it is obvious that the clauses originally consisted of two propositions. By taking into account the usage of mental verbs in discourse, we can see different stages of grammaticalization synchronically, and these will shift/change over time: formulaic mental verbs may acquire a real adverbial use, other mental verbs may become more formulaic. As a consequence, the analysis of sentences we now call "complex" will change over years too.

The same is true for Piraha. Although we have no records of the language older than a few decades, some of the suffixes have a striking similarity to verbs (e.g. *xáagahá*, which comes from the verb "be" and a COMP_CERT affix). This could mean that at an earlier stage Piraha had lexical mental verbs, maybe even embedded syntactic structures, which have now grammaticalized into verbal suffixes.

Since in such a view syntactic complexity can increase and decrease over time, it becomes more difficult to maintain the assumption that it is the only essential and unchangeable property of human language. One might wonder to what extent our linguistic theories, which assume syntactic complexity as default, have imposed this on structures where it may not be appropriate. More generally, one could ask why in most syntactic theories complexity is taken as a default assumption and simplicity has to be demonstrated, rather than the other way round. In most other natural processes of evolution and development we see a pathway where simple structures become gradually more complex.

To use complexity in the explanation of the differences between humans and other species, it is crucial to be clear about whether one is talking about complexity in syntax or in cognition. Data presented here and elsewhere (Deutscher 2000; Karlsson 2007a) make it more likely that the source of the increase in complexity has been in general cognition rather than syntax. Even now we have many complex thoughts every day, but they are comparatively infrequently expressed by complex syntax (Karlsson 2007a), and there is no reason to assume that thoughts have to be reflected in language structure to be able to exist. Such a view would assume profound differences between human minds according to the languages they speak.

It is more plausible that the brain and its cognitive structures are the connecting factor between all minds and thus between languages, since it is the physical mediator between the mind and its expression. Tendencies and possible universals in language in this view come about by constraints on cognitive structures and human reasoning. This does not imply, however, that there is only one way to structure language. As in most areas of evolution and development, there are several ways to reach the same goal (to move, to breathe, to represent the world to others), all influenced by physical constraints, by the environment, and partly by chance.

As a tentative last thought, one could consider the possibility that language structures occur in a normal distribution. Some ways to conceive and represent the world are more likely to occur than others, because of the way our brains work. This does not mean, however, that other structures occurring at the tails of the normal distribution are less effective. They are just less likely to occur cross-linguistically. With respect to language complexity, this means that the default for languages might be to have complex structures that mirror complex thoughts, but that there can be languages that have other devices to express complex thoughts.

A view like this explains why some structures are more common than others, but leaves room for rare structures without seeing them as quirks. They fit perfectly within their own system.

17

"Overall complexity": a wild goose chase?

GUY DEUTSCHER

1 "Equal complexity" as an urban legend

The statement that "All Languages are Equally Complex" (ALEC) is often portrayed as one of the fundamental tenets of modern linguistics.[1] It is repeated in introductory courses, enshrined in all manner of textbooks, and occasionally invoked as an axiom in theoretical arguments (for instance, about the admissibility or otherwise of particular reconstructions of proto-languages). ALEC is sometimes presented as a "finding": "a central finding of linguistics has been that all languages, both ancient and modern, spoken by both 'primitive' and 'advanced' societies, are equally complex in their struc-ture" (Forston 2004: 4). However, references to where the "finding" was made are never supplied. The intellectual pedigree of ALEC is often claimed to go back to Edward Sapir, but Sapir does not seem to have made such a statement in print. Some of the statements he did make, in fact, make it clear he did not subscribe to ALEC. In the following passage, for instance, Sapir is at pains to stress the lack of correlation between complexity of culture and of language, but he strongly implies that languages can differ in their complexity:

[If the complexity of the vocabulary is taken into account] it goes without saying that there is a constant correlation between complexity of language and culture. If, however, as is more usual, linguistic complexity be used to refer to degree of morphologic and syntactic development, it is by no means true that such a correlation exists. In fact, one might almost make a case of an inverse correlation and maintain that morphologic development tends to decrease with increase of cultural complexity....On the other hand, too much must not be made of this. The existence of numerous relatively simple

[1] This chapter was written during a stay at the Research Centre for Linguistic Typology in Melbourne. I am grateful to the directors and to the other members of the institute for their comments on an earlier version.

forms of speech among primitive peoples discourage the idea of any tangible correlation between degree or form of culture and form of speech. (Sapir [1912] 1949: 95)

The closest to ALEC Sapir seems to have come in print is the following general and purposely vague statement, from an article on "communication" in the *Encyclopaedia of the social sciences*:

It is exceedingly important to observe that whatever may be the shortcomings of a primitive society judged from the vantage point of civilization, its language inevitably forms as sure, complete and potentially creative an apparatus of referential symbolism as the most sophisticated language that we know of. What this means for a theory of communication is that the mechanics of significant understanding between human beings are as sure and complex and rich in overtones in one society as in another, primitive or sophisticated. (Sapir [1931] 1949: 105)

Sapir talks about "the mechanics of significant understanding between human beings" in pre-theoretical terms, and the level of epistemological presumption here is thus very modest. But Sapir's caution had been thrown to the wind by the 1950s, when ALEC seems to have become an established slogan. For example, in the article on "language" in the fourteenth edition of the *Encyclopaedia Britannica* (1956), George Trager asserts:

All languages of today are equally complex and equally adequate to express all the facets of the speakers' culture, and all can be expanded and modified as needed. There are no "primitive" languages, but all languages seem to be equally old and equally developed.

And a more famous pronouncement was made by Charles Hockett in 1958, already quoted by Geoffrey Sampson on p. 2 above:

Objective measurement is difficult, but impressionistically it would seem that the total grammatical complexity of any language, counting both morphology and syntax, is about the same as that of any other. (Hockett 1958: 180)

By the 1950s, then, the argument has taken two new turns, both unfortunate. First, Trager's formulation makes a misguided equation between ALEC and the claim that "there are no primitive languages". (In practice, the latter by no means implies the former. If a "primitive language" is thought of, for instance, as one that resembles a restricted pidgin, or perhaps what might have been spoken at the early stages of language evolution, then it is clear that no natural language today is "primitive". But this says nothing about the "equal complexity" of languages.) And second, Hockett has upgraded Sapir's vague statement about the "mechanics of significant understanding between human beings" to an explicit claim about morphology and syntax, whose sum total of complexity, in all languages, he claimed to be "about the same". Note, however, that Hockett is at least careful not to report ALEC as a "fact" or a "finding", but merely as an impression, hedged with multiple modalities.

After Hockett, even the disclaimers were forgotten, and any quick search of books and articles written in the last few decades brings up dozens of instances of ALEC, often stated categorically without caveats and provisos. ALEC thus turns out to be an urban legend: it seems to gain its validity merely from the fact that one has heard it mentioned by an eminent source. But in the chain of imperfect transmission, what had started as at best a report of an impression eventually assumed the status of a dogma, an axiom, or even a "finding", but one whose empirical basis has never been revealed by any of its proponents.

2 Two flawed pre-theoretical arguments for ALEC

Let us think of the overall complexity of a language, for the moment, as some yet-to-be-exactly-defined measure of the amount of different forms a language has, the amount of semantic distinctions it makes, the amount of rules in its grammar, the difficulty it poses to learners or speakers or hearers, or some combination of these. Are there any *a priori* reasons to expect that all languages spoken today are even roughly of equal complexity? Clearly, languages do not compare complexity among themselves. So if all languages were equal in complexity, it would be as a result of some internal mechanism that stems from human communication patterns, or from the limitations of the human brain, or from both, and steers any language to converge on a certain degree of complexity.

Two main arguments have been suggested to account for such convergence. We may call them the "minimum argument" and the "maximum argument" respectively. The "minimum argument" was suggested by Hockett himself, in the continuation of the passage quoted above:

...the total grammatical complexity of any language, counting both morphology and syntax, is about the same as that of any other. This is not surprising, since all languages have about equally complex jobs to do, and what is not done morphologically has to be done syntactically. Fox, with a more complex morphology than English, thus ought to have a somewhat simpler syntax; and this is the case. (Hockett 1958: 180)

There is no doubt that languages have a complex task to perform, and this must impose a certain minimum of complexity on them. (Indeed, this argument fully justifies the claim that "there are no primitive languages".) However, as McWhorter (2001a) and others have argued, languages can be far more complex than merely the minimum required for effective communication.

A great deal of complexity is redundant historical baggage. And there is no reason why reduction in irregularity or redundancy in one subsystem should increase it in another. One need only replace "Fox" in the quotation above with "German", to see how weak the argument is. Johanna Nichols in Chapter 8, above, using heuristic measurements of complexity in different subsystems of language, shows that complexity in one subsystem is not generally compensated by simplicity in another.

The second main argument that could be advanced to argue for convergence in the overall level of complexity can be termed the "maximum argument". The idea of an upper limit of complexity has been put forward, for instance, by Levinson (who is, however, not arguing for ALEC):

> I propose the following hypothesis: Cultures will tend to become more complex over time, up to the limits of the transmission process (where transmission is constrained by what is individually learnable on the one hand, and by social and cultural constraints... on the other). (Levinson 2005: 20)

Applying this idea to language in particular, one could claim that language naturally tends to increase in complexity over time, but at some stage it reaches an upper limit, which is due either to the limitations of transmission between generations (learnability), or to the brain's capacity to process, or both. Since all languages today (except creoles) have had enough time to develop and reach this upper limit of complexity, they should all converge on this same maximum limit and thus be of equal complexity.

But the maximum argument fails for a variety of reasons, as has been argued by Kusters (2003). The widespread phenomenon of bilingualism and multilingualism proves that individual languages do not even begin to exhaust the brain's capacity to learn and process language. In addition, languages do not always become more complex over time. Some (although by no means all) types of contact tend to result in simplification (Aikhenvald 2007: 42).

The minimum level of complexity required for communication is far below the maximum limit of complexity the human brain can handle, and as there are processes which both increase complexity and decrease it, there is no *a priori* reason why all languages should converge on even roughly the same point for overall complexity.

3 Beyond ALEC: why "overall complexity" cannot be quantified as a single measure

ALEC implies that the "overall complexity" of a language is a meaningful concept, one that can be non-arbitrarily quantified. The discussion so far has granted this assumption, for the sake of argument. But in this section, I argue that it is in fact impossible to define the notion of overall complexity in an objective meaningful way. At best, the "overall complexity" of a language can be understood as a vector (one-dimensional matrix) of separate values.

If the notion of "overall complexity" is to be defined in a way that justifies scientific interest in it, the concept should capture, at least partly, our intuitive notions of what complexity in language is about. Unfortunately, however, intuitions can be vague, and ultimately even inconsistent. In particular, our intuitive ideas of what is meant by complexity include a list of separate notions, which do not coincide, and which require different measures.

Miestamo (2008) insightfully divides our different intuitive notions of complexity in language into two main groups: those that broadly depend on difficulty or cost for the language users, and those that depend on the information content of a language: the "number of parts" in the language system. These two camps correspond to the two basic meanings of the word "complex" in everyday speech: "1. composed of many interrelated parts. 2. complicated; involved; tangled" (*Chambers 21st century dictionary*). As Miestamo and others have pointed out, the two notions do not coincide. There may be a rough correlation between the number of parts in a system and the difficulty it poses to users, but the relation is not one-to-one. Therefore, even if our intuition of complexity involves both difficulty and number of parts, a scientific definition of the term could only be based on one of the measures. But which?

For some linguists, such as Trudgill (2001: 371), the answer is clearly the notion of difficulty: "my thinking was, and is, that 'linguistic complexity', although this . . . is very hard to define or quantify, equates with 'difficulty of learning for adults.'" A similar approach is taken by Kusters (2003). However, others (Dahl 2004; Miestamo 2008) argue against difficulty as the basis of comparison of overall complexity between languages. To start with, L2 learners are not the only group of language users for which language poses difficulties. What is difficult for L1 learners, for instance, does not coincide with what is difficult for L2 learners. But even for L2 learners themselves, the difficulty posed by a language *X* largely depends on the distance of *X* from the first language of the learner *Y*. So while it may be possible to compare objectively the difficulty posed by two closely related languages (on the assumption that they are equidistant from almost any given *Y*), such a measure cannot be generalized to compare the difficulty of any two given languages. Thus, although difficulty for L2 learners is unquestionably a part of our intuition about complexity, difficulty cannot be measured independently of the learner's first language.

If "overall complexity" of a language is to be measured objectively, therefore, the basis of the definition cannot be the notion of difficulty. However, I shall now argue that a single non-arbitrary measure for overall complexity cannot be devised on the basis of the "number of parts" either.

As has already been pointed out by several contributors to this volume, the information-theoretic concept of "Kolmogorov complexity" defines the complexity of an object as the length of the shortest possible specification or description of that object. It has been suggested that the overall complexity of a language may be defined, at least in theory, on the basis of the notion of Kolmogorov complexity. But this idea is misguided. Kolmogorov complexity requires a given "object" (for example, a fixed text) which can be described and specified completely. "Language", however, is not such an object. Language is in itself an abstraction, a term used in a variety of vague senses, and one which has never been completely specified.

One could claim that the object in question is the "knowledge of language" in the Chomskyan sense. In theory, it may be possible one day to describe precisely the neural systems that account for an individual's ability to speak and understand a language. (Or alternatively, it may be possible to describe a computer program that simulates this knowledge.) If so, it will be possible to apply the notion of Kolmogorov complexity to the resulting "object" (granting, for the sake of argument, that the systems involved in the knowledge of language can be separated from those that code knowledge of the world more generally). However, it is clear that even if the information content of this object could one day be measured, the resulting measure would have little to do with our intuition of "linguistic complexity". For one thing, this measure will crucially depend on the size of the lexicon, and it will vary enormously between individuals.

In practice, when linguists talk about the "complexity of language", they usually have in mind the complexity of grammar. However, "grammar" is an even vaguer and less well-defined abstraction than "language". It is an arbitrarily drawn set of supposedly regular patterns, whose delineation depends on the descriptive theory, on the desired level of resolution, and so on. In particular, as one proceeds up the ladder of subsystems of language, from phonology to morphology to syntax and finally to semantics, it becomes more difficult to draw the line between the set of supposedly recurrent patterns (grammar) and the set of idiosyncrasies (lexicon) in anything but an arbitrary way. This is why in practice, almost all discussions of complexity in language have concentrated on phonology and morphology, and on some restricted areas of syntax. McWhorter (2001a: 134) professes that he is unaware of any precise arguments as to why syntax and semantics would be, in contrast [to phonology and morphology], inherently unamenable to complexity rankings. It is much less likely that any such unamenability exists than that the issue, its difficulties acknowledged, simply has not had occasion to receive much attention from modern linguists.

But the increasing arbitrariness of the dividing line between grammar and lexicon in syntax and especially semantics is precisely such an argument. So it is not possible, even in principle, to apply the notion of Kolmogorov complexity to "grammar" as a holistic entity.

4 "Overall complexity" as a vector of values

If any measure for the "number of parts" in a grammar can be well defined, which nevertheless corresponds to our intuitions about complexity, then it has to be approached through a bottom-up approximation. We would need to define specific subdomains within language in such a way that the parts in each subdomain can be counted. If a range of such measurable subdomains can be defined which is broad enough to cover all the areas which linguists consider under the label "grammar", the resulting series of measures could be considered to satisfy our intuition of the "overall complexity".

However, the series of values which will result from these subdomains will not be amenable to summation, since the parts to be counted in the different subdomains will be of very different natures, and will thus be incommensurable. (For a full discussion, see Miestamo 2008.) Some of the measures will be based on the number of (obligatory or optional) semantic distinctions made by the grammar in particular functional domains. Such measures correspond to the "explicitness" or perhaps the "sophistication" of a grammar. Other measures will be counting the number of distinct forms, even when these do not correspond to semantic distinctions. Such measures will depend on the amount of "irregularity" in the language. Measures of both "explicitness/sophistication" and "irregularity" firmly belong in our intuition of complexity, but there is no non-arbitrary way of weighing up their relative importance. Still other measures will be based on the size of the phonemic inventory, and thus count building blocks which are not comparable with either "irregularity" or "explicitness" measures.

Since it is not possible to collapse the list of complexity measures (the number of parts in particular well defined subdomains) into one overall figure, no non-arbitrary single measure of overall complexity of grammar can be defined. The overall complexity of a language A can only be viewed as a vector (one-dimensional matrix) of separate values $(A_1 \ldots A_n)$, each representing the measure for one of the n sub-domains. In set-theoretic terms, the n different subdomains will give n distinct total orders on the set of languages, and as these orders do not necessarily coincide, the result will only be a partial order on the set of languages. This means that it will not be possible to compare any two given languages in the set for overall complexity.

However, in some special cases, a pair of languages A and B may be found, where for every j, $A_j \geq B_j$. In this case, the overall complexity of A could be meaningfully declared to be greater or equal to that of B (and in particular, greater than B if for some j, $A_j > B_j$). When can such two languages be found? The simplest case is when A and B are two closely related languages (as in the Scandinavian case discussed by Östen Dahl in Chapter 4), or two diachronic stages of the same language, which are identical for practical purposes in almost all areas but differ only in one subdomain (or consistently in a few subdomains).

It is also possible, of course, that two unrelated languages A and B may be found, where B scores lower or equal to A for each and every subdomain to be measured. In this case, the overall complexity of B could meaningfully be called lower than that of A. McWhorter (2001a), for example, identifies a set of languages, creoles, which he argues are overall less complex than non-creoles. To prove the claim, one would need to show that for every single subdomain of grammar (not just for an eclectic range of subdomains), all creoles score lower or equal to all non-creoles. Note, moreover, that in a complexity measure based on the number of parts in the system (rather than on the notion of difficulty), the cross-linguistic rarity of the particular parts is irrelevant. (A watch made of gold cogs is no more complex than one with aluminium cogs.) Thus, the list of subdomains to be compared should not be based on notions such as markedness or overspecification, which discriminate between parts on the basis of their cross-linguistic rarity. Rather, the measures should only count the number of parts in each subdomain.

5 Summary

I have argued that it is impossible to define a single measure of overall complexity for a language's grammar. There is thus no total order on the set of languages by which any two languages can be compared for overall complexity. What then is the truth-value of ALEC? Is it meaningless, or is it just wrong? Strictly speaking, ALEC can be proved wrong (and thus not meaningless) if there are even just two languages whose "overall complexity" can be compared, and which turn out to be unequal. Given the above definition of overall complexity as a vector of values, there may indeed be at least one pair of languages in the world whose overall complexity can be compared and found unequal. However, the relative respectability of being proved wrong in the strict logical sense would not entirely clear ALEC from the greater ignominy of meaninglessness. Linguists who assert ALEC are suggesting, at least by implication, that any two languages are equal on a single measure called "overall complexity". As this single measure is nonexistent, the assertion is meaningless in spirit (even if just wrong in the strict logical sense).

The above discussion, which aimed to expose the inherent weakness in the concept of overall complexity, was not meant to imply that aspects of complexity in language are unworthy of study. Far from it. There are many questions about complexity which deserve linguists' full attention and best efforts: the evaluation of complexity in well-defined areas; the diachronic paths which lead to increases and decreases in complexity of particular domains; the investigation of possible links between complexity in particular domains and extra-linguistic factors, such as the size and structure of a society. All these, and others, are important to our understanding of language. But the investigation of questions relating to complexity in language will only be hampered by a chase after a non-existent wild goose in the form of a single measure for "overall complexity".

18

An efficiency theory of complexity and related phenomena

JOHN A. HAWKINS

1 Introduction

Theories of complexity in language share the guiding intuition that "more [structural units/rules/representations] means more complexity". Despite its plausibility, this intuition has proved hard to define. See, for example, the lively debate in the papers of Plank (2001) responding to McWhorter (2001a). The discussion went to the heart of the fundamental question: what exactly is complexity? and how do we define it?

Some current problems include:

Trade-offs. Simplicity in one part of the grammar often results in complexity in another; some examples are given in section 2.

Overall complexity. The trade-offs make it difficult to give an overall assessment of complexity, resulting in unresolvable debates over whether some grammars are more complex than others, when there is no clear metric of overall complexity for deciding the matter.

Defining grammatical properties. The (smaller) structural units of grammars are often clearly definable, but the rules and representations are anything but, and theories differ over whether they assume "simplicity" in their surface syntactic structures (see e.g. Culicover and Jackendoff 2005), or in derivational principles (as in N. Chomsky 1995), making quantification of complexity difficult in the absence of agreement over what to quantify.

Defining complexity itself. Should our definition be stated in terms of rules or principles that generate the structures of each grammatical area (i.e. in terms of the "length" of the description or grammar, as discussed most recently in Dahl 2004), or in terms of the structures themselves (the outputs of the grammar)? Definitions of this latter kind are inherent in metrics such as G. A. Miller and Chomsky's (1963) using non-terminal to terminal node ratios, and in the metrics of Frazier (1985), Hawkins (1994), and Gibson (1998). Do these rule-based and structure-based definitions give the same complexity ranking or not?

In this chapter I argue that we can solve some of these problems if metrics of complexity are embedded in a larger theory of efficiency. Efficiency relates to the basic function of language, which is to communicate information from the speaker (S) to the hearer (H). I propose the following definition:

> *Communication is efficient when the message intended by S is delivered to H in rapid time and with minimal processing effort.*

and the following hypothesis:

> *Acts of communication between S and H are generally optimally efficient; those that are not occur in proportion to their degree of efficiency.*

Complexity metrics, by contrast, are defined on the grammar and structure of language. An important component of efficiency often involves structural and grammatical simplicity. But sometimes efficiency results in greater complexity. And it also involves additional factors that determine the speaker's structural selections, leading to the observed preferences of performance, including:

- *speed* in delivering linguistic properties in online processing;
- *fine-tuning* structural selections to (i) frequency of occurrence and (ii) accessibility;
- *few online errors* or garden paths.

These factors interact, sometimes reinforcing, sometimes opposing one another. In Hawkins (1994, 2004) I have presented evidence that grammatical conventions across languages conventionalize these performance factors and reveal a similar interaction and competition between them. Comparing grammars in terms of efficiency, rather than complexity alone, gives us a more complete picture of the forces that have shaped grammars and of the resulting variation (including creoles). Cross-linguistic variation patterns also provide quantitative data that can be used to determine the relative strength of different factors and the manner of their interaction with one another.

2 Trade-offs

Four brief examples of grammatical variation will be given that point to a trade-off: simplicity in one area of grammar is matched by complexity in another. More generally, efficiency in one area is matched by inefficiency in another. The evidence for these trade-offs comes from descriptive patterns across languages and within languages.

2.1 *Simple SVO structures with complex theta-role assignments*

English NP–V–NP sequences, with simple adjacency of NPs and V, must often be mapped onto complex argument structures in ways that many (often most) languages do not permit, even the closely related German. Some less common theta-role assignments to transitive subjects that are grammatical in English but ungrammatical in German and that depart from the Agent–Verb–Patient prototype of (1) are illustrated in (2)–(4) (Rohdenburg 1974; Hawkins 1986; Müller-Gotama 1994; König and Gast 2007).

(1)   a. The professor wrote an important book.   [Agent]
      b. Der Professor hat ein wichtiges Buch geschrieben.

(2)   a. A few years ago a penny would buy two to three pins.   [Instrument]
      b. *Vor einigen Jahren kaufte ein Pfennig zwei bis drei Stecknadeln.

(3)   a. This tent sleeps four.   [Location]
      b. *Dieses Zelt schläft vier.

(4)   a. The book sold 10,000 copies.   [Theme]
      b. *Das Buch verkaufte 10,000 Exemplare.

German regularly uses semantically more transparent prepositional phrases for these non-agentive subjects of English, resulting in translations such as (6a–i) for English (5a–i):

(5)   a. This advert will sell us a lot of dog food.
      b. Money can't buy everything.
      c. This statement overlooks the fact that the situation has changed.
      d. This loses us our best midfield player.
      e. The lake prohibits motor boats.
      f. The Langdon (river) could and frequently did drown people.
      g. My guitar broke a string mid-song.
      h. The latest edition of the book has added a chapter.
      i. . . . Philips, who was streaming blood, . . .

(6)   a. Mit dieser Werbung werden wir viel Hundefutter verkaufen.
      b. Mit Geld kann man nicht alles kaufen.
      c. Mit dieser Aussage übersieht der Autor, dass . . .
      d. Damit verlieren wir unseren besten Mittelfeldspieler.
      e. Auf dem See sind Motorboote nicht zugelassen.

    f. <u>Im Langdon</u> konnte man ertrinken, was übrigens häufig genug vorkam.

    g. <u>An meiner Gitarre</u> riss mitten im Lied eine Seite.

    h. <u>Zur letzten Ausgabe des Buches</u> wurde ein Kapitel angefügt.

    i. . . . Philips, <u>von dem</u> Blut herunter strömte, . . .

English transitive and ditransitive clauses are syntactically and morphologically simple. The NP–V–(NP)–NP surface structure is minimal and contains fewer syntactic categories than its German counterpart with PPs. English also lacks the case morphology of German, except residually on its pronouns. The rules that generate these English surface forms are also, arguably, more minimal than their German counterparts and generate a larger proportion of the outputs of English grammar. Yet in any formalization of the mappings from surface forms to argument structures and semantic representations, the set of English mappings must be regarded, by anyone's metric, as more complex than the German set. There are more argument structure types to be linked to NP–V–(NP)–NP than to the corresponding transitive and ditransitive structures of German (containing NPs only and without PPs). This adds "length" and complexity to the grammar of English. It also makes processing more complex. The assignment of an Instrument to the subject NP in (2a) and of a Locative in (3a) requires crucial access by the processor to the verbs in these sentences, to their lexical semantics and co-occurrence structure, and also possibly to the postverbal NP. More disambiguation needs to be carried out by the English processor, and greater access is needed to more of the surface structure for this disambiguation, i.e. the processing domains for theta-role assignments in English are less minimal (Hawkins 2004).

By what logic, therefore, can it be said that these SVO orders, which are typical of so many inflectionally impoverished languages and of creoles, are simple? The rules mapping these forms onto meanings have been conventionalized in English, i.e. they constitute conventions of grammar, and these conventions have changed in the recorded history of English: Old English used to be much more like German (Rohdenburg 1974).

Even if one were to argue that these mappings from form to meaning have not been conventionalized and are purely pragmatic and perhaps derived inferentially from basic structural and semantic information available to the processor, this would not affect my point. It would merely shift the trade-off. In one theory, simplicity in one part of the grammar would be matched by complexity in another. In a more radical pragmatic theory, simplicity in the grammar would be matched by complexity in the mapping to pragmatically constituted conceptual representations (cf. Walter Bisang's Chapter 3, above). David Gil's (2001) account of Indonesian appeared to assume this more radical alternative (though Gil himself has subsequently rejected that assumption, most explicitly in his (2008)). There is still a trade-off, I suggest, in either analysis.

It is no accident that German has richly case-marked NPs, whereas Modern English does not. In Müller-Gotama's (1994: 143) sample of fifteen languages comparing theta-role assignments to NPs, it was the languages with the most minimal surface structures (Chinese, Indonesian, and English) that had the widest and least semantically transparent mappings onto argument structures. Other richly case-marked languages (e.g. Korean, Japanese, Russian, Malayalam) behaved like German. This provides empiricial support for the trade-off; and while more languages and theta-role assignment rules need to be investigated, Müller-Gotama's sample provides initial general support for it.

2.2 *Extrapositions: good for some phrases, often bad for others*

One structure that has figured prominently in psycholinguistic metrics of complexity is Extraposition (G. A. Miller and Chomsky 1963; Frazier 1985; Hawkins 1994; Gibson 1998). An English clause with a sentential subject, *that their time should not be wasted is important*, would be more complex, according to Miller and Chomsky's non-terminal to terminal node ratio, than its extraposed counterpart *it is important that their time should not be wasted*. This latter has one additional terminal element (*it*), but the same amount of higher non-terminal structure, resulting in a (slightly) lower non-terminal to terminal node ratio. In general, complexity increases by their metric in proportion to the amount of higher structure associated with the words of a sentence.

The more local metric of Hawkins (1994, 2004), stated in terms of Phrasal Combination Domains (PCDs) and the principle of Early Immediate Constituents (section 3 below), defines complexity differently. These two sentences would be compared as follows, with higher overall percentages corresponding to more efficient structures for parsing:

(7)   a. [$_S$ [that their time should not be wasted] [$_{VP}$ is   important]]
PCD:s   ————————————————————————   2/8 = 25%
PCD:vp   ———— 2/2 = 100%

        b. [$_S$ it [$_{VP}$ is important [that their time should not be wasted]]]
PCD:s   ————   2/2 = 100%
PCD:vp   ————————————   3/3 = 100%

The sentential subject in (7a) results in a complex PCD for the matrix S. Eight words must be processed for the recognition of two immediate constituents (resulting in a 2/8 IC-to-word ratio, or 25 per cent). The PCD for the VP has just two words constructing two ICs (2/2 = 100 per cent IC-to-word ratio). By extraposing in (7b), both S and VP domains become optimally efficient. The written corpus of Erdmann (1988) provides empirical support for these ratios: structures like (7b) are massively preferred over (7a), by 95 per cent to 5 per cent.

But Erdmann's corpus data also point to a trade-off in English performance. In some cases adding the sentential subject to the VP makes its PCD less efficient. Compare (8a) and (8b), in which the VP has a PP *for us all* to the right of *important*. This PP can be parsed and projected from the preposition *for*. The three ICs of the VP can accordingly be recognized by three adjacent words in (8a), *is important for*, without the parser having to access the remainder of the PP (IC-to-word ratio 3/3 = 100 per cent). But when the sentential subject is added to the VP in (8b), becoming a fourth IC in the VP, the added clause reduces the efficiency of the VP. Six adjacent words must now be processed, *is important for us all that*, in order to construct the four ICs of the VP, which lowers the IC-to-word ratio from 100 per cent in (8a) to 67 per cent in (8b):

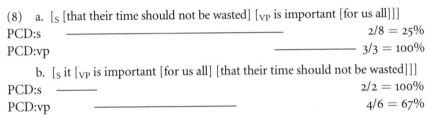

(8) a. [s [that their time should not be wasted] [vp is important [for us all]]]
PCD:s   ————————————————————————   2/8 = 25%
PCD:vp   ——————— 3/3 = 100%

     b. [s it [vp is important [for us all] [that their time should not be wasted]]]
PCD:s   ———   2/2 = 100%
PCD:vp   ————————————————   4/6 = 67%

The overall benefit from extraposing is now less than in (7), and Erdmann's corpus reflects this. There are almost five times as many sentential subjects in structures corresponding to (8a) (24 per cent) compared with (8b), than there are for (7a) (5 per cent) compared with (7b). This follows from the efficiency approach to complexity given here. The VP in (8b) has a worse ratio than it does in (8a), even though the S domain is better.

We can use these efficiency ratios to make fine-tuned predictions for structural selections in performance, on the assumption that there are trade-offs in these different word orders. One clear case that has been investigated in detail involves extraposition of a relative clause from an NP in German, illustrated by (9b) which alternates with the unextraposed relative in (9a). The idiomatic English translation would be "Yesterday he read the book that the professor wrote".

(9)   "He has   the book that the professor written has   yesterday read"

a. *Er hat* [$_{VP}$ [$_{NP}$ *das Buch das der Professor geschrieben hat*] [$_{XP}$*gestern*] *gelesen*]

PCD:vp   3/9 = 33%

PCD:np   ⎯⎯⎯⎯⎯⎯⎯⎯   3/3 = 100%

b. *Er hat* [$_{VP}$ [$_{NP}$ *das Buch*] [$_{XP}$ *gestern*] *gelesen*] [$_{NP}$ *das der Professor geschrieben hat*]

PCD:vp   3/4 = 75%

PCD:np   3/5 = 60%

Example (9a) has an efficient NP in which three adjacent words *das Buch das* suffice to construct three ICs (the determiner, the head noun, and the relative clause constructed by the relative pronoun *das*), i.e. 3/3 = 100 per cent, but at the expense of a lengthened VP whose processing domain proceeds from *das Buch* through *gelesen*, i.e. 3/9 = 33 per cent. (9b), with Extraposition from NP, has the reverse costs and benefits: a less efficient NP with separation of *das Buch* from the relative pronoun *das*, i.e. 3/5 = 60 per cent, but a shorter and more efficient VP resulting from the extraposition, 3/4 = 75 per cent.

By quantifying the trade-offs we can predict which variant will be preferred in performance, on the assumption that structures selected will be those that are most efficient overall. For example, depending on the length of the XP preceding V in (9) one soon reaches the point (after only a two-word XP) when benefits for the VP from extraposing are outweighed by disadvantages for the NP, and extraposition is predicted to be disfavoured (Hawkins 2004: 142–6). Uszkoreit et al. (1988) tested this prediction, and the following data from their German corpus support it. Extraposition from NP is favoured with a one-word intervening XP; it is disfavoured with an XP of three or more words; while two-word XPs are transitional.

(10) Uszkoreit et al.'s (1988) corpus data: Extraposition from NP frequencies
XP(1 word) + V = 77%, XP(2) + V = 35%, XP(3–4) + V = 8%, XP(5+) + V = 7%

My point here is not to argue for the correctness of this particular processing theory and its predictions. The point is to show a clear trade-off between keeping a phrasal constituent in situ or moving it, as a function of the size of a potentially intervening constituent (XP in (9)). This can be analysed in terms of competing efficiency benefits for NP versus VP phrases.

2.3 Competing head orderings for complex phrases

The typology of relative clause ordering points to a trade-off between competing forces in head-final (OV) languages. VO languages almost without exception have head noun before relative clause (NRel), as in English, *the students$_i$ [that I teach O$_i$]*. OV languages are mixed, either NRel (Persian) or RelN (Japanese). The distribution of NRel to RelN appears to correlate with the degree of head-finality: the more rigidly verb-final languages like Japanese prefer RelN, the less rigid ones have NRel. This suggests that consistent head ordering across phrases is one factor influencing the typology of relative clause ordering. A competing factor appears to be the preference for a head noun (filler) to occur to the left of its gap or resumptive pronoun within the relative. Both preferences can be realized in VO languages, but at most one in OV languages, resulting in consistent and almost exceptionless VO and inconsistent OV languages, with these latter selecting RelN in proportion to their degree of head finality elsewhere (Hawkins 2004: 208):

(11)

VO	OV
NRel (English)	NRel (Persian)
*RelN	RelN (Japanese)

2.4 *Complex inflections and functional categories benefit online processing*

Complex inflections, marking for example nominal cases, and functional categories like definite articles have been much discussed in the literature on complexity (cf. e.g. Plank 2001). It is commonly observed that these morphological and syntactic categories arise as a result of lengthy grammaticalization processes and are not characteristic of the earliest and simplest systems, such as creoles. I have argued in Hawkins (2004) that grammaticalization makes processing of the relevant grammars more efficient. If true, this means that there are benefits that compensate for added morphological and syntactic complexity: complexity in form processing is matched by simplicity with respect to the processing functions performed by rich case marking and definite articles.

Japanese has rich case marking (Hawkins 2002, 2004: 248), illustrated in (12):

(12) *John   ga   tegami   o   yonda*
      John   NOM   letter   ACC   wrote

I mentioned in section 2.1 that such languages generally have transparent and consistent mappings of cases onto theta-roles, avoiding the one-to-many mappings of English. The result is especially favourable for verb-final languages, since this permits theta-roles to be assigned early in parsing prior to the verb (Bornkessel 2002). The productivity of case marking in these languages can be seen in the language samples referenced in (13):

(13)   V-final with rich case marking: 89% (Nichols 1986), 62–72% (Dryer
              2002, Hawkins 2004: 249)
          V-initial with rich case marking: 38%, 41–47% respectively
          SVO with rich case marking: 14–20% (Dryer 2002)

Definite articles generally arise historically out of demonstrative determiners (Lyons 1999). Their evolution is especially favoured, in the analysis of Hawkins (2004: 82–93), in languages that have VO or other head-initial phrases (e.g. OVX languages) and in which the article can serve an NP "construction" function. The following data from the *World atlas of language structures* database (Haspelmath et al. 2005) clearly show a strong correlation with head-initiality (Hawkins 2007):

(14)	Def word distinct from Dem	No definite article
OV	19% (6)	81% (26)
VO	58% (62)	42% (44)
Non-rigid OVX	54% (7)	46% (6)

There is a trade-off in both complex morphology and definite articles between additional form processing on the one hand and certain complementary benefits on the other resulting from the presence of these forms, arguably of the kind hypothesized in Hawkins (2004).

3 Efficiency factor 1: Minimize Domains

Hawkins (2004) proposes three general principles of efficiency that are supported by a wide range of data from performance and grammars. These principles motivate a number of interacting and partially competing forces, they make predictions for the trade-offs we have just seen, and they provide a general basis for describing when and why they arise. In sections 3–5 I summarize these principles briefly and relate them to the data in section 2.

Efficiency is increased, first, by minimizing the domains (i.e. the sequences of linguistic forms and their conventionally associated properties) within which certain properties are assigned. This reduces the time and the processing effort required for the assignment of these properties. This principle is defined in (15):

(15)   Minimize Domains (MiD)

The human processor prefers to minimize the connected sequences of linguistic forms and their conventionally associated syntactic and semantic properties in which relations of combination and/or dependency are processed. The degree of this preference is proportional to the number of relations whose domains can be minimized in competing sequences or structures, and to the extent of the minimization difference in each domain.

Combination: Two categories *A* and *B* are in a relation of combination iff they occur within the same syntactic mother phrase or maximal projection (phrasal combination), or if they occur within the same lexical co-occurrence frame (lexical combination).

Dependency: Two categories *A* and *B* are in a relation of dependency iff the parsing of *B* requires access to *A* for the assignment of syntactic or semantic properties to *B* with respect to which *B* is zero-specified or ambiguously or polysemously specified.

In section 2.2 we saw one application of this principle when discussing extraposed and unextraposed word orders. Minimize Domains predicts that Phrasal Combination Domains (PCDs), defined in (16), should be as short as possible, and the degree of this preference should be proportional to the minimization difference between competing orderings.

(16)   Phrasal Combination Domain (PCD)

The PCD for a mother node *M* and its immediate constituents consists of the smallest string of terminal elements (plus all *M*-dominated non-terminals over the terminals) on the basis of which the processor can construct *M* and its ICs.

When there are big differences between competing PCDs, the optimal and minimal one is generally chosen. When differences are smaller, a less efficient and less minimal one may be chosen, in proportion to its efficiency relative to the optimal order.

By the general parsing principles of Hawkins (1994), some linear orderings reduce the number of words needed to recognize a mother phrase *M* and its immediate constituent daughters, assuming that (heads and head-like) categories such as P immediately project to mother nodes such as PP, making phrasal combination faster. The particular version of Minimize Domains that I have defined for ordering preferences is called Early Immediate Constituents (EIC) and is defined in (17):

(17)   Early Immediate Constituents (EIC, Hawkins 1994: 69–83)

The human processor prefers linear orders that minimize PCDs (by maximizing their IC-to-word ratios), in proportion to the minimization difference between competing orders.

When PCDs are smaller, fewer words need to be processed for recognition of the relevant phrase, resulting in higher IC-to-word ratios. This was illustrated in (7–9) for S, VP, and NP domains. Numerous predictions made by EIC for alternative orderings in performance are tested in Hawkins (1994, 2004). Grammatical conventions across languages reveal the same degrees of preference for minimal domains, with the relative quantities of languages reflecting the preferences as in the following "Greenbergian correlations" (data from Dryer's 1992 sample):

(18)   a. $[_{VP}$ V $[_{PP}$ P NP$]] = 161$ (41%)   b. $[_{VP}$ $[_{PP}$ NP P$]$ V$] = 204$ (52%)
    IC-to-word: $2/2 = 100\%$ IC-to-word: $2/2 = 100\%$

    c. $[_{VP}$ V $[_{PP}$ NP P$]] = 18$ (5%)   d. $[_{VP}$ $[_{PP}$ P NP$]$ V$] = 6$ (2%)
    IC-to-word: $2/4 = 50\%$ IC-to-word: $2/4 = 50\%$

    Assume: V $= 1$ word; P $= 1$ word; NP $= 2$ words
    EIC-preferred (18a) + (b) $= 365/389$ (94%)

The adjacency of V and P in (18a, b) guarantees the smallest possible domain for construction of VP and its two ICs (V and PP), and these optimal word order types account for 94 per cent of grammars. EIC can also explain when exceptions to these majority patterns will occur, and it accounts for many other word order universals (Hawkins 1994, 2004).

EIC gives us a ready means of quantifying the competing preferences in the trade-off data of section 2.2. (8a) and (8b) showed that a minimal domain for the processing of S can make the VP less minimal, and vice versa. (9a) and (9b) showed that the benefits for the VP could be at the expense of those for NP, and vice versa. This approach enables us to calculate an overall benefit for the sentence as a whole resulting from one variant versus another, and to predict the selection of different variants in performance.

4 Efficiency factor 2: Maximize Online Processing

A second general efficiency factor involves the timing with which linguistic properties are introduced in online processing. There is a clear preference for selecting and arranging linguistic forms so as to provide the earliest possible access to as much of the ultimate syntactic and semantic representation as possible. This preference, called Maximize Online Processing, also results in a preference for error-free online processing since errors delay the assignment of intended properties and increase processing effort. Clear examples can be seen across languages when certain common categories {A, B} are ordered asymmetrically A + B, regardless of the language type, in contrast to symmetries in which both orders are productive [A + B/B + A], e.g. Verb + Object [VO] and Object + Verb [OV].

Some examples of asymmetries are summarized in (19):

(19)   Some asymmetries (Hawkins 2004):
   (i) Displaced WH preposed to the left of its (gap-containing) clause
      (almost exceptionless; Hawkins 2002, 2004)
      Who$_i$ [did you say O$_i$ came to the party]

   (ii) Head Noun (Filler) to the left of its (gap-containing) Relative
      Clause
      e.g. *the students$_i$ [that I teach O$_i$]*
      If a language has basic VO, then with rare exceptions it is NRel
      rather than RelN, cf. (11) (Hawkins 1983)

   (iii) Antecedent precedes Anaphor (highly preferred cross-linguistically)
      e.g. *John washed himself* (SVO), *Washed John himself* (VSO), *John himself washed* (SOV) highly preferred over e.g. *Washed himself John* (VOS)

   (iv) Wide Scope Quantifier/Operator precedes Narrow Scope Quantifier/Operator (preferred)
      e.g. *Every student a book read* (SOV lgs) $\forall\exists$ preferred
      A book every student read (SOV lgs) $\exists\forall$ preferred

In these examples there is an asymmetric dependency of B on A: the gap is dependent on the head-noun filler in (ii) (for gap-filling), the anaphor on its antecedent in (iii) (for co-indexation), the narrow scope quantifier on the wide scope quantifer in (iv) (the number of books read depends on the quantifier in the subject NP in *Every student read a book/Many students read a book/Three students read a book*, etc.). The assignment of dependent properties to B is more efficient when A precedes, since these properties can be assigned to B immediately in online processing. In the reverse order, B + A, there will be delays in property assignments online ("unassignments") or misanalyses ("misassignments"). If the relative clause precedes the head noun, the gap is not immediately recognized and there are delays in argument structure assignment within the relative clause; if a narrow scope quantifier precedes a wide scope quantifier, a wide scope interpretation will generally be (mis)assigned online to the narrow scope quantifer; and so on.

Maximize Online Processing is defined in (20):

(20)   Maximize Online Processing (MaOP)
The human processor prefers to maximize the set of properties that are assignable to each item X as X is processed, thereby increasing online property (OP) to ultimate property (UP) ratios. The maximization difference between competing orders and structures will be a function of the number of properties that are unassigned or misassigned to X in a structure/sequence S, compared with the number in an alternative.

I have argued that MaOP competes with EIC and Minimize Domains in head ordering asymmetries like (11): a head before relative clause preference is visible in both VO and OV languages, with only rigid V-final languages resisting this preference to any degree (and preferring EIC-motivated consist-ent ordering of lexical heads), Hawkins (2004: 203–10).

5 Efficiency factor 3: Minimize Forms

A third general efficiency factor defended at length in Hawkins (2004) is Minimize Forms:

(21)   Minimize Forms (MiF)
The human processor prefers to minimize the formal complexity of each linguistic form F (its phoneme, morpheme, word, or phrasal units) and the number of forms with unique conventionalized property assignments, thereby assigning more properties to fewer forms. These minimizations apply in proportion to the ease with which a given property P can be assigned in processing to a given F.

The basic premise of MiF is that the processing of linguistic forms and of conventionalized property assignments requires effort. Minimizing forms and form–property pairings reduces that effort by fine-tuning it to the informa-tion that is already active in communication through accessibility, inferen-cing, and frequency. These processing enrichments avoid duplication in communication and are efficient.

This principle is visible in two complementary sets of cross-linguistic and intralinguistic variation data. One set involves complexity differences between surface forms (morphology and syntax), with preferences for minimal ex-pression (e.g. zero) in proportion to ease of processing, including frequency. Nominative case is more frequent than accusative, singular more frequent than plural, etc. Correspondingly, nominative and singular are more often expressed by zero forms than are accusative and plural respectively. Another data set involves the number and nature of lexical and grammatical distinctions conventionalized by languages. The preferences are again in proportion to ease of processing, including frequency of use in performance. Thus, there are preferred lexicalization patterns across languages, certain grammatical distinctions are cross-linguistically preferred (number, tense, aspect, causativity, some basic speech acts, thematic roles Agent/Patient), etc.

The general predictions made by MiF are summarized in (22):

(22) a. The formal complexity of each *F* is reduced in proportion to the frequency of that *F* and/or the processing ease of assigning a given *P* to a reduced *F* (e.g. to zero).

b. The number of unique *F:P* pairings in a language is reduced by grammaticalizing or lexicalizing a given *F:P* in proportion to the frequency and preferred expressiveness of that *P* in performance.

For further definition and testing, for example in relation to the kind of performance and grammatical data motivating Greenberg's (1966) markedness data, see Hawkins (2004). In the present context note that these MiF preferences compete with others.

5.1 *MiF competes with semantic transparency*

Assume (with Newmeyer 2005) that iconicity of syntactic structure with semantic representation is one fundamental determinant of syntax, with semantic transparency the result. MiF reduces this transparency through compression of semantic distinctions onto fewer syntactic forms, with much ambiguity and vagueness, all in order to reduce the formal and lexical units of a language that need to be stored and processed. This compression can be seen particularly clearly in compounds: *paper plate* for *plate made of paper*, *paper factory* for *factory that makes paper*, *paper clip* for *clip for use on paper*, etc. Compounds can convey pretty much any meaning that is compatible with real-world knowledge-based inferencing applied to a structure with a right-hand syntactic and semantic head (cf. Sperber and Wilson 1995).

Variation in the assignment of diverse argument structure types onto a common and minimal SVO (see section 2.1) can be profitably viewed from this perspective. This variation should be, by MiF, in proportion to the ease and frequency of making such assignments without explicitly coding the different argument types. Agent–Predicate–Patient sequences (*the professor wrote a book*) are the easiest and commonest argument structures to assign to a transitive clause, at the one end; Locative–Predicate–Agent (*this tent sleeps four*) is one of the least common reductions from a more semantically transparent *four can sleep in this tent*, and is one of the rarest within languages that permit it (English) and across languages (most of which do not).

5.2 *MiF competes with MaOP and MiD*

Complex morphology in the form of rich case marking is dispreferred by MiF, but provides early online information about theta-roles in advance of a verb, which is favoured by MaOP, and which is especially beneficial for V-final languages (cf. (13); Hawkins 2004: 249). Definite articles separate from demonstratives result in less minimal forms for NP than bare NPs but have numerous processing advantages, especially in head-initial languages (cf. (14)). These advantages include early construction of mother NP nodes, favoured by both MiD and MaOP. Hence MiF competes with both MaOP and MiD here.

6 Conclusions

The trade-offs in section 2 are the result of interacting efficiency factors that sometimes reinforce each other but sometimes compete in the relevant structures and languages. These competitions are summarized in (23):

(23)   §2.1: SVO and complex theta-roles: MiF versus transparent one-to-one theta-role assignments (MiF leads to one-to-many assignments in proportion to the ease/frequency of making such assignments without distinctive semantic coding);

§2.2: competing MiD preferences in different phrases (S v. VP, or VP v. NP);

§2.3: competing head orders in complex phrases (MaOP v. MiD advantages);

§2.4: complex morphology and definite articles (MiF v. MiD and MaOP advantages).

Variation results when factors compete or when different structures satisfy one and the same factor (e.g. Minimize Domains) in different ways. Performance preferences are motivated by a number of factors, therefore, of which relative complexity measured by size of domains and amount of structure is just one. Cross-linguistic grammatical conventions point to a similar interaction and competition between multiple factors. According to the Performance–Grammar Correspondence Hypothesis (Hawkins 2004), the more efficiency there is in a given structure, the more grammars incorporate it as a convention. This is defined in (24):

(24)   Performance–Grammar Correspondence Hypothesis (PGCH)
       Grammars have conventionalized syntactic structures in proportion to their degree of preference in performance, as evidenced by patterns of selection in corpora and by ease of processing in psycholinguistic experiments.

If this PGCH is correct, then the classic picture of the performance–grammar relationship presented in N. Chomsky (1965) (which is still widely held in generative theorizing) needs to be revised. For Chomsky, grammar is an integral part of a performance model, but it has not been shaped by performance to any significant extent. Instead, grammar is autonomous and Universal Grammar is innate. The PGCH is built on the opposite assumption of a deep interconnection between principles of performance and principles of grammar; and it is supported by the extensive correspondences between language-internal variation patterns in performance and cross-linguistic grammatical variation (Hawkins 1994, 2004).

Ranking grammars according to overall complexity is problematic for the reasons given in section 1:

- the trade-offs;
- unclarity over the measurement of overall complexity;
- unclarity over how best to describe many grammatical properties;
- different (rule- or structure-based) definitions of complexity itself.

Discussions of evolving (overall) complexity are no less problematic. The most we can do is say that languages are more or less complex in certain individual areas of grammar. For example, we can measure consonant inventory sizes and rank languages according to the number and nature of their consonant phonemes (Lindblom and Maddieson 1988). We can measure the amount of structure within a given noun phrase, in performance, or in the limit defined by a grammar, or we can measure the size of a larger piece of structure like a clause.

On the other hand, comparing grammars in terms of efficiency in communication as defined in section 1 enables us to model more of the factors that ultimately determine the preferences of performance and of grammars, in addition to complexity itself:

- speed in the delivery of linguistic properties;
- fine-tuning structural selections to frequency, accessibility, and inference;
- error avoidance.

This provides a more general theory of performance and of grammars, it puts structural complexity in its proper context, and it helps us understand the trade-offs better: preferred structures can be simpler in one respect, more complex in another; and the trade-off may involve simplicity competing with some other efficiency factor, e.g. speed of online property assignments in processing.

Having identified the multiple factors determining efficiency, we can then use quantitative data from both performance and grammars to guide our theorizing about the strength of each, about their relative strength in combination, and about their strength of application in different linguistic structures. Performance data such as (10) involving Extraposition from NP frequencies, grammatical frequencies such as (13) and (14), as well as distributional asymmetries such as (11), all shed light on this crucial issue: how strong is each factor, intrinsically and relatively? I have argued that the kind of multi-factor model of grammar and language use that we now need (and any serious model of these two domains has to be a multi-factor one) is best characterized in terms of different ways of achieving efficiency in communication, rather than in terms of simplicity and complexity alone.

19

Envoi

THE EDITORS

The preceding chapters have offered many diverse views about language complexity; and they speak for themselves. It would be neither practical nor appropriate for us to draw a specific set of "conclusions" on behalf of the contributors. Nevertheless, it may be worthwhile to round the book off with some brief comments on general themes that emerge.

A first point is the sense that the book is pushing at an open door. It is no surprise that our contributors themselves are scholars who see language complexity as a variable property – who reject or are sceptical about the dogma which Guy Deutscher calls "ALEC", All Languages are Equally Complex. The organization of the workshop from which the book emerges probably made that inevitable. (In principle we would have been glad to welcome participants who defended the traditional orthodoxy; but when a meeting is announced as being about variable language complexity, one must expect that those interested in attending will be people who believe that the phenomenon exists.) However, Geoffrey Sampson's introductory chapter portrayed ALEC sceptics as isolated voices in a sea of true believers. A few years ago that may have been so, but it is not the scenario which emerges from subsequent chapters here. Many contributors evidently take variation in language complexity for granted, and do not see this as so controversial a position as to require much defence. They are interested in exploring the detailed ramifications of the phenomenon, without evincing any expectation that critics will reject the fundamental assumptions of their research. It seems that a discipline-wide consensus may be changing.

Another noticeable feature of the contributions, taken together, is the centrality of grammar (in the British sense, meaning syntax and morphology), and particularly of clause structure and clause subordination, to assessments of language complexity. That is not to say that these are the only aspects of language structure to interest our contributors – far from it. But it seems fair to see them as the "centre of gravity" for the book taken as a whole. When relative language complexity was previously a live issue in linguistics, early in the twentieth century, syntax was not specially central to the discussions. Franz Boas's argument against the idea that American Indian languages are "primitive" relative to European languages began by considering the claim that the sounds of the former are imprecisely defined (Boas [1911] 1966: 12), and issues of phonology were perhaps as important as any in the debate as conducted in those years by other linguists. Some of our contributors discuss phonology, but in the book as a whole it is a peripheral topic.

To some extent this merely reflects a change in emphasis within linguistics in general. Leaving aside the question of degrees of language complexity, it is certainly true that the proportions of attention devoted to grammar and to phonology in general linguistic description and theorizing have been respectively greater and smaller over the past forty years than they were earlier. But the centrality of clause syntax in this book seems too marked to be explained purely as a reflection of the overall shape of the discipline.

It is surely fair to see this as a consequence of the "Chomskyan revolution". On the whole, and with exceptions, our contributors are not very sympathetic to Noam Chomsky's ideas about language. This is natural: Chomsky's leading idea is that language structure is universal and genetically fixed, so his approach is not likely to commend itself to scholars who see language structures as differing in significant ways – particularly when a number of them point to correlations between those differences and the particular cultures of the respective speech communities. Nevertheless, credit should be given where it is due: it is Chomsky who has led linguists to think of recursive syntactic rules as central to the cognitive endowments which distinguish language-using human beings from the other animal species. Only, Chomsky sees the structure of rules as genetically built-in to our common cognitive inheritance, whereas many of our contributors see the inheritance as giving human groups the ability to create and learn grammatical rules, with some cultures finding more use for this ability than others.

Another recurring theme is that just alluded to of relationships between language structures and (other aspects of) speakers' cultures. Whorf's hypothesis about the influence of a language on its speakers' world-view has been much discussed for decades, but that relates more to the semantic content of different languages than to their abstract structural properties (the division between these things is admittedly not easy to pin down). On the other hand the traditional assumption, as Kaius Sinnemäki rightly points out, has been that there is no influence in the other direction, from external factors onto language: "language structure has nothing to do with its geographical or sociocultural setting." Languages differ in abstract type, but any type of language might be found spoken in any kind of place.

Our contributors do not share that assumption, and several give solid reasons to disbelieve it. If people's language is part of their culture, one might wonder why the assumption ever seemed plausible. Universities have to define boundaries between subjects for practical administrative purposes; but there is surely little reason to expect the real world to contain barriers between various aspects of human life reflecting arbitrary academic boundaries.

If our contributors have been able to move beyond traditional linguistic assumptions, part of the reason is that we are better informed nowadays than linguists used to be about the basic facts of languages of very different kinds. Thirty years ago, it might have been difficult or impossible to assemble the level of detailed data on numerous remote and little-known languages that is represented in the preceding pages. Even nowadays, one encounters publications which claim to explore the nature of human language in general, and yet which are based just on the standard languages of a few highly literate modern societies, with no acknowledgement that these may not necessarily be representative. Happily, today there is a better way to do linguistics.

References

In this list, alphabetization of authors' names ignores lower-case prefixes (such as 'de' or 'van') and accents (thus Ä is alphabetized as A rather than as AE).

Many recent papers are available online, but the efficiency of current search engines is such that it has not seemed worth including URLs here other than for a few items which are difficult to access in other ways. For those URLs which are included, the protocol prefix http:// is assumed.

Admoni, W. G. (1970). *Der deutsche Sprachbau.* (German translation of 1966 Russian original.) Munich: Beck.

—— (1974). *Die Entwicklungstendenzen des deutschen Satzbaus von heute.* Munich: Hueber.

—— (1980). *Zur Ausbildung der Norm der deutschen Literatursprache im Bereich des neuhochdeutschen Satzgefüges (1470–1730): ein Beitrag zur Geschichte des Gestaltungssystems der deutschen Sprache.* Berlin: Akademie.

—— (1990). *Historische Syntax des Deutschen.* Tübingen: Niemeyer.

Aikhenvald, A. Y. (2000). *Classifiers: a typology of noun categorization devices.* Oxford: Oxford University Press.

—— (2007). Grammars in contact: a cross-linguistic perspective. In A. Y. Aikhenvald and R. M. W. Dixon (eds.), *Grammars in contact: a cross-linguistic typology.* Oxford: Oxford University Press.

Åkerberg, B. (2004). *Grammatik 2004: för kurser och självstudier i älvdalska.* MS.

Akmajian, A. (1984). Sentence types and the form–function fit. *Natural Language and Linguistic Theory* 2: 1–23.

Allcott, H., Karlan, D., Möbius, M., Rosenblat, T., and Szeidl, A. (2007). Community size and network closure. *American Economic Review Papers and Proceedings* 97: 80–5.

Ambrazas, V. (ed.) (1997). *Lithuanian grammar.* Vilnius: Baltos Lankos.

Andersen, H. (1988). Center and periphery: adoption, diffusion, and spread. In J. Fisiak (ed.), *Historical dialectology: regional and social.* Berlin: Mouton de Gruyter.

Anglin, J. M. (1993). *Vocabulary development: a morphological analysis.* Monographs of the Society for Research in Child Development, 58(10), serial no. 238.

Ansaldo, U., and Lim, L. (2004). Phonetic absence as syntactic prominence: grammaticalization in isolating tonal languages. In O. Fischer, M. Norde, and H. Perridon (eds.), *Up and down the cline: the nature of grammaticalization.* Amsterdam: Benjamins.

Arends, J. (2001). Simple grammars, complex languages. *Linguistic Typology* 5: 180–2.

——, and Perl, M. (eds.) (1995). *Early Suriname creole texts.* Frankfurt: Vervuert.

Armbruster, C. (1960). *Dongolese Nubian: a grammar.* Cambridge: Cambridge University Press.

Arndt, P. P. (1933). *Grammatik der Ngad'a Sprache. Verhandelingen: Koninklijk Bataviaasche Genootschap van Kunsten en Wetenschappen,* 72.3. Bandung: Nix.

Arppe, A. (forthcoming). Univariate, bivariate and multivariate methods in corpus-based lexicography: a study of synonymy. Ph.D. dissertation, University of Helsinki.

Atkinson, R. C., and Schiffrin, R. M. (1968). Human memory: a proposed system and its control processes. In K. W. Spence and J. T. Spence (eds.), *The psychology of learning and motivation,* vol. 2: *Advances in research and theory.* New York: Academic Press.

Bailey, C.-J. N. (1973). *Variation and linguistic theory.* Arlington, VA: Center for Applied Linguistics.

Baker, P. (1999). Investigating the origin and diffusion of shared features among the Atlantic English creoles. In P. Baker and A. Bruyn (eds.), *St. Kitts and the Atlantic creoles.* London: University of Westminster Press.

Barnes, J. (ed.) (1984). *The complete works of Aristotle: the revised Oxford translation,* vol. 2. Princeton, NJ: Princeton University Press.

Baruzzi, A. (1982). Effects of degree of education on the comprehension of syntactic structures in normal and aphasic populations. *McGill Working Papers in Linguistics* 2: 56–74.

Bateman, J. (1986). *Iau verb morphology.* NUSA: Linguistic Studies of Indonesian and Other Languages in Indonesia, 26. Jakarta: Universitas Katolik Indonesia Atma Jaya.

Bates, E., Bretherton, I., and Snyder, L. S. (1988). *From first words to grammar: individual differences and dissociable mechanisms.* Cambridge: Cambridge University Press.

Bates, E., McNew, S., MacWhinney, B., Devescovi, A., and Smith, S. (1982). Functional constraints on sentence processing: a cross-linguistic study. *Cognition* 11: 245–99.

Beck, I. L., and McKeown, M. G. (1991). Social studies texts are hard to understand: mediating some of the difficulties. *Language Arts* 68: 482–90.

Becker, K. F. (1870). *Ausführliche deutsche Grammatik als Kommentar der Schulgrammatik,* vol. 2. 2nd rev. edn. Prague: Tempsky.

Becker, N. (2005). Numeralklassifikatoren im Thai. Ph.D. dissertation, University of Mainz.

van den Berg, R. (1989). *A grammar of the Muna language.* Dordrecht: Foris.

Bergman, G. (1968). *Kortfattad svensk språkhistoria.* Stockholm: Prisma.

Berlin, B., and Kay, P. (1969). *Basic color terms: their universality and evolution.* Berkeley: University of California Press.

Bernstein, B. (1971). *Class, codes and control,* vol. 1: *Theoretical studies towards a sociology of language.* London: Routledge & Kegan Paul.

Berwick, R. C. (1998). Language evolution and the Minimalist Program: the origins of syntax. In J. R. Hurford, M. Studdert-Kennedy, and C. Knight (eds.), *Approaches to the evolution of language: social and cognitive bases.* Cambridge: Cambridge University Press.

Biber, D. (1988). *Variation across speech and writing.* Cambridge: Cambridge University Press.

——Finegan, E., Johansson, S., Conrad, S., and Leech, G. N. (1999). *Longman grammar of spoken and written English.* Harlow: Longman.

BibleWorks 5 (2001). Software for Biblical exegesis and research. Bigfork, MT: Hermeneutika.

Bickel, B., and Nichols, J. (2002ff.). The Autotyp research program. Available at: www.uni-leipzig.de/~autotyp/

——(2005). Inflectional synthesis of the verb. In Haspelmath et al. (2005).

Bickerton, D. (1990). *Language and species.* Chicago: University of Chicago Press.

Bisang, W. (1992). *Das Verb im Chinesischen, Hmong, Vietnamesischen, Thai und Khmer: Vergleichende Grammatik im Rahmen der Verbserialisierung, der Grammatikalisierung und der Attraktorpositionen.* Tübingen: Narr.

——(1999). Classifiers in East and Southeast Asian languages: counting and beyond. In J. Gvozdanović (ed.), *Numeral types and changes worldwide.* Berlin: Mouton de Gruyter.

——(2004). Grammaticalization without coevolution of form and meaning: the case of tense–aspect–modality in East and mainland Southeast Asia. In W. Bisang, N. Himmelmann, and B. Wiemer (eds.), *What makes grammaticalization? A look from its fringes and its components.* Berlin: Mouton de Gruyter.

——(2006). South East Asia as a linguistic area. In K. Brown (ed.), *Encyclopedia of language and linguistics,* vol. 11. New York: Elsevier.

——(2003). Grammaticalization and the areal factor: the perspective of East and mainland Southeast Asian languages. In M. J. López-Couso and E. Seoane (eds.), *Rethinking grammaticalization: new perspectives.* Amsterdam: Benjamins.

Blackings, M., and Fabb, N. (2003). *A grammar of Ma'di.* Berlin: Mouton de Gruyter.

Blatt, F. (1957). Latin influence on European syntax. *Travaux du Cercle Linguistique de Copenhague* 11: 33–69.

Blaubergs, M. S., and Braine, M. D. S. (1974). Short term memory limitations on decoding self-embedded sentences. *Journal of Experimental Psychology* 102: 745–8.

Bloom, L., Rispoli, M., Gartner, B., and Hafitz, J. (1989). Acquisition of complementation. *Journal of Child Language* 16: 101–20. Repr. in L. Bloom (ed.), *Language development from two to three.* Cambridge: Cambridge University Press, 1991.

Bloomfield, L. (1933). *Language.* New York: Holt.

Boas, F. (1911). Introduction to *Handbook of American Indian languages.* Bureau of American Ethnology, *Bulletin* 40, part I, pp. 1–83. Repr. 1966 in one volume with J. W. Powell, *Indian linguistic families of America north of Mexico.* Lincoln: University of Nebraska Press.

Boast, R. (2006). Tragic Piraha past? *New Scientist,* 15 Apr.

Boivie, P. G. (1834). *Försök till en svensk språklära jemte inledning, innehållande allmänna grammatikan,* rev. edn. Uppsala: Palmblad.

Boretzky, N. (1983). *Kreolsprachen, Substrate und Sprachwandel.* Wiesbaden: Harassowitz.

Borgman, D. M. (1990). Sanuma. In Derbyshire and Pullum (1990), vol. 2.

Bornkessel, I. (2002). The Argument Dependency Model: a neurocognitive approach to incremental interpretation. Ph.D. dissertation, University of Potsdam.

Bowe, H. J. (1990). *Categories, constituents and constituent order in Pitjantjatjara: an Aboriginal language of Australia.* London: Routledge.

Braunmüller, K. (1990). Komplexe Flexionssysteme: (k)ein Problem für die Natürlichkeitstheorie? *Zeitschrift für Phonetik, Sprachwissenschaft und Kommunikationsforschung* 43: 625–35.

——(1995). Morphologische Undurchsichtigkeit: ein Charakteristikum kleiner Sprachen. In K. Braunmüller (ed.), *Beiträge zur skandinavistischen Linguistik.* Oslo: Novus.

Broadbent, S. (1964). *The Southern Sierra Miwok language.* Berkeley: University of California Press.

Broca, P. (1878). Anatomie comparée des circomvolutions cérébrales: le grand lobe limbique et la scissure limbique dans la série des mammifères. *Revue anthropologique* 1: 385–498.

Bruce, L. (1984). *The Alamblak language of Papua New Guinea (East Sepik).* Canberra: Pacific Linguistics (Australian National University).

Bryant, P. E., MacLean, M., Bradely, L. L., and Crossland, J. (1990). Rhyme and alliteration, phonemic detection, and learning to read. *Developmental Psychology* 26: 429–38.

Burling, R. (2005). *The talking ape: how language evolved.* Oxford: Oxford University Press.

Burzio, L. (1981). Intransitive verbs and Italian auxiliaries. Ph.D. dissertation, MIT.

Bybee, J., Perkins, R., and Pagliuca, W. (1994). *The evolution of grammar: tense, aspect and modality in the languages of the world.* Chicago: University of Chicago Press.

Byrne, F. X. (1987). *Grammatical relations in a radical creole.* Amsterdam: Benjamins.

Cadely, J.-R. (1994). Aspects de la phonologie du créole haïtien. Ph.D. dissertation, Université du Québec à Montréal.

Calvet, L.-J. (1998). *Language wars and linguistic politics.* (Translation of a 1987 French original.) Oxford: Oxford University Press.

Campbell, L. (1985). *The Pipil language of El Salvador.* Berlin: Mouton de Gruyter.

Carlisle, J. F. (2000). Awareness of the structure and meaning of morphologically complex words: impact on reading. *Reading and Writing* 12: 143–341.

Carlson, R. (1994). *A grammar of Supyire.* Berlin: Mouton de Gruyter.

Carroll, S. B. (2005). *Endless forms most beautiful: the new science of Evo Devo and the making of the animal kingdom.* New York: Norton.

Casad, E. (1984). Cora. In R. Langacker (ed.), *Studies in Uto-Aztecan grammar,* vol. 4: *Southern Uto-Aztecan grammatical sketches.* Dallas, TX: Summer Institute of Linguistics.

Chafe, W. (1994). *Discourse, consciousness, and time.* Chicago: Chicago University Press.

Chamoreau, C. (2000). *Grammaire du purépecha.* Munich: LINCOM.

Chelliah, S. L. (1997). *A grammar of Meithei.* Berlin: Mouton de Gruyter.

Childs, G. T. (1995). *A grammar of Kisi: a Southern Atlantic language.* Berlin: Mouton de Gruyter.

Chipere, N. (1997). *Individual differences in syntactic skill.* Working Papers in Applied Linguistics of the Research Centre for English and Applied Linguistics, 4, University of Cambridge.

—— (2001). Native speaker variations in syntactic competence: implications for first language teaching. *Language Awareness* 10: 107–24.

—— (2003). *Understanding complex sentences: native speaker variation in syntactic competence.* Basingstoke: Palgrave Macmillan.

—— (2006). A constructivist epistemology for the language sciences. In H. Pishwa (ed.), *Language and memory: aspects of knowledge representation.* Berlin: Mouton de Gruyter.

Chomsky, C. (1969). *The acquisition of syntax in children from 5 to 10.* Cambridge, MA: MIT Press.

Chomsky, N. (1965). *Aspects of the theory of syntax.* Cambridge, MA: MIT Press.

—— (1968). *Language and mind.* New York: Harcourt, Brace & World.

—— (1976). *Reflections on language.* London: Temple Smith.

—— (1980). *Rules and representations.* Oxford: Blackwell.

—— (1991). Linguistics and cognitive science: problems and mysteries. In A. Kasher (ed.), *The Chomskyan turn.* Oxford: Blackwell.

—— (1995). *The Minimalist Program.* Cambridge, MA: MIT Press.

—— (2005). Three factors in language design. *Linguistic Inquiry* 36: 1–22.

Clark, E., Hecht, B. F., and Mulford, R. C. (1986). Coining complex compounds in English: affixes and word order in acquisition. *Linguistics* 24: 7–29.

Clark, G. (1977). *World prehistory in new perspective.* Cambridge: Cambridge University Press.

Colapinto, J. (2007). The interpreter: has a remote Amazonian tribe upended our understanding of language? *New Yorker,* 16 Apr. 2007.

Cole, P. (1985). *Imbabura Quechua.* London: Croom Helm.

——, Hermon, G., and Tjung, Y. N. (2006). Is there *Pasif Semu* in Jakarta Indonesian? *Oceanic Linguistics* 45: 64–90.

Comrie, B. (ed.) (1987). *The world's major languages.* London: Croom Helm; repr. 1990 by Oxford University Press.

—— (1992). Before complexity. In J. A. Hawkins and M. Gell-Mann (eds.), *The evolution of human languages.* New York: Addison-Wesley.

—— (2005). Alignment of case marking. In Haspelmath et al. (2005).

Conrad, R. J., and Wogiga, K. (1991). *An outline of Bukiyip grammar.* Canberra: Pacific Linguistics (Australian National University).

Corbett, G. G. (1979). The agreement hierarchy. *Journal of Linguistics* 15: 203–24.

—— (1991). *Gender*. Cambridge: Cambridge University Press.

Court, C. (1985). Fundamentals of Iu Mien (Yao) grammar. Ph.D. dissertation, University of California at Berkeley.

Covington, M., and Rosenfelder, M. (2002). The sci.lang FAQ: frequently asked questions about linguistics, version 2.29. Available at: www.zompist.com/langfaq.html

Cowan, H. K. J. (1965). *Grammar of the Sentani language*. The Hague: Nijhoff.

Croft, W. (1991). *Syntactic categories and grammatical relations: the cognitive organization of information*. Chicago: University of Chicago Press.

—— (2003). *Typology and universals*, 2nd edn. Cambridge: Cambridge University Press.

Cromer, W. (1970). The Difference Model: a new explanation for some reading difficulties. *Journal of Educational Psychology* 61: 471–83.

Culicover, P. W., and Jackendoff, R. (2005). *Simpler syntax*. Oxford: Oxford University Press.

Cupples, L., and Holmes, V. M. (1987). Reading skill and interpretation of temporary structural ambiguity. *Language and Cognitive Processes* 2: 179–203.

——, and —— (1992). Evidence for a difference in syntactic knowledge between skilled and less skilled adult readers. *Journal of Psycholinguistic Research* 21: 249–75.

Curnow, T. J. (1997). A grammar of Awa Pit (Cuaiquer): an indigenous language of south-western Colombia. Ph.D. dissertation, Australian National University.

Dąbrowska, E. (1997). The LAD goes to school: a cautionary tale for nativists. *Linguistics* 35: 735–66.

——, and Street, J. (2006). Individual differences in language attainment: comprehension of passive sentences by native and non-native English speakers. *Language Sciences* 28: 604–15.

Dahl, Ö. (2004). *The growth and maintenance of linguistic complexity*. Amsterdam: Benjamins.

—— (forthcoming). Definitions of complexity. In *Proceedings of the Symposium on Complexity, Accuracy, and Fluency*, Brussels, 29–30 Mar. 2007.

Dahlstrom, A. (1991). *Plains Cree morphosyntax*. New York: Garland.

Dayley, J. (1985). *Tzutujil grammar*. Berkeley: University of California Press.

Deacon, T. W. (1997). *The symbolic species: the co-evolution of language and the brain*. New York: Norton.

Dearborn, W. F., and Anderson, I. H. (1973). A new method for teaching phrasing and increasing the size of reading fixations. *Psychological Record* 1: 459–75.

DeGraff, M. (1993). A riddle on negation in Haitian. *Probus* 5: 63–93.

—— (2001). On the origin of creoles. *Linguistic Typology* 5: 213–310.

Déprez, V. (1992). Is Haitian Creole really a pro-drop language? *Travaux de recherche sur le créole haïtien* 11: 23–40.

Derbyshire, D. C. (1979). *Hixkaryana*. Amsterdam: North-Holland.

——, and G. K. Pullum (eds.) (1986, 1990). *Handbook of Amazonian Languages*, vols. 1 and 2. Berlin: Mouton de Gruyter.

Deutscher, G. (2000). *Syntactic change in Akkadian: the evolution of sentential complementation.* Oxford: Oxford University Press.

—— (2002). The Akkadian relative clause in cross-linguistic perspective. *Zeitschrift für Assyriologie und vorderasiatische Archäologie* 92: 86–105.

Devoto, G. (1968). *Geschichte der Sprache Roms.* Heidelberg: Winter.

Diamond, J. (1998). *Guns, germs and steel: a short history of everybody for the last 13,000 years.* London: Vintage.

Dickinson, D. K., and Snow, C. E. (1987). Interrelationships among prereading and oral language skills in kindergartners from two social classes. *Early Childhood Research Quarterly* 2: 1–25.

Diessel, H., and Tomasello, M. (2001). The acquisition of finite complement clauses in English: a usage based approach to the development of grammatical constructions. *Cognitive Linguistics* 12: 97–141.

van Dijk, T. A., and Kintsch, W. (1983). *Strategies of discourse comprehension.* New York: Academic Press.

Dixon, R. M. W. (2004). *The Jarawara language of Southern Amazonia.* Oxford: Oxford University Press.

Dol, P. H. (1999). A grammar of Maybrat. Ph.D. dissertation, University of Leiden. Published 2007 as *A grammar of Maybrat: a language of the Bird's Head Peninsula, Papua Province, Indonesia.* Canberra: Pacific Linguistics (Australian National University).

Donohue, M. (2004). A grammar of the Skou language of New Guinea. MS, National University of Singapore. www.papuaweb.org/dlib/tema/bahasa/skou/

——, and Sawaki, Y. (2007). Papuan Malay pronominals: forms and functions. *Oceanic Linguistics* 46: 253–76.

Douglas, K. (2006). Lost for words. *New Scientist,* 18 Mar.

Dryer, M. S. (1980). The positional tendencies of sentential noun phrases in universal grammar. *Canadian Journal of Linguistics* 25: 123–96.

—— (1989). Large linguistic areas and language sampling. *Studies in Language* 13: 257–92.

—— (1992). The Greenbergian word order correlations. *Language* 68: 81–138.

—— (2002). Case distinctions, rich verb agreement, and word order type. *Theoretical Linguistics* 28: 151–7.

—— (2005). Genealogical language list. In Haspelmath et al. (2005).

Du Bois, J. W., Chafe, W. L., Meyer, C., and Thompson, S. A. (2000). *Santa Barbara Corpus of Spoken American English,* part 1. Philadelphia: Linguistic Data Consortium.

Dulay, H. C., and Burt, M. K. (1973). Should we teach children syntax? *Language Learning* 23: 245–58.

—— (1974). Natural sequences in child second language acquisition. *Language Learning* 24: 37–53.

Enfield, N. (ed.) (2002). *Ethnosyntax: explorations in grammar and culture.* Oxford: Oxford University Press.

—— (2003). *Linguistic epidemiology: semantics and grammar of language contact in mainland southeast Asia.* London: Routledge Curzon.

Engdahl, S. (1962). *Studier i nusvensk sakprosa: några utvecklingslinjer.* Skrifter utgivna av Institutionen för nordiska språk vid Uppsala universitet, 11.

Erdmann, P. (1988). On the principle of 'weight' in English. In C. Duncan-Rose and T. Vennemann (eds.), *On language: rhetorica, phonologica, syntactica: a Festschrift for Robert P. Stockwell from his friends and colleagues.* London: Routledge.

Ericsson, K. A., and Kintsch, W. (1995). Long-term working memory. *Psychological Review* 102: 211–45.

Erman, K. B. (1913). Beziehungen zwischen stellung und funktion der nebensätze mehrfacher unterordnung im ahd. *Zeitschrift für deutsche Philologie* 45: 1–46, 153–216, 426–84.

Evans, N. D. (1995). *A grammar of Kayardild, with historical-comparative notes on Tangkic.* Berlin: Mouton de Gruyter.

—— (1997). Head class and agreement class in the Mayali dialect chain. In M. Harvey and N. Reid (eds.), *Nominal classification in Aboriginal Australia.* Amsterdam: Benjamins.

——, Brown, D., and Corbett, G. G. (2002). The semantics of gender in Mayali: partially parallel systems and formal implementation. *Language* 78: 111–55.

Everett, D. L. (1985). Syllable weight, sloppy phonemes, and channels in Pirahã discourse. In M. Niepokuj et al. (eds.), *Proceedings of the Eleventh Annual Meeting of the Berkeley Linguistics Society.* Berkeley, CA: BLS.

—— (1986). Pirahã. In Derbyshire and Pullum (1986), vol. 1.

—— (1993). Sapir, Reichenbach, and the syntax of tense in Pirahã. *Journal of Pragmatics and Cognition* 1: 89–124.

—— (2004). Coherent fieldwork. In P. van Sterkenberg (ed.), *Linguistics today.* Amsterdam: Benjamins.

—— (2005). Cultural constraints on grammar and cognition in Pirahã: another look at the design features of human language. *Current Anthropology* 76: 621–46.

—— (2007). Cultural constraints on grammar in Pirahã: a reply to Nevins, Pesetsky, and Rodrigues (2007). Available at: ling.auf.net/lingBuzz/000427

—— (forthcoming a). *Don't sleep, there are snakes: life and language in the Amazonian jungle.* New York: Pantheon.

—— (forthcoming b). *Linguistic fieldwork: a student guide.* Cambridge: Cambridge University Press. Available at: ling.auf.net/lingBuzz/000442

Fabb, N. (1984). Syntactic affixation. Ph.D. dissertation, MIT.

Fabian, G., Fabian, E., and Waters, B. (1998). *Morphology, syntax and cohesion in Nabak, Papua New Guinea.* Canberra: Pacific Linguistics (Australian National University).

Feldpausch, T., and Feldpausch, B. (1992). Namia grammar essentials. In J. Roberts (ed.), *Namia and Amanab grammar essentials.* Data Papers on Papua New Guinea Languages, vol. 39. Ukarumpa: Summer Institute of Linguistics.

Ferguson, C. A. (1979). Phonology as an individual access system: some data from language acquisition. In C. J. Fillmore, D. Kempler, and W. S.-Y. Wang (eds.), *Individual differences in language ability and language behavior.* New York: Academic Press.

Filppula, M., J. Klemola, J., and Paulasto, H. (eds.) (forthcoming). *Vernacular universals and language contacts: evidence from varieties of English and beyond.* London: Routledge.

Fitch, W. T. (1997). Vocal tract length and formant frequency dispersion correlate with body size in rhesus macaques. *Journal of the Acoustical Society of America* 102: 1213–22.

Foley, W. A. (1991). *The Yimas language of New Guinea.* Stanford, CA: Stanford University Press.

Forby, R. (1830). *The vocabulary of East Anglia.* London: Nichols. Repr. New York: Kelley, 1969.

Forston, B. W. (2004). *Indo-European language and culture: an introduction.* Oxford: Blackwell.

Fortescue, M. (1984). *West Greenlandic.* London: Croom Helm.

Fowler, R. L. (1984). Aristotle on the period. *Classical Quarterly* 32: 89–99.

Fox, B. A., and Thompson, S. A. (2007). Relative clauses in English conversation: relativizers, frequency, and the notion of construction. *Studies in Language* 31: 293–326.

Frajzyngier, Z., with Shay, E. (2002). *A grammar of Hdi.* Berlin: Mouton de Gruyter.

Frank, P. (1990). *Ika syntax.* Summer Institute of Linguistics and the University of Texas at Arlington.

Frayne, D. R. (1993). *The royal inscriptions of Mesopotamia: early periods,* vol. 2: *Sargonic and Gutian periods (2334–2213 BC).* Toronto: University of Toronto Press.

Frazier, L. (1985). Syntactic complexity. In D. Dowty, L. Karttunen, and A. Zwicky (eds.), *Natural language parsing.* Cambridge: Cambridge University Press.

Freedle, R., and Craun, M. (1969). Observations with self-embedded sentences using written aids. *Perception and Psychophysics* 7: 247–9.

Freeman, D. (1983). *Margaret Mead and Samoa: the making and unmaking of an anthropological myth.* Cambridge, MA: Harvard University Press.

Freyd, P., and Baron, J. (1982). Individual differences in acquisition of derivational morphology. *Journal of Verbal Learning and Verbal Behavior* 21: 282–95.

von der Gabelentz, G. (1891). *Die Sprachwissenschaft, ihre Aufgaben, Methoden und bisherigen Ergebnisse.* Leipzig: Weigel Nachfolger. Repr. Tübingen: Narr, 1972.

Gachelin, J.-M. (1991). Transitivity and intransitivity in the dialects of south-west England. In Trudgill and Chambers (1991).

Galloway, B. D. (1993). *A grammar of Upriver Halkomelem.* Berkeley: University of California Press.

Geer, S. E., Gleitman, H., and Gleitman, L. (1972). Paraphrasing and remembering compound words. *Journal of Verbal Learning and Verbal Behavior* 11: 348–55.

Gell-Mann, M. (1994). *The quark and the jaguar: adventures in the simple and the complex.* London: Little Brown.

Gibson, E. (1998). Linguistic complexity: locality of syntactic dependencies. *Cognition* 68: 1–76.

Gil, D. (1994). The structure of Riau Indonesian. *Nordic Journal of Linguistics* 17: 179–200.

——(2000). Syntactic categories, cross-linguistic variation and universal grammar. In P. M. Vogel and B. Comrie (eds.), *Approaches to the typology of word classes*. Berlin: Mouton de Gruyter.

——(2001). Creoles, complexity, and Riau Indonesian. *Linguistic Typology* 5: 325–71.

——(2002a). Ludlings in Malayic languages: an introduction. In B. K. Purwo (ed.), *PELBBA 15, Pertemuan Linguistik Pusat Kajian Bahasa dan Budaya Atma Jaya: Kelima Belas*. Jakarta: Unika Atma Jaya.

——(2002b). The prefixes *di-* and *N-* in Malay/Indonesian dialects. In F. Wouk and M. Ross (eds.), *The history and typology of Western Austronesian voice systems*. Canberra: Pacific Linguistics (Australian National University).

——(2004a). Learning about language from your handphone: *dan, and* and *&* in SMSs from the Siak River Basin. In K. E. Sukatmo (ed.), *Kolita 2, Konferensi Linguistik Tahunan Atma Jaya*. Jakarta: Pusat Kajian Bahasa dan Budaya, Unika Atma Jaya.

——(2004b). Riau Indonesian *sama*: explorations in macrofunctionality. In M. Haspelmath (ed.), *Coordinating constructions*. Amsterdam: Benjamins.

——(2005a). Isolating-Monocategorial-Associational Language. In H. Cohen and C. Lefebvre (eds.), *Categorization in cognitive science*. Oxford: Elsevier.

——(2005b). Word order without syntactic categories: how Riau Indonesian does it. In A. Carnie, H. Harley, and S. A. Dooley (eds.), *Verb first: on the syntax of verb-initial languages*. Amsterdam: Benjamins.

——(2006). Early human language was Isolating-Monocategorial-Associational. In A. Cangelosi, A. D. M Smith, and K. Smith (eds.), *The evolution of language: proceedings of the 6th International Conference (EVOLANG6)*. Singapore: World Scientific.

——(2007). Creoles, complexity and associational semantics. In U. Ansaldo and S. J. Matthews (eds.), *Deconstructing Creole: new horizons in language creation*. Amsterdam: Benjamins.

——(2008). How complex are isolating languages? In Miestamo et al. (2008).

Givón, T. (1979). *On understanding grammar*. New York: Academic Press.

——(2008). Toward a diachronic typology of relative clauses. Paper given at the Symposium on the Genesis of Syntactic Complexity, Rice University, March.

Gleitman, L. R., and Gleitman, H. (1970). *Phrase and paraphrase*. New York: Norton.

Gordon, L. (1986). *Maricopa morphology and syntax*. Berkeley: University of California Press.

Gordon, R., Jr. (ed.) (2005). *Ethnologue: languages of the world*, 15th edn. SIL International (Dallas). Available at: www.ethnologue.com

Goswami, U., and Bryant, P. (1992). Rhyme, analogy and children's reading. In P. B. Gough, L. C. Ehri, and R. Treiman (eds.), *Reading acquisition*. Mahwah, NJ: Erlbaum.

Grace, G. (1990). The 'aberrant' (vs. 'exemplary') Melanesian languages. In P. Baldi (ed.), *Linguistic change and reconstruction methodology*. Berlin: Mouton de Gruyter.

Graesser, A. C., Hoffman, N. L., and Clark, L. F. (1980). Structural components of reading time. *Journal of Verbal Learning and Verbal Behavior* 19: 135–51.

Greenbaum, S. (1996). *Comparing English worldwide: the International Corpus of English*. Oxford: Clarendon Press.

——, and Quirk, R. (1970). *Elicitation experiments in English: linguistic studies in use and attitude*. London: Longman.

Greenberg, J. H. (1960). A quantitative approach to the morphological typology of language. *International Journal of American Linguistics* 26: 178–94.

—— (1963). Some universals of grammar with particular reference to the order of meaningful elements. In J. H. Greenberg (ed.), *Universals of language*, 2nd edn. Cambridge, MA: MIT Press, 1966.

—— (1966). *Language universals, with special reference to feature hierarchies*. 2nd edn. The Hague: Mouton.

—— (1974). Numeral classifiers and substantival number: problems in the genesis of a linguistic type. In *Proceedings of the 11th International Congress of Linguists, Bologna–Florence, August–September 1972*. Bologna.

Grinevald-Craig, C. (1988). A grammar of Rama. Report to National Science Foundation, BNS 8511156.

Gruber, H. E., and Vonèche, J. J. (eds.) (1977). *The essential Piaget*. New York: Basic Books.

Guasti, M. T. (2002). *Language acquisition: the growth of grammar*. Cambridge, MA: MIT Press.

Guilfoyle, E., and Noonan, M. (1992). Functional categories in language acquisition. *Canadian Journal of Linguistics* 37: 241–72.

Guirardello, R. (1999). A reference grammar of Trumai. Ph.D. dissertation, Rice University.

Haan, J. (2001). The grammar of Adang: a Papuan language spoken on the island of Alor, East Nusa Tenggara – Indonesia. Ph.D. dissertation, University of Sydney.

Hagman, R. S. (1977). *Nama Hottentot Grammar*. Language Science Monographs, 15. Bloomington: Indiana University.

Haiman, J. (1983). Iconic and economic motivation. *Language* 59: 781–819.

——, and Thompson, S. A. (eds.) (1988). *Clause combining in grammar and discourse*. Amsterdam: Benjamins.

Hakulinen, A., Karlsson, F., and Vilkuna, M. (1980). *Suomen tekstilauseiden piirteitä: kvantitatiivinen tutkimus*. Publications of the Department of General Linguistics, University of Helsinki, 6.

Hale, K. (1976). The adjoined relative clause in Australia. In R. M. W. Dixon (ed.), *Grammatical categories in Australian languages*. Canberra: Australian Institute of Aboriginal Languages.

——, and Keyser, S. J. (2002). *Prolegomena to a theory of argument structure*. Cambridge, MA: MIT Press.

Hansson, I.-L. (2003). Akha. In G. Thurgood and R. J. LaPolla (eds.), *The Sino-Tibetan languages*. London: Routledge.

Hardman, M. (2000). *Jaqaru*. Munich: LINCOM Europa.

Harriehausen, B. (1988). Hmong Njua, syntaktische Analyse einer gesprochenen Sprache mit Hilfe datenverarbeitungstechnischer Mittel und sprachvergleichende Beschreibung des südostasiatischen Sprachraumes. Ph.D. dissertation, Georg-August-Universität zu Göttingen.

Harrington, M. (1987). Processing transfer: language specific strategies as a source of interlanguage variation. *Applied Psycholinguistics* 8: 351–78.

Harris, A. (1981). *Georgian syntax: a study in relational grammar*. Cambridge: Cambridge University Press.

Harris, M. (1988). Concessive clauses in English and Romance. In Haiman and Thompson (1988).

Harris, Z. S. (1947). *Methods in structural linguistics*. Chicago: University of Chicago Press. (Later republished as *Structural linguistics*.)

Harvey, M. (2002). *A grammar of Gaagudju*. Berlin: Mouton de Gruyter.

Haspelmath, M. (1993). *A grammar of Lezgian*. Berlin: Mouton de Gruyter.

——, Dryer, M., Gil, D., and Comrie, B. (eds.) (2005). *The world atlas of language structures*. Oxford: Oxford University Press.

Haudricourt, A.-G. (1961). Richesse en phonèmes et richesse en locuteurs. *L'Homme* 1: 5–10.

Hauser, M. D., Chomsky, N., and Fitch, W. T. (2002). The faculty of language: what is it, who has it, and how did it evolve? *Science* 298: 1569–79.

Hawkins, J. A. (1983). *Word order universals*. New York: Academic Press.

—— (1986). *A comparative typology of English and German: unifying the contrasts*. Austin: University of Texas Press and London: Routledge.

—— (1994). *A performance theory of order and constituency*. Cambridge: Cambridge University Press.

—— (1995). Argument-predicate structure in grammar and performance: a comparison of English and German. In I. Rauch and G. F. Carr (eds.), *Insights in Germanic linguistics*, vol. 1. Berlin: de Gruyter.

—— (2002). Symmetries and asymmetries: their grammar, typology and parsing. *Theoretical Linguistics* 28: 95–149.

—— (2004). *Efficiency and complexity in grammars*. Oxford: Oxford University Press.

—— (2007). An asymmetry between VO and OV languages: the ordering of obliques. In G. G. Corbett and M. Noonan (eds.), *Case and grammatical relations: essays in honour of Bernard Comrie*. Oxford: Oxford University Press.

Hawkins, R. (2001). *Second language syntax: a generative introduction*. Oxford: Blackwell.

Hay, J., and Bauer, L. (2007). Phoneme inventory size and population size. *Language* 83: 388–400.

Heath, J. (1999). *A grammar of Koyra Chiini*. Berlin: Mouton de Gruyter.

Henderson, J. (1995). *Phonology and grammar of Yele, Papua New Guinea*. Canberra: Pacific Linguistics (Australian National University).

Hermann, E. (1895). Gab es im Indogermanischen nebensätze? *Zeitschrift für vergleichende Sprachforschung* 33: 481–535.

Hernández, N. (2006). User's guide to FRED. Freiburg: English Dialects Research Group. Available at: www.freidok.uni-freiburg.de/volltexte/2489

Hewitt, G. (1996). *Georgian: a learner's grammar*. London: Routledge.

Hill, A. A. (1961). Grammaticality. *Word* 17: 1–10.

Hiltunen, R. (1990). Chapters on legal English: aspects past and present of the language of the law. *Annales Academiæ Scientiarum Fennnicæ* B 251. Helsinki: Suomalainen Tiedeakatemia (Academia Scientiarum Fennica).

Hockett, C. F. (1958). *A course in modern linguistics*. New York: Macmillan.

Höftmann, H. (2003). *Dictionnaire fon-français, avec une esquisse grammaticale*. Cologne: Köppe.

Holligan, C., and Johnston, R. S. (1991). Spelling errors and phonemic segmentation ability: the nature of the relationship. *Journal of Research and Reading* 14: 21–32.

Holm, G. (1967). *Epoker och prosastilar: några linjer och punkter i den svenska prosans stilhistoria*. Lundastudier i nordisk språkvetenskap A17. Lund: Studentlitteratur.

Hualde, J. I., and Ortiz de Urbina, J. (2003). *A grammar of Basque*. Berlin: Mouton de Gruyter.

Hudson, R. A. (1981). 83 things linguists can agree about. *Journal of Linguistics* 17: 333–44.

Huey, E. B. (1968). *The psychology and pedagogy of reading*. Cambridge, MA: MIT Press.

Hyltenstam, K. (1984). The use of typological markedness conditions as predictors in second language acquisition: the case of pronominal copies in relative clauses. In R. Andersen (ed.), *Second languages*. Rowley, MA: Newbury House.

Hyslop, C. (1993). Towards a typology of spatial deixis. BA thesis, Australian National University.

Ihalainen, O. (1976). Periphrastic *do* in affirmative sentences in the dialect of East Somerset. *Neuphilologische Mitteilungen* 67: 608–22.

——(1991). On grammatical diffusion in Somerset folk speech. In Trudgill and Chambers (1991).

Isaacson, R. L. (1982). *The limbic system*, 2nd edn. New York: Plenum Press.

Itkonen, E. (1966). *Kieli ja sen tutkimus*. Helsinki: Söderström.

Iwasaki, S., and Ingkaphirom, P. (2005). *A reference grammar of Thai*. Cambridge: Cambridge University Press.

Jackendoff, R. (1993). *Patterns in the mind: language and human nature*. Hemel Hempstead: Harvester Wheatsheaf.

——(1999). Possible stages in the evolution of the language capacity. *Trends in Cognitive Sciences* 3: 272–9.

——(2002). *Foundations of language: brain, meaning, grammar, evolution*. Oxford: Oxford University Press.

Janssen, D. B., Bickel, B., and Zúñiga, F. (2006). Randomization tests in language typology. *Linguistic Typology* 10: 419–40.

Jespersen, O. (1905). *Growth and structure of the English language.* 9th edn, Oxford: Blackwell, 1967.

Joos, M. (ed.) (1957). *Readings in linguistics.* New York: American Council of Learned Societies.

Just, M. A., and Carpenter, P. A. (1992). A capacity theory of comprehension: individual differences in working memory. *Psychological Review* 99: 122–49.

Kail, M. (1989). Cue validity, cue cost, and processing types in sentence comprehension in French and Spanish. In MacWhinney and Bates (1989).

Kakumasu, J. (1986). Urubu-Kaapor. In Derbyshire and Pullum (1986), vol. 1.

Kalmár, I. (1985). Are there really no primitive languages? In D. R. Olson, N. Torrance, and A. Hildyard (eds.), *Literacy, language and learning: the nature and consequences of reading and writing.* Cambridge: Cambridge University Press.

Karlsson, F. (2007a). Constraints on multiple initial embedding of clauses. *International Journal of Corpus Linguistics* 12: 107–118.

——— (2007b). Constraints on multiple centre-embedding of clauses. *Journal of Linguistics* 43: 365–392.

——— (2007c). Genuine data on multiple centre-embedding of clauses. Available at: www.ling.helsinki.fi/~fkarlsso/ceb_data.pdf

———, Miestamo, M., and Sinnemäki, K. (2008). Introduction: the problem of language complexity. In Miestamo et al. (2008).

Kaye, J. (1989). *Phonology: a cognitive view.* Mahwah, NJ: Erlbaum.

Keenan, E., and Comrie, B. (1977). Noun phrase accessibility and universal grammar. *Linguistic Inquiry* 8: 63–99.

Kibrik, A. E. (1998). Archi (Caucasian – Daghestanian). In A. Spencer and A. M. Zwicky (eds.), *The handbook of morphology.* Oxford: Blackwell.

Kihm, A. (2003). Inflectional categories in creole languages. In I. Plag (ed.), *Phonology and morphology of creole languages.* Tübingen: Niemeyer.

Kilborn, K., and Cooreman, A. (1987). Sentence interpretation strategies in adult Dutch-English bilinguals. *Applied Psycholinguistics* 8: 5–31.

———, and Ito, T. (1989). Sentence processing strategies in adult bilinguals. In MacWhinney and Bates (1989).

Kimball, G. D. (1991). *Koasati grammar.* Lincoln: University of Nebraska Press.

King, G. (1993). *Modern Welsh: a comprehensive grammar.* London: Routledge.

Kiparsky, P. (1968). Tense and mood in Indo-European syntax. *Foundations of Language* 4: 30–57.

Kirby, S. (1997). Competing motivations and emergence: explaining implicational hierarchies. *Linguistic Typology* 1: 5–31.

Kirk, J. (1992). The Northern Ireland Transcribed Corpus of Speech. In G. Leitner (ed.), *New directions in English language corpora.* Berlin: Mouton de Gruyter.

Kiss, K. (2002). *The syntax of Hungarian.* Cambridge: Cambridge University Press.

Kitagawa, Y. (1986). Subjects in English and Japanese. Ph.D. dissertation, University of Massachusetts.

Klamer, M. (1998). *A grammar of Kambera.* Berlin: Mouton de Gruyter.

van Kleeck, A. (1990). Emergent literacy: learning about print before learning to read. *Topics in Language Disorders* 10: 25–45.

Klein, W., and Perdue, C. (1997). The basic variety (or: Couldn't natural languages be much simpler?) *Second Language Research* 13: 301–47.

Koefoed, G., and Tarenskeen, J. (1996). The making of a language from a lexical point of view. In Wekker (1996).

Kolk, H. (2006). How language adapts to the brain: an analysis of agrammatic aphasia. In Progovac et al. (2006).

König, E., and van der Auwera, J. (1988). Clause integration in German and Dutch. In Haiman and Thompson (1988).

——, and Gast, V. (2007). *Understanding English-German contrasts.* Berlin: Schmidt.

Koopman, H., and Sportiche, D. (1991). The position of subjects. *Lingua* 85: 211–58.

Kortmann, B., Schneider, E., Burridge, K., Mesthrie, R., and Upton, C. (eds.) (2004). *A Handbook of Varieties of English.* Berlin: Mouton de Gruyter.

——, and Szmrecsanyi, B. (2004). Global synopsis: morphological and syntactic variation in English. In Kortmann et al. (2004).

Kracke, O. (1911). *Die Entwicklung der Mittelstellung des deutschen Nebensatzes.* Darmstadt: Otto.

Kramer, P. E., Koff, E., and Luria, Z. (1972). The development of competence in an exceptional language structure in older children and young adults. *Child Development* 43: 121–30.

Kriebel, W. (1873). *Der Periodenbau bei Cicero und Livius.* Prenzlau: Mieck.

Kruspe, N. (1999). A grammar of Semelai. Ph.D. dissertation, University of Melbourne. Published 2004 by Cambridge University Press.

Kusters, W. (2003). *Linguistic complexity: the influence of social change on verbal inflection.* Utrecht: Landelijke Onderzoekschool Taalwetenschap (LOT).

—— (2008). Complexity in linguistic theory, language learning and language change. In Miestamo et al. (2008).

Kutsch Lojenga, C. (1994). *Ngiti: a Central-Sudanic language of Zaire.* Cologne: Köppe.

Langacker, R. W. (1987). *Foundations of cognitive grammar: theoretical prerequisites.* Stanford, CA: Stanford University Press.

Langenberg, D. N. (ed.) (2000). *Report of the National Reading Panel: teaching children to read.* Washington, DC: US Department of Health and Human Services.

Languages of Suriname: Sranan-English dictionary. Available at: www.sil.org/americas/suriname/Sranan/English/ SrananEngDictIndex.html

LaPolla, R., with Chenglong Huang (2003). *A grammar of Qiang.* Berlin: Mouton de Gruyter.

Larsen, J. A., and Nippold, M. A. (2007). Morphological analysis in school-age children: dynamic assessment of a word learning strategy. *Language, Speech, and Hearing Services in Schools* 38: 201–12.

Laurence, S. (1998). Convention-based semantics and the development of language. In P. Carruthers and J. Boucher (eds.), *Language and thought: interdisciplinary themes*. Cambridge: Cambridge University Press.

Lebeaux, D. (1989). Language acquisition and the form of the grammar. Ph.D. dissertation, University of Massachusetts.

Lee, R. B., and DeVore, I. (1968). *Man the hunter*. Chicago: Aldine.

Lefebvre, C., and Brousseau, A.-M. (2001). *A grammar of Fongbe*. Berlin: Mouton de Gruyter.

Lefever, M. M., and Ehri, L. C. (1976). The relationship between field independence and sentence disambiguation ability. *Journal of Psycholinguistic Research* 5: 99–106.

Lehmann, C. (1982). *Thoughts on grammaticalization: a programmatic sketch*. Arbeiten des Kölner Universalienprojekts, 48. Cologne University. Rev. edn published Unterschleißheim, Bavaria: LINCOM, 1995.

—— (1985). Grammaticalization: synchronic variation and diachronic change. *Lingua e stile* 20: 303–18.

—— (1988). On the function of agreement. In M. Barlow and C. A. Ferguson (eds.), *Agreement in natural language: approaches, theories, descriptions*. Stanford, CA: Center for the Study of Language and Information.

Lehmann, W. P. (1974). *Proto-Indo-European syntax*. Austin: University of Texas Press.

Leino, P. (1975). Äidinkieli ja vieras kieli: rahvaanrunouden metriikkaa. *Kalevala-seuran vuosikirja* 55: 25–48.

Lenneberg, E. H (1967). *Biological foundations of language*. New York: Wiley.

Leong, C. K. (2000). Rapid processing of base and derived forms of words and grades 4, 5 and 6 children's spelling. *Reading and Writing* 12: 277–302.

Levander, L. (1909). *Älvdalsmålet i Dalarna: ordböjning ock syntax*. Nyare bidrag till kännedom om de svenska landsmålen ock svenskt folkliv, 4:3. Stockholm.

Levin, H., and Kaplan, E. L. (1970). Grammatical structure and reading. In H. Levin and J. P. Williams (eds.), *Basic studies in reading*. New York: Basic Books.

Levinson, S. C. (2000). *Presumptive meanings: the theory of generalized conversational implicatures*. Cambridge, MA: MIT Press.

—— (2005). Introduction: the evolution of culture in a microcosm. In S. C. Levinson and P. Jaisson (eds.), *Evolution and culture*. Cambridge, MA: MIT Press.

Li, M., and Vitányi, P. (1997). *An introduction to Kolmogorov complexity and its applications*, 2nd edn. Berlin: Springer.

Lieberman, P. (2000). *Human language and our reptilian brain: the subcortical bases of speech, syntax, and thought*. Cambridge, MA: Harvard University Press.

Limber, J. (1973). The genesis of complex sentences. In T. E. Moore (ed.), *Cognitive development and the acquisition of language*. New York: Academic Press.

Lindblom, B., and Maddieson, I. (1988). Phonetic universals in consonant systems. In L. M. Hyman and C. N. Li (eds.), *Language, speech and mind: studies in honour of Victoria A. Fromkin*. New York: Routledge.

Lindskog, C. (1896). Beiträge zur Geschichte der Satzstellung im Latein. *Acta Universitatis Lundensis* 32: 1–60.

Lindstedt, T. (1927). Tendenser i nusvensk meningsbildning. *Nysvenska studier* 7: 1–29.

Lindström, E. (2002). Topics in the grammar of Kuot, a non-Austronesian language of New Ireland, Papua New Guinea. Ph.D. dissertation, Stockholm University.

Littlewood, W. (2006). Second language learning. In A. Davies and C. Elder (eds.), *The handbook of applied linguistics*. Oxford: Blackwell.

Locke, J. L., and Bogin, B. (2006). Language and life history: a new perspective on the development and evolution of human language. *Behavioral and Brain Sciences* 29: 259–325.

Longacre, R. E. (1964). *Grammar discovery procedures: a field manual.* The Hague: Mouton.

Longobardi, G. (1994). Reference and proper names: a theory of N-movement in syntax and logical form. *Linguistic Inquiry* 25: 609–65.

Lord, A. B. (1960). *The singer of tales.* 2nd edn, Cambridge, MA: Harvard University Press, 2000.

Lyons, C. G. (1999). *Definiteness.* Cambridge: Cambridge University Press.

Lytinen, S. L. (1987). Integrating syntax and semantics. In S. Nirenburg (ed.), *Machine translation.* Cambridge: Cambridge University Press.

Maas, U. (2007). Die Grammatikalisierung der satzinternen Großschreibung. In A. Redder (ed.), *Diskurse und Texte: Festschrift für S Konrad Ehlich.* Tübingen: Stauffenburg.

——, and Mehlem, U. (2003). Schriftkulturelle Ressourcen und Barrieren bei marokkanischen Kindern in Deutschland. Osnabrück: IMIS. Available at: zentrum.virtuos.uni-osnabrueck.de/utz.maas/Main/BerichteAusForschungsprojekten.

——, and —— (2005). Schriftkulturelle Ausdrucksformen der Identitätsbildung bei marokkanischen Kindern und Jugendlichen in Marokko. Osnabrück: IMIS. Available at same URL as previous item.

Macaulay, M. (1996). *A grammar of Chalcatongo Mixtec.* Berkeley: University of California Press.

McDonald, J. (1989). The acquisition of cue-category mappings. In B. MacWhinney and E. Bates (eds.), *The crosslinguistic study of sentence processing.* Cambridge: Cambridge University Press.

MacDonald, L. (1990). *A grammar of Tauya.* Berlin: Mouton de Gruyter.

McGregor, W. (1990). *A functional grammar of Gooniyandi.* Amsterdam: Benjamins.

MacLean, P. D. (1949). Psychosomatic disease and the 'visceral brain': recent developments bearing on the Papez theory of emotion. *Psychosomatic Medicine* 11: 338–53.

MacWhinney, B., and Bates, E. (eds.) (1989). *The crosslinguistic study of sentence processing.* Cambridge: Cambridge University Press.

McWhorter, J. H. (2000). *The missing Spanish creoles.* Berkeley: University of California Press.

—— (2001a). The world's simplest grammars are creole grammars. *Linguistic Typology* 6: 125–66. Repr. in McWhorter (2005).

—— (2001b). *The power of Babel: a natural history of language.* Repr. London: Arrow, 2003.

—— (2001c). What people ask David Gil and why: rejoinder to the replies. *Linguistic Typology* 6: 388–413.

—— (2002). What happened to English? *Diachronica* 19: 217–72. Repr. in McWhorter (2005).

—— (2005). *Defining creole.* Oxford: Oxford University Press.

—— (2007). *Language interrupted: signs of non-native acquisition in standard language grammars.* Oxford: Oxford University Press.

Maddieson, I. (2005a). Vowel quality inventories. In Haspelmath et al. (2005).

—— (2005b). Syllable structure. In Haspelmath et al. (2005).

—— (2005c). Tone. In Haspelmath et al. (2005).

Mahony, D., Singson, N., and Mann, V. (2000). Reading ability and sensitivity to morphological relations. *Reading and Writing* 12: 191–218.

Maratsos, M. P. (1976). *The use of definite and indefinite reference in young children.* Cambridge: Cambridge University Press.

Marcus, M. P. (1980). *A theory of syntactic recognition for natural language.* Cambridge, MA: MIT Press.

Maslova, E. (1999). A grammar of Kolyma Yukaghir. Ph.D. dissertation, University of Bielefeld.

Matisoff, J. A. (1972). Oy, ve! Lahu nominalization, relativization, and genitivization. In J. Kimball (ed.), *Syntax and semantics,* vol. 1. New York: Seminar Press.

Matthews, S., and Yip, V. (1994). *Cantonese: a comprehensive grammar.* New York: Routledge.

Mead, M. (1928). *Coming of age in Samoa: a psychological study of primitive youth for Western civilization.* New York: Morrow.

Meader, C. L. (1905). Types of sentence structure in Latin prose writers. *Transactions and Proceedings of the American Philological Association* 36: 32–51.

Mendoza-Denton, N. (1999). Turn-initial No: collaborative opposition among Latina adolescents. In M. Bucholtz, A. C. Liang, and L. A. Sutton (eds.), *Reinventing identities: the gendered self in discourse.* Oxford: Oxford University Press.

Mesthrie, R. (2004). Introduction: varieties of English in Africa and south and southeast Asia. In Kortmann et al. (2004).

Miestamo, M. (2004). Grammatical complexity of languages: a cross-linguistic point of view. Paper given at the 20th Scandinavian Conference of Linguistics, Helsinki, 7 Jan.

—— (2005). *Standard negation: the negation of declarative verbal main clauses in a typological perspective.* Berlin: Mouton de Gruyter.

—— (2006). On the feasibility of complexity metrics. In K. Kerge and M.-M. Sepper (eds.), *FinEst Linguistics: Proceedings of the Annual Finnish and Estonian Conference of Linguistics, Tallinn, May 6–7, 2004.* Tallinn: Tallinn University Press.

—— (2008). Grammatical complexity in cross-linguistic perspective. In Miestamo et al. (2008).

Miestamo, M., Sinnemäki, K., and Karlsson, F. (eds.) (2008). *Language complexity: typology, contact, change*. Amsterdam: Benjamins.

Mihajlović, V. (1992). *Ime po zapovesti* [Name by command]. Belgrade: Nolit.

Miller, A. (2001). *A grammar of Jamul Tiipay*. Berlin: Mouton de Gruyter.

Miller, G. A. (1956). The magical number seven, plus or minus two: some limits on our capacity for processing information. *Psychological Review* 63: 81–97.

—— and Chomsky, N. (1963). Finitary models of language users. In R. D. Luce, R. Bush, and E. Galanter (eds.), *Handbook of mathematical psychology*, vol. 2. New York: Wiley.

——, and Isard, S. (1964). Free recall of self-embedded English sentences. *Information and Control* 7: 292–303.

Miller, J., and Fernandez-Vest, M. M. J. (2006). Spoken and written language. In J. Bernini and M. L. Schwartz (eds.), *Pragmatic organisation of discourse in the languages of Europe*. Berlin: Mouton de Gruyter.

——, and Weinert, R. (1998). *Spontaneous spoken language: syntax and discourse*. Oxford: Oxford University Press.

Mills, J. A., and Hemsley, G. D. (1976). The effect of level of education on judgements of grammatical acceptability. *Language and Speech* 19: 324–42.

Milroy, J., and Milroy, A. L. (1985). Linguistic change, social networks and speaker innovation. *Journal of Linguistics* 21: 339–84.

Mithun, M. (1984). How to avoid subordination. In C. Brugman and M. Macaulay (eds.), *Proceedings of the Tenth Annual Meeting of the Berkeley Linguistics Society*. Berkeley, CA: BLS.

—— (2007). A typology of recursion. Paper presented at the conference on Recursion in Human Languages, Illinois State University (Normal, Ill.), 27–9 Apr.

Morais, J., Mousty, P., and Kolinsky, R. (1998). Why and how phoneme awareness helps learning to read. In C. Hulme and R. M. Joshi (eds.), *Reading and spelling: development and disorders*. Mahwah, NJ: Erlbaum.

Morwood, M. J., and Cogill-Koez, D. (2007). *Homo* on Flores: some early implications for the evolution of language and cognition. In A. C. Schalley and D. Khlentzos (eds.), *Mental states*, vol. 1: *Evolution, function, nature*. Amsterdam: Benjamins.

Moussay, G. (1981). *La langue minangkabau*. Paris: Archipel.

Mühlhäusler, P. (1977). *Pidginization and simplification of language*. Canberra: Pacific Linguistics (Australian National University).

—— (2001). Typology and universals of pidginization. In M. Haspelmath et al. (eds.), *Language typology and language universals: an international handbook*. Berlin: de Gruyter.

Müller-Gotama, F. (1994). *Grammatical relations: a cross-linguistic perspective on their syntax and semantics*. Berlin: de Gruyter.

Muncer, S. J., and Bever, T. G. (1984). Sensitivity to propositional units in good reading. *Journal of Psycholinguistic Research* 13: 275–9.

Murane, E. (1974). *Daga grammar, from morpheme to discourse*. Norman, OK: Summer Institute of Linguistics.

Muter, V., Hulme, C., Snowling, M., and Taylor, S. (1997). Segmentation, not rhyming, predicts early progress in learning to read. *Journal of Child Psychology and Psychiatry and Allied Disciplines* 35: 293–310.

von Nägelsbach, K. F. (1846). *Lateinische Stilistik für Deutsche.* 9th edn repr. Darmstadt: Wissenschaftliche Buchgesellschaft, 1963.

Nakayama, T. (2001). *Nuuchahnulth (Nootka) morphosyntax.* Berkeley: University of California Press.

Naslund, J. C., and Schneider, W. (1996). Kindergarten letter knowledge, phonological skills, and memory processes: relative effects on early literacy. *Journal of Experimental Child Psychology* 62: 30–59.

Nettle, D. (1999). *Linguistic diversity.* Oxford: Oxford University Press.

Nevins, A. I., Pesetsky, D., and Rodrigues, C. (2007). Pirahã exceptionality: a reassessment. Available at: ling.auf.net/lingBuzz/000411

Newmeyer, F. J. (2005). *Possible and probable languages: a generative perspective on linguistic typology.* Oxford: Oxford University Press.

Nichols, J. (1986). Head-marking and dependent-marking grammar. *Language* 62: 56–119.

—— (1992). *Linguistic diversity in space and time.* Chicago: University of Chicago Press.

—— (2007a). The distribution of complexity in the world's languages: prospectus. Presented at Linguistic Society of America annual meeting, Anaheim, CA, 4–7 Jan.

—— (2007b). Linguistic complexity: a comprehensive definition and survey. Presented at Association for Linguistic Typology 7th Biennial Meeting, Paris, 25–8 Sept.

—— (2008). Variation in the distribution of source gender in Nakh-Daghestanian. Presented at the Workshop on Variation and Change in Languages of the Caucasus, 13th International Morphology Meeting, Vienna, Feb.

—— with Barnes, J., and Peterson, D. A. (2006). The robust bell curve of morphological complexity. *Linguistic Typology* 10: 96–108.

—— and Bickel, B. (2005). Possessive classification (alienable/inalienable possession). In Haspelmath et al. (2005).

——, Peterson, D. A., and Barnes, J. (2004). Transitivizing and detransitivizing languages. *Linguistic Typology* 8: 149–211.

Noonan, M. (1985). Complementation. In T. Shopen (ed.), *Language typology and syntactic description*, vol 2: *Complex constructions.* Cambridge: Cambridge University Press.

Olson, R., Wise, B., Conners, F., and Rack, J. (1990). Organization, heritability, and remediation of component word recognition and language skills in disabled readers. In T. H. Carr and B. A. Levy (eds.), *Reading and its development: component skills approaches.* New York: Academic Press.

O'Neil, W. (1976). Clause adjunction in Old English. *General Linguistics* 17: 199–211.

Ong, W. (1982). *Orality and literacy: the technologizing of the word.* London: Methuen.

Osterhout, L. (1997). On the brain responses to syntactic anomalies: manipulations of word position and word class reveal individual differences. *Brain and Language* 59: 494–522.

Otto, W. (1928). *Handbuch der Altertumswissenschaft*, II:2. Munich: Beck.

Ouhalla, J. (1991). *Functional categories and parametric variation*. London: Routledge & Kegan Paul.

Paddock, H. (1991). The actuation problem for gender change in Wessex versus Newfoundland. In Trudgill and Chambers (1991).

Parker, A. R. (2006). Evolution as a constraint on theories of syntax: the case against minimalism. Ph.D. dissertation, University of Edinburgh.

Payne, D. L., and Payne, T. E. (1990). Yagua. In Derbyshire and Pullum (1990), vol. 2.

Pearlmutter, N. J., and MacDonald, M. C. (1995). Individual differences and probabilistic constraints in syntactic ambiguity resolution. *Journal of Memory and Language* 34: 521–42.

Penchoen, T. (1973). *Tamazight of the Ayt Ndhir*. Los Angeles: Undena.

Pericliev, V. (2004). There is no correlation between the size of a community speaking a language and the size of the phonological inventory of that language. *Linguistic Typology* 8: 376–83.

Perkins, R. (1992). *Deixis, grammar, and culture*. Amsterdam: Benjamins.

Piattelli-Palmarini, M. (ed.) (1980). *Language and learning: the debate between Jean Piaget and Noam Chomsky*. London: Routledge & Kegan Paul.

Pinker, S. (1994). *The language instinct: the new science of language and mind*. London: Allen Lane.

—— (2007). *The stuff of thought: language as a window into human nature*. New York: Viking.

—— and Bloom, P. (1990). Natural language and natural selection. *Behavioral and Brain Sciences* 13: 707–84.

——, and Jackendoff, R. (2005). The faculty of language: what's special about it? *Cognition* 95: 201–36

Pitkin, H. (1984). *Wintu grammar*. Berkeley: University of California Press.

Plank, F. (ed.) (2001). *Linguistic Typology* 5(2/3), special issue on creoles and complexity.

Platzak, C. (1990). A grammar without functional categories: a syntactic study of early child language. *Nordic Journal of Linguistics* 13: 107–26.

Potts, C., and Roeper, T. (2006). The narrowing acquisition path: from expressive small clauses to declaratives. In Progovac et al. (2006).

Price, R., and Price, S. (n.d.). Transcriptions of Saramaccan folk tales. MS, given to John McWhorter by Val Ziegler in 2006.

Primus, B. (1999). *Cases and thematic roles: ergative, accusative and active*. Tübingen: Niemeyer.

Progovac, L. (2006a). The syntax of nonsententials: small clauses and phrases at the root. In Progovac et al. (2006).

—— (2006b). Fossilized imperative in compounds and other expressions. Online Proceedings of the First Inaugural Meeting of SLS (Slavic Linguistics Society), Bloomington, IN. Available at: www.indiana.edu/~sls2006/page6/page6.html

—— (2007a). *Exocentric compounds: from evolution to extinction*. MS.

—— (2007b). What is there when little words are not there: possible implications for evolutionary studies. Paper presented at Georgetown University Round Table on Languages and Linguistics (GURT 2007), 8–11 May.

—— (2007c). When clauses refuse to be recursive: an evolutionary perspective. Paper presented at Conference on Recursion in Human Languages, Illinois State University, Normal, 27–9 Apr.

——, Paesani, K., Casielles, E., and Barton, E. (eds.) (2006). *The syntax of nonsententials: multidisciplinary perspectives*. Amsterdam: Benjamins.

Pulleyblank, E. G. (1995). *Outline of classical Chinese grammar*. Vancouver: UBC Press.

Pulman, B. (2004). Malinowski and ignorance of physiological paternity. *Revue française de sociologie* 45, supplement, pp. 125–46.

Quintero, C. (2004). *Osage grammar*. Lincoln: University of Nebraska Press.

Quirk, R., Greenbaum, S., Leech, G. N., and Svartvik, J. (1989). *A comprehensive grammar of the English language*, 7th (corrected) impression. Harlow: Longman.

R Development Core Team (2007). *R: a language and environment for statistical computing*. Vienna: R Foundation for Statistical Computing. Available at: www. R-project.org

Radford, A. (1988). Small children's small clauses. *Transactions of the Philological Society* 86: 1–43.

—— (1990). *Syntactic theory and the acquisition of English syntax*. Oxford: Blackwell.

Reh, M. (1985). *Die Krongo-Sprache (nìino mó-dì): Beschreibung, Texte, Wörterverzeichnis*. Berlin: Reimer.

—— (1996). *The Anywa language*. Cologne: Köppe.

Rice, K. (1989). *A grammar of Slave*. Berlin: Mouton de Gruyter.

—— (2004). Language contact, phonemic inventories, and the Athapaskan language family. *Linguistic Typology* 8: 321–43.

Riddle, E. M. (2008). Complexity in isolating languages: lexical elaboration v. grammatical economy. In Miestamo et al. (2008).

Ridley, M. (1993). *Evolution*. Oxford: Blackwell Scientific.

—— (1999). *Genome: the autobiography of a species in 23 chapters*. London: Fourth Estate.

Roberts, I. (1999). Verb movement and markedness. In M. DeGraff (ed.), *Language creation and language change*. Cambridge, MA: MIT Press.

Roebrooks, W. (2001). Hominid behavior and the earliest occupation of Europe: an exploration. *Journal of Human Evolution* 41: 437–61.

Roeper, T. (1999). Universal bilingualism. *Bilingualism: Language and Cognition* 2: 169–86.

——, and Siegel, D. (1978). A lexical transformation for verbal compounds. *Linguistic Inquiry* 9: 199–260.

Rohdenburg, G. (1974). *Sekundäre Subjektivierungen im Englischen und Deutschen.* Bielefeld: Cornelson-Velhagen & Klasing.

Rolfe, L. (1996). Theoretical stages in the prehistory of grammar. In A. Lock and C. R. Peters (eds.), *Handbook of human symbolic evolution.* Oxford: Clarendon Press.

Romero-Figueroa, A. (1997). *A reference grammar of Warao.* Munich: LINCOM Europa.

Rosch Heider, E., and Olivier, D. C. (1972). The structure of the color space in naming and memory for two languages. *Cognitive Psychology* 3: 337–54.

Ross, M. D. (1996). Contact-induced change and the comparative method: cases from Papua New Guinea. In M. Durie and M. D. Ross (eds.), *The comparative method reviewed.* Oxford: Oxford University Press.

—— (1997). Social networks and kinds of speech-community event. In R. Blench and M. Spriggs (eds.), *Archaeology and language I: Theoretical and methodological orientations.* London: Routledge.

Roth, M. T. (1997). *Law collections from Mesopotamia and Asia Minor,* 2nd edn. Atlanta, GA: Scholars Press.

Rounds, C. (2001). *Hungarian: an essential grammar.* London: Routledge.

Rountree, S. C. (1972). Saramaccan tone in relation to intonation and grammar. *Lingua* 29: 308–25.

Saeed, J. (1999). *Somali.* Amsterdam: Benjamins.

Sakel, J. (2004). *A grammar of Mosetén.* Berlin: Mouton de Gruyter.

—— (in preparation). Dictionary Pirahã–English–Portuguese.

——, and Stapert, E. (forthcoming). Pirahã in need of recursive syntax? *Linguistic Review.*

Samarin, W. J. (1967). *Field linguistics: a guide to linguistic field work.* New York: Holt, Rinehart & Winston.

Sampson, G. R. (1997). *Educating Eve: the 'language instinct' debate.* London: Continuum.

—— (2001). Demographic correlates of complexity in British speech. In G. R. Sampson, *Empirical linguistics.* London: Continuum.

—— (2005). *The 'language instinct' debate,* rev. edn of Sampson (1997). London: Continuum.

—— (2006). Does simple imply creole? In *A man of measure: Festschrift in honour of Fred Karlsson on his 60th birthday.* Turku: Linguistic Association of Finland.

—— (2007). Minds in uniform: how generative linguistics regiments culture, and why it shouldn't. In M. Grein and E. Weigand (eds.), *Dialogue and culture.* Amsterdam: Benjamins.

Sanders, L. J. (1971). The comprehension of certain syntactic structures by adults. *Journal of Speech and Hearing Research* 14: 739–45.

Sapir, E. (1921). *Language: an introduction to the study of speech.* Repr. London: Hart-Davis, 1963.

—— (1949). *Selected Writings of Edward Sapir in language, culture, and personality,* ed. D. G. Mandelbaum. Berkeley: University of California Press.

Sasaki, Y. (1997). Individual variation in a Japanese sentence comprehension task: forms, functions and strategies. *Applied Linguistics* 18: 508–37.

de Saussure, F. (1983). *Course in general linguistics* (trans. by R. Harris from 1916 French original). London: Duckworth.

Schachter, P. (1987). Tagalog. In Comrie (1987).

Schaub, W. (1985). *Babungo*. London: Croom Helm.

Schiering, R. (2006). Cliticization and the evolution of morphology: a cross-linguistic study on phonology and grammaticalization. Ph.D. dissertation, University of Konstanz.

Schnitzer, M. L. (1993). Steady as a rock: does the steady state represent cognitive fossilization? *Journal of Psycholinguistic Research* 22: 1–19.

Schulze, U. (1975). *Lateinisch-deutsche Parallelurkunden des dreizehnten Jahrhunderts*. Munich: Fink.

Schumann, C. L. (1783). *Neger-Englisches Wörterbuch*, 3rd edn. Available at: www.sil. org/americas/suriname/Schumann/National/SchumannGerDict.html

Schütze, T. C. (2001). On the nature of Default Case. *Syntax* 4: 205–38.

Schwyzer, E. (1950). *Griechische Grammatik auf der Grundlage von Karl Brugmanns Griechischer Grammatik*, vol. 2: *Syntax und syntaktische Stilistik*. Munich: Beck.

Seiler, W. (1985). *Imonda, a Papuan language*. Canberra: Pacific Linguistics (Australian National University).

Seuren, P., and Wekker, H. (1986). Semantic transparency as a factor in creole genesis. In P. Muysken and N. Smith (eds.), *Substrata versus universals in creole genesis*. Amsterdam: Benjamins.

Shanks, L. (ed.) (1994). *A buku fu Okanisi anga Ingiisi wowtu* [Aukan-English dictionary]. Paramaribo: Summer Institute of Linguistics.

Sharpe, M. (1972). *Alawa phonology and grammar*. Canberra: Australian Institute of Aboriginal Studies.

Shosted, R. K. (2006). Correlating complexity: a typological approach. *Linguistic Typology* 10: 1–40.

Singson, N., Mahony, D., and Mann, V. (2000). The relation between reading ability and morphological skills: evidence from derivational suffixes. *Reading and Writing* 12: 219–52.

Sinnemäki, K. (2008). Complexity tradeoffs in core argument marking. In Miestamo et al. (2008).

Siple, P. (2006). Nonsententials and agrammatism. In Progovac et al. (2006).

Smeets, C. (1989). A Mapuche grammar. Ph.D. dissertation, University of Leiden.

Sneddon, J. N. (1996). *Indonesian: a comprehensive grammar*. London: Routledge.

—— (2006). *Colloquial Jakartan Indonesian*. Canberra: Pacific Linguistics (Australian National University).

Snow, C. E., Burns, S. M., and Griffin, P. (eds.) (1998). *Preventing reading difficulties in young children*. Washington, DC: National Academy Press.

Spencer, A. (1991). *Morphological theory*. Oxford: Blackwell.

Spencer, N. J. (1973). Differences between linguists and nonlinguists in intuitions of grammaticality–acceptability. *Journal of Psycholinguistic Research* 2: 83–98.

Sperber, D., and Wilson, D. (1995). *Relevance: communication and cognition*, 2nd edn. Oxford: Blackwell.

Sridhar, S. (1990). *Kannada*. London: Routledge.

Stahl, S. A., and Murray, B. A. (1994). Defining phonological awareness and its relationship to early reading. *Journal of Educational Psychology* 86: 221–34.

Stapert, E., Frank, M., Everett, D. L., and Gibson, E. (in preparation). Embedded structures in Pirahã: the expression of relative clauses, possessives and conditionals.

Stassen, L. (1992). A hierarchy of main predicate encoding. In M. Kefer and J. van der Auwera (eds.), *Meaning and grammar*. Berlin: Mouton de Gruyter.

—— (1997). *Intransitive predication*. Oxford: Clarendon.

Steinhauer, H. (1993). Notes on verbs in Dawanese (Timor). In G. P. Reesink (ed.), *Topics in descriptive Austronesian linguistics*. Leiden: Vakgroep Talen en Culturen van Zuidoost-Azië en Oceanië.

Stevanović, M. (1966). *Gramatika srpskohrvatskog jezika*. Cetinje: Obod.

—— (1974). *Savremeni srpskohrvatski jezik II: Sintaksa*. Belgrade: Naučna Knjiga.

Stolz, W. (1967). A study of the ability to decode grammatically novel sentences. *Journal of Verbal Learning and Verbal Behavior* 6: 867–73.

Stowell, T. (1981). Origins of phrase structure. Ph.D. dissertation, MIT.

—— (1983). Subjects across categories. *Linguistic Review* 2/3: 285–312.

Strickberger, M. W. (2000). *Evolution*, 3rd edn. Boston, MA: Jones & Bartlett.

Szmrecsanyi, B., and Kortmann, B. (forthcoming). Vernacular universals and anglo-versals in a typological perspective. In Filppula et al. (forthcoming).

Teleman, U., Hellberg, S., and Andersson, E. (1999). *Svenska Akademiens grammatik* (4 vols.). Stockholm: Norstedts Ordbok.

Terrill, A. (2003). *A grammar of Lavukaleve*. Berlin: Mouton de Gruyter.

Thompson, S. A. (2002). Object complements and conversation: towards a realistic account. *Studies in Language* 26: 125–64.

Thomsen, M.-L. (1984). *The Sumerian language*. Copenhagen: Akademisk.

Thurston, W. (1994). Renovation and innovation in the languages of north-western New Britain. In T. Dutton and D. Tryon (eds.), *Language contact and change in the Austronesian world*. Berlin: Mouton de Gruyter.

Torgesen, J. K., Wagner, R. K., and Rashotte, C. A. (1994). Longitudinal studies of phonological processing and reading. *Journal of Learning Disabilities* 27: 276–86.

de la Torre, I. (2004). Omo revisited: evaluating the technological skills of Pliocene hominids. *Current Anthropology* 45: 439–65.

Towell, R., and Hawkins, R. (1994). *Approaches to second language acquisition*. Clevedon, Som.: Multilingual Matters.

Trudgill, P. (1983). Language contact and language change: on the rise of the creoloid. In P. Trudgill, *On dialect: social and geographical perspectives*. Oxford: Blackwell.

—— (1989). Interlanguage, interdialect and typological change. In S. Gass, C. Madden, D. Preston, and L. Selinker (eds.), *Variation in second language acquisition*, vol. 2: *Psycholinguistic issues*. Clevedon, Som.: Multilingual Matters.

—— (1992). Dialect typology and social structure. In E. H. Jahr (ed.), *Language contact: theoretical and empirical studies*. Berlin: Mouton de Gruyter.

—— (1995). Grammaticalization and social structure: nonstandard conjunction-formation in East Anglian English. In F. R. Palmer (ed.), *Grammar and semantics: papers in honour of John Lyons*. Cambridge: Cambridge University Press.

—— (1996a). Dual-source pidgins and reverse creoloids: northern perspectives on language contact. In E. H. Jahr and I. Broch (eds.), *Language contact in the Arctic: northern pidgins and contact languages*. Berlin: Mouton de Gruyter.

—— (1996b). Dialect typology: isolation, social network and phonological structure. In G. Guy et al. (eds.), *Towards a social science of language: papers in honour of William Labov*, vol. 1: *Variation and change in language and society*. Amsterdam: Benjamins.

—— (1998). Typology and sociolinguistics: linguistic structure, social structure and explanatory comparative dialectology. *Folia Linguistica* 31: 349–60.

—— (1999). Language contact and the function of linguistic gender. *Poznań Studies in Contemporary Linguistics* 35: 133–52.

—— (2001). Contact and simplification: historical baggage and directionality in linguistic change. *Linguistic Typology* 5: 371–3.

—— (2002). Linguistic and social typology. In J. K. Chambers, N. Schilling-Estes, and P. Trudgill (eds.), *Handbook of linguistic variation and change*. Oxford: Blackwell.

—— (2003). *The Norfolk dialect*. Cromer: Poppyland.

—— (2004a). Linguistic and social typology: the Austronesian migrations and phoneme inventories. *Linguistic Typology* 8: 305–20.

—— (2004b). On the complexity of simplification. *Linguistic Typology* 8: 384–88.

—— (2008). Contact and sociolinguistic typology. In R. Hickey (ed.), *Handbook of language contact*. Oxford: Blackwell.

—— (forthcoming a). Vernacular universals and the sociolinguistic typology of English dialects. In Filppula et al. (forthcoming).

—— (forthcoming b). *Language in contact and isolation: sociolinguistic typology and linguistic complexity*. Oxford: Oxford University Press.

——, and Chambers, J. K. (eds.) (1991). *Dialects of English: studies in grammatical variation*. Harlow: Longman.

Uszkoreit, H., Brants, T., Duchier, D., Krenn, B., Konieczny, L., Oepen, S., and Skut, W. (1998). Studien zur performanzorientierten Linguistik: Aspekte der Relativsatzextraposition im Deutschen. *Kognitionswissenschaft* 7: 129–33.

Valenzuela, P. (1997). Basic verb types and argument structures in Shipibo-Konibo. MA thesis, University of Oregon.

van Valin, R., Jr. (1977). Aspects of Lakhota syntax: a study of Lakhota (Teton Dakota) syntax and its implications for universal grammar. Ph.D. dissertation, University of California at Berkeley.

de Villiers, J. (1999). Language and theory of mind: what are the developmental relationships? In S. Baron-Cohen, H. Tager-Flusberg, and D. J. Cohen (eds.), *Understanding other minds: perspectives from developmental cognitive neuroscience*, 2nd edn. Oxford: Oxford University Press.

Voorhoeve, J. (1962). *Sranan syntax.* Amsterdam: North-Holland.

van der Voort, H. (2004). *A grammar of Kwaza.* Berlin: Mouton de Gruyter.

de Vries, L. (1993). *Forms and functions in Kombai, an Awyu language of Irian Jaya.* Canberra: Pacific Linguistics (Australian National University).

—— (2004). *A short grammar of Inanwatan, an endangered language of the Bird's Head of Papua, Indonesia.* Canberra: Pacific Linguistics (Australian National University).

Vygotsky, L. S. (1981). The genesis of higher mental functions (translation of 1960 Russian original). In J. V. Wertsch (ed.), *The concept of activity in Soviet psychology.* Armonk, NY: Sharpe.

Webster, T. B. L. (1941). A study of Greek sentence construction. *American Journal of Philology* 62: 385–415.

Weekley, E. (1916). *Surnames.* New York: Dutton.

Wekker, H. (ed.) (1996). *Creole languages and language acquisition.* Berlin: Mouton de Gruyter.

Wells, J. C. (1982). *Accents of English* (3 vols.). Cambridge: Cambridge University Press.

Werner, O. (1984). Morphologische Entwicklungen in den germanischen Sprachen. In J. Untermann and B. Brogyanyi (eds.), *Das Germanische und die Rekonstruktion der Indogermanischen Grundsprache.* Amsterdam: Benjamins.

White, T. G., Graves, M. F., and Slater, W. H. (1990). Growth of reading vocabulary in diverse elementary schools: decoding and word meaning. *Journal of Educational Psychology* 82: 281–90.

Wierzbicka, A. (2005). Commentary on Everett (2005). *Current Anthropology* 46: 641.

Wiesemann, U. (1991). Tone and intonational features in Fon. *Linguistique africaine* 7: 65–90.

Wilhelm, F. (ed.) (1932–63). *Corpus der altdeutschen Originalurkunden bis zum Jahre 1300.* Lahr, Schwarzwald: Schauenberg.

Wouk, F. (1989). The impact of discourse on grammar: verb morphology in spoken Jakarta Indonesian. Ph.D. dissertation, University of California at Los Angeles.

—— (1999). Dialect contact and koineization in Jakarta, Indonesia. *Language Sciences* 21: 61–86.

Wulfeck, B., Juarez, L., Bates, E., and Kilborn, K. (1986). Sentence interpretation in healthy and aphasic bilingual adults. In J. Vaid (ed.), *Language processing in bilinguals: psycholinguistics and neuropsychological perspectives.* Mahwah, NJ: Erlbaum.

Zhou, M. (1998). *Tense/aspect markers in Mandarin and Xiang dialects, and their content.* Sino-Platonic Papers, 83. Philadelphia: Department of Asian and Middle Eastern Studies, University of Pennsylvania.

Zipf, G. K. (1949). *Human behavior and the principle of least effort.* New York: Hafner.

Zúñiga, F. (2000). *Mapudungun.* Munich: LINCOM Europa.

Index

Höftmann, H. 155
Holligan, C. 180
Holm, G. 201
Holmes, V. M. 181–2
Homer 200
Hopi 221
Horace 3–4
Hua 123, 125
Hualde, J. I. 85, 87
Hudson, R. A. 7
Huey, E. B. 182
Hungarian 123, 125, 134, 140
Hyltenstam, K. 70
hypotaxis 195; *see also* embedding,
    recursion
Hyslop, C. 110

Iau 133–4, 140
Icelandic 102, 201
Ihalainen, O. 107–8
Ika 134, 140
Immediacy of Experience Principle
    (IEP) 223–5
Imonda 85, 88
Inanwatan 85, 95
incredulity clauses 203–4
Indonesian 16–17, 22–31, 110, 134, 140,
    212, 255–6
Ingkaphirom, P. 85, 140
Ingush 121, 123, 125
injunctive 205n, 206n, 211
International Corpus of English
    (ICE) 67
Inuktitut 195
Isaacson, R. L. 210
Isard, S. 183–5
Isolating-Monocategorial-
    Associational (IMA)
    Language 20–31, 35, 212
Itkonen, E. 195
Ito, T. 182
Iwasaki, S. 85, 140

Jackendoff, R. 6, 11, 204n, 208–9,
    232, 252

Jamaican Creole 66
Janssen, D. B. 95n, 137
Japanese 122, 124, 256, 259
Jaqaru 134, 140
Jarawara 85
Jespersen, O. 202
Johnston, R. S. 180
Joos, M. 2
Just, M. A. 184–6

Kail, M. 182
Kakumasu, J. 140
Kalevala 195
Kalmár, I. 195
Kambera 85, 90–1
Kannada 130, 133–4, 140
Kaplan, E. L. 182
Karlsson, F. G. 10, 192–202, 234, 242
Kathlamet 195
Kay, P. 11
Kayardild 85, 123, 125
Kaye, J. 126
Keenan, E. 83
Ket 123, 125
Keyser, S. J. 206
Khmer 38–40
Khoekhoe 85, 89, 95, 115, 134, 140
Kibrik, A. E. 3
Kihm, A. 162
Kikongo 149
Kilborn, K. 182
Kimball, G. D. 85, 140
King, G. 140
Kintsch, W. 185–6, 189–90, 200
Kiparsky, P. 205n, 211
Kirby, S. 84
Kiriwina *see* Trobriands
Kirk, J. 67
Kisi 134, 140
Kiss, K. 140
Kitagawa, Y. 206
Kiwai 123–4
Klamer, M. 85, 90
van Kleeck, A. 180
Klein, W. 70, 77

Studies in the Evolution of Language

General Editors
Kathleen R. Gibson, *University of Texas at Houston,*
and James R. Hurford, *University of Edinburgh*

In Preparation

Darwinian Linguistics
Evolution and the Logic of Linguistic Theory
Stephen R. Anderson

The Evolution of Morphology
Andrew Carstairs McCarthy

The Evolution of Linguistic Form
Language in the Light of Evolution 2
James R. Hurford

Biolinguistic Approaches to Language Evolution
Edited by Anna Maria di Sciullo and Cedric Boeckx

To be Published in Association with the Series

The Oxford Handbook of Language Evolution
edited by Maggie Tallerman and Kathleen R. Gibson

Published in Association with the Series

Language Diversity
Daniel Nettle

Function, Selection, and Innateness
The Emergence of Language Universals
Simon Kirby

The Origins of Complex Language
An Inquiry into the Evolutionary Beginnings of Sentences, Syllables, and Truth
Andrew Carstairs McCarthy